SCRIBES, SCRIPT AND BOOKS

The Book Arts
from Antiquity to
the Renaissance

The royal scribe Nebmertof, Egypt, ca. 1400 B.C.E.
Louvre, Départment des Antiquités Egyptiennes

SCRIBES, SCRIPT AND BOOKS

The Book Arts from Antiquity to the Renaissance

LEILA AVRIN

Illustrations by Malla Carl
and Noah Ophir

American Library Association / The British Library
Chicago   London
1991

Composed in Bembo by the Clarinda Company on a Xyvision system using a
Linotron 202 typesetter

The paper used in this publication meets the minimum requirements of American
National Standard for Information Sciences—Permanence of Paper for Printed
Library Materials, ANSI Z39.48-1984. ∞

Library of Congress Cataloging-in-Publication Data
Avrin, Leila.
　　Scribes, script and books : the book arts from antiquity to the Renaissance /
Leila Avrin.
　　　　p.　　cm.
　　Includes bibliographical references.

　　　1. Books—History.　2. Writing—History.　3. Manuscripts—History.
4. Scriptoria—History.　5. Scribes—History.　I. Title.
Z4.A88　1990
002—dc20
　　　　　　　　　　　　　　　　　　　　　　　　　　　　　89-18024

British Library Cataloguing in Publication Data
Avrin, Leila
　　Scribes, script and books : the book arts from antiquity to the Renaissance.
　　1. Books. Production. History
　　I. Title
　　686

　　ISBN 978-0-8389-1038-2

First published in 1991 by the American Library Association, 50 East Huron
Street, Chicago, IL 60611, and The British Library, Great Russell Street, London
WC1B 3DG.

Printed in the United States of America.

To my daughters
Elissa and Eve

Contents

CHAPTER 1

Writing 17

CHAPTER 2

The Alphabet 45

CHAPTER 3

The Book in the Ancient World: Mesopotamia 63

CHAPTER 4

The Egyptian Book 81

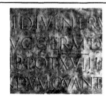

Plates

Figures

Maps

Tables

Preface

Writing this book required two idiosyncrasies in the character of the writer: chutzpah and courage of imperfection. "Courage of imperfection" (an expression coined by Rollo May) is evident in my willingness to expose myself to academic critics who will call attention to the lack of primary research. I have written this book to gather the scattered information on writing and the handmade book into a continuous history, whose progress has been determined by the principles of tradition and change.

The aim of *Scribes, Script and Books* is to demonstrate just how these principles of tradition and change have determined the form of the Western book from ancient times to the age of printing. In viewing the book of each culture, I hope to examine the script found on its surface, the materials on which the book was written and how they were manufactured and assembled, the tools employed in writing the book, and briefly, the literature found in the book and its illustration, with a few examples of the culture's great books and documents. Where possible, we will glimpse at the scribes who wrote these books, and read the colophons they left to posterity.

I am aware as I write that for each generalization there is an exception, and for every "earliest known" there soon will be a new discovery to prove it obsolete. Imperfection is inherent in one's own work — how much more so in interpreting the work of others. I have "chutzpah" (a Hebrew word popularized by the *New York Times*), because for each chapter here there could be and often are far more detailed books written on its single subject. And chutzpah because I am not an expert in 99 percent of the areas discussed in this book. I have depended on the research of others, whose names appear in the bibliography, and hope that the reader will find this synthesis of their original works coherent and useful.

Some technical details: Diacritical marks have been omitted here where scholars would have them on the assumption that they are meaningless to the general reader and that their precise assistance is not needed by specialists, who will recognize the word or name. Renderings of ancient and medieval names generally have followed the usage of encyclopedias with a few favorite modifications. In plate captions, dimensions have been included only for illuminated European manuscripts where such information may be useful for comparative study.

In addition to the scholars from whose original work I have drawn information, I would like to thank those experts, scholars, and craftspersons who have answered my questions patiently for the past several years, and those who have read and improved individual chapters and directed me to additional sources: Malachi Beit-Arié, Michelle Brown, James W. Craven, Sarah Scott Gibson, Mordechai Glatzer, Moshe Henry Goshen-Gottstein, Jonas Greenfield, Abraham Malamat, Yehuda Miklaf, Hermineh Miller, Asher Ovadiah, Benjamin Richler, Aaron

Shaffer, Moshe Sharon, Denise Schmandt-Besserat, Joyce Schmidt, Nellie Stavisky, Susan Otis Thompson, and Joan Goodnick Westenholz. Any errors of transmission of their knowledge and skills are mine, not theirs. I am also grateful to the department chairmen, deans, and professors at the Hebrew University of Jerusalem and the University of Michigan, where I have taught the History of Books and Printing, who have inspired and guided me, particularly Russell E. Bidlack, Andrew S. Ehrenkreutz, Marvin J. Eisenberg, Raymond Lincoln Kilgour, Bluma Peritz, Dov Schidorsky, and Robert M. Warner.

For encouragement in undertaking and completing the work, I am indebted to members of my family and friends: Toby Asch, Eve Avrin and Ross Halpern, Marcia Silber Boxman, Martha Avrin Hencken, Esther and the late Max A. Kopstein, the late Revella R. Kopstein, the late Dr. Robert L. Leslie, Elissa Avrin, and Louis Sherby, and Michele and Paul Vishny.

I would like to express my gratitude for the efficiency and kindness of the librarians, curators, and photographers of the libraries and museums credited herein for their efforts in providing me with photographs, and to the institutions and individuals who have granted permission to reproduce the works they have preserved. More thanks to those I pestered the most: Brian F. Cook, T. G. H. James, Irène Lewitt, T. C. Mitchell, Annie de Sainte Maréville, Diana Rowland-Smith, A. J. Spencer, and Zalman Zand. To artist, calligrapher, and friend Malla Carl-Blumenkranz, words of praise will never equal the drawings and calligraphy she accomplished to enhance this book. When most of the figures were lost, graphic artist Noah Ophir graciously, speedily, and skillfully replaced them.

Finally, I am grateful to David Way of The British Library for his help and for the work of the staff of the American Library Association: Senior Editor Herbert Bloom; Associate Editor Bettina MacAyeal; former Associate Editor Joseph Brinley; Helen Cline, Managing Editor; Mary Huchting; Harriett Banner; Marcie Lange; and Gil Taylor.

Having exhausted the thesaurus entry for "gratitude," rather than thank all of the students who once sat in my History of Books course, I will instead beg their forgiveness for any misinformation I may have passed along to them in class. I trust those errors have been corrected here, and that I now have answered any questions that were left unanswered years ago. Knowledge is imperfect; there is more we do not know than we do know (and what is unknown is so much more interesting!). But there is always the hope that tomorrow we may know a little more.

Introduction

The book we know today is a product of tradition. Although we live in an age of technological revolution, particularly in methods of printing and manufacturing books, the contemporary printer and book designer still respect tradition. Even with all the changes wrought in the past five millennia, the entity of the book has remained the same—a collection of surfaces to receive writing for the purpose of communicating ideas. Some of our book traditions go back five thousand years, some were born with the medieval manuscript, and some were established in the Renaissance with the earliest presses. Here we will follow the development of the book until the first technological revolution in the fifteenth century, printing from movable type. We will see how the book was made in the ancient and medieval worlds (pl. 1), how writing and the alphabet evolved, how the materials used in making the book originated in the same earth on which its readers walked, and how scribes and craftsmen based their techniques on the traditions of preceding and neighboring cultures. We will see, as far as is possible, who the scribes were, how they learned to write, and how their work was valued by their own society.

Pl. 1. Ceremony of the Opening of the Mouth from the Hunefer Papyrus. Egypt, early XIX Dynasty, ca. 1300 B.C.E. British Museum Department of Egyptian Antiquities, Papyrus 9901. Courtesy of the British Museum

If we take a contemporary book in hand (pl. 2), we can analyze its components, materials, and methods of manufacture in terms of past books to find its ultimate sources in Antiquity and the Middle Ages. For example, the tradition of covering the book originates with clay tablets of Mesopotamia. Over four thousand years ago in Sumer and Akkad, documents and correspondence deemed worthy of protection were provided with envelopes (pl. 3); Assyrian and Roman wax tablets were shielded by their wood or ivory frames; Egyptian and Hebrew scrolls were protected by ceramic jars (pl. 4) and cylindrical cases of leather and wood; Hebrew and Roman scrolls were covered with fabric jackets; medieval European parchment codices were laced to heavy wooden boards, at times covered with gilt silver, silver, ivory, or leather. When books became more portable, their protective coverings became lighter—cardboard replaced wood; parchment, velvet, and silk were used for outer wrappers; and later leather was replaced by cloth and then by paper.

The materials of the contemporary book, too, are ancient in their origins. Paper was invented in the second century B.C.E. ("Before the Common Era," equivalent to B.C.). It was used for books in China, its place of origin, for hundreds of years before knowledge of its use and manufacture spread to the Near East in the eighth century C.E. ("Common Era," equivalent to A.D.). In the late Middle Ages,

Pl. 2. Doves Bible (London: Doves Press, 1903–1905). Courtesy of the University of Michigan Library, Department of Rare Books and Special Collections. Photo: Patrick J. Young

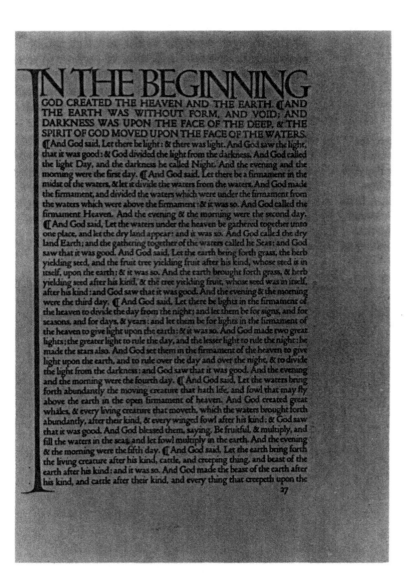

European scribes were already writing books on paper. When printing was introduced, the cost would have been prohibitive had this inexpensive substitute for parchment not been available.

Animal skin, the forerunner of paper as a surface for books, was used for scrolls in Egypt as early as 2500 B.C.E. and perhaps that early in western Asia. Leather was well known there in the first millennium B.C.E. Parchment, hides that are processed in a manner different from leather, came into common use in the early centuries of Christianity. Before parchment, papyrus was the writing material of the Mediterranean world; it gave its Egyptian name *ppr* to paper, which began to replace it in the Near East in the eighth century C.E. Paper did not serve as a substitute for parchment in western Europe until much later. Parchment and vellum, the thinner and softer variety of parchment, never disappeared entirely; fine editions continued to be printed on this luxury material even though the task was difficult, and vellum continued to be used for binding. The Jewish Torah (Pentateuch) and other scrolls read in the synagogue are still written on parchment and vellum.

Pl. 3. Clay tablet business letter in Old Assyrian, *right,* with sender's seal rolled on the envelope, *left.* From Kanish (Kultepe, Turkey), ca. 1900 B.C.E. British Museum Department of Western Asiatic Antiquities, No. 113572. Courtesy of the British Museum

Pl. 4. Isaiah Scroll and clay jars. Qumran, Israel, ca. 125–100 B.C.E. Courtesy of Shrine of the Book, Israel Museum, Jerusalem. Photo: David Harris

The format of the modern book was inherited from the Roman codex—wax tablets that were fastened at their inner edges. When parchment leaves replaced wax tablets with their wood or ivory boards, both the cover and the manner of securing the sheets at the inner edge were retained. This was in contrast to the Far Eastern method of folding the scroll into an accordion or fanfolded book. In the Western medieval codex, after the text was written, parchment sheets were cut and sewn in gatherings or quires, usually of four sheets, that is, eight leaves or sixteen pages. When printing began, gatherings came to be called signatures, still composed of multiples of two, but there eventually could be twelve-, sixteen-, eighteen-, or twenty-four-page signatures because paper was thinner and could be folded and cut easily. The binding of a book by hand today is accomplished in the same manner as it was in the Middle Ages—it is sewn to cords that are strung vertically onto a sewing frame. Binders' tools and the techniques of blind and gold stamping are essentially the same as they were five hundred years ago.

The layout of the page is older than the codex; ancient scrolls exhibit a rectangular block of text with margins around it. Earlier Mesopotamian clay tablets and multi-sided prisms even display a rectangle of script. The proportions of blank space above, below, and between the scroll's columns of writing were transferred to the codex, and the relative proportion of text to blank space is the same now as it was two thousand years ago. It is as if the golden mean of book design were inborn in all makers of books, past and present, and as if master handed down that aesthetic to apprentice from generation to generation. The two-column layout found in Bibles and reference works today has its origin in the fourth-to-twelfth century codex, which in turn based its layout on the scroll. When one opened a large, early luxury codex, four, six or eight columns of text appeared across the two pages so that it looked very much like an open scroll (compare pl. 5 with pl. 133, p. 149). As

Pl. 5. Codex Vaticanus. Greek Bible Manuscript, Uncial script. Fourth century C.E. Vatican Library, cod. gr. 1209. Courtesy of the Biblioteca Apostolica Vaticana, Vatican City

the average manuscript became smaller, book designers in Europe in the late Middle Ages found the two-column layout the most readable, as it still is for quick scanning of the page. Practicality and readability guide the book designer now as they did then. The reader's eye can take in about five to nine units at a time; this was about the width of a column in ancient and medieval times. Newspapers, multicolumn magazines, dictionaries, and encyclopedias still have this layout. Today, psychophysiological testing may prove this to be the best design, but in the ancient and medieval worlds the scribe knew it instinctively, or simply followed the traditions he found in the scroll or codex he copied.

Justification of the right-hand margin was well established by the Middle Ages, and printers simply followed this tradition. Indeed, the early printed book was an imitation of the manuscript in many ways—in its typography that duplicated script, in its use of medieval contractions and ligatures, in its proportions of text to blank space, in its spacing between lines, and in its decoration and illuminations (pl. 6). Not that printers of incunabula (books printed before 1501) were willful plagiarists; they knew of no other way to make a book with their new technology except to copy what came before, just as many scribes had done.

Pl. 6. The Gutenberg Bible. (Mainz: Gutenberg, Fust and Schoeffer, 1455?) Staatsbibliothek Preussischer Kulturbesitz, Berlin, Inc. 1511, f. 5r. Courtesy of the Staatsbibliothek Preussischer Kulturbesitz

Other materials and techniques of the handmade book, such as carbon ink, linen thread for binding, gold leaf for enhancement, and the use of red for eye-catching headings called "rubrics," have been known since Egyptian, Hellenistic, and Roman times. Practical apparatus to assist reading, such as punctuation, pagination, marginal or interlineal notes called glosses, running heads, contents notes and concordances, and even the *ex libris,* made their appearance in preprinting days, although a continuous tradition for many of these was not established firmly until relatively recent times. Some of the everyday book terminology now taken for granted comes from earlier Greek or Latin roots (Chapter 6); easily recognizable are *paragraphos, pagina, titulus, liber, volumen. Liber* was the inner bark of a tree, which may have been an early Roman writing surface. From this term came the word for book and for the copyist and bookseller in ancient and medieval times, *librarius;* in modern English it gives us the home for books and their keeper, the library and librarian. In French, *libraire* is the bookseller. Although *book* may come from a Germanic root (the Middle English *beech*), all things bibliophilic come from *biblos,* the Greek name for papyrus. Law codes come from *codices.*

The written word, now in typographic form, is even more conservative than the book's materials and format. Letter forms have changed little since the beginning of the Latin alphabet, and only slightly more so from the first Semitic alphabet that came into being in the middle of the second millennium B.C.E. Our capital letters are identical to the Roman Capitals on monuments of the early second century C.E. because these very letters were an inspiration to fifteenth-century Italian printers; the term *capitals* even reflects their first architectural application. Our small printed letters developed from the hand of Renaissance humanist calligraphers who in turn copied the minuscule script of Carolingian monastic scribes. The first printers of Germany and Italy based their movable types on scribal hands of the cities in which they printed because their designers were on the spot and because they wanted their books to be read with ease by the local public. In the sixteenth century, Roman typefaces, which at first were based on the Humanistic hand but soon were copied from successful Roman typefaces, triumphed over Gothic types in most parts of Europe.

Illustrations do not appear in all books today, nor did they in the past, but their traditions derive from the earliest Mesopotamian and Egyptian books (see pl. 1). In Mesopotamia, text was superimposed on illustration on palace walls, or figures appeared independently on small, carved cylinder seals used as name stamps. The author's or patron's portrait appeared at the head of the text from the time of the Code of Hammurabi in the eighteenth century B.C.E., even though King Hammurabi was not the true author or editor, but the royal Babylonian publisher. Roman and Byzantine authors had their portraits painted, whether real or imaginary, among the preliminary pages in codices and probably in the scrolls that preceded them. Even the inexpensive editions of Virgil were reported to have included his portrait. When the Gospel book became the major manuscript produced in Europe, a picture of the evangelist served as author portrait. At times the writer appeared alone at the beginning of each Gospel, at times as one of a group portrait at the opening of the book, or both. The tradition of the author portrait is still with us, except that the writer's photograph has moved from frontispiece to book jacket.

Illustrations were not accidental, and when they existed they were planned in advance. If they did appear, the problem of integrating text with illustration and decoration always had to be solved. Should writing be interrupted by pictures at intervals, or should the picture occupy a full page opposite the text? Or should all the pictures be grouped together for the sake of harmony and economy? Should there be decorations other than illustrations? These problems were solved in various ways in the past, as they are today. The enlarged or decorated initial letter at the beginning of the book or chapter has been a consistent feature of book decoration since the introduction of parchment codices, even when there was no other ornamentation. Ornamental initial letters existed before a system of capitalization was developed by Carolingian scribes in the late eighth and ninth centuries.

The tradition of the colophon began long before this Greek term came into being for the notice of production details left by the scribe and later by the printer. Some attribute the origin of the term with this meaning to the humanist Erasmus (1466?–1536). The colophon itself can be found in ancient Mesopotamian tablets and monuments, where it would state the purpose of the work, or that it was a true copy of the original. In the Egyptian scroll, the colophon revealed the place of writing and an expression of thanks or satisfaction upon completion of the work. In Hellenistic and Roman books it recorded the number of lines written by the scribe or the name of the corrector. The medieval scribe, in his colophon, told the reader his name, the place and date of the manuscript's writing, and, at times, how he felt about his work. Curses against the bookthief and mutilator also originate in the ancient Near East; Jewish and Muslim scribes of the Middle Ages preserved this tradition and perhaps passed along the idea to their Christian counterparts in Europe. The colophon today (not the publisher's emblem but the note at the end of the book) extends the medieval tradition by giving information about the paper, design, edition, typography, binding, and printer. At times there is an autograph. Without a colophon, today's printer is anonymous, and the publisher takes all the credit for production. But colophons are rare today in commercial publications, and seldom does an author know who printed the book. Colophons exist in examples of private printing and fine printing, where craftspersons take pride in their work and publishers take pride in their printers and designers.

One of the more humble writing surfaces was universal. This was the tablet with handle, a square or rectangular paddle that was held easily by a schoolchild. Modest tablets such as these have been excavated from ancient sites. Some were whitewashed, some held wax. Some still had their *ABC's* on them, and are known as abecedaries. The Marsiliana tablet is the Etruscan version (pl. 7). Greek-speaking Egyptians used elongated, knob-handled tags as mummy labels (pl. 8). The Roman version, the *tabella ansata* (small-handled tablet), was a familiar everyday object, so

Pl. 7. Marsiliana Tablet, an Etruscan abecedary, ca. 700 B.C.E. Department of Antiquities, Florence (Inn. N. 93480). Courtesy of Soprintendenza Alle Antichità d'Etruria, Firenze

much so that it served as a model for inscription frames in monuments and in smaller objects, such as jewelry (pl. 9), sometimes with a triangular handle on each side. We see *tabellae ansata* in the hands of students in Islamic and European manuscripts (pl. 10, 11). These tablets also inspired the decorative *ansa* (handle) of carpet-page designs in Irish and English illuminated manuscripts, the earliest Hebrew manuscripts, and Islamic manuscripts (pl. 12, 13). In English-speaking countries, the ubiquitous tablet became the hornbook (pl. 14). A lesson sheet of paper or parchment was pasted to a wooden tablet and covered with transparent horn. Modern calculator users, like ancient Mesopotamian clay-tablet writers, are less in need of the handle because their devices are small enough to fit in the palm of the hand. But look at the twentieth century's Monotype matrix case (pl. 15). Is it the same shape because of practical necessity, or was its inventor conforming to tradition?

The changes that have come about since the book's inception may seem greater in number than its traditions. After all, the book today does not resemble a Mesopotamian clay tablet, and only a good imagination and knowledge of book history would equate it with the Egyptian papyrus scroll. The medieval parchment codex often impresses one with its weight, and it is not practical for everyday reading even for those who understand the text. But the makers of the modern book must thank their ancestors—the scribes and makers of clay tablets, papyrus and parchment scrolls, and vellum codices—for setting the book in the right direction. Today's type director and book designer have the same goals as those early scribes—clarity, beauty, and readability. The book would not look the way it does today without this foundation.

So much for type and its precursor, script, and books and their predecessors, scrolls and codices. What about the ancestors of the printer and designer? Who were the scribes? Like today's printers, most of them were anonymous. They served in

Pl. 8. Mummy label. "Premposirios, son of Taus, his father Hatres the club-footed." Upper Egypt, second to fourth century C.E. University of Michigan, Harlan Hatcher Graduate Library, Papyrology Collection, P. Mich. Inv. 4533.9. Courtesy of the University of Michigan Library, Department of Rare Books and Special Collections

different capacities in different times and places. The scribe could be a copyist, a clerk, a notary, a calligrapher, a scholar, a writing master, a grammarian, a drudge, a general, a prime minister. Exactly which role he filled depended on when and where he lived, his training, his skill, and the need for his services by his society. Information on the scribes themselves varies from time to time and from place to place. Nearly all were men. Some scribes extolled the joys of their profession; some complained bitterly. Some had portraits made of themselves; one included his mother (pl. 16). But most of them were silent. The personality of the scribe does not enter into the manufacture of the book. The individuality of the scribe and his handwriting is even more subtle than the style of the artist, and the ordinary eye probably would not notice that more than one medieval scribe worked on a single codex. The scribe was a craftsman, not a creative artist determined to express himself in his work. His creativity was subtle, to be seen only in the shapes of letters.

Pl. 9. Gold *tabella ansata*, with inscription, "Take Courage!" Provenance unknown, Roman period. Adornments such as these were often placed in tombs over the mouth of the deceased. Courtesy of the Israel Antiquities Authority, Jerusalem

Pl. 10. School scene, with schoolboys holding tablets. *Maqamat al-Hariri,* from the 46th maqama. Cairo, 1337. Bodleian Library, Ms. Marsh. 458, f. 116r. Courtesy of the Bodleian Library, Oxford

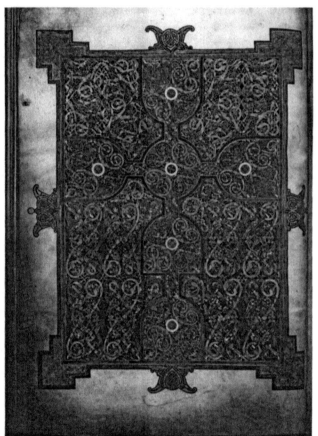

Pl. 11. The Deacon Petrus, holding tablet, catches a glimpse of the Holy Spirit inspiring St. Gregory. From a twelfth century *Registrum Gregorii*. Trier City Library, Cod. 171/1626. Courtesy of the Stadtbibliothek, Trier

Pl. 12. Cruciform carpet page, with ansa on each side. Lindisfarne Gospels, British Library, Ms. Cotton Nero D. IV, f. 26v. Lindisfarne, ca. 700 C.E. Courtesy of the British Library

The work of the scribe and his position in society varied according to the age, place, and culture. One would think a more literate society would better appreciate the scribe. In truth, the scribe's services were more highly valued when writing was not as widespread. When writing was universal, he was appreciated only if he was a superior calligrapher.

Pl. 13. Sura ornament from Qur'ān, ca. ninth century. Kufic script. Chester Beatty Library, Ms. 1407, f. 2v. Courtesy of the Chester Beatty Library, Dublin

Pl. 14. Hornbook with counting device. Eighteenth century. Courtesy of Library of Congress, John Davis Batchelder Collection

Pl. 15. Monotype matrix case. Courtesy of The Monotype Corporation, Redhill, England

Pl. 16. Stele of the Neo-Hittite scribe Tarhunpiyas with his mother. Inscription in Hittite hieroglyphics. Marash, Anatolia (Turkey), late eighth century B.C.E. Basalt. Louvre, AO 19222. Courtesy of the Louvre

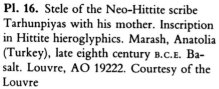

At the dawn of Sumerian history, the scribe may have been attached to the temple, and it was in Sumer that scribes were first trained in schools. But one must not forget that the temple in Mesopotamia was also the trade center, so early scribal writings were not necessarily religious but economic in character. A school, in the ancient Near East, was the place where one learned to read and write to become a professional scribe. In Greece and Rome, however, "school" meant getting an education. A mere copyist, working for an author or publisher (there were publishers in ancient Rome) was undoubtedly paid poorly. In the days when Rome conquered Greece, the scribe could have been a Greek slave, his captivity having reduced his status, to say nothing of his income (pl. 17). In Byzantine times, the professional writer was remunerated according to the number of lines he wrote and by the quality of his script. The best Muslim scribes were honored not only with extravagant fees and status, but by students and plagiarists who signed their masters' names.

Pl. 17. Poet and Muse on an ivory codex. Ca. 500 C.E. Courtesy of the Museo del Duomo, Monza

In Antiquity as well as in the Middle Ages, scribes specialized. In the ancient Near East, some scribes were public notaries, some were private secretaries, some worked in temple or palace library copying literature, some were teachers of script, some were court messengers, and some were palace administrators. In pharaonic Egypt, writing was a key to advancement in government. The fact that army officers and ministers held scribal implements in their sculptured portraits demonstrates how proud they were of their writing skills (pl. 18). In Syria and Mesopotamia, a royal scribe could have been rewarded with an estate. At the palace, a son had a good chance of inheriting his father's scribal position. In the biblical age, Ezra the Scribe was the Jewish spiritual leader; later the Jewish scribe had the status of a scholar or grammarian. In Hebrew, *sofer* means "author" as well as "scribe." High status was also enjoyed by the monastic scribe of early medieval Christian Europe. In Gospel books, the evangelists are portrayed as scribes at work (pl. 19). Literacy was not common in medieval Europe, and the monastic scribe seems to have had a more enviable job than his brethren who tended the flocks and farm, even though he complained about his disagreeable working conditions. His pay? The same as the farming monk—he worked for his heavenly reward.

Pl. 18. Haremhab, scribe and commander-in-chief of the armies of Tutankhamon, who eventually became king himself. Memphis, XVIII Dynasty, ca. 1355 B.C.E. Diorite. MMA 23.10.1, gift of Mr. and Mrs. V. Everit Macy. Courtesy of the Metropolitan Museum of Art, New York

Pl. 19. St. Matthew, Gospel Book of Ebo. Hautvillers, ca. 820. Bibliothèque Municipale, Epernay, Ms. 1., f. 18v. (10¼ × 8¼″, 260 × 210 mm). Courtesy of Bibliothèque Municipale, Epernay

In Jewish society, where writing was widespread both in the Near East and in Europe, the Torah scribe, who wrote the scrolls read in the synagogue service, was respected much more than the notary who wrote documents or personal correspondence or worked for the rabbinical courts. (This does not mean he was overpaid.) Torah scribes wrote codices as well as scrolls. But codices also were written by people of other professions: doctors, teachers, or goldsmiths. They wrote to have books for their own study, or because they considered the writing of a Bible codex a meritorious act, just as Muslim princes viewed the writing of a Qur'ān.

In the late Middle Ages in Europe, with the growth of cathedral schools and afterwards the universities, reading and writing were no longer limited to the monastic scriptorium, the ruler's chancery, and the merchant class. Scribes were hired by publishers, the *stationarii*, in university towns, or by students themselves.

Or students could pick up extra income by serving as scribes. Textbooks were not as beautiful and legible as those written in the monastic book hand. Once printing was invented, the gap between the ordinary transcriber (the compositor) and the scribe, now thought of as a calligrapher, grew. Calligraphers' labors came to be valued, not because they reproduced a text, but because with their writing they could create a work of art on parchment or paper. For when the eye grows weary of art, it turns for satisfaction to the abstraction of script, and when the senses are jaded by paint and marble, the hand turns the crisp leaf of paper or parchment to discover a fresh delight.

CHAPTER 1

Writing

I t is relatively easy for us to see the dependence of today's printed letters on the alphabet used by the Romans in the first century C.E., and only slightly more difficult to see their origin in the ancient Semitic alphabet of ca. 1500 B.C.E. Yet the alphabet grew from an even earlier writing system that few would recognize as an ancestor—the hieroglyphics of Egypt. This was not an alphabet but a mixed system of writing, a system also used by two other civilizations of the ancient world—Mesopotamia and China. Although the signs of these three scripts in no way resembled one another visually, the system underlying all of them combined the same elements of script—logographic (pictographic and ideographic) and phonographic, and phonetic (sound) signs. Is it a coincidence that the underlying principles of the three major scripts of the ancient world were the same? Did each civilization develop its system independently? Did one influence the other? Did the human mind progress from one stage of a system to a higher one? Was it necessary for human society, or speech, to reach a certain stage, or for the brain to develop in a certain way for the mind to invent and perfect a system of recording ideas and words? We cannot promise answers to all of these questions.

EMBRYO WRITING

Long before there was a decipherable system of writing at all, there was graphic recording of thoughts, or protowriting, of the most primitive kind. As far back as the Stone Age, from 30,000 to 15,000 B.C.E., from the time weapons and tools were first made, the needs of society both to express itself visually and to record the former by means of art and the latter with signs were present in the human consciousness. Writing implies communication between two people using the same system. Some systems are more sophisticated than others, and we like to think that ours, the alphabet, is the best. But today, along with the alphabet, we still use the same primitive kind of writing first used in the Stone Age—embryo writing. Embryo writing consists of signs that are invented for the writer alone or that represent an idea known only to others with the same frame of reference. Memory devices belong to this class of writing, for example, the tying of a knot around the finger as a reminder, or the pre-Columbian Peruvian *quipu,* made of knotted cords of different colors and lengths to designate numerical values (pl. 20). Heraldic devices from the Middle Ages and printers' and publishers' marks can be classified as embryo writing but they also can be considered the first stage of true writing—logograms. So may the clog almanac, used in England in medieval times through the seventeenth century (pl. 21). This wooden calendar recorded the feast days of saints by means of their attributes: the wheel for St. Catherine, arrows for St. Sebastian, the harp for David. Today we see trademarks, cleaning instructions for fabrics, international road signs, and many other examples of embryo writing (or logograms).

In Europe, especially in southern France and northern Spain, from Paleolithic to Neolithic times (30,000 to 9,000 B.C.E.), embryo writing consisted of marks and signs painted on cave walls (pl. 22, 23) and scratched on stones and on bones of birds (pl. 24, 25). By the number and pattern of repeated signs on a single surface, it has been hypothesized by Alexander Marshack that prehistoric people noted the passage of days and phases of the moon on these surfaces. Perhaps they recorded the number of animals killed, wrote memory devices to help recall the tales of their clan, invented symbols to assist in magic, or created a calendar. The exact message of this pre- and protowriting remains obscure, and this is precisely the difficulty with reading embryo script, whether ancient or modern. Without an outside explanation of each sign or full knowledge of the context of the signs, or without frequent repetition of the same signs to aid in decipherment, the writing cannot be interpreted accurately. Modern embryo writing is accessible because it is verified easily or explained by other media. Even the clog almanac is not completely obscure because

Pl. 20. Peruvian *quipu,* from Chancay. Courtesy of American Museum of Natural History, New York (Reproduced from Leslie LeLand Locke, *The Ancient Quipu*)

Pl. 21. Clog almanacs from England (*second from top,* Norwegian; *bottom,* a perpetual pocket clog almanac). Courtesy of the Museum of the History of Science, Oxford University

many people still recognize some of the symbols. If the Christian frame of reference were lost, the calendar would be unintelligible. Embryo writing is limited culturally. Furthermore, one can neither write sentences with it nor present ideas to others without an accompanying explanation.

SYSTEMS AND STAGES

True writing, which has been defined as the graphic communication of ideas between people separated by time and space, is divided into three stages of development. The human race is believed to have progressed from one so-called

Pl. 22. Embryo writing with the "Chinese horse" from the Lascaux caves. 15,000–10,000 B.C.E. Courtesy of Caisse Nationale des Monuments Historiques et des Sites, Arch. Phot./S.P.A.D.E.M., Paris

Pl. 23. Stencil print of hand. Cave at Pech-Merle à Cabrerets, Lot, France. 15,000–10,000 B.C.E. Courtesy of Musée de Prehistoire Amedee Lemozi, Lot

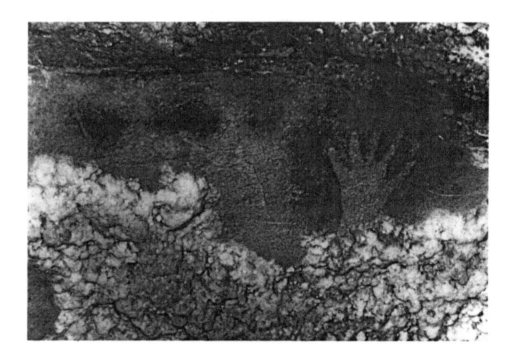

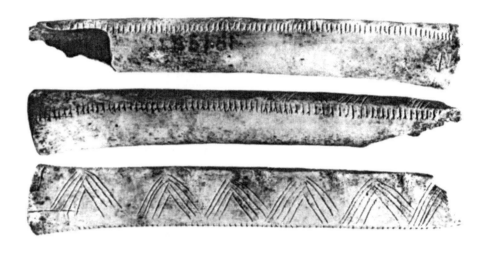

Pl. 24. Eagle bone tool with engraved marks. Ishango, Congo, Mesolithic (10,000–4000 B.C.E.). Reproduced from *The Roots of Civilization,* © Alexander Marshack. Published by McGraw-Hill

Pl. 25. Engraved and shaped bone plaque from rock shelter site of Abri Blanchard (Dordogne). Aurignacian (20,000 B.C.E.). Courtesy of Musée des Antiquités Nationales, Saint-Germaine-en-Laye

stage to the next, although at least two stages have almost always existed simultaneously in the civilizations of the Fertile Crescent. For example, in ancient times, cylinder seals were used at the same time as a mixed system of writing, and today embryo writing and logograms exist alongside the alphabet. One stage did not interfere with the other; at times they complemented each other and even may have speeded development of a better system. Writing itself is conservative, even holy to some; people are reluctant to give up an old system even when a new one is more functional, either for the sake of tradition or because it continues to serve a purpose for its users.

Stages or subsystems of writing are classified as logographic, phonographic, and phonetic. Logographic writing is picture writing—the sign is bound up with the image of an object (although the logographic sign became more and more abstract and eventually did not look at all like the object that had originally inspired it; figs. 1 and 2). In phonographic writing the sign is bound to the *sound* of the name of an object but, by punning, it could represent the homophone, a word of a different meaning. In phonetic script, the sign represents a sound with no apparent relationship to a depicted object, although we will see that in the original Semitic alphabet there was once a relationship between the two. These three writing stages, or subsystems, can be subdivided further. The term *stages* does not imply that writers necessarily advanced from one to the next. Cuneiform, Egyptian hieroglyphics, and Chinese script combined all three stages. Mixed systems formerly were called "analytic" by some historians of the alphabet.

Fig. 1. Cuneiform in its pictorial form: logograms (pictograms and ideograms) and determinatives

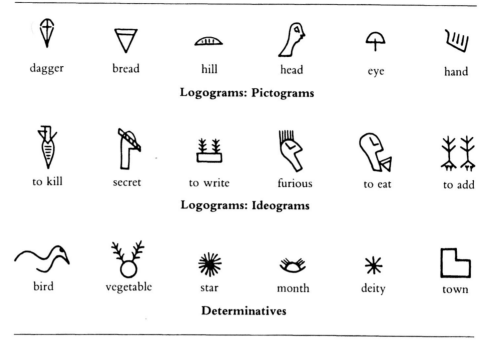

| | dagger | bread | hill | head | eye | hand |

Logograms: Pictograms

| | to kill | secret | to write | furious | to eat | to add |

Logograms: Ideograms

| | bird | vegetable | star | month | deity | town |

Determinatives

Fig. 2. Sumerian and Egyptian logograms

	Sumerian	Egyptian		Sumerian	Egyptian
man			sun		
king			water		
ox			house		
sky			land		

Logograms

The borderline between embryo writing and the single logogram is a fine one, and some signs seem to fall into both categories. Trademarks or logos, for example, can be seen as embryo writing when they are so new that they cannot be identified without an explanation. Once the signs become familiar, they can be considered logograms. Another distinction between the two is that embryo writing consists of isolated, individual signs not at all or seldom repeated, or signs that have a single context limited in time or intended for use by very few people. Logographic script attempts to impose a universally recognized graphic sign within a given time or place, or a system by which sentences can be composed, even if they are not grammatically correct by our standards.

Logographic writing consists of two types of signs—pictographic and ideographic. Pictograms are graphic representations of objects: ⚆ means sun, ⚇ means man, ⚇ means hand. Theoretically, pictographic script should be universal; the spoken language should not be necessary to write or interpret these signs. It is doubtful, however, that a complete system of writing could be based on pictograms alone, just as sentences could not be composed only of nouns. It is more likely that pictograms were combined with ideograms as soon as the writer wished to present a series of ideas graphically. In ideographic writing, the sign represents concepts associated with the picture. Thus ⚆ could represent a number of ideas suggested by the sun—it could be a noun meaning "heaven," "sky," "day," "the gods"; an adjective meaning "warm," "light," or "shiny"; or a verb, "to brighten" or "to shine." It could be used as a phrase within a longer sentence; "when the sun came up." The meaning of the individual ideogram must be taught and, because this teaching depends on culture and oral communication, ideographic writing is less international than pictographic. A purely logographic system is very limited for communicating ideas outside the immediate environment, and it was almost never used exclusively. Until twenty years ago, it was believed that the preconquest Mayans of Central America wrote with a logographic system, using a few sound signs for proper names (pl. 26). Their logographic numerical system was deciphered first, and the subjects of their calendars and almanacs were interpreted with the help of oral communication between the Mayans themselves and sixteenth-century Spanish priests. Now it is known that from one-quarter to one-third of the signs have syllabic value, and there is hope of deciphering more with new tools of linguistic analysis. Logograms seen daily in our time include road signs, numerals, astrological signs, commercial and corporate logos, bar codes, and the dollar sign ($).

Complete logographic messages occasionally are still invented to communicate. When the *Pioneer 10* satellite was sent into orbit in 1972, Carl Sagan designed a plaque carrying a message for the spaceship's extraterrestrial finders, who presumably would have human or superhuman scientific intelligence (pl. 27). Whether Sagan's logograms are understood by these beings depends on their knowledge of our civilization. Their interpretation of his message could be as uncertain as our understanding of cave art and other ancient embryo writing. It is interesting that one of the finest science writers of our age turned to the most primitive and least decipherable form of writing to communicate. A story or greetings in one language and script, long enough to repeat signs, would have sufficed, as would the same inscription written in several languages. This is what the ancients did in their biscripts and triscripts. Because they wrote the same message in two or three languages, scholars since the nineteenth century have been able to decipher cuneiform and hieroglyphics. A subsequent message, also devised by Sagan, was multilingual but there was a different message in each language. This will certainly drive outer spaceniks crazy. Better to send a videocassette or disk with written operating instructions in several languages and scripts.

Phonograms

In phonographic writing, the sign or unit does not represent the object or an idea connected with it, but the *sound* of the object's name. It is tied to the specific spoken language; the reader mentally pronounces the picture. One sounds out ⚆ as "sun." In this way, what looks like a logogram or picture writing in reality can be a phonogram. The numeral 1 is both a logogram for the concept of "one," and a phonogram for "un," or "uno," depending on the reader's language. In the ancient

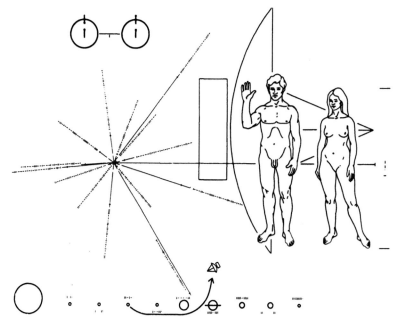

Pl. 27. Pioneer 10 plaque. 1972. Reproduced from Carl Sagan, *The Cosmic Connection*. Courtesy of Doubleday, Anchor Press

Pl. 26. New Year's ceremonies. The Dresden Codex, Chapter 10. Mayan book. Bars and dots are numerals. Courtesy of the Sächsische Landesbibliothek, Dresden

Near East, practical phonographic script made use of homophones, or words that sound alike but have different meanings—puns. Thus ⊙ could be "son" as a phonogram. Words of several syllables could be made up of sound-pictures for each syllable. For example "sensible" could be written ⊙ ∽ ∽ ⬠ (sun-see-bull). In English we make a game of it, a written form of charades called rebus-writing (pl. 28). In Mesopotamia and Egypt this was serious writing.

Logograms were combined with phonograms in the earliest examples of a true writing system. Today, phonograms, such as the ampersand (&) for "and" are used as space savers. "Xmas" for "Christmas" combines a phonogram with the alphabet. In reading mixed script in ancient times, however, readers had to be told whether the sign they were looking at was to be read as a logogram or as a phonogram—was ⊙ to be read as a logogram for "heavens" or as a phonogram for "sun" or "son"? An auxiliary sign, called a determinative, was invented to guide the reader in correctly interpreting a sign: ⬚ would mean a plant, ⬚ a name of a city. The Egyptian cartouche ▭ contained the name of royalty. This type of determinative is also known as a semantic indicator.

There were phonetic indicators as well, signs that reinforced pronunciation so there would be no mistake in the previous syllable. For example, a tree would follow "pantry" to tell the reader not to pronounce it "try." Mixed systems of logograms and phonograms served the writing needs of ancient Mesopotamia and Egypt for three thousand years. The Chinese system was fully developed by 1200 B.C.E. It was composed of word signs: logograms and phonograms that could employ homophones (rebus writing), accompanied by an additional sign that was a classifier (a semantic indicator, sometimes called a radical). Linear signs have been found on fourth millennium B.C.E. pottery, but as these inscriptions are not continuous and are unrelated to later writing, they cannot be read or considered part of the Chinese writing system. When ancient scripts abstracted their pictorial forms, the signs nevertheless remained logographic and phonographic. "Pictorial" should not be confused with "pictographic"; the former refers to the shape of the sign, the latter to the stage or aspect of a system.

Phonetic Script

The most advanced stage of writing is fully phonetic, and does not need to be accompanied by other stages or subsystems; it is a system in itself. In phonetic writing, elements of speech (its consonants and vowels) are represented by signs. Phonetic script can be viewed as growing from phonograms, although reference to the object once represented is no longer necessary. Phonetic writing can be accomplished with a syllabic script or an alphabetic one. In syllabic writing, each unit represents a consonant-and-vowel combination. In the two previously mentioned systems, logographic and phonographic, hundreds of signs were required for pictograms, ideograms, phonograms, determinatives, and other indicators. A syllabic system, on the other hand, needs only one hundred or fewer signs, enough to represent the number of possible consonant-and-vowel combinations in speech—ba, be, bi, bo, bu, ca, ce, ci, co, cu, and so forth. Two ancient Aegean systems of writing were partly syllabic: Linear B, used in Crete and Mycenae from the twelfth to the fifth centuries B.C.E. (pl. 29), and the later, related Cypriot script,

Pl. 28. Phonograms in two greeting cards by Sandra Boynton. *a.* "Ewer Great" *b.* "Happy Birthday to You." Courtesy of Recycled Paper Products, Chicago

used from the seventh to the first centuries B.C.E. Two formal Japanese syllabaries have been in use since the ninth century C.E.: *katakana,* used mainly for scientific literature and public documents, and *hiragana,* the everyday script found in newspapers and general literature. The Eskimo of Baffinland were provided with a syllabary based on that of the Cree Indians, an artificial script invented by nineteenth-century Christian missionaries in order to translate the Bible.

The alphabet further reduced the units of script to a number between twenty-two and thirty. There is one sign for one sound in the alphabetic system, at least in theory, although no alphabet is perfect and in all of them we can find examples of one sign for two sounds that are very similar, or two signs for one sound, or accent marks to assist in pronunciation. The original Semitic alphabet worked on the acrophonic principle, that is, each sign carried the initial sound in the name of the object that the sign represented (see Chapter 2). Subsequent users of alphabets who were not speakers of Semitic languages, such as the Greeks, were unaware of the principle of acrophony; they simply borrowed the Semitic alphabet's shapes and sound values and sometimes the names of the letters, with slight modifications. Eventually the Semitic alphabet replaced all other systems in the Near East and in Europe but not in the Far East. While there have been attempts in recent years to introduce an alphabetic system in China, its script is still basically logographic, comprised of some fifty thousand signs. It does have a syllabary of sixty-two signs developed in the fifth or sixth century C.E. to aid in pronouncing foreign names. Traditions of writing do not die easily.

It is doubtful that the inventors of script consciously thought out the steps from logographic to phonographic to phonetic in logical order, just as the first speakers did not work out rules of grammar. When the giant steps from logograms to phonograms and from phonograms to the alphabet were made, no one claimed credit.

Logograms, phonograms, and determinatives are modern terms, although ancient users of the alphabet undoubtedly called it the alphabet, or *alef-bet,* after the names of its first two letters. Civilized people devised script as their needs demanded that they count, record, and do business, or express themselves culturally or religiously in a form that would be permanent. The shapes of the signs were determined by objects seen and used in their daily life or found in the local surroundings. The surfaces on which they recorded and the tools with which they wrote were composed of the materials most available to them and most convenient for writing. As agriculture and commerce developed, society improved on the system, either by trial and error or by absorbing influences from the systems of others. This phenomenon of outside influence in script is known as "idea-diffusion," a thought process described by David Diringer, a historian of writing. One culture may have

Pl. 29. Linear B clay tablet from Knossos, recording chariot wheels made of wood and bronze. Fourteenth century B.C.E. Ashmolean Museum, 1910.211 (So 894 DMG 278). Courtesy of the Ashmolean Museum, Oxford

seen the writing system of another culture but, instead of taking over the system wholesale, applied the *idea* of writing or particular aspects of the system to its own language, materials, and culture.

THE ANCESTORS OF WESTERN SCRIPT

Let us now look at the two major scripts of the ancient Near East—cuneiform and hieroglyphics. Both of these were based on the same mixed system but the signs employed were as different as the materials and tools used by their writers.

Cuneiform

In the Near East, the first steps toward a viable writing system were taken in Mesopotamia and around the Persian Gulf. The phrase *History Begins at Sumer* (the title of Samuel Noah Kramer's book) is still accepted because of the nineteenth-century notion that "history" meant the beginning of written records. The Sumerians were the first to use a fully developed mixed system of logograms and phonograms. Their writing is called cuneiform, meaning wedge-shaped, because of the triangular marks made on clay by the stylus. Cuneiform was used for different writing systems (even an alphabetic one, Ugaritic; see fig. 10, p. 54), and for writing several languages that had no linguistic relationship to one another—the Sumerian language differed from Semitic Akkadian and both differed from Persian.

With archeological discoveries and a new interpretation of the data, we are able to trace the steps that led to cuneiform writing. As people of the Near East settled down from a hunting-gathering life to a herding-planting life around 9000 B.C.E. and began to build cities and engage in trade, they required some system for recording agricultural products as well as for recalling and verifying business transactions. In Mesopotamia, lumps of clay fashioned into different shapes were used in pre- and protohistoric times (pl. 30). These became the basis for the first systems of writing and counting. Excavations concentrated at Neolithic (ca. 9000–8000 B.C.E.) sites in Anatolia, Mesopotamia, Iran, Syria, and Palestine have yielded clay tokens in various shapes, such as cones, cylinders, disks, and flattened pellets. At first these were believed to be toys or small sculptures, but now, thanks to the research of Denise Schmandt-Besserat, it has been proven that the tokens are evidence of an ancient recording system used by a commercially oriented Near Eastern society. Schmandt-Besserat has distinguished between two kinds of clay tokens—one that engendered numerals and one that gave us the first true writing system. The earliest were simple, unmarked tokens of various shapes—spheres, cones, disks, tetrahedrons, and cylinders. These were at times encased in clay envelopes with marks on the outside that duplicated the shape of the token inside. More complex tokens, not as common and found generally at southern Mesopotamian sites (especially at Uruk, Ur, Nippur, and also at Susa), seem to be a Sumerian innovation in protoscript of the late fourth millennium. The shapes are more sophisticated—bent coils, rhomboids, and parabolae—and they could represent a wide variety of products and vessels, crafted objects, and foodstuffs produced in these cities, such as bread, oil, and perfume. The surfaces of complex tokens were marked or punched (pl. 31), and at times had holes so they could be strung together. If they were strung, attached to the string was a *bulla,* a piece of oblong clay stamped with a seal (pl. 32, 33 and fig. 3). In some instances, both simple and complex tokens were found together. Simple tokens were used for counting agricultural products on a one-to-one basis according to their shape; at times they were marked with dots resembling patterns on dice. Sometimes complex tokens had clay envelopes similar to simple ones. In other words, two kinds of protowriting were used simultaneously and not always consistently.

Pl. 30. Clay tablet impressed with to-
kens. From Susa, Iran, ca. 3100 B.C.E.
Courtesy of the Louvre, Départment des
Antiquités Orientales. Photo provided by
Denise Schmandt-Besserat

Pl. 31. Complex tokens. Susa, Iran, ca. 3300 B.C.E. *Top row:* oil,
honey(?), textile(?), one sheep. *Bottom row:* metal, wool(?). Courtesy of
the Louvre, Départment des Antiquités Orientales. Photo provided by
Denise Schmandt-Besserat

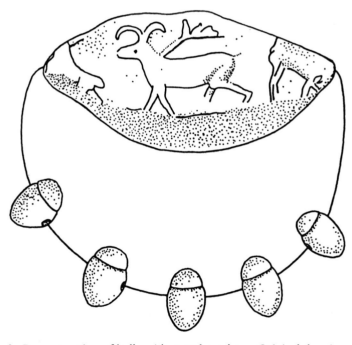

Pl. 32. Bulla that would have been
strung with tokens. From Habuba Kabira,
Syria, late fourth millennium B.C.E. Courtesy of Eva Strommenger, Museum für
Vor- und Frühgeschichte, Schloss Char-
lottenburg, Berlin. Photo provided by
Denise Schmandt-Besserat

Fig. 3. Reconstruction of bulla with complex tokens. Original drawing
by Ellen Simmons. Courtesy of Denise Schmandt-Besserat

Pl. 33. Bulla envelope. Susa, ca. 3300 B.C.E. The seal, which anticipates the first cylinder seals, was carved with scenes of everyday life. Louvre, Sb 1979. Courtesy of Louvre, Départment des Antiquités Orientales

At the Sumerian city-state of Uruk, complex tokens from 3350–3100 B.C.E. were found in the temple district. They represented deliveries of offerings to the temple, such as furniture, vessels, and prepared edibles, from the flocks and farms of the inhabitants of the area. Were these offerings to the gods or taxes in a theocratic city-state? These fine distinctions may not have been made at that time, when the temple district also included the palace and shopping center. The shapes of the tokens and their markings, made either by a pointed stylus or stamped as a negative imprint, can be related to early Sumerian pictorial and cuneiform signs on clay tablets. The bullae, with artistic renderings, are possibly ownership stamps that can be related to later cylinder seals (pl. 34). The discovery of this embryonic counting and recording system using plain and marked tokens sheds light on the transition from simple recording to the use of logograms as well as on the early pictorial aspect of cuneiform (pl. 35). It also explains the choice of materials used for the first Sumerian and subsequent Mesopotamian writing. Although the earliest clay tablets have not been deciphered thoroughly to everyone's satisfaction, they are obviously economic: records of transactions, administrative notes, or offerings to the temple in a society in which politics, religion, and the economy were interwoven.

Schmandt-Besserat's theory explains the logographic origin of cuneiform, for the earliest signs were drawn or sculpted as tokens. It does not explain the leap from logograms to phonograms; this development is still obscure. Nor does it explain the abstraction of once-pictorial signs into wedge-shaped units. This undoubtedly was determined by the tools and materials, possibly when the writing system itself became so complex that one needed a specialist for the task of recording, that is, a scribe. Perhaps then, it was necessary to formalize not only the script but methods of teaching it as well, and schools were established. Mesopotamian writers distinguished clearly between art and script, as Stone Age cave painters and bone writers had done. But even before Sumerian script was formalized into the wedge shapes of cuneiform, phonograms were an aspect of the script.

In the first decipherable Sumerian tablets, ca. 3200–3000 B.C.E., one logographic sign could mean several words: ✳ stood for a star, the sky, a deity, ⊐ meant "sun" or its ideographic associations, "light" and "day"; ⌂ could mean "land" or "mountain" or "foreign country." Man and food combined meant "to eat" ⟨ ; man and mountain together meant "a male slave" who came from the mountains. Also found from this early period were clay tags impressed with cylinder seals, ownership marks of individuals who sent to the temple the items to which these tags were attached (pl. 34 and pl. 73, p. 74). These were the descendants of the bullae attached to a string of tokens. They were Mesopotamia's contribution to the art of printing.

It could have been the need to write out names to replace those on cylinder seals that inspired the phoneticization of signs. During the late fourth millennium B.C.E., a Sumerian writer must have realized that writing could be augmented if a "pun word" or homophone were used for writing another word. For example, an arrow was *ti* ➤— in Sumerian. The word *ti* also meant "life." Then "life" could also be written ➤— . In a language of many homophones, the opportunity for phonographic writing was unlimited. Sumerians could break down many of their words into syllables with depictable homophones. The phonographic aspect of Sumerian had

Pl. 34. Cylinder seal and impression of an Akkadian royal scribe, Ibnisharrum. Mesopotamia, ca. 2280 B.C.E. Serpentine. Louvre, AO 22303. Courtesy of the Louvre, Départment des Antiquités Orientales

Pl. 35. Early pictorial Sumerian clay tablet. A list of proper names and land-owners, associated with the king. Lower Mesopotamia, late fourth millennium B.C.E. Louvre, AO 19936. Courtesy of the Louvre, Départment des Antiquités Orientales

some 100 to 150 signs, in addition to two thousand logograms, many of which were found in early tokens and tablets. The number of logograms was eventually reduced to eight hundred. Determinative and other semantic indicators were necessary to identify signs as words for persons, animals, plants, cities, rivers, and mountains. Phonetic indicators were used as well; for example, the crown, called *en*, after a sign ensured the pronunciation of the previous word as *men*.

Sumerian script was not fully phonetic; consonants and vowels at the end of syllables overlapped with the previous or following syllable. Syllables themselves were structured as consonant-vowel-consonant (CVC). Many different signs could be used to express the same syllable: *du*, for example, had twenty-two signs. Depending on the scribe's conventions, period, and place, syllabaries were limited; at other times cuneiform script was composed primarily of syllabic signs.

Very soon after the mixed system developed in Sumer, the shapes of the signs changed from schematic pictorial outlines to the more angular wedge shapes. This was due not only to inherent abstracting and simplifying but to the practical use of clay as the writing material. Impressed clay was the natural surface for writing not only because of its availability but because it was already the traditional material, long in use for tokens. The change to wedge-shaped writing was accomplished by 2800 B.C.E. (fig. 4).

Fig. 4. Development of cuneiform signs from pictorial logograms to abstract signs, to Akkadian, and to classic Assyrian

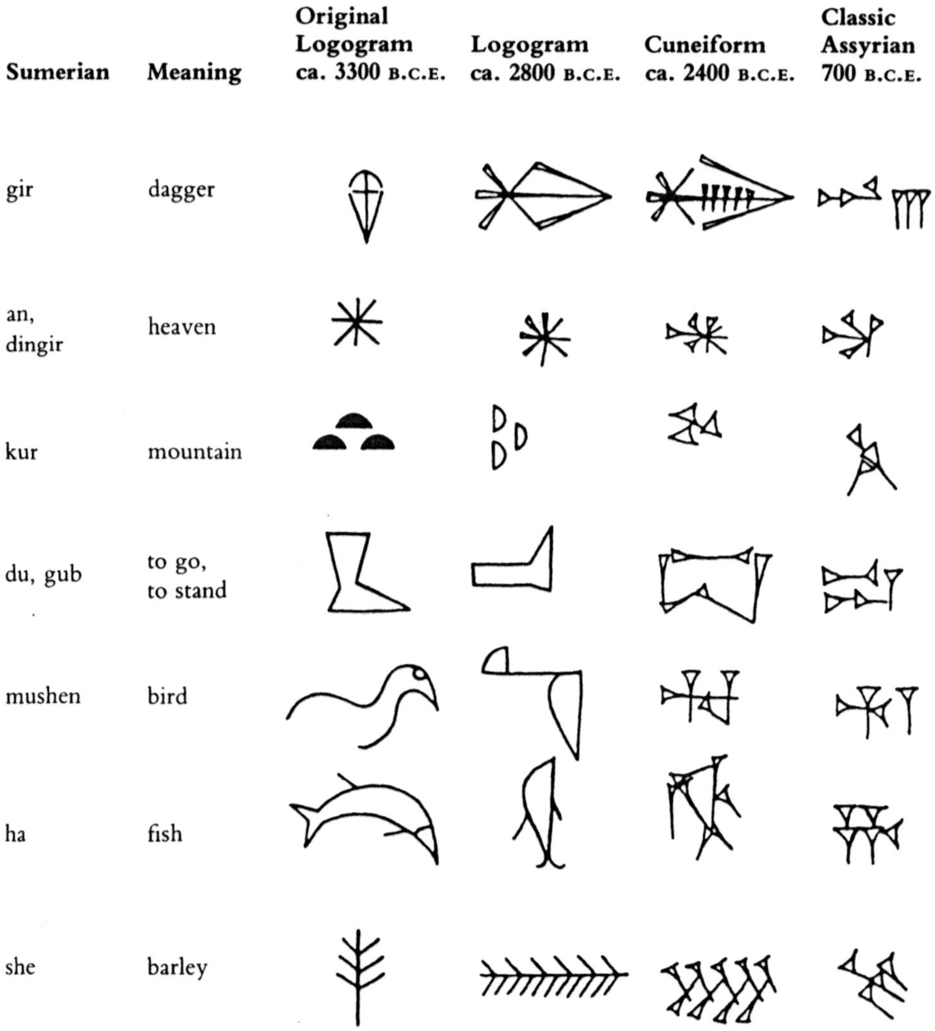
Sumerian
Meaning
Original Logogram ca. 3300 B.C.E.
Logogram ca. 2800 B.C.E.
Cuneiform ca. 2400 B.C.E.
Classic Assyrian 700 B.C.E.
gir
dagger
an, dingir
heaven
kur
mountain
du, gub
to go, to stand
mushen
bird
ha
fish
she
barley

The origins of the Sumerians, both linguistically and ethnically, as yet are unknown. Their cuneiform script was adopted by the Akkadians of northern Mesopotamia in the middle of the third millennium B.C.E. for their own Semitic language. The Akkadians, the ancestors of the Assyrians and Babylonians, dominated the area for almost two thousand years. Akkadian was the *lingua franca,* the diplomatic language of the Near East in the second millennium B.C.E., and Akkadian cuneiform tablets have been found as far away from Mesopotamia as the Egyptian site of El-Amarna, where trade between the two Fertile Crescent cultures flourished in the fourteenth century B.C.E. (pl. 36). As other ethnic groups and city-states rose to power in Mesopotamia and Iran, they wrote their own languages in cuneiform script. Among them were the Elamites, who adopted cuneiform at the

Pl. 36. Cuneiform clay tablet letter from King Tushratta of Mitanni (northern Syria-northern Mesopotamia) to Pharaoh Amenophis III, his father-in-law, in Egypt, requesting gifts. El-Amarna, fourteenth century B.C.E. British Museum, Department of Western Asiatic Antiquities, No. 29791. Courtesy of the British Museum

same time as did the Akkadians, after dropping their earlier (and still undeciphered) script. Elamite writing contained 25 logograms, 131 phonograms, and 7 determinatives. Other groups who inhabited the Tigris-Euphrates valley and Anatolia used cuneiform for languages such as Hurrian, Urartian, Hattic, Luvian, and Palaic. These were primarily syllabic scripts, with a few logograms. Hieroglyphic Hittite, a script that represented one of the two languages used at the court of the powerful Hittite Empire (which dominated Anatolia and Syria ca. 1900–1200 B.C.E.), contained four hundred logograms and about sixty syllabic signs. Although the term *hieroglyphic* is used, it is not related to the Egyptian script. The Hittites had their own cuneiform script as well. Other Near Eastern peoples wrote with wedge-shaped characters that looked like cuneiform, undoubtedly because these shapes best suited the native clay, the cheapest and most available writing surface. But the script was not always based on Akkadian. In the fourteenth and thirteenth centuries B.C.E. at Ugarit (Ras Shamra) in Syria, scribes wrote with a thirty-letter alphabet based on the Semitic model, in addition to writing in Akkadian syllabic cuneiform (see fig. 10, p. 54). Alphabetic cuneiform also has been found in a few sites in Israel, at Taanach, Nahal Tavor, and Beth Shemesh, near Jerusalem. Later, the Persians used cuneiform for a syllabic script, also unrelated to the earlier Mesopotamian mixed systems.

The Akkadians wrote dictionaries of equivalents for their own language and for Sumerian as well as for other languages. These helped nineteenth-century scholars decipher Sumerian and other early scripts. In borrowing cuneiform, Akkadian writers at times took the Sumerian unit, either a phrase, logogram, or syllable, and used it in their own script, even though their term for the same object or concept differed. This phenomenon of borrowed signs is called *xenography*. There are hundreds of these "sumerograms" in Akkadian script. For example, Akkadians used the Sumerian sign for king, *lugal,* for their word for king, *sharrum.* The xenographic principle was used in the scripts of other cultures: Hittite cuneiform took Akkadian spellings, and Pahlavi (middle Persian) script frequently borrowed Aramaic written words to spell Persian words. For example, the Aramaic *malka,* "king," was used for the Persian *shah.* Xenography is still used in script today. We write "i.e." (*id est*) for "that is," "lb." (*libra*) for "pound," and "etc." (*et cetera*) for "and so forth."

By the late Assyrian and Babylonian periods (the seventh and sixth centuries B.C.E.), there were still six hundred signs in cuneiform, of which 100 to 150 were syllabic. When the Persians borrowed cuneiformlike signs for their own Indo-European language, they reduced the number to forty-one syllabic signs, having been influenced by the Aramaic alphabet. Aramaic script eventually replaced cuneiform for the Persian tongue and, much later, in the seventh century C.E., Arabic script replaced Aramaic for Persian. Cuneiform script ceased to be written by the first century C.E. The script was then forgotten and, unlike Egyptian hieroglyphics, there was no knowledge of cuneiform's existence in Europe until visitors to Persia in the seventeenth century found inscriptions at Persepolis, Persia's ancient capital. Even then, few were curious about the script. In 1787, a Sassanian Persian inscription in Aramaic identifying the founder of that dynasty, Ardashir (d. 240 C.E.) from Naqsh-i-Rustam, near Persepolis, was read with the aid of the accompanying Greek by Silvestre de Sacy (1758–1838), a professor of Arabic in Paris. His method of first isolating names as a key to decipherment was then used by Georg Grotefend (1775–1853), a German schoolteacher who worked on the cuneiform Persian inscription from foundation-stone plaques found at the palace at Persepolis at the turn of the nineteenth century (pl. 37). Grotefend identified the names and titles of the Achaemenid dynasty's builders of this capital, known from Greek history. From these he assigned the phonetic value of a third of the cuneiform signs, which he assumed to be alphabetic: "Darius, mighty [the great] king, king of kings, king of the Dahae [countries], son of Hystaspes, the race of the rulers of the world [the Achaemenid]. . . ." His mistakes were corrected (corrections in brackets) by others whose knowledge of Old Persian and the new field of comparative philology was greater and who classified the script as syllabic. An adventurous and scholarly army officer of the British East India Company, Major Henry Rawlinson (1810–1895), climbed the great Rock of Behistun (or Bisutun, in the province of Kurdistan) to copy the long trilingual inscription also commissioned by Darius (pl. 38). He sent the results of his work to the Royal Asiatic Society in 1839 and again in 1845–46. Although others arrived at similar results simultaneously, no one achieved as much in the decipherment and translation of the Achaemenid Persian cuneiform script as did the nonacademic Rawlinson.

The other two languages of the Persepolis and Rock of Behistun inscriptions were Elamite and Babylonian. By 1850, Rawlinson had identified many of the Babylonian characters but these amounted to only a tenth of the total number of signs. By 1857, Assyrian cuneiform was read and translated by scholars (one of whom was William Henry Fox Talbot, the British pioneer of photography). The document used by English and French scholars as a test of their successful decipherment was a clay prism of Tiglath-Pileser I, itself a kind of history book

Pl. 37. Gold foundation plaque of Darius with trilingual inscription. Persepolis, late sixth century B.C.E. Archeological Museum, Teheran. Reproduced from *Art of Ancient Iran*. Courtesy of Golden Press

Pl. 38. Detail of Rock of Behistun. Relief of Darius with trilingual cuneiform inscription. Sixth century B.C.E. Courtesy of the Cameron Archive of Behistun, Kelsey Museum of Archeology, University of Michigan

from ca. 1100 B.C.E. (pl. 39). Elamite script proved to be the most difficult to recover for the language was unknown, but by the end of the nineteenth century it too was understood.

Hieroglyphics

The origin of the Egyptian system of writing may be traced to the influence of Sumer on Egypt ca. 3100–3000 B.C.E. The presence in Egypt of cylinder seals and the potter's wheel, the form of the pyramid (from the ziggurat), and the use of brick as a building material all testify to the cultural impact of Mesopotamia on the other end of the Fertile Crescent. Writing, too, is a concrete example of idea-diffusion: Egypt adopted a mixed system combining logograms (see fig. 2, p. 21) with phonograms and determinatives but with her own pictorial signs (fig. 5). The most familiar determinative is the cartouche, which framed a royal name (pl. 40). This Sumerian influence probably took place before writers of Mesopotamia transformed their script into its exclusively wedge-shaped forms. The earliest "document" to display Egyptian hieroglyphics comes from Hierakonpolis in upper Egypt, about

Pl. 40. Queen Nefertari playing sennet, from a wall painting in her tomb. Her name is in the cartouche. Thebes, Valley of the Queens, XIX Dynasty, thirteenth century B.C.E. Courtesy of the Egyptian Museum, Cairo

Pl. 39. Octagonal clay prism of Tiglath-Pileser I, recording his campaigns, hunting expeditions and building programs. Ashur, Assyria, ca. 1100 B.C.E. British Museum Department of Western Asiatic Antiquities, No. 91033. Courtesy of the British Museum

Fig. 5. Hieroglyphic logograms, phonograms, and
determinatives

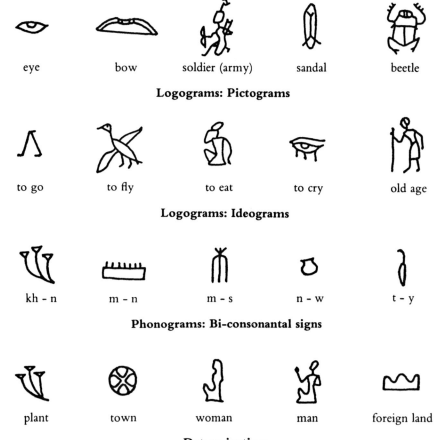

eye   bow   soldier (army)   sandal   beetle

Logograms: Pictograms

to go   to fly   to eat   to cry   old age

Logograms: Ideograms

kh - n   m - n   m - s   n - w   t - y

Phonograms: Bi-consonantal signs

plant   town   woman   man   foreign land

Determinatives

fifty miles south of Thebes (Luxor). It is the Narmer Palette, a royal ceremonial slate slab that served as a receptacle for ocular sunblock ointment (pl. 41). The central name-sign at the top of both sides of the palette reads "Nar-mer" (*nar,* sea creature and *mer,* nail), identified as Menes, the founder of Egypt's first dynasty who conquered lower Egypt and united it with upper Egypt ca. 3100–3000 B.C.E. Other phonograms, possibly names, appear on the palette along with conquest imagery and logograms but the pictorial style of script and image is so similar that it is difficult to distinguish between symbolic images and actual writing. The identical nature of script and picture continues to be characteristic of hieroglyphics and art; script appears to be miniatures of Egyptian art (pl. 40). Both art and script remained relatively static throughout the pharaonic age, with some exceptions. While there are additional examples of phonogram-names on other slate palettes from Hierakonpolis, no evidence has yet been found for the evolution from logograms to phonograms to the fully developed mixed system that appeared so soon thereafter. This development was either very speedy or the whole system may have been created at once on the Sumerian model.

Hieroglyphics from its very beginnings in the early third millennium was a mixed script that included about six hundred logograms and determinatives, one hundred phonograms, and twenty-four uniconsonantal (alphabetlike) signs. Its Greek name, *hieroglyphica grammata,* "sacred carved letters," was given at the end of the second century C.E. by Clement of Alexandria, who believed the script to have been employed exclusively for holy purposes. Although this was not the case, hiero-glyphics was the formal, monumental script of Egypt. It also appeared in papyrus manuscripts. In addition to hieroglyphics, two cursive (running) scripts, hieratic

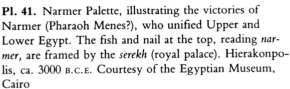

Pl. 41. Narmer Palette, illustrating the victories of Narmer (Pharaoh Menes?), who unified Upper and Lower Egypt. The fish and nail at the top, reading *narmer,* are framed by the *serekh* (royal palace). Hierakonpolis, ca. 3000 B.C.E. Courtesy of the Egyptian Museum, Cairo

(holy) and demotic (public), were noticed by Herodotus in the fifth century B.C.E. and by later writers (pl. 42, 43; fig. 6). Both of these nonpictorial scripts were derived from hieroglyphics. Hieratic appeared ca. 2500 B.C.E. (pl. 43, 44). Demotic, which was based on hieratic but was even more cursive, was introduced about 700 B.C.E. (pl. 43, 48). Cursive script developed because it was much quicker and easier to write in this manner with a reed pen-brush on papyrus. Thus the limitations of materials shaped the more practical but less legible script. Both hieratic and demotic were sign-for-sign transcriptions of hieroglyphics, and their use in manuscripts had nothing to do with their Greek names (also given by Clement). The phonetic system did not develop any further in either hieratic or demotic, despite their resemblance to cursive alphabetic script. Both scripts were written from right to left, whereas hieroglyphic script was at times written in both directions on the same surface and in rows from top to bottom. Direction depended on the overall design of the wall inscription or scroll section because symmetry was important to the scribe and to the designer of the monument or scroll.

Hieroglyphics were used exclusively by the Egyptians to represent their own speech. No other script now termed hieroglyphic, that is, Mayan or Minoan or

Fig. 6. Signs in hieroglyphic, hieratic, and
demotic

Hieroglyphic   **Hieratic**   **Demotic**

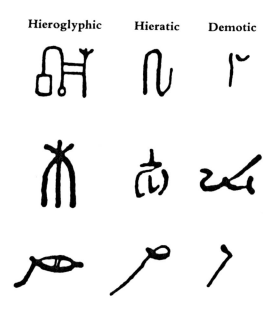

Pl. 42. Poetic account of
Ramses II's Battle of
Qadesh, against the Hittites.
Hieratic script on papyrus,
written ca. 1200 B.C.E.
Louvre, Raifé Collection,
AE/E4892. Photo courtesy
of the Réunion des Musées
Nationaux

Pl. 44. Clay tablet letter from Tushratta of Mitanni to Amenophis III, sending regards to his daughter Taduhepa, one of pharaoh's wives. Cuneiform, with endorsement in hieratic in ink. El-Amarna, fourteenth century B.C.E. British Museum, Department of Western Asiatic Antiquities, No. 29791. Courtesy of the British Museum

Pl. 43. A farming contract written on papyrus in demotic script. Egypt, 533 B.C.E. Louvre, Départment des Antiquités Egyptiennes, E 7836, ancienne coll. Eisenlohr. Photo courtesy of the Réunion des Musées Nationaux

Hittite, is related to it. For its three-thousand-year existence, the Egyptian system, like its pictorial forms, remained almost unchanged, although orthography varied at different times. When homophones were used to compose phonographic signs, the structure of the syllable differed from that of the Sumerians, who used overlapping sounds in their CVC or CV syllables (e.g., *tam* written *ta-am*). In Egyptian, the syllable would have been written *tm,* omitting the vowel sound. The problem with reading the hundred Egyptian syllabic–phonographic signs is that we cannot with certainty reconstruct their vowels, which were provided automatically by ancient Egyptian readers, as readers of Hebrew do today. Nineteenth- and early-twentieth-century scholars transliterated as they believed the vowels should have been. A few of these syllabic signs were triconsonantal, such as *mdt* and *s-sh ntr,* the words for writing (literally, "the speech or writing of a god"). About eighty signs were biconsonantal, or biliteral—one sign for two sounds. The twenty-four uniconsonantal or alphabetic signs existed in Egyptian writing since its beginning. For example, the sign for the *el* sound would be represented by the lion, *labo* in Egyptian; this worked on the principle of acrophony, as did the first Semitic alphabet (see Chapter 2). The existence of systematic uniconsonantal signs on the acrophonic principle within the mixed hieroglyphic system gives the impression that the Egyptians invented an alphabet (fig. 7). Even if they had been aware of the advantages of this "alphabet" for representing speech, they never used it exclusively and never dropped all of the other logograms, phonograms, and determinatives of their mixed hieroglyphic system. If you were to look at a typical text page that had about five hundred hieroglyphic characters, about 54 percent would be alphabetic. Several different signs could be used for the same consonantal sound, even in the same period.

Fig. 7. The hieroglyphic alphabet

Sign	Sound	Object Represented
𓄿	*ꜣ*	vulture
𓇋	*ỉ*	reed
(1) 𓇌 (2) 𓏭	*y*	reed flowers, strokes
𓂝	*ꜥ*	forearm
𓅱	*w*	quail
𓃀	*b*	leg
𓊪	*p*	seat
𓆑	*f*	horned viper
𓅓	*m*	owl
𓈖	*n*	water
𓂋	*r*	mouth
𓉔	*h*	courtyard
𓎛	*ḥ*	twisted flax
𓐍	*ḫ*	placenta(?)
𓄡	*ẖ*	belly of animal with teats
(1) 𓊃 (2) 𓋴	*s*	bolt, folded cloth
𓈙	*š*	pool
𓈎	*ḳ*	hill, slope
𓎡	*k*	basket with handle
𓎼	*g*	stand for jar
𓏏	*t*	loaf, bread
𓍿	*ṯ*	halter for cattle
𓂧	*d*	hand
𓆓	*ḏ*	snake

Hieroglyphics did play a part in inspiring the alphabet, and certain aspects common to the two should not be ignored. The Semitic alphabet, like Egyptian script, was solely consonantal in the beginning, with vowels supplied by the reader. Some of the hieroglyphic uniconsonantal signs are similar in shape to early Semitic alphabetic forms (hand, mouth), although pronunciation of the signs was not the same. The *n-t* sign ⌇ (water) in Egyptian can be identified with the Semitic *mem* (water) and *nun* (fish). *Z-n,* an Egyptian arrow, sounds like the Hebrew *zayin,* dagger. Other than these, few alphabetic letters are identical in sound, shape, and meaning to hieroglyphic uniconsonants. But idea-diffusion was operative.

Hieroglyphics were written well into the period of the Roman occupation of Egypt in the first centuries B.C.E. and C.E., but by that time only priests knew how to write them. Quite a few biscripts were commissioned by Roman rulers, but ancient writers who observed hieroglyphics viewed the script with curiosity and never delved into how the mixed system operated. The last dated hieroglyphic inscription was made in 374 C.E. in Philae. The only surviving element of Egyptian script was the use of seven demotic characters that were added to the Greek alphabet by the Copts (natives of Egypt who converted to Christianity) to form the Coptic alphabet (fig. 8). These characters-turned-letters were necessary for writing sounds in the ancient Egyptian language the Copts continued to speak. The Greek language and alphabet arrived in Egypt on a permanent basis with the Hellenistic conquerors in the late fourth century B.C.E., and Greek persisted even after the Roman conquest

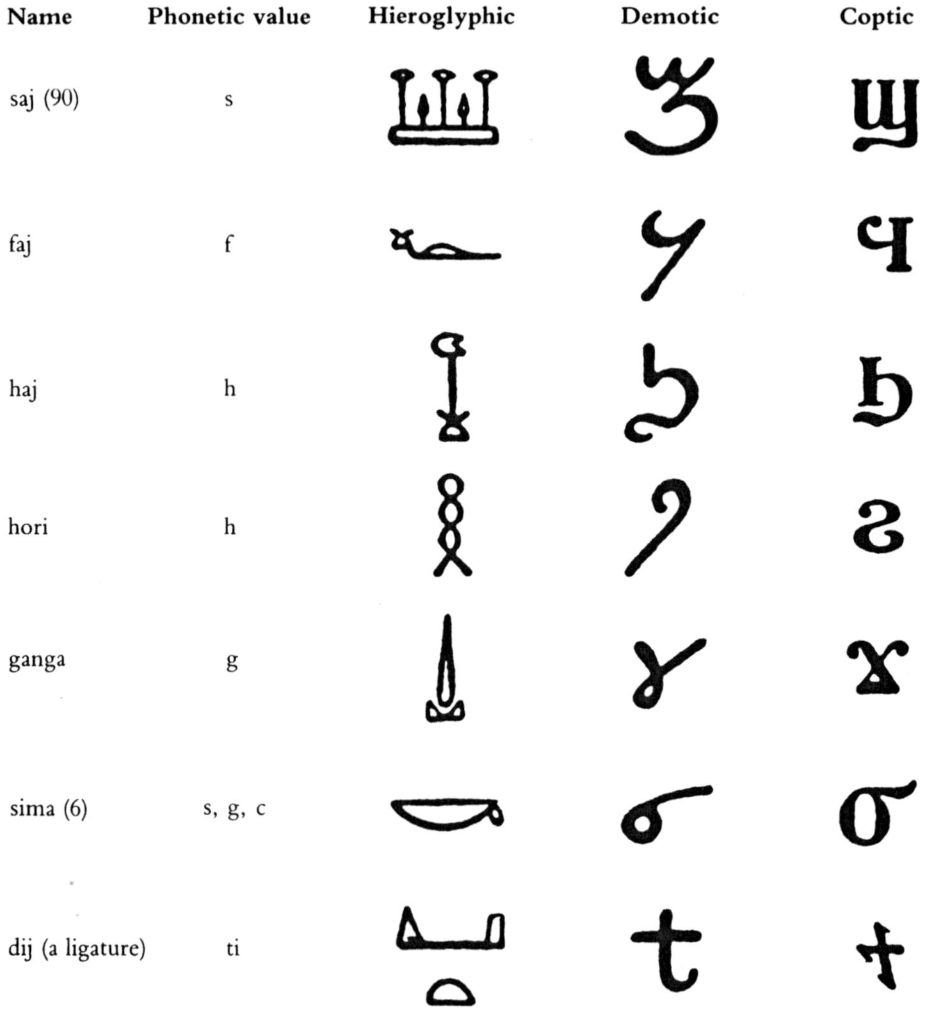

Fig. 8. Demotic signs added to Greek to make the Coptic alphabet. After Jensen, *Sign, Symbol and Script*

Name	Phonetic value	Hieroglyphic	Demotic	Coptic
saj (90)	s			
faj	f			
haj	h			
hori	h			
ganga	g			
sima (6)	s, g, c			
dij (a ligature)	ti			

as the language and script of administration. The Coptic church preserved its Greek-plus-demotic script, as it did the Egyptian language, for its liturgy, writings, and everyday use (pl. 45); but once Arabic was spoken after the Arab conquest of Egypt in 641 C.E., Coptic fell into disuse and, by the seventeenth century, the language ceased to be spoken altogether. Shortly thereafter, European scholars began to study the ancient language and Coptic manuscripts were sought by collectors.

The Romans looked on Egypt rather romantically. They carried obelisks from Egypt as souvenirs to be displayed in their capital. Although the last of these inscribed obelisks was destroyed in Rome by the eleventh century C.E., a few sculptures with hieroglyphic inscriptions remained, such as a pair of lions that stood in front of the Pantheon from the twelfth century and were moved to the fountain of Acque Felice in 1506. Other inscribed sculptures remained in the Vatican collection. To the people of the late Middle Ages and Renaissance, hieroglyphics became synonymous with "mysterious." The humanists of the Italian Renaissance, interested in Egyptian as well as Greek and Roman antiquities, revived hieroglyph-

Pl. 45. Coptic manuscript. Fourteen Epistles of St. Paul. From the Monastery of St. Michael of the Desert, in the Fayyum (Hamouli, Egypt), ninth century. Pierpont Morgan Library, Ms. 570, f. 2r. Courtesy of the Pierpont Morgan Library, New York

ics without understanding their meaning. They believed the writing to be symbolic of wisdom, and attributed mystic, moralistic, and philosophical connotations to the signs. This misunderstanding gave rise to the pseudohieroglyphic Emblem book, fashionable from the late fifteenth through the seventeenth centuries (pl. 46, 47). No one looked on hieroglyphics as true writing until the eighteenth century.

The key to the recovery of the ancient Egyptian script was the discovery of the Rosetta Stone by troops at Fort Saint Julien de Rosetta (Rashid) in the Nile Delta in Napoleon's time (pl. 48). It then became a prize of the English victory over Napoleon, and is now in the British Museum. The Rosetta Stone is a triscript, written in hieroglyphics, demotic, and Greek—a decree carved in honor of Ptolemy V in 196 B.C.E. To assist the reader, the Greek inscription noted that the "local writing" (*encorial*) in the other two scripts bore the same text. Jean-François Champollion (1790–1832) was the decipherer of hieroglyphics. A scholar of Near Eastern languages, including Coptic, he was an expert in ancient Egyptian place and personal names and their Greek, Latin, Coptic, and Arabic equivalents. Others had attempted to decipher the script, including Champollion's teacher Silvestre de Sacy, who had deciphered the Sassanian Persian inscription of Naqsh-i-Rustam. The young scholar succeeded in assigning the phonetic value of "Ptolemy" to the name in the cartouche and in proving the identity of the Rosetta Stone's demotic and

Pl. 46. Elephant and obelisk, from Francesco Colonna's *Hypnerotomachia Poliphili* (Venice: Aldus Manutius, 1499). Hieroglyphics were emblems or symbols of moral wisdom in the Renaissance. Courtesy of the Jewish National and University Library, Jerusalem. Photo: Albert Ben-Yaacov

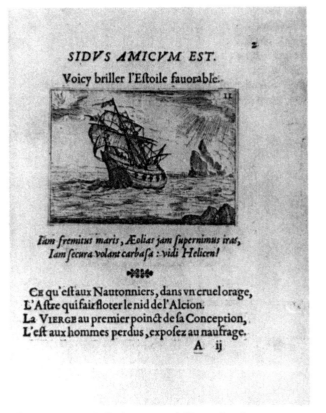

Pl. 47. Jacques Callot's engraved illustration in an emblem book, *Vita Beatae Mariae Virginis Matris Dei, Emblematibus Delineata* (Paris, 1646). Courtesy of the Jewish National and University Library, Jerusalem

hieroglyphics. He surmised that the two cursive scripts were "ideographic" as well, and that demotic was the equivalent of hieratic known from other documents. And, realizing that the extra letters of Coptic came from demotic, he assigned the sound values to the demotic as well as to the hieroglyphic inscription. Then, from other cartouches with names foreign to Egyptian, he transliterated hieroglyphs on obelisks, realizing that more than one sign could represent a single sound. Champollion thus was able to deduce the names and titles of the Roman emperors and, from these, the names of the pharaohs. When he realized that the signs outside the cartouches were phonetic as well as ideographic, he was on his way to decipherment. The identification of determinatives other than the cartouche, such as 𓀀 "man" and ⌒ "woman," and his knowledge of grammatical forms in Coptic and Semitic languages, along with the conclusion that Egyptians had multiple sound signs and homophones, led to the essentially correct reading of their scripts. In his *Précis du système hiéroglyphique des anciens Egyptiens* (Paris, 1824), Champollion brilliantly described the Egyptian writing system and its three scripts, which opened the ancient Egyptian book to the modern reader.

Pl. 48. The Rosetta Stone. Triscript decree, in hieroglyphics, demotic, and Greek, in honor of Ptolemy V Epiphanes, 196 B.C.E. Black basalt. Discovered at Fort Julien near Rashid (Rosetta), in the Delta. British Museum, Department of Egyptian Antiquities, No. 24. Courtesy of the British Museum

CHAPTER 2

The Alphabet

PRINCIPLE AND SYSTEM

he Semitic alphabet, created between 1700 and 1500 B.C.E., was the most important development in the history of writing. While the alphabet can be viewed as a natural outgrowth of one aspect of Egyptian hieroglyphic script, it can also be considered both a liberation from a pictorial form of writing and a revolution against the complicated mixed systems of the time.

We have already seen that the mixed system of Egypt included twenty-four unconsonantal signs. From this "alphabet" the first Semitic writers borrowed the operative principle of acrophony. With acrophony, each letter is a sound sign whose name is that of the object depicted and whose form is the shape of the object (outlined and simplified in the case of Semitic script). Three elements are involved in the acrophonic principle: the sound of the letter, the name of the letter, and the appearance of the letter. The alphabet's inventor (if there were a single inventor, which is doubtful) was no artist, and the aesthetics of the inscription were of no concern to the early Semitic writer; the linear Semitic sign was not so beautiful as it was functional. It may take some imagination on the reader's part to see the relationship of the original letter to the object depicted. Furthermore, the origin and meaning of a few letters are still obscure or at times controversial.

The Letters

The Semitic (often referred to as North Semitic or West Semitic) alphabet will be examined in detail to illustrate the principle of acrophony as well as to demonstrate how little the letters have changed since the alphabet's invention in the second millennium B.C.E. We will trace the letters' progress from their first appearance in Sinaitic, Canaanite, and Hebrew inscriptions to their present English (Latin) form (fig. 9). At the head of the alphabet stood alef, the chief ox (*alp* in Canaanite, *aluf* in Hebrew), which initially resembled an ox head ⊃⊂, but later was abstracted to ⊄ and ⊅. The Greeks and Romans turned the letter around to the *alpha* and *A* and it became a vowel; originally it was a voiceless consonant. The second letter, *bet,* was a house, with the sound value of *b*. It looked more like a house in its South Semitic

Fig. 9. Sinaitic, North Semitic, Greek, and Latin alphabets. Slight variations in signs found in text and chart reflect different dates and places of alphabet's use.

Hebrew names	Greek names	Sinai script	North Semitic	Earliest Greek	Classical Greek	Modern Greek	Early Latin
alef	alpha						
bet	beta						
gimmel	gamma						
dalet	delta						
he	epsilon						
vav	digamma						
zayin	zeta						
het	eta						
tet	theta						
yod	iota						
kaf	kappa						
lamed	lambda						
mem	mu						

form п than in its North Semitic form 𐤄. Although the South Semitic alphabet appeared in southern Arabia later than the Northern branch (about 1300 B.C.E. according to Joseph Naveh), its very existence led some scholars to believe that both North and South Semitic were derived from some earlier prototype alphabet for which there is no material evidence. *Bet* passed into archaic Greek as *beta* in similar

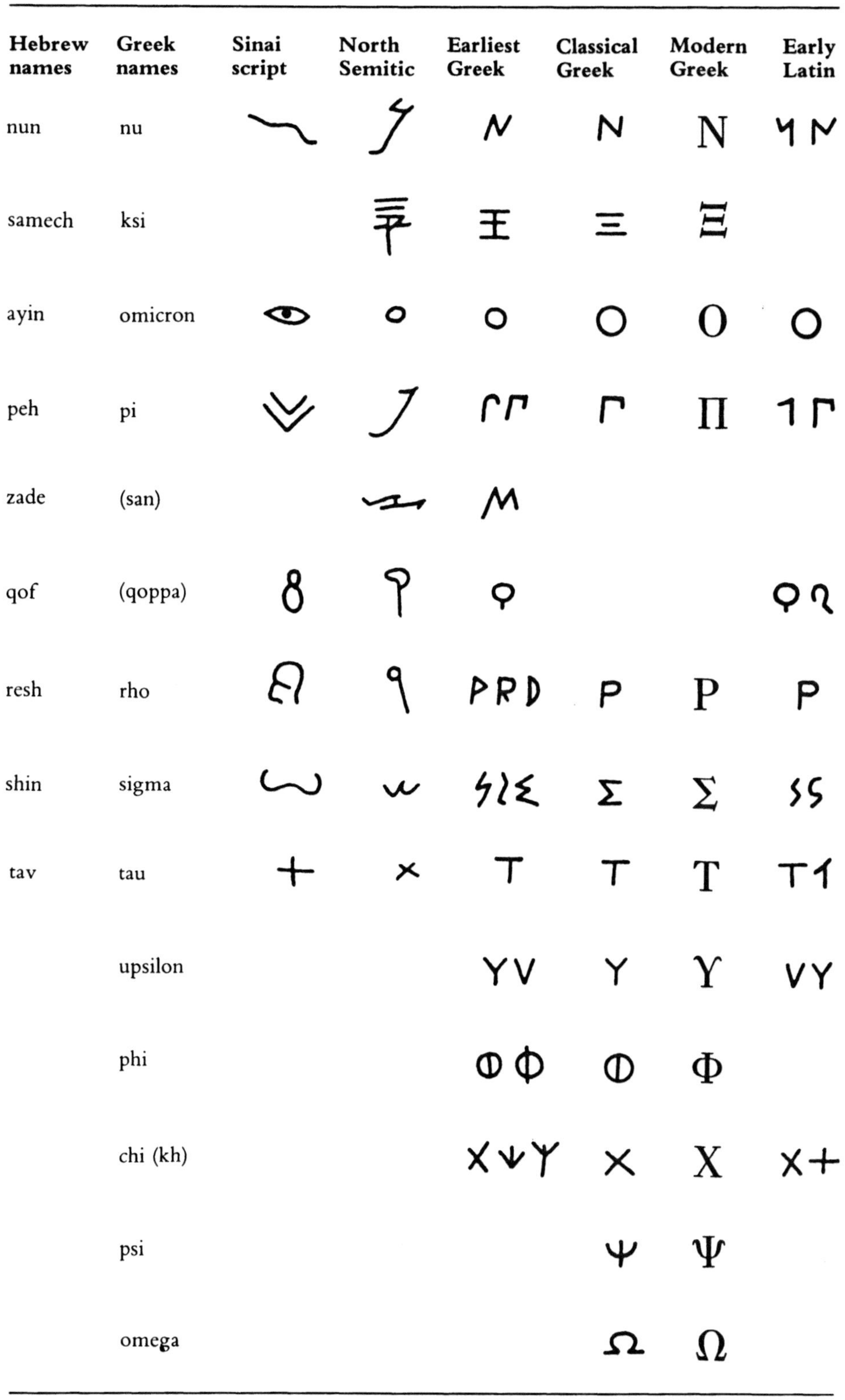

Hebrew names	Greek names	Sinai script	North Semitic	Earliest Greek	Classical Greek	Modern Greek	Early Latin
nun	nu	∿	𐤍	N	N	N	ꓨ N
samech	ksi		𐤎	Ξ	Ξ	Ξ	
ayin	omicron	◉	o	O	O	O	O
peh	pi	⋁	𐤐	ΓΓ	Γ	Π	ꓘΓ
zade	(san)		⤳	M			
qof	(qoppa)	8	𐤒	Ϙ			ϘϞ
resh	rho	ᘱ	𐤓	ΡΡD	P	P	P
shin	sigma	�	ᱜ	ꟿᔑƐ	Σ	Σ	ꟅꟅ
tav	tau	+	×	Τ	Τ	Τ	Τꓕ
	upsilon			ΥV	Υ	Υ	VΥ
	phi			ΦΦ	Φ	Φ	
	chi (kh)			Χ↓Υ	Χ	Χ	Χ+
	psi				Ψ	Ψ	
	omega				Ω	Ω	

form 𝟜𝟛 and eventually became our *B*. Several of the Semitic letters were reversed in classical Greek and Latin and are mirror images of earlier Semitic script.

The third letter of the Semitic alphabet is *gimmel*, pronounced *g* (as in girl) and written ⅂ or Γ . It could have represented the hump of the camel (*gamal* in Hebrew), or the camel goad. This goad looked like a boomerang ⌒, and was a common domestic object in Egypt and in the rest of the Near East. The Greek *gamma* ∧ or Γ was also used for the *g* sound, but the Romans transformed the archaic Greek *gamma* into two sound signs, *C* and *G*. This transformation came about because the Etruscans, forerunners of the Romans, did not have the *g* sound in their language. The early Romans changed the sound of the sign to *k*, while keeping the rounded form of *C* in its place as the third letter of the alphabet. Then, in order to express the *g* sound in writing, they modified the *C* by adding a short horizontal stroke, and inserted the *G* in the slot of the dropped Greek *zeta,* for which the Romans had no use at first. Although the *G* was differentiated from the *C* by the third century B.C.E., the capital *C* as *G* was retained into imperial times, as in Gaius Caesar's initial, written C. Caesar.

The Semitic letter now called *dalet* in Hebrew was a fish ⌑ (*dag*) in its earliest form, but at some point its name became a door (*delet*) ◁ △ . In the earliest inscriptions from Serabit el-Khadem in the southern Sinai desert, the *dalet* is a fish. We know from the Bible that ancient Hebrews were not very interested in fish because there are no names for different species, not even for Jonah's big fish. The letter's Greek name, *delta,* would indicate that the name had already changed from "fish" to "door" while the triangular form was retained, before the Phoenicians spread the alphabet throughout the Mediterranean basin. The Romans turned the triangle around another forty-five degrees, and rounded it off (as they did with many of their letters) into the *D*.

The origin of the letter *he* ⋏ (pronounced "hay") in the Semitic alphabet, the *epsilon* in Greek Ε and the *E* in Latin is probably the most mysterious of all letters because the acrophonic principle cannot be explained easily. There is no object whose Hebrew name can explain the initial sound and name aspects of the acrophonic principle. The biblical Hebrew *hoi* (lo) does not explain the letter's form. The closest logogram in Egyptian hieroglyphics is a figure in an attitude of prayer 𝓧 . This logogram meant "high," "rejoiced," or "mourner," and one of its sounds began with an *h*. The South Semitic form of the letter was similar: ꙡ . The earliest North Semitic form is ꙅ . Since this letter appears twice in the name of God ⅂Υ⅂ꙅ (YHVH) as it is abbreviated in biblical texts, there is the possibility that *he* is the only letter of the alphabet to represent an abstract idea. Its original name then could have been obscured deliberately by a monotheistic culture that discouraged the magical use of the Deity's name.

Vav looks like the hook that it represents in Hebrew: Υ . The letter became complicated only when Europeans adopted it. The Greeks took it over as the archaic *vau* or *digamma* (a later name), at first ⋏ and Υ . They later dropped it, but a similar letter had been placed toward the end of the alphabet, the vowel *upsilon* Υ and ∨, probably very soon after the alphabet was adopted. The Romans were able to use the *vau* as an *F* and kept it in the same position as the Hebrew *vav*. The Greek *upsilon,* as used by the Romans, then branched out into two Latin letters, the *V* and *Y*, and in the Middle Ages the *V* gave birth to two more letters, the *U* and the *W*. The Semitic ⅃ *(zayin)* was a dagger. Its form and name may have been inspired by the Egyptian *z-n* or *zwn* for an arrow ⟶ . The *zayin* was taken over as the *zeta* in archaic Greek in the same shape and in the same position in the alphabet. In classical Greek and later in Latin the form changed slightly to *Z*. The Romans originally had no *z* sound in their language so the letter was not required until after the conquest of Greece in the second century B.C.E., when Rome's incorporation of Greek words necessitated adding *Z*, at the end. The original position of *Z* had already been usurped by *G*.

The origin of the eighth letter of the Semitic alphabet, *het* ⏁, is open to several interpretations. It is frequently explained as a fence because it resembles one, but since *het* did not mean "fence" in Hebrew, it is difficult to apply the acrophonic principle. The modern meaning of "canine tooth" or "plow" for *het* also can be seen in the shape of the letter, but this would not account for its original name. The letter at times is also associated with the Egyptian logogram of twisted rope ⏃, whose initial sound was *h*. The similarity in sound of *het* to the letter *he* (in Hebrew speech) and its similar shape, if you add a vertical stroke on the left side of the *he* ⏁, may indicate that there was a division of one letter into two when distinctions in speech necessitated the invention of two signs to accommodate each variation, *he* and *het*. The archaic Greek scripts took over the *het* as *eta* in the form of ⊟ or Η. Classical Greek used the letter *eta* for the long vowel *e*, as opposed to the short vowel *epsilon*. Later it would also serve as the short vowel *i* as opposed to the long vowel *iota*. The spoken Latin *H* is close to the original Semitic *het* sound and even closer to the Semitic *he*, which had already become the vowel *E*. The *H* remained a consonant in Latin.

The *tet* ⊕ may have been added to a shorter "original" Semitic alphabet because it appears in the Phoenician and Moabite alphabets but not in an earlier version sometimes called the Sinaitic or proto-Sinaitic alphabet. It is not among the letters that appear in the inscriptions found at Serabit el-Khadem in Southern Sinai (pl. 49). It could have been a broom, *(ma)tateh* in Hebrew. In shape and sound it resembles the *tav* ✕, the last letter of the Semitic alphabet, which may have been a doublet for the *t* sound. Since the signs and sounds are so similar, either could have been the final letter. Several letters in the Semitic alphabet seem to be doublets such as these. Greek retained the *tet* as *theta* ⊕⊙, but Latin dropped it because one *T* was enough for their language and they chose the *tav* at the end of the Semitic alphabet for *T*.

The principle of acrophony is on firmer ground when we trace the next four letters. The *yod* was undoubtedly the hieroglyphic hand ⇌, pronounced *d* or *t-t* when it was a uniconsonantal sign. *Yod* is its Semitic name, also meaning hand, which it sketches in profile ∿. Classical Greek and Latin straightened it out into the Ι after it went through the forms ∫ and ⟨ in the archaic period. As the Greek *iota*, the letter was used as a vowel or as a consonant *y* in conjunction with other vowels. As the Latin *I*, it also served as both consonant and vowel until the *j* sound necessitated the creation of its own letter in the Middle Ages.

The *kaf* ⨌ is the palm of the hand and also a bough, and its pictorial origin as either is evident in the earliest Sinaitic inscriptions. It is also pronounced *kh*, something like the *het*; Hebrew speakers of Western Europe and America do not distinguish between the *het* and *khaf* in speech, but those from Islamic countries do. In other early Semitic texts the *kaf* was abstracted into ⟨, ≻, and ⋗, and was eventually reversed by the Greeks into *kappa* Κ, and by the Romans into *K*, a seldom-used letter.

The *lamed* Ϲ is related to the camel goad, *gimmel*, in both shape and meaning but not in sound. The curved stick employed for training and directing animals also functioned as a human teaching instrument, euphemistically called "the rod of instruction"; *lamad* is the Hebrew word for "learn." Archaic Greek script tried the *lambda* in all directions: Γ, ∨, and ∧, until classical Greek settled on Λ. The Latin *L* is closer to the original Semitic form. *Mem* ∿ᴈ is related to the Hebrew word for water, *mayim*, which it resembles in hieroglyphics (pronounced *n-t*) ▬. Its obvious heirs are the archaic and classical Greek *mu* ∾ Μ and the Latin *M*. The development of *nun* from Semitic to Greek and Latin is parallel to that of *mem*: ⅄ to Ν to *N*. The sound of *nun* remained the same from Sinaitic script to Hebrew, but the name may have changed, for the Sinaitic inscriptions have it as a snake ⌒, *nahash*. *Nun* is a fish in Aramaic, which would render its name closer to the Greek *nu*. But as in the case of the *dag* and *dalet,* the name changed before the alphabet was passed to the Greeks. Either way, the acrophonic principle was operative.

Samech 𐤎 may have been a fish, but it was related to the Hebrew word for "support" as well, and could have been a functional object on the farm, such as a lean-to. Its present *s* sound is related to the *zayin,* the *zade (tz),* and the *sin,* and it could have been an added doublet to distinguish between variations in *s, z,* and *tz* sounds as Semitic languages developed. The Greeks were able to use the sign for their *ksi* in its archaic form 𐌙; in its classic form Ξ, but the Romans dropped it at first. Later, when the Romans needed a letter to express the *ks* sound, they used the Greek *xi*'s shape but not its sound, and transplanted it toward the end, as they had done with the *V* and *Z,* for Greek words adopted after the mid-second century B.C.E.

The *ayin* o meaning eye, was a conservative letter-form that even in its English descendant still resembles the original shape. It appeared as an eye in Sinaitic inscriptions ⟴, and was ₒ in its later Semitic form; it then became the Greek omicron and Latin *O.* Its ancient sound is believed to have been *ng,* the sound still used by Hebrew speakers from Islamic countries. European Jews (Ashkenazim) do not distinguish between the aspirate *alef,* the *ayin* and the final *he.*

The *peh,* meaning "mouth" in Hebrew, first appears as ⌐ in North Semitic script; in South Semitic it resembles a mouth even more: ◊ . The Hebrew word for the corner of a field, *pe'ah,* better suits its North Semitic shape; perhaps the name of the letter was shortened later to *peh,* as *nahash* had been shortened to *nun.* From the tenth century B.C.E. *peh* was further abstracted into ⎤, and passed into archaic Greek reversed and squared off: Γᴦ. Eventually the right vertical stroke was lengthened to make the classical and modern *pi* π. The Romans rounded the archaic Greek form Γ into the *P.*

The *zade* ⟿ was originally a grasshopper, pronounced *tz.* The letter passed into archaic Greek as the *san* Ϻ in some sites, such as Thera and Crete, but it was dropped in others, and there is no equivalent for it in Latin. The Latin *Q* originated in the Semitic *qof,* φ or φ, which is usually explained as a monkey but also means the eye of a needle. The principle of acrophony works for either source of the letter. The archaic Greek letter was *qoppa* ϙ , which was used only as a numeral in classical Greece. The *resh* is an abstracted head (*rosh* in Hebrew): ꓷ in Sinaitic script and in the early Canaanite Lachish Dagger, and eventually ᠲ in early Hebrew. The Greeks reversed it and called it *rho,* and it looked more like the Latin *P.* A short stroke was added by the Romans for *R.*

The *shin,* according to its modern Hebrew name, would indicate that the original sign was a tooth. It resembled teeth in its Phoenician form Ѡ, but in earlier Sinaitic and Canaanite inscriptions, one can speculate that the sign's name and pictorial origin was *shaddaim,* "breasts" ᴗᴗ . In the period of the Israelite conquest of Canaan (the late thirteenth to eleventh centuries B.C.E.), the letter already had two sounds, *s* and *sh.* We know this from Judges 12:6: when the Gileadites wanted to identify men from the Israelite tribe of Ephraim they asked them to pronounce *shibboleth.* Ephraimites pronounced it with an initial *s,* and were discovered thereby. It was not until vowel points were introduced for Hebrew in about the ninth century C.E. that the two sounds for the same letter could be distinguished graphically: *s* ש and *sh* שׁ. Archaic Greek turned the *shin* on its side: ⟨ or ⟩. In classical Greek it is the *sigma* Σ, and in Latin the *S.* The last letter of the Semitic alphabet is *tav,* ✗ or +, meaning "mark" and having a *t* sound. Obviously, it was the ancestor of the Greek *tau* and the Latin *T.*

Acrophony has a marvelous built-in teaching mechanism that worked in Semitic languages of the first millennium B.C.E., and probably made it much easier for a child to learn the alphabet. Many children's alphabet books today teach with the "a is for apple" technique. A small cursive *a* may resemble an apple with a stem, lying on its side ɑ, but the visual aspect of acrophony does not work for the other letters of the alphabet. Even in modern Hebrew, letters do not look enough like their Semitic ancestors to take advantage of this teaching device. In ancient Canaan, Judea, Israel, Phoenicia, and Moab, however, acrophony greatly aided all those who learned to read and write each slight variation on the Semitic alphabet.

There is no doubt that the Semitic alphabet grew out of Egyptian hieroglyphics, even though only a few signs resemble the uniconsants from the older script. The greatness of the alphabet as an invention lies in its *exclusive* use and in the rejection of other complicated aspects of the mixed hieroglyphic system. This was no accident. Semitic culture is essentially antivisual. Both the Israelite and the later Islamic religions deny the physical form of the deity. In the literature of both of these Semitic groups, words and sounds are more important than the images that are created by them. Oral traditions are revered not only as the medium for transmitting culture but also in food taboos and symbolism. The alphabet, as a truly *oral* (or "oral-aural," as Marshall McLuhan would have it) invention, can thus be seen as the reaction of an iconoclastic culture to a writing system that emphasized the visual aspect of the word—in both its pictorial form and its logographic nature. The alphabet, therefore, was not merely an outgrowth or a simplification of an existing system.

The names and shapes of the Early Semitic alphabet's letters are all parts of the human body as well as household and farming or herding objects and creatures, reflecting its invention by an agrarian or herding society and not by a mercantile or seafaring people such as the Phoenicians, who at one time were believed to have been the alphabet's inventors. No scholar of the past half-century has believed that the Phoenicians invented the alphabet; nevertheless, it is still referred to as "the Phoenician alphabet" in popular and scholarly literature.

The direction of writing in early Sinaitic and Canaanite inscriptions is not always in the retrograde (right to left) direction of the later Phoenician, Hebrew, Moabite, and Aramaic script; it also could be vertical or horizontal, depending on the surface on which it was written (pl. 49, 50). By the eleventh century, Semitic peoples in Palestine settled on retrograde writing, possibly under the influence of Egyptian hieratic script (pl. 51, 52, 53, 54, 55). Direction may have been fixed by the Israelite

Pl. 49. Sandstone sphinx with early Semitic (Sinaitic) inscription, *L'Baalat* ("to the lady," the goddess). Serabit el-Khadem, fourteenth–thirteenth century B.C.E. British Museum, Department of Egyptian Antiquities, No. 41748. Courtesy of the British Museum

Pl. 50. Lachish Bowl. *B'shlsht* ("in three"). Early Semitic (Canaanite) script. Thirteenth century B.C.E. Courtesy of the Israel Antiquities Authority, Jerusalem

Pl. 51. Gezer Calendar. List of agricultural activities by months. Semitic (Hebrew) incised on soft limestone. Tenth century B.C.E. Original in the Archeological Museum, Istanbul. Photo of replica courtesy of the Israel Museum, Jerusalem

Pl. 52. Moabite Stone. Commemorates triumphs of Mesha, king of Moab over Israel. Semitic (Moabite) script incised on black basalt. Dibon (Dhiban, Jordan), ca. 840–820 B.C.E. Louvre, AO 5066 + AO 2142. Photo courtesy of the Israel Museum, Jerusalem

Pl. 53. Siloam Inscription. Commemorates the meeting of teams of workmen hewing an aqueduct through limestone during Hezekiah's reign. Semitic (Hebrew) script. Jerusalem, late eighth century. Original in the Archeological Museum, Istanbul. Photo from cast courtesy of the Israel Museum, Jerusalem

Pl. 55. Uzziah Stone. Epitaph: "Hence were brought the bones of Uzziah, King of Judah, not to be opened." Square Hebrew incised on marble. Jerusalem, first century B.C.E./C.E. Israel Museum, No. 68.56.38. Courtesy of the Israel Museum, Jerusalem. Photo: David Harris

Pl. 54. Silver shekel from the first Jewish revolt against Rome. Inscription in style of earlier Semitic script. Obverse: "shekel of Israel, y[ear] 2" Reverse: "Jerusalem the holy." Jerusalem, 67 C.E. Courtesy of the Israel Museum, Jerusalem

tribe of Ephraim, known to be left-handed (retrograde script is natural for left-handed people). The order of the alphabet's letters must have been determined by the fourteenth century B.C.E. This is known from two documents. The first is an abecedary from the fourteenth-century town of Ugarit, in Syria, where the cuneiform alphabet follows almost the same order as North Semitic script (fig. 10). The Ugaritic alphabet was not related to Akkadian cuneiform, which also was known in this town; it simply used Mesopotamia's materials and tools and wedge-shaped signs. Ugaritic displayed twenty-seven consonants, *A–T,* with three added vowels (fig. 9). The second abecedary is proto-Canaanite, found at the twelfth-century B.C.E. site of Izbet Sarta in Israel: an ostracon (potsherd) bearing twenty-two letters (fig. 11). The *peh* and *ayin* are reversed but this reversal is also found in some biblical acrostic poetry (Lam. 2, 3, 4) and in inscriptions as late as the eighth century B.C.E. For these two letters, at least, order was not finalized until well into the first millenium B.C.E.

Fig. 10. The Ugaritic
alphabet

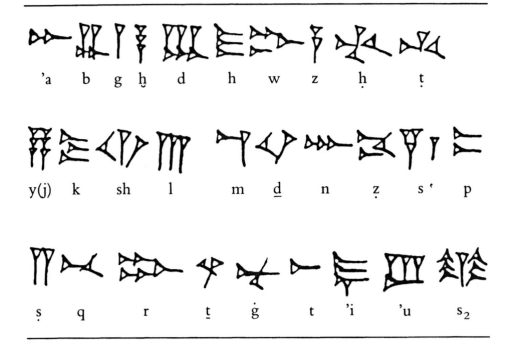

'a   b   g   ḫ   d   h   w   z   ḥ   ṭ

y(j)   k   sh   l   m   ḏ   n   ẓ   sʿ   p

ṣ   q   r   ṯ   ġ   t   'i   'u   s₂

Fig. 11. Izbet Sarta abecedary. Courtesy of Moshe
Kokhavi

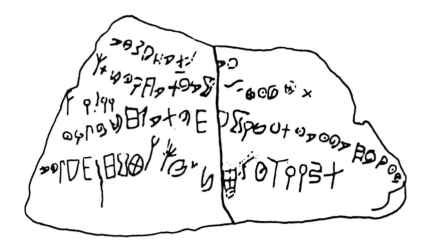

DIFFUSION OF THE ALPHABET

The Greek Alphabet

Long before the Greeks used the Semitic alphabet, other scripts existed in the Mediterranean world but these were forgotten by the time the alphabet was introduced. These scripts, used by the Minoans and Myceneans in the second millennium B.C.E., were not related to Egyptian or Semitic writing. One pictographic script and two so-called linear scripts, classified A and B, were uncovered at the turn of the twentieth century. Linear A was used in Crete to record a language as yet unknown. Linear B, a syllabic script of some eighty-eight phonetic signs (consonant + vowel) and logograms, was deciphered in 1953 by Michael Ventris, who proved that the script represented the ancient Greek language (see pl. 29, p. 25). Some one hundred inscriptions were found on painted vases from Knossos (Crete), Tiryns, Mycenae, Thebes, and a few other sites, and close to four thousand unfired clay tablets were found at Knossos (1400–1300 B.C.E.), Thebes (1350–1300 B.C.E.), and Mycenae and Pylos (1250–1150 B.C.E.). These texts were nonliterary, with few real sentences. John Chadwick, who continued the work after Ventris's death, believed that the clay tablets could have been the scratch paper of the culture, and that the final copies, and perhaps even literature, were written on papyrus, which has disappeared. Linear B was lost with the Dorian invasions of the twelfth century B.C.E. (except in its descendant on Cyprus and Crete). It is assumed that the Greeks then remained scriptless (that sounds nicer than "illiterate") until the Semitic alphabet was introduced between the eleventh and eighth centuries B.C.E. by the Phoenicians, the merchants of the Mediterranean world. The Greek historian Herodotus acknowledged the Phoenician origin of the alphabet.

There were local variations of the Phoenician-to-Greek forms of letters in each of the Mediterranean sites where the archaic Greek script has been found, just as there were local dialects and just as there had been variations of the North Semitic alphabet that were used for Hebrew, Canaanite, Moabite, and Phoenician. A few of the archaic Greek letters resemble Semitic forms of the tenth century, although material evidence for Greek script does not come from so early a date. According to Lilian Jeffery, extended residence of one group in the territory of another was necessary to accommodate the Semitic script to the Greek language, or to produce bilingual teachers and students. This means that either Phoenicians who colonized Greek sites taught the alphabet, or that trading Greeks who settled in Phoenician territory in the mid- or late eighth century brought the alphabet back to their homeland.

The earliest evidence for the Greek alphabet is from late eighth-century B.C.E. Rhodes and Crete, both key trading centers between mainland Greece and Phoenicia, and from Thera (Santorini) and Athens. One of the earliest "documents" of archaic Greek script is the Athens Dipylon Oinochoe of ca. 725 B.C.E. (pl. 56). Another early example is the Françoise Vase (pl. 57). Many inscriptions from the

Pl. 56. Attic Dipylon Oinochoe. "This is the prize for the best dancer." Athens, ca. 725 B.C.E. Early Greek script painted on pottery. Courtesy of the National Museum, Athens

same period are found on other pottery vessels as well as on ostraca (broken pottery), stone (marble and limestone), bronze sculpture, and utensils. There are dedications and epitaphs, abecedaries, name lists, and graffiti.

Pl. 57. Françoise Vase, top row. Attic black-figure krater. Early Greek writing reads in both directions. Chiusi, ca. 575 B.C.E. Archeological Museum, Florence, 4209. Courtesy of Soprintendenza Archeologica per la Toscana-Firenze

Pl. 58. Greek stone fragment, showing boustrophedon script (reverse epsilon, lambda, nu). Regulations for sacrifices at the Dipoleia, festival honoring Zeus. Athens, ca. 550 B.C.E. British Museum, Department of Greek and Roman Antiquities, GIBM 74. Courtesy of the British Museum

When the Greeks began to write they almost always accepted the retrograde direction of Semitic script, at least for one-line inscriptions. In some North Semitic inscriptions the lines had run in alternating directions, and in a few instances the second line was written from left to right with the letters reversed. This phenomenon is known as *boustrophedon* writing—the way the ox ploughs a field. Boustrophedon script began early in Greek writing history and was common in the seventh and sixth centuries. When the scribe wrote more than one paragraph, each section began with retrograde script, as if tradition dictated that this was the correct way to begin a thought (pl. 58). Two centuries of such impractical writing may seem strange to modern readers but it is entirely in keeping with the conservative nature of script (and perhaps is more practical—the computer printer works boustrophedon). Since twelve of the letters were symmetrical and six needed little modification when reversed, only eight letters appeared to be different in the boustrophedon stage: B, E, F, K, M, N, π (r) and R. The inner needs of the right-handed scribe writing on hides or papyrus finally prevailed by the fifth century B.C.E., when nearly all examples of Greek script show the present right-reading direction. Obviously, this is the reason that several of our letters are the reverse of their Semitic ancestors.

Of some thirty-three local early Greek scripts that have been identified, the universal alphabet of late classical Greece grew from the script now classified as the Eastern Ionic type, formally adopted by Athens in 403 B.C.E. Standardization of script came quite late if one considers the other artistic and literary achievements of Athens. The Greeks squared off or rounded their letters once they paid heed to calligraphic niceties. One would have expected perfected letter shapes from such a visually sensitive culture for whom balance, harmony, and perfect proportions were the aesthetic ideal. But aesthetic concerns for script did not seem to interest the Greeks as early in their history as their interest in sculpture and architecture. We do not have manuscripts of the fifth century B.C.E. to prove this, but writing on pottery of this time is amateurish, and writing on classical monuments of the mid-fifth century is rare, unlike the monuments of imperial Rome where perfect script is contemporary to the best art and literature. This does not mean, however, that monumental inscriptions are entirely lacking (pl. 59, 60).

The Greek names of the letters were based on those of their Semitic predecessors: *alpha, beta, gamma, delta,* and so forth. These words had no meaning in Greek. The slight variations, especially the added *a* or *i* at the end, were due to the assimilation of the Semitic names into Greek speech, which preferred final vowel sounds. In accommodating the Phoenician alphabet to their tongue, the Greeks changed the sound of some signs and added letters. While preserving the basic order, they added four new letters at the end: *phi* Φ, *chi* ✕, *psi* Ψ, and *omega* Ω. In doing so they did not apply the acrophonic principle, of which they were unaware. The *chi* may have had its visual origin in the eleventh-century Semitic *kaf* ⅄ (also pronounced *kh*), →, or ↓, for it was written several ways in archaic Greek but was fixed to the end of the alphabet with the other new letters. The *omega* Ω was a doublet of the *omicron*. The Semitic *vav* became *vau* Υ *(digamma)*, which was used temporarily then dropped except as a numeral. The *upsilon* Υ, having also come from the *vav* but apparently not considered the same letter by the Greeks, was placed after the *tau* and before the other four additional letters. Classical Greece dropped the *vau*, as it did the *san* Ϻ and the *sampi* ⋊, both derived from the Semitic *zade*. *Sampi* was retained as a numeral representing nine hundred and *vau* was kept for six, and *qoppa* Ϙ reserved for ninety.

The great contribution of the Greeks to the alphabet was the use of certain Semitic consonants as vowels. The aspirates, the voiceless *alef* ✦, the *he* ⅁, and the *ayin* Ο, were useless in Greek as consonants, but they must have sounded enough like their own vowels to become the vowels *alpha, epsilon,* and *omicron* (and *omega*). *Eta* can be seen as a long-vowel *E* or a short-vowel *I*. The Semitic semi-vowels *yod* and *vav*

Pl. 60. Wall with Greek inscription of manumission of slaves. Sanctuary of Apollo at Delphi, last quarter of the sixth century B.C.E. Courtesy of Ecole Française d'Archéologie, Athens

Pl. 59. Hellenistic Greek inscription from statue base, honoring athlete Lucius for his victory at the Great Didymaean Games. Decorative leaf, inscribed on Roman monuments as well, later inspired printers. From Didyma. British Museum, Department of Greek and Roman Antiquities, GIBM 928. Courtesy of the British Museum

became the *iota* and the *upsilon*. Unlike the early Semitic writers of the alphabet, who had to supply their own vowel sounds when they read, the Greeks now had a phonetic alphabet that truly represented speech. Some historians of the alphabet, notably Ignace Gelb, are loath to call it an alphabet until the Greeks wrote with it because, they claim, a true alphabet must have vowels. This may be hair-splitting over names and definitions; with similar logic it can be claimed that, since the Hebrews or other Semitic peoples invented the name, *alef-bet,* from the first two letters, they also invented the entity.

The Latin Alphabet

The source of the Roman alphabet was the western Greek alphabet, by way of Etruria, and the earliest examples occur a century later than their Greek equivalents. The boustrophedon stage does not last as long. The Etruscans themselves may have taken their alphabet from the people of Cumae, a Chalcidian colony near Naples, or from some other western Greek colony. The earliest example of Etruscan is an abecedary, ca. 700 B.C.E., written from right to left on the frame of a wax tablet and found at Marsiliana near Orbetello (see pl. 7, p. 7). The Etruscan alphabet itself changed over the centuries, and it was from the earlier version that Rome borrowed, probably in the seventh century B.C.E., when Etruscan kings ruled over Rome (616–509). One of the oldest Latin inscriptions comes from the sixth century B.C.E. from the Forum in Rome; it is the *Lapis Niger*, or Black Stone (pl. 61). The inscription runs vertically on four sides of a volcanic limestone pillar, in boustrophedon style. Similar to the Greek are the early Latin letters of Ⱶ for *H*, *P* for *R*, and *Y* for *V*. The Etruscans had no use for the *B, D, G, O,* and *X,* and hardly used the *K* and *Q*.

The archaic Latin alphabet had twenty-one letters. It lacked the Semitic *tet* (the Greek *theta*), *samekh*, and *zade,* but included the Greek *upsilon* and *chi*. Even in the Etruscan and early Latin alphabets, certain letter forms already differed enough from their Greek counterparts to account for the divergent shapes of equivalent letters in modern Greek and Latin alphabets: the *C, D, L, P,* and *S* were written Ɔ, ◁, ↲, ۹ or Ρ, and ∫. An extra stroke had to be added to the closed *rho* of Greek in order to form the *R*. The *C* was used initially for both the *g* and the *k* sounds and, by the third century B.C.E. the short horizontal bar of the *G* was added to distinguish between the two. The Romans used the *K,* as did the Etruscans, only when it was followed by an *A* or a consonant, and later it was seldom used. The *C* always was followed by *E* and *I,* the *Q* by *U*. Unlike classical Greek script, Latin retained the archaic *vau* ↗, pronounced *f*. In early Etruscan and Latin alphabets, the Greek *digamma* Y and the Ⱶ were sometimes combined to represent *F,* but the Ⱶ element was later separated to become the consonant *H*. When the *F* became the dominant sound, the *V* was pushed out of its Semitic slot and placed after the *T* (where the *upsilon* was), and used as both a consonant and a semivowel. The distinction between the shapes of *U* and *V* was a development of medieval script, and the

Pl. 61. Lapis Niger (Black Stone). One of the earliest Latin inscriptions; displays boustrophedon script. Roman Forum, sixth century B.C.E. Reproduced from Károly Földes-Papp, *Vom Felsbild zum Alphabet.* Courtesy of Chr. Belser Verlag

phonetic distinction came later with printing. In the late second and first centuries B.C.E., when many Greek words entered Latin, *Y* and *Z* were readopted. Before that, *V* and *I* had been used for the *y* sound, and *S* and *SS* for *z*. Thus the Semitic *vav* split into three (eventually five) Latin letters: *F, V* (*U* and *W*), and *Y*. The *Z*, which had been dropped to make way for the *G*, became and remained the last letter of the twenty-three letters of the Roman alphabet. It was only in the first century C.E. that *Y* and *Z* were mentioned officially.

The Romans used letters as numerals; thus, as with all numerals, they can be viewed as logograms. Unlike Hebrew, where letters in sequence represented their numerical value (*alef* to *tet* = 1–9, *yod* = 10, *kaf* = 20, etc.), and Greek, which followed the Hebrew but also employed the unused Semitic letters as numerals, Roman numerals have no relation to their position in the alphabet. The Romans used *C* for 100 (centum) and *M* for 1,000 (mille). Another numeral one often finds in printed books for 1,000, cıɔ , may have originated in the Greek *phi* ɸ (which in Greek was 500, not 1,000). It was modified by the Romans to ⊕ and later to ∞ and cıɔ. Half of the cıɔ was ıɔ , eventually *D*, the Roman numeral for 500. I, V, and X for 1, 5, and 10, respectively, came from finger computation: I was one finger, V was the space between the thumb and the flat open palm with fingers closed, and X was the profile of two hands crossed. The L for 50 was originally the Greek *chi*, written ѵ or ⊥ before the letter was standardized. The Romans drew a horizontal line above and below their numerals to distinguish them from letters. Roman numerals are important for the history of the Western book because they were retained for printing the book's publication date long after Arabic numerals were common in Europe. Some private printers today still maintain this tradition.

The names of Latin letters obviously differ from their Semitic equivalents. They are simply the sound of the consonant either preceding or following a vowel: *be, ce, de,* or *el, em, en*. The names of the vowels are their sound as long vowels: I = eye. At different times names varied slightly, for example, H = *ha*, and pronunciation of individual letter-names differs slightly in modern English and Romance languages. The naming system is believed to have been an Etruscan invention, although there is no documentary proof for this. These Latin names were in existence by the first century B.C.E.

When the Roman alphabet achieved visual perfection on monumental inscriptions in the second century C.E., it possessed twenty-three letters. The only ones missing from the modern alphabet were *J, U,* and *W*. The *W* was a doubling of the *V*, which occurred in the eleventh or twelfth century. In classic imperial Roman Capital script, the *V* represented the *u, v,* and *w* sounds, although in cursive script the consonantal *v* sound was sometimes written as a double *V* (*VV*). In tenth-century minuscule (small-letter) script when majuscule (capital) letters were used as initials, the capital *V* form became the initial and the *U* form became the minuscule *v*, used in the middle of words or sentences; its rounding already had appeared in the earlier Uncial script. Since more Latin words begin with the consonantal *V* than with the vowel *U*, the division was a natural one. Complete distinction between the *V* and *U* as different sound signs did not occur until the sixteenth century. The separation of the consonant *J* from the vowel *I* took place around this same time, although the J-shape had been used as a capital letter in the Middle Ages, and letters resembling the *J* can be found in Irish and Italian scripts. The absence of the letters *J, U,* and *W*, from the original Latin alphabet has given rise to another modern book tradition: When the printed book's signatures (sections or gatherings) are lettered alphabetically to keep them in proper order for binding, these three letters (or the *V* instead of *U*) are missing from the sequence.

In addition to rounding the letters to a greater degree than had the Greeks, the Romans brought beauty and symmetry to the alphabet (pl. 62 and pl. 148, p. 178). They valued the aesthetics of script more than did their classical Greek predecessors, although Hellenistic and later Greek scribes were more concerned with letters as art.

Study of the further development of Latin into the printed alphabet belongs to paleography (Chapter 8). The Romans carved their inscriptions on monuments all over their empire, but it was not these monuments that were responsible for transmitting writing traditions in the Middle Ages. Traditions were made and broken by monastic scribes, with a little help from chancery scripts and the common cursive. The perfectly proportioned capital letters of second century C.E. Rome did serve as an inspiration to the late fifteenth-century printers of Italy, who sought a harmonious majuscule for the Roman typography that was based on the minuscule Humanistic hand (pl. 63).

Throughout its history, the shape taken by writing, as opposed to the underlying system, was determined by the materials used to record it. This we will see when we look at the books made by the various cultures of the ancient and medieval worlds: the wedge-shaped cuneiform was written thus because of clay and stylus; the cursive forms of Egyptian hieratic and demotic, Aramaic, Greek, and Latin suited the reed pen on papyrus or processed animal skin; Roman Capitals on monuments were fashioned by hammer and chisel into stone; and Uncials were the result of the movement of the quill on parchment. At its finest, each script seems to have been delineated perfectly by the tools employed to write it and by the surface on which it was written.

Pl. 62. Roman Square Capital sepulchral inscription in *tabula ansata*. Museo Nazionale Romano, inv. no. 39507; CIL 6.37075. Marble. Rome, ca. 17 B.C.E.–12 C.E. Reproduced from Arthur E. and Joyce S. Gordon, *Album of Dated Latin Inscriptions*. Courtesy of University of California Press, Berkeley

POLIPHILO QVIVI NARRA, CHE GLI PAR VE AN-
CORA DI DORMIRE, ET ALTRONDE IN SOMNO
RITROVARSE IN VNA CONVALLE, LAQVALE NEL
FINE ERA SERATA DE VNA MIRABILE CLAVSVRA
CVM VNA PORTENTOSA PYRAMIDE, DE ADMI-
RATIONE DIGNA, ET VNO EXCELSO OBELISCO DE
SOPRA. LAQVALE CVM DILIGENTIA ET PIACERE
SVBTILMENTE LA CONSIDEROE.

 A SPAVENTEVOLE SILVA, ET CONSTI-
pato Nemore euafo, & gli primi altri lochi per el dolce
fomno che fe haueua per le feffe & profternate mébre dif-
fufo relicti, me ritrouai di nouo in uno piu delectabile
fito affai piu che el præcedente. El quale non era de mon
ti horridi, & crepidinofe rupe intorniato, ne falcato di
ftrumofi iugi. Ma compofitamente de grate montagniole di non tro-
po altecia. Siluofe di giouani quercioli, di roburi, fraxini & Carpi-
ni, & di frondofi Efculi, & Ilice, & di teneri Coryli, & di Alni, & di Ti-
lie, & di Opio, & de infructuofi Oleaftri, difpofiti fecondo lafpecto de
gli arboriferi Colli. Et giu al piano erano grate filuule di altri filuatici

Pl. 63. Francesco Colonna, *Hypnerotomachia Poliphili* (Venice: Aldus Manutius, 1499). Roman Capitals in an incunable. Courtesy of the Jewish National and University Library, Jerusalem

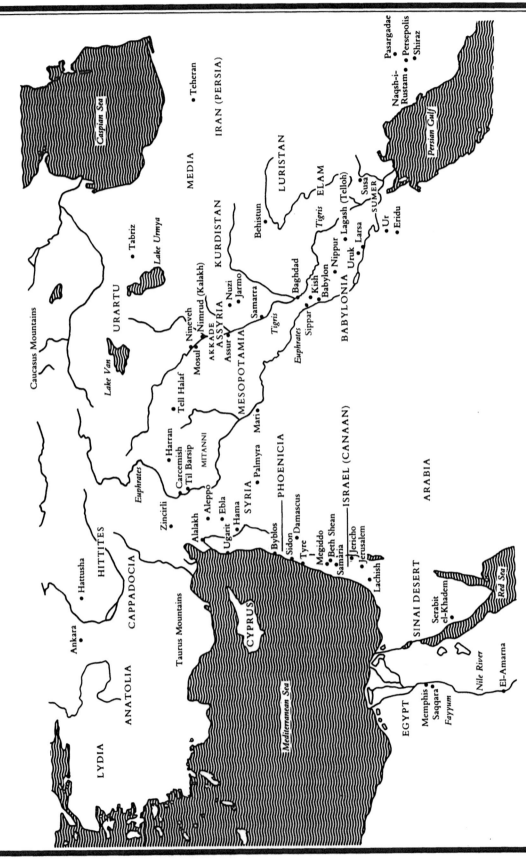

The Fertile Crescent—The Ancient Near East

CHAPTER 3

The Book in the Ancient World: Mesopotamia

he study of history is the study of documents—books. We are able to reconstruct the history of a literate society only on the basis of the documents it left for us, sometimes, it seems, rather capriciously. When a culture wrote on a fragile writing surface, the evidence for that society—its literature and its records of everyday activities—disappeared, unless succeeding peoples made a conscious effort to continue the preceding culture's traditions by translating and copying its books or by writing descriptions of it. This was the fate of Greek literature of the classical period, the fourth century B.C.E. The Greeks must have written everything important on papyrus or animal skins, which deteriorated in the relatively damp Mediterranean climate. All that we know of the rich literary activity of the Greeks comes from what was copied and recopied for many centuries after their culture flourished, or from what was rediscovered in the form of fragments of the literature copied by Hellenistic scribes in Egypt, where the papyri on which poetry and drama were written were preserved by the dry climate. Greek literature was also preserved in later Latin translations and in Byzantine manuscripts.

The study of the history of books involves the examination of how these documents were made and the materials used to make them. The materials, or descriptions of the materials and methods of book production, like the writings themselves, have been left to us by intention as well as by chance. Fire, either deliberate or accidental, destroyed many a library throughout history, but a fire in Mesopotamia fortunately enhanced preservation, at least of documents that were written on clay. Part of Assurbanipal's great library of Nineveh was preserved in this way. Once the languages were deciphered, Sumerian, Assyrian, and Babylonian literature and everyday life were the simplest to reconstruct. The Mycenaeans may have written their literature or official reports on perishable materials, such as papyrus, but all that has been left for us to read are their account books on clay tablets. From the biblical land of Israel, other than a few isolated inscriptions on stone or metal or clay bullae, nearly all that is known are lists or correspondence on ostraca, broken pottery that was the scratch paper of the ancient Near East. It seems ironic that the cheapest writing material should have proved to be the most durable. The survival of the Hebrew Bible is due to its having been recopied continuously from ancient times to the present.

The apparent obsession of pharaonic Egypt with death may be due to the practice of burying some of its literature in tombs and cemeteries, for, along with Egypt's dry climate, the sands preserved what was interred. The soil of Mesopotamia did not offer the same service; the only letters on leather that have survived were sent from Persia to Egypt. We also know of Assyrian writing on leather from illustrations in wall paintings or on reliefs. The small number of papyri that have surfaced in Israel were found in the arid Negev and in the desert near the Dead Sea. Some of the ancients were aware of the destructibility of their writing materials. Clay tablets eventually were fired to strengthen them and, if a king had something important to proclaim, he had it engraved on stone, often in two or three languages. Books were even written on the walls of palaces. The scribe of the Isaiah Scroll, the most important of the biblical Dead Sea Scrolls, sealed it in a jar. Other works were wrapped in linen to preserve them before they were encased in earthenware jars and hidden in caves.

Today we think of a book as a gathering of paper pages bound together with a protective cover. For the books of older, partially lost civilizations, we must expand our imagination to include all kinds of writing instruments and bookmaking materials we would not have considered otherwise, such as stone, metal, trees (wood, bark, bamboo, and palm leaves), glass, ivory, clay, wax, fabric, and the bones and skins of animals. All of these were surfaces for books and documents. Some materials were ordinary, some exotic. Probably the most exotic handmade book of recent times, now in the British Library, was made in nineteenth-century Burma of cotton cloth stiffened with black lacquer, cut into the shape of a traditional palm-leaf book, and inlaid with mother-of-pearl letters (pl. 64). This is almost rivaled in beauty by the books of the contemporary Private Press movement and other examples of the book arts today (pl. 2, p. 2).

HISTORY OF MESOPOTAMIA: SUMER, ASSYRIA, BABYLONIA

Just as the various inhabitants of Mesopotamia adopted and adapted the mythology, literature, religion, arts, and the cuneiform script of the Sumerians of the third millennium B.C.E., so did they maintain and develop Sumerian techniques of making books. Although the region of the Tigris-Euphrates river valley was dominated by different ethnic and linguistic groups, methods of book production remained relatively constant. The traditional Sumerian techniques continued, even as new materials and methods were introduced by succeeding cultures. The unity of materials and methods, however, was determined by place more than by historical, ethnic, socioeconomic, and cultural factors.

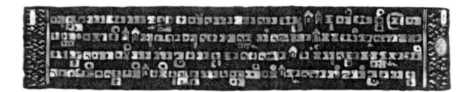

Pl. 64. Nineteenth-century Burmese book of cotton cloth, with mother-of-pearl inlay letters. British Library, Department of Oriental Manuscripts and Printed Books, Add. 23939. Courtesy of the British Library

The Sumerians, whose ethnic and linguistic origins are still a mystery, occupied the southern region of Mesopotamia, north of the Persian Gulf, from at least the middle of the fourth millennium B.C.E. Their major cities were Uruk (the biblical Erech, modern Warka), Kish, Nippur, Ur, and Lagash. Their gods, in human form, represented the forces of nature, not always friendly to humans in a land of sudden thunderstorms, scorching sun, and intermittently uncontrollable rivers. The Sumerian economy was based on irrigation agriculture that had developed in the region in the millennia preceding the development of cuneiform script. Their city-states were fortified and their army strengthened. The arts of sculpture, wheel-thrown pottery, seal carving, glassmaking, and architecture flourished. The Sumerians were musicians, merchants, astronomers, and bookkeepers. Their army, however, was not strong enough for them to remain masters of this turbulent region; eventually Semites known as Akkadians, who were already urbanized and settled to the north of the Sumerian cities by the middle of the third millennium B.C.E., began to dominate Mesopotamia. The Akkadian king Sargon (ca. 2300 B.C.E.) established a dynasty which controlled Mesopotamia at Akkade (Agade) and ruled for over a century. The Akkadians were overthrown by nomads from the north, the Guti, who were never able to rule over the entire area, so the Neo-Sumerians reestablished their kingdom, rebuilding their city of Ur and initiating a second golden age. One Neo-Sumerian king, Gudea of Lagash, reigned for only fifteen years but managed to immortalize himself by commissioning over thirty statues of himself, some of which were also written documents (pl. 65). Ur declined slowly with the incursions of the Semitic Amorites, who had entered the

Pl. 65. Gudea, ruler of Lagash. The inscription glorifies Gudea as a builder of temples. Telloh, Lower Mesopotamia, ca. 2150 B.C.E. Calcite. Louvre, AO 22126. Courtesy of the Louvre, Départment des Antiquités Orientales

region around 2200 B.C.E.; the final blow came from the Elamites around 2000 B.C.E. Amorite Babylonian kings began to rule about 1900 B.C.E.; the most famous of them was Hammurabi (ca. 1790–1750) (see pl. 74, p. 76). Although the Hittites, who spoke an Indo-European language but adopted cuneiform as one of their scripts, conquered Babylon in the early sixteenth century B.C.E., they withdrew to Anatolia (Turkey), leaving Mesopotamia to be dominated by the Kassites (1570–1350) and the Mitanni, an Indo-Aryan aristocracy over a Hurrian substratum, until the mid-twelfth century B.C.E. The Mitanni held sway over Assyria but never over Babylonia. A period of cultural stagnation followed until the Assyrians, from northern Mesopotamia, revitalized the region.

The Semitic Assyrians had been in Mesopotamia since the third millennium, but they dominated it only for short periods. When they began to gain military control around 1245, they accepted the literary and artistic culture that had preceded them, just as the Babylonians had done. Their kingdom grew steadily by colonization and conquest, especially between 900 and 612 B.C.E., to include Syria and northern Israel. The great Assyrian cities were Nimrud (Kalakh), Khorsabad, Assur, and Nineveh; in all of them books were made and illustrated on a variety of surfaces, depending on availability of materials and imports. We even have pictures of their scribes. Just when the Assyrians seemed to be at the height of their power, they were brought down by the Medes and Neo-Babylonians. The Neo-Babylonian Empire lasted for nearly a century, from the fall of Nineveh in 612 B.C.E. to the fall of Babylon to King Cyrus of Persia in 539. The Achaemenid kings of Persia were masters of the Near East from 538, and even conquered Egypt in 525 B.C.E. In turn, Persia was conquered by Alexander the Great in 331 B.C.E.

Table 1 lists the masters of Mesopotamia, their kings, and their major cities. Gaps in dates represent anarchic periods; overlapping dates occur when no single empire had established hegemony.

BOOKS: MATERIALS AND TECHNIQUES

Mesopotamian books were written on the most durable materials—stone and clay—and on the most perishable of them, leather, and possibly papyrus. One may not ordinarily think of stone as a material for books, but a rock-cut mountain, such as the Rock of Behistun in Persia, was perfect for a permanent royal inscription, and it became a history book for us. Stone was rare in Assyria and nonexistent in Babylonia and had to be imported. In Assyria, inscriptions were written on a variety of native stones: marble, limestone, and igneous rocks such as basalt and dolerite. Diorite was imported. Boundary stones, permanent records of land grants, were common in Babylonia. Dedicatory inscriptions and records of the conquests and accomplishments of kings were written on royal buildings and on sculpted figures of softer stone such as steatite (talc), alabaster, and gypsum. Marble, onyx, and lapis lazuli (medium-hard stones) displayed incised writing. Gudea, king of Lagash, commissioned many statues of himself with accounts of his abilities as an administrator and as a patron of literature and the arts (see pl. 65). The palaces of kings such as Assurnasirpal at Nimrud (Kalakh) in the ninth century B.C.E. and Assurbanipal at Nineveh in the seventh century B.C.E. were faced with relief sculpture that included standardized cuneiform texts (pl. 66). King Sennacherib of Assyria took along an artist to Judea to document his victory at Lachish in 701 B.C.E. so that the event could be recorded in a room in his palace at Nineveh, just as a television crew or photojournalist today would be dispatched to a faraway war to relay visual information to the people back home.

Small, semi-precious stones were used as cylinder seals from the late fourth millennium: serpentine, limestone, quartz, jasper, chalcedony, agate (a banded chalcedony), carnelian (a red chalcedony), hematite, magnetite, rock crystal, lapis lazuli, and marble (see pl. 34, p. 29, and pl. 73, p. 74). These early examples of printing served as ownership marks and signatures for most men and even for some

Table 1. Chronology of the Mesopotamian World

Date (B.C.E.)	Dominating Group	Major Kings	Major Cities
2600–2350	Early dynastic city-states		Ur, Uruk, Lagash, Nippur, Kish, Mari
2334–2154	Akkadian	Sargon I Naram Sin	Akkade, Ur, Susa, Mari
2154–2112	Guti invasions	Gudea	Lagash
2112–2004	Neo–Sumerian, third Dynasty of Ur		Ur, Nippur, Uruk
2025–1763	Isin, Larsa dynasties		Larsa, Lagash, Ur
1894–1595	Babylonian	Hammurabi (1780–1750)	Babylon, Susa, Mari
1570–1155	Kassite		
	Elamite raids, without dominating; take Code of Hammurabi in 1165		Susa
1950–1813	Old Assyrian Period	Assur	
1400–1000	Middle Assyrian Period	Tiglath-Pileser I (1112–1074)	Assur
1000–625	Neo-Assyrian Period	Assurnasirpal II (884–859)	Nimrud, Assur
		Shalmaneser III (858–824)	Assur
		Sargon II (721–705)	Khorsabad
		Tiglath-Pileser III (745–727)	Nimrud
		Sennacherib (704–681)	Assur, Nineveh
		Esarhaddon (680–669)	Til Barsip, Nineveh
		Assurbanipal (668–631)	Til Barsip, Nineveh
625–539	Neo-Babylonian	Nebuchadnezzar	Babylon
538–331	Persian–Achaemenid	Cyrus II (559–529)	Pasargade
		Darius I (521–485)	Susa, Persepolis
		Xerxes I (485–465)	Persepolis

Pl. 66. Bas relief from the palace of Assurnasirpal II at Nimrud. Standard inscription of the building's dedication runs across the illustration. Nimrud (Kalakh), 875 B.C.E. Gypseous alabaster. British Museum, Department of Western Asiatic Antiquities, No. 124563. Courtesy of the British Museum

slaves and women. Inscriptions usually were set off in frames. Seals were universal in ancient Near Eastern society; commoners as well as kings had them, and they were as necessary for identification then as a driver's license or major credit card is today. In Mesopotamia, contributions to the temple were stamped with cylinder seals, as were contracts. Stamp seals were replaced in lower Mesopotamia in the fourth millennium B.C.E. by cylinder seals, but by the Persian period, stamp seals in all materials were used once again. Those who could not write stamped documents written for them by professional scribes. Kings approved appointments and signed decrees with seals, and important rooms of the palace, such as the treasury and kitchen, were secured with a lock covered with sealed clay (which was broken, it is hoped, for official entries only). To ensure that a letter would not be tampered with, from the late third millennium to the first half of the second millennium, clay was wrapped around the document and rolled with the sender's cylinder seal. When we say that a letter is sealed, we don't mean it as literally as did a person in ancient or even medieval times, but the equivalent is still quite common for legal and other formal documents: stamped by embossing. Art and book collectors and libraries use seals as well, and in the Far East they have been as important historically as they were in the ancient Near East. In Sumer, Assyria, and Babylonia, seal cutters were a special group of artisans, working in miniature, as were Greek and Roman cameo carvers.

Metals, too, were used for inscriptions, either as stamp seals or as tablets or as crafted objects and weapons; antimony, copper, bronze, silver, and gold were all used. At his capital of Persepolis in the late sixth century B.C.E., Darius buried gold and silver foundation plaques in stone boxes under the *apadana,* his large audience hall, engraved with trilingual inscriptions (see pl. 38, p. 33). Mementos for the future are still embedded in foundation stones.

Wax tablet books were used in Assyria in the time of Tiglath-Pileser I (the late twelfth and early eleventh centuries), and again in the eighth and early seventh centuries B.C.E. during the reigns of Sargon II and Sennacherib. Made of ivory or wood (tamarisk, cypress, cedar, or walnut), these rectangular tablets were recessed to hold beeswax on both sides (pl. 67, 68). The surface of the board was crisscrossed to grip the wax. Orpiment and arsenic sulfide dyed the wax yellow and black and slowed down its hardening so the scribe could write with ease. The scribe wrote with an ivory, bone, or bronze stylus. The tablets were hinged together to form a fanfolded book. The longest one extant seems to have been made of fifteen boards; each board measures about 15 × 6 inches (38 × 15 cm), and is 1/2 inch (1.4 cm) thick. Wooden boards were slightly larger than ivory ones. In the longest, if there was no title page, there could be 250 lines on each of the thirty pages, for a total of 7,500 lines. The text was written in two columns. The outside of the first tablet served as a title page; it sometimes included the name of the scribe and the library to which the book belonged in addition to the title, which consisted of the opening words of the book. The verso of the title page was not inscribed, nor was the last page. Hinges and pins that enabled the ivory polyptychs to fold in either direction have not survived, but we still see the hinge grooves. These hinges may have been made of gold. One of these wax-tablet books found at Nimrud contained an astrological text commissioned by Sargon II, *Enuma Anu Enlil,* a compilation of omens taken from observations of the sun, moon, planets, and fixed stars. The editor was Nabuzuqupkena, scribe-astrologer to Sargon and Sennacherib. The Neo-Hittites (1209–709 B.C.E.), early Greeks, and Etruscans also used waxed writing boards such as these, prototypes of the Roman codex.

Neither parchment nor leather has been found from so early a date, although leather was known to have been used in western Asia by the first millennium. It was natural to write Aramaic on a soft material with a reed pen. The Greek historian Ctesias (d. 398) noted that Persian records were written on royal hides (*diphterai*

Pl. 67. Ivory and wax writing tablet, its hinges missing, on which an astronomical work was written. Nimrud (Kalakh), eighth century B.C.E. British Museum, Department of Western Asiatic Antiquities, No. 3566. Courtesy of the British Museum

Pl. 68. Wooden writing board with Aramaic script. Egypt, ca. fifth century B.C.E. Louvre, AO 17204. Courtesy of the Louvre, Départment des Antiquités Orientales

basilikai) and that the *Avesta* was written on skins of oxen. From Egypt, where the dry climate has preserved so many documents, there has come a collection of some fourteen letters (one of which crumbled), written in Aramaic in the fifth century B.C.E. The exact findspot is unknown, but the Arsham letters, as they are called, are now preserved in the Bodleian Library, Oxford. Most of the correspondence was written by Arsham, the Persian satrap of Egypt, when he returned to Persia in 411–410 B.C.E., to his officer Nehtihur; a few other official letters were in the same leather pouch. They prove that during the time Persia ruled the Near East leather must have been a common writing surface in western Asia.

There was a Sumerian term for the scribe who wrote on animal skin, *lu-kush-sar*. In Akkadian, there was a term for papyrus, *niyaru*, taken from the Egyptian *ni(t)r(w)*, the "stuff of the river," first mentioned in the reign of Sargon II. (The Hebrew *neyyar* was used for "papyrus" in talmudic times and *niyyar* still is the word for "paper.") When parchment was invented (we do not know the exact date), it may have been the Mesopotamian or western Asiatic desire to refine animal skin into a writing surface that imitated papyrus. Some of the leather of the Dead Sea Scrolls is very thin and almost white, and we can assume that leather such as this had been manufactured for centuries in the Near East. We see it illustrated on the walls of a Syrian palace of the eighth century B.C.E. (pl. 77, p. 78).

Clay Tablets

When one thinks of the classic Sumerian book and its Assyrian and Babylonian descendants, one thinks of clay tablets (pl. 69). These have been found as far away from their original home between the Tigris and Euphrates rivers as Anatolia in the north and Lachish, Taanach, Gezer, and other sites in Israel and El-Amarna at the western end of the Fertile Crescent (see pl. 36, p. 31, pl. 44, p. 38), and as far east as Tepe Yahya in the Kerman plain, Iran, Shahr-i Sokhta in Sistan, eastern Iran (proto-Elamite writing from about 3200 B.C.E., the same time that writing appears in Uruk), and Pakistan (Harappan texts from around 2000 B.C.E.). Tablets unrelated to those in Mesopotamia have also been found in Romania. Clay tablets were used from the end of the fourth millennium B.C.E. until about 100 C.E. The earliest were found at four sites in southern Mesopotamia—Uruk, Jamdat Nasr, Ur, and Farah—as well as at Kish, near Babylon, and Lagash. The earliest tablets were squarish, with a slightly convex surface and rounded corners, but they soon took on an oblong form. Eventually there was a wide range of tablet shapes and sizes, which sometimes depended on the nature of the text and its function, sometimes on the bookmaking style of the culture. Circular tablets were used for land contracts, maps, plans, and school texts; egg-shaped tablets or three-sided cones were used for ownership tags; olive-shaped tablets were used as amulets; and nail or wedge-shaped tablets were set in building foundations. Cylinder or barrel-shaped tablets were used from Sumerian times on, and the Babylonians and Persians continued these forms for historical inscriptions. Assyrians preferred prisms of six, eight, or ten sides for writing their history books from the twelfth to the eighth centuries B.C.E. A few editions of Sennacherib's campaign in Judea were published in this polygonal format (pl. 70). Animals inspired shapes as well; some tablets were in the form of a hoof or a paw. From the nineteenth to the sixteenth centuries B.C.E., Babylonians employed liver-shaped tablets for hepatoscopy, fortune-telling with the aid of a sheep's liver (pl. 71). The sheep was slaughtered for this purpose, and its liver was "read" for signs according to their correspondence to a master copy written in cuneiform on the clay tablet. The Etruscans, too, practiced hepatoscopy, and perhaps the idea of

Pl. 69. Old Babylonian deed of sale in cuneiform. The envelope repeats the text of the contract and records names of witnesses. Uruk, ca. 1750 B.C.E. British Museum, Department of Western Asiatic Antiquities, No. 33236. Courtesy of the British Museum

prophecy with livers, like the form of wax-tablet books, spread from Mesopotamia to Etruria.

The most popular form of clay tablet was the slightly oblong, pillow-shaped tablet, with flattened topside and slightly more convex underside, which could be held easily in the left hand of the scribe. The average size was 2 × 1-¼ inches (50 × 25–30 mm). The clay, so readily available in Mesopotamia, was first kneaded. Sometimes small impurities remained but they were flattened out, and the tablets were rounded off at the edges. If the tablet was big—some were as large as 18 × 12 inches (46 × 30 cm)—it was wrapped in wet cloth to keep it damp as the scribe wrote. Polygonal tablets were thrown on a wheel like a jar so that they were hollow inside, and the outer sides were flattened for writing. One can see the finger ridges of the potter on the inside if the handled lid is missing. The text was written freehand in a compact, minute, clear script in horizontal rows starting at the top, left-hand corner and ending in the lower right-hand corner on the flatter side of the tablet. Fine lines were drawn between the rows of script; each acted as a guideline for the following row. If the text was too long for one side, the scribe turned the tablet over and covered the reverse side with script, so that the writing was upside down from that on the obverse. If still more writing surface was needed, the scribe wrote across the upper edge and along the left and right sides of the tablet. Some sort of support board may have been used when two-sided or polygonal tablets were written because the writing on the first side is never smeared from having been turned over on the other side; none of these has been found, however.

Pl. 70. Sennacherib's Prism. Polygonal clay tablet. Akkadian cuneiform inscription describes the king's military campaign against Hezekiah of Judah in 701 B.C.E. Nineveh, Assyria, 691 B.C.E. Courtesy of the Israel Museum, Jerusalem

Pl. 71. Clay tablet in the shape of a sheep's liver, for divination, with omens and magic formulae. Babylonian, ca. nineteenth–sixteenth century B.C.E. British Museum, Department of Western Asiatic Antiquities, No. 92668. Courtesy of the British Museum

The stylus was a reed, or perhaps a very hard wood, or bone and ivory, at times. Reed and wood styli have perished. Reeds were as accessible as the native clay; they grew naturally and abundantly in Mesopotamia, and were perfectly suited to cuneiform writing. The reed was hard on the outside, with tough fibers inside. A stone or pumice was used for sharpening the reed, but it is not certain if the tip was squared off or cut into a triangular shape, or whether it was flat or beveled, for the wedge-shaped signs could be made in clay with any of these shapes. Perhaps the cutting of the tip varied over the centuries and in different locations; the strokes of cuneiform were not consistent in different schools of writing. Corrections could be made while the clay was still wet, and even a sun-dried tablet could be remoistened. Erasures were made with the other end of the stylus, or with a damp cloth for larger surfaces. A bone stylus was found at Nimrud; the flat end of it was probably used for smoothing the clay and the other, pointed end for scoring it. When a large tablet was written, the scribe drew lines around the text with a string or a straightedge. The spaces between these lines provided the same function as margins did in scrolls and later in codices, and cause the layout of the large clay tablet or the Assyrian wax tablet with two columns of text to look familiar to the reader of the modern Bible or dictionary. The columns ran from left to right on the front, and right to left on the reverse of the clay tablet. Several tablets written on both sides could make up a single book. Business and legal documents and correspondence at times were provided with protective envelopes, especially in early Babylonian days (see pl. 3, p. 3, and pl. 69). When the tablet was dry, either clay was molded over it or the tablet was slipped into its protective case and sealed with fresh clay. The scribe tried to leave some space between the inner tablet and its envelope so that the writing would not be obliterated by pressure. Then an identical text or a summary thereof was written to preserve the integrity of the contract or letter inside. A cylinder seal could also be rolled across the envelope. Clay-tablet envelopes were not true ancestors of modern book covers, but the need to protect the text was always present in bookmaking. A Sumerian legend told that Sargon, the Akkadian king, was the messenger who carried the very first tablet to have a clay envelope. He did not know its contents instructed the recipient to murder him.

After writing the tablet, the scribe dried it in the sun. More important texts were fired in a kiln from about 1800 B.C.E. In the kiln they were probably supported by tripods of clay and covered with a dome-shaped lid to prevent fire from damaging the writing. Holes were made in large tablets to prevent breakage during firing.

Books and documents were stored in reed baskets, earthenware jars, and wooden and clay boxes. Some were laid on shelves in archives and libraries, as at Nineveh in Assyria and at Ugarit and Ebla in Syria. Other libraries were found at Nippur, Lagash, and Mari. Libraries, archives, and scribal chanceries were standard features in temples and palaces of the Near East. A scribal office from the late eighth century B.C.E. was excavated at Nimrud's northwest palace. In it were burnt brick benches that were either seats or tables for scribes, and two rows of brick boxes that may have served as filing cabinets and contained many kinds of clay tablets, ranging from letters about stocks of grain and dispatches of horses and camels to complaints about the unreliability of the mail, problems of tax evasion, and the resettlement of captive populations—in other words, the trivia of palace administration. Some libraries had catalogs; two were found at Nippur. One listed sixty-two tablets and the other sixty-eight, with forty-three books in common. Altogether, seven library catalogs from the second millennium B.C.E. have been found. Ebla's archives, from the second half of the third millennium B.C.E., are among the earliest organized collections of this type. Round tablets with economic and administrative texts were stacked on the floor; square tablets with texts of other kinds were arranged in filing cabinet manner on wood shelves supported by wooden poles. The contents or opening phrase was written along the edge of the tablet (just as a title is written on the spine of a book today) to identify it as it rested on the shelf.

LITERATURE

A great variety of work is represented by the tens of thousands of clay tablets unearthed thus far in Mesopotamia. More than 90 percent of them are economic and administrative: accounts of agriculture and industries of Mesopotamia, contracts, legal texts and other commercial records, political correspondence, astronomical and astrological calculations, magic texts, mathematics books, maps and building plans, and medical and technical treatises and formulas, such as one for the manufacture of glass. From these many documents we get a picture of the activities of the kings, officials, and common people of Babylonia probably more accurate than what is known for any other long-destroyed civilization. Lexical texts begin to appear after 2500 B.C.E., at first monolingual Sumerian editions. Then bilingual dictionaries and word lists became common, and continued to be written in the first millennium B.C.E. One classic work from the second millennium lists some 9,700 terms on twenty-four tablets: *Har-ra Hubullu* ("Loan with Fixed Interest"). This Sumerian-Akkadian work, with its descriptions of society, court, costume, flora and fauna, mineralogy, and even beer making, is virtually an encyclopedia of ancient Mesopotamian life. About five thousand tablets from Sumer, many of them fragmented, are literary; the Sumerians had been writing for about five hundred years before tablets were used for transcribing their *belles lettres*.

The Semitic Assyrians and Babylonians adopted and revised Sumerian literature, just as they did the Sumerian plastic arts and cuneiform script. The Old Assyrians and Babylonians left a large number of personal letters from the eighteenth century B.C.E., and both Babylonians and Assyrians left history books, that is, long accounts of their kings' accomplishments, particularly their military victories. Why not? It was the kings who commissioned these books. Royalty usually did not read and write but had secretaries to do this work for them. King Assurbanipal of Assyria was an exception; he boasted that he had "read the beautiful clay tablets from Sumer and the obscure Akkadian writing which is hard to master." His greatest achievement, however, was the establishment of a library at Nineveh, the largest library in ancient Mesopotamia, for which he commissioned new editions of Sumerian and Akkadian literature. At the end of the texts in his library the tablets were stamped "Property of the Palace of Assurbanipal." Assurbanipal's chief librarian-scribe was Ishtarshumeresh, son of Sargon's scribe Nabuziqupkena. The names of other scribes from this family are known, covering a period of two centuries.

We have seen that it was not easy to read and write a complicated script like cuneiform, with its mixed system of logograms, phonograms, determinatives, and syllables (Chapter 1). Mesopotamian literature, therefore, was not intended for a wide audience of intelligent readers but for the royal collection and for the shelves of the school library, where belles lettres were copied for study and teaching. Special editions were ordered and housed at the Sumerian city of Nippur, the Hittite capital at Boğhazköy, and the Assyrian cities of Assur in 1100 B.C.E. and Nimrud between 705 and 614 B.C.E. But Assurbanipal's mid-seventh-century library at Nineveh is remembered today as the most famous of them all. One of the Great Books it contained was the Babylonian Creation poem, *Enuma Elish* ("When on High"), recited on the fourth day of the New Year festival. It is believed to have been written down first in the nineteenth century B.C.E. When the final edition was published for Assurbanipal, it filled seven large clay tablets.

Even more famous today because it has been translated so many times is the *Gilgamesh Epic* (pl. 72). The earliest Sumerian versions date back to the late third millennium B.C.E.; by the early second millennium there was an Old Babylonian Akkadian version, and by 1300 B.C.E. the Akkadian form of the epic was standardized. In it, the Sumerian king-hero Gilgamesh and his savage friend Enkidu combat monsters and share other adventures. When Enkidu dies, Gilgamesh seeks immortality, which previously had been granted to Utnapishtim, a survivor of the deluge. Gilgamesh undertakes a voyage to the underworld to visit Enkidu, who has nothing good to report about the Land of No Return. As in other works of Mesopotamian literature, there are parallels to the Bible. Copies of the *Gilgamesh Epic* must have circulated far and wide; a fragment of the epic from the fifteenth or fourteenth century B.C.E. was found at Megiddo in Israel. Some of its heroic tales must have been told even before there were written versions, for the iconography associated with Gilgamesh can be found in the art of cylinder seals as early as the beginning of the third millennium, before the real Sumerian King Gilgamesh of Uruk reigned, in about 2650 B.C.E. (pl. 73).

Pl. 72. Gilgamesh Epic, Tablet 11. Utnapishtim, the Babylonian counterpart of Noah, tells of the flood. Nineveh, seventh century B.C.E. Clay. British Museum, Department of Western Asiatic Antiquities, No. K 3375. Courtesy of the British Museum

Pl. 73. Man (Gilgamesh?) grappling with the lion. Akkadian agate seal and impression, 2500–2000 B.C.E. British Museum, Department of Western Asiatic Antiquities, No. 89147. Courtesy of the British Museum

ILLUSTRATION

Illustrated literature such as we know from medieval and modern books did not seem to exist in ancient Mesopotamia. Although Assyrian clay- and wax-tablet editions of the classics were not illustrated, sometimes their mythological figures appeared independently in cylinder seals, which can be viewed as illustrated miniature books, printed as the seal was rolled across the clay. But one must be careful in the identification of all mythological themes in seals, because the name of the individual who purchased it from the sealmaker's stock or the dedication on it to a particular god frequently had no relationship to the depicted subject as it was known from later written literature. Some glyptic heroes whose images are engraved on seals cannot be identified at all. Where texts are lacking, iconography is disputed by scholars.

If documents required illustrations such as diagrams, mathematical figures, or architectural plans, or if documents were intended to receive a seal, the scribe left space for this purpose. There were exceptions to this rule: there is a boundary stone, for example, on which the procedure was the opposite—the sculpture was accomplished first and the text incised afterward.

Assyrian relief sculpture was narrative in nature, even when no text accompanied it. Sometimes, however, relief sculptures had supplementary texts inscribed on them, as at the palace at Nimrud, where Mosul marble (gypsum) reliefs outside and in the throne room of Assurnasirpal II display a remarkable integration of script and illustration, executed with an artistic flair not to be encountered again until the manuscripts of the Carolingian period (see pl. 66). The cuneiform recorded the king's titles, his early conquests, and the extent of his realm; it described the palace he built and how he resettled the city of Nimrud. Other illustrations on his palace walls had summaries of the main inscription. In a way, these relief "books" were larger publications than wax-tablet books or medieval manuscripts; more people saw and read these wall inscriptions than saw or read the private clay tablets in the king's library or the later manuscripts on parchment commissioned by such patrons as the Duc de Berry.

Some books with historical content, such as stelae, were illustrated, particularly with a picture of the king or god or the two together. Law books also were illustrated. The Code of Hammurabi is the most famous of these, published by the eighteenth-century B.C.E. king of Babylon (pl. 74). Its 282 laws governing economic and social life were expressed succinctly and incised clearly on the eight-foot black diorite monument that stood in Babylon for six centuries. At the top of the monument is an investiture portrait: the seated god of justice, the sun god Shamash, commissions Hammurabi to promulgate the statutes carved thereon. Illustration of many public books was accomplished in this way with a portrait at the top, a prototype author or patron portrait, which we will see in medieval and modern books. Some of Hammurabi's laws, which had existed in earlier versions but here were edited and codified, were removed by the Elamites who carried off the stele to their capital at Susa in the twelfth century B.C.E. These laws can be reconstructed with the help of copies that were made after the code was first published. The code was studied and rewritten in scribal schools for a thousand years after it was carved, even though its laws were not always followed.

SCRIBES

Although literacy was not common in Mesopotamia because of the complex writing system (perhaps 2 percent to 5 percent of the population could read and write), it is a mistake to believe that writing was accomplished only by a small group of priests. Scribes were trained in special schools attached to the palace and temple (pl. 75). In Sumer there were schools by 2500 B.C.E. By the Babylonian period, schools were no longer connected to temples at all. From the towns of Uruk and Ur, word lists and exercise tablets as well as bilingual dictionaries have been found. Tuition was paid by the student's father, who came from the higher classes; if he was not a scribe

Pl. 74. *a*. Code of Hammurabi. Found in Susa; originally in Babylon or Sippar, ca. 1760 B.C.E. Basalt. Louvre, Sb 8. Courtesy of the Louvre *b*. (*above right*) Detail of Babylonian cuneiform inscription on Code of Hammurabi

Pl. 75. Scribes from relief on Tiglath-Pileser III's palace at Nimrud. Eighth century B.C.E. One scribe writes on a clay tablet, the other on a softer material, leather or papyrus. British Museum, Department of Western Asiatic Antiquities, No. 118882. Courtesy of the British Museum

himself he was a military officer, a high official, or an accountant. A few women became scribes, but most students were boys, and they attended school from sunrise to sunset until they reached adulthood. From the many school texts in the form of exercise tablets, we get a picture of school life at the Sumerian *edubba,* or "tablet house." As in the crafts and manual trades, children were sent to apprentice with the master scribe, the *ummia,* the "father" or principal of the school. Instructors, or "big brothers," assisted them in writing out their daily lessons—the literary and lexical school texts that the students simply copied over and over again. First the students learned the cuneiform signs; then they copied lists of words and synonyms, and vocabularies of the different branches of learning, such as geography, natural science, and law. After copying texts they wrote out literary quotations from memory. One wonders whether the *ummia* knew and revealed the underlying principles of logograms and phonograms and determinatives, or whether he and the students simply accepted the system without question. Once a student could write out all of the standard literary texts and could copy more than thirty thousand lines from dictation, he qualified for a specialty. By the time Akkadian became the spoken language, the student was expected to be bilingual and, in later times in Meso-potamia, scribes specialized in other languages, such as Aramaic and Egyptian. Upon graduation, the scribe specialized in law, medicine, or technology. He could take a job as an estate scribe, work for the government, serve as an army scribe, or provide his scribal services to the illiterate of the city. He could become a literary person, copying texts for the *edubba* library, or he could even become an *ummia.* This professorship, however, did not pay very well.

At Ugarit (Ras Shamra) on the northern coast of Syria, excavations that began in 1929 revealed that from the fourteenth to the thirteenth centuries B.C.E., when the king was a vassal of the Hittite Empire, the school for scribes was also the library of the high priest. Written works included myths, incantations, lists of gods and rituals, wisdom literature, magic and medical texts, public and private contracts, legal decisions and enactments, real estate, purchases of slaves and tax records, diplomatic correspondence, palace administrative archives—even versions of the Gilgamesh cycle.

According to the research of Anson F. Rainey, there were scribes who served as public notaries and scribes who served as messengers, reading their missives to the recipient. Some Ugaritic scribes were not only expert in their own western Semitic language but were trained in Sumerian, Akkadian, Hittite, and Hurrian. They compiled multicolumn lexicons with equivalents in these languages. The position of the official court scribe at times was held by father and son, and some royal scribes were rewarded with land grants in other Near Eastern cultures. The scribe could rise to a position of importance, even to become vizier. Ugarit's documents provide us with an example of a "library" whose destruction by fire preserved it—a burnt archive.

By 2500 B.C.E., there may have been thousands of scribes in Sumer. As with many crafts, the occupation was frequently hereditary, and by the second millennium some families boasted that they descended from many generations of scribes. The typical scribe portrait can be found in the relief sculpture from Nimrud (pl. 75) and Nineveh (pl. 76), and on a wall painting from Til Barsip (Tell Ahmar) (pl. 77), an Aramaean town on the left bank of the Euphrates in northern Syria, which had been conquered by Shalmaneser III in the ninth century B.C.E. Scribes are depicted because they record the booty taken from captives or because they count the heads of the dead. This eighth-century B.C.E. scribal iconography shows us the various tools and writing surfaces used in Mesopotamia at that time: pens, styli, clay tablets, wax tablets, and a flexible material that is white in the copy of the Til Barsip painting—either papyrus because this was a known Egyptian export item or, more likely, leather. These scribes must have been language-and-script specialists; each

Pl. 76. Scribes from relief on Sennacherib's palace at Nineveh, ca. 702 B.C.E. One scribe writes on a wax tablet, the other on papyrus or leather. British Museum, Department of Western Asiatic Antiquities, No. 124955. Courtesy of the British Museum

Pl. 77. Scribes from Til Barsip, ca. eighth century B.C.E. One writes on a soft material, the other on clay. Wall painting (Tell Ahmar, Syria), copy by L. Cavro, Paris. Reproduced from *The Arts of Assyria.* Courtesy of Golden Press

wrote in the script suitable to the material. Cuneiform was written with a stylus on wax or clay tablets, Aramaic with a reed pen on papyrus or leather.

COLOPHONS

In the literature found in Mesopotamian libraries there was often a colophon in the last column. The tradition of the colophon is much older than its Greek name implies; it flourished in ancient Mesopotamia and Egypt. The colophon's information and composition varied. It gave the standard title, that is, the book's opening words, and the name of the scribe, at times with his patronym. Seldom was the book's author named. Sometimes the colophon verified that this edition was a true copy of the original book, giving the name of the scribe of the prototype and its date and owner. Then the date of the copy would be given along with the name of the patron who commissioned the book and the nature of the work. If the book was composed of several tablets, each one would be numbered and identified by the work's title. Catchlines were also used, that is, the first line of each tablet was written at the bottom of the preceding one. At times the total number of lines on the following tablet would be recorded as well. Other books-in-series would be subdivided into parts and numbered, so that books using both catchlines and numbered sections were doubly protected against the loss of their pages. The longest clay book found has seventy-one tablets containing eight thousand lines, which would make it less convenient bedtime reading than the fifteen-board, wax-tablet book of a similar text, where twice as much could be written on each page. Another aspect of the Mesopotamian colophon was the blessing upon the reader who preserves the text and a curse upon the one who would try to alter it, burn it, dissolve it in water, lose it, lend it, or allow anyone to steal it. Neo-Babylonian books have curses in them. The curse continued to be the custom in colophons of Hebrew and Arabic books into the Middle Ages, and the practice continued in European manuscripts as well. One is reminded of these when one reads the words of caution against copyright infringement in contemporary books, although these are mild in comparison to a good Near Eastern book curse.

The Code of Hammurabi ends with a long epilogue, a typical device for a royal inscription from the third millennium and much longer than the colophon. It is replete with self-praise. This is part of it, quoted from the third edition of James B. Pritchard's *Ancient Near Eastern Texts:*

> In the days to come, for all time, let the king who appears in the land observe the words of justice which I wrote on my stele; let him not alter the law of the land which I enacted, the ordinances of the land which I prescribed; let him not rescind my statutes. . . . If that man did not heed my words which I wrote on my stele, and disregarded my curses, and did not fear the curses of my gods, but has abolished the law which I enacted, has distorted my words, has altered my statutes, effaced my name inscribed [thereon], and has written his own name . . . may the mighty Anum, father of the gods . . . deprive him of the glory of his sovereignty, may he break his scepter, may he curse his fate![1]

Mesopotamians were printers, too. Cylinder seals and their stamped bullae existed even before there was a fully developed mixed system of writing. Bricks used in buildings were stamped with dies of inscriptions; the earliest of these come from the time of Sargon I. In later periods, molds of old inscriptions were made, reversing their texts. But as with most inventions, ancient printing did not establish itself as a continuous and permanent tradition because the Western world was not ready for it.

Note

1. James Bennett Pritchard, ed., *Ancient Near Eastern Texts Relating to the Old Testament,* 3rd ed. (Princeton, N.J.: Princeton Univ. Pr., 1969), 178–79.

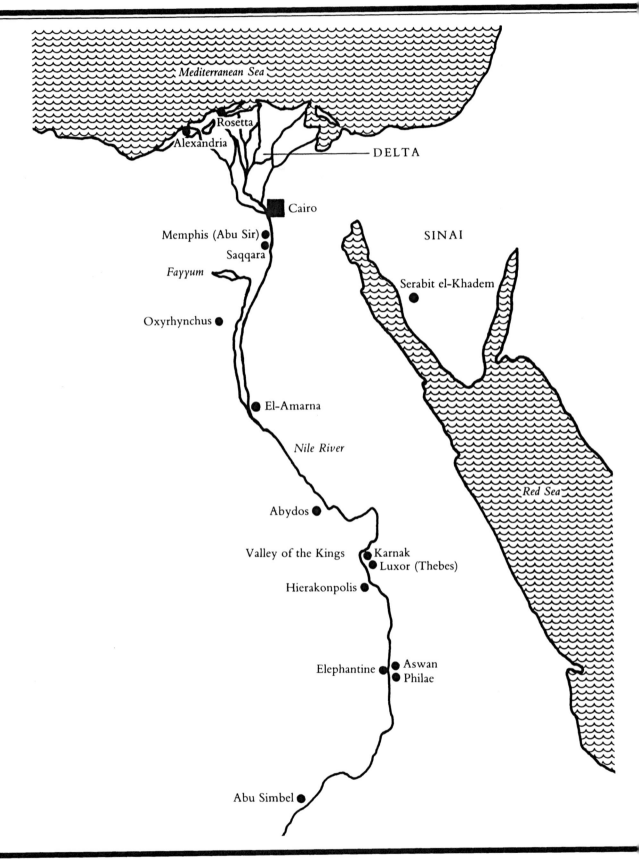

Mediterranean Sea

Rosetta

Alexandria

DELTA

SINAI

Cairo

Memphis (Abu Sir)

Saqqara

Serabit el-Khadem

Fayyum

Oxyrhynchus

El-Amarna

Nile River

Red Sea

Abydos

Valley of the Kings

Karnak

Luxor (Thebes)

Hierakonpolis

Elephantine

Aswan

Philae

Abu Simbel

Egypt

The Egyptian Book

The geographic position of Egypt, isolated from her neighbors by mountains and desert, enabled her to develop a religion, art, and script independent of all others; possible influences from the outside world were limited. At the beginning of her history, the late fourth millennium B.C.E., certain forms in art and architecture and the idea for a mixed system of writing undoubtedly came from the eastern end of the Fertile Crescent. But commerce with Nubia, the Sudan, and Libya during the Old Kingdom, and with Syria and Palestine during the Twelfth Dynasty (ca. 1991–1786), and the eventual incursions of Asiatic and Semitic peoples in the delta did not affect or modify Egypt's writing and books. By the time of the New Kingdom (the Eighteenth Dynasty, ca. 1580), Egypt expanded her horizons as far as the Euphrates by conquest and colonization of Palestine and Syria, ushering in an age of great wealth, international trade, and revitalization of her crafts and art. It is only from the half-century beginning about 1400 that one finds a significant number of documents of international diplomacy and one sees the impact of the non-Egyptian realm on Egypt's religion and art. These documents are from El-Amarna, where Amenhotep IV, who changed his name to Ikhnaton when he recognized the sun god Aton as supreme, established his capital. Because of her early isolation, Egypt's books, script, and literature developed quite independently of those of the rest of the Near East. Indeed, once she came in contact with the outside world, first through expansion and trade and then through conquest by the Greeks and Romans, it was Egypt who influenced the shape and materials of the books of others.

Because of her early seclusion, Egypt considered herself to be the entire civilized world. Life along the Nile was the epitome of status quo. Unlike Mesopotamia, where various populations were constantly beset by invasions and threatened by forces of nature, Egypt enjoyed a life that was peaceful, regular, dependable, orderly, rhythmic, and good. It seldom rained in ancient times, and one could depend on the Nile to overflow its banks in June and July each year so that a fertile strip of land could be cultivated. Beyond that green strip lay desert and mountains. The cycle of life was as fixed as the seasons. Just as the sun rose in the east and set in the west each day, death was not the end of life; humans went on living the same good life in the afterworld. Egyptian religion tolerated many gods; sometimes there were two with the same function. The gods varied in form from city to city, each city having its favorites and chief god. One manifestation of a god did not cancel the other with the same name or bodily form. A king who wanted to change his principal god changed his capital city as well. The king himself was a god, in life associated with Horus, in death with Horus's father, Osiris. The king also acted as intermediary between man and the gods.

Just as in Mesopotamia, where the materials for making books were determined by the native soil and its products, in Egypt the Nile provided both papyrus, which was the major writing surface of the Egyptians, and reeds, which were their pens. The lowly acacia provided an important ingredient for their ink, gum arabic. Bookmakers took advantage of all the Nile had to offer in providing raw materials. The preservation of Egypt's books was assured by the arid climate.

Although the earliest hieroglyphs were associated with temples and tombs, it is incorrect to assume that writing in Egypt was always in the hands of a priestly caste who jealously guarded its secrets for thousands of years (pl. 78). Perhaps the workmen who carved and painted the inscriptions on the walls of tombs in Saqqara during the Fifth Dynasty or in Thebes during the Eighteenth Dynasty were able to read the little pictures; perhaps they copied them without understanding. But by the beginning of the second millennium B.C.E. there was definitely a professional class of scribes, independent of the temples. The god who was associated with scribes and writing was Thoth, seen either as an ibis-headed figure or as a baboon, considered by the Egyptians to be the most intelligent of the animals (pl. 79). It is the priest of Thoth wearing an ibis mask whom we see in the Papyrus of Ani and other Books of the Dead, recording the weighing of the deceased's soul; Thoth as a baboon sits atop the balance (see pl. 89, p. 94). At all official functions, the scribe is there to take notes, even in the afterworld.

With the unification of lower and upper Egypt by Menes at the end of the fourth millennium, Egyptian history commenced. The relationship between Menes and Narmer, whose palette is among the first hieroglyphic documents, is unknown, but many scholars believe they were the same person (pl. 41, p. 36).

Egyptian chronology varies with different modern historians. This variation occurs because the division into three kingdoms and a further breakdown into dynasties were recorded by the Egyptian priest Manetho in the third century B.C.E. He listed the length of each pharaoh's reign, but did not record the number of years during which two kings reigned at the same time. About two hundred years are missing from many chronologies. The Egyptians preserved lists of kings, but sometimes omitted the ones considered heretical, such as Hatshepsut, the female ruler, and Ikhnaton, both of the Eighteenth Dynasty. Consequently, none of the dates is absolutely certain, and it is simpler for historians to speak of "dynasties" rather than specific dates. One will find a variety of dates for the beginning and end of each dynasty, traditionally written in Roman numerals. Table 2 provides a guide to Egyptian chronology.

MATERIALS

Our knowledge of Egyptian materials and tools comes from many sources: from the hieroglyph for scribe, which appears in the first historic period; from formal portraits of scribes and relief, carved, and painted illustrations of scribes at work; from paintings of papyrus harvesting and processing; from actual implements that have been excavated, and from the books and documents that were preserved either deliberately or fortuitously.

Pl. 79. The royal scribe, priest, and archivist Nebmertof with the god of writing, Thoth. New Kingdom, XVIII Dynasty, ca. 1400 B.C.E. Schist. Louvre, Départment des Antiquités Egyptiennes, AE/E 11154. Courtesy of Réunion des Musées Nationaux

Pl. 78. Hesire panel. Hesire was chief of the royal scribes (and chief dentist), not a priest. From the tomb of Hesire, Saqqara. Old Kingdom, III Dynasty, ca. 2700–2650 B.C.E. Wood. Egyptian Museum, JE 28504 = CG 1427. Courtesy of the Egyptian Museum, Cairo

Papyrus

The classic Egyptian book was the papyrus scroll. Papyrus (*Cyperus papyrus L.*) grew wild in the marshy delta region of the Nile in Lower Egypt, although once it was put to practical use it certainly was cultivated with a crop that could be harvested at least once a year, perhaps when the pool of labor was not occupied with the grain harvest. In addition to serving as a writing surface, papyrus provided Egyptians with the raw material for boats, sails, shoes, clothing, rope, mats, fuel, even chewing gum, and its roots were eaten by the poor. Papyrus may have existed as a writing support from the First Dynasty, but the earliest scroll to be found was a blank one, buried in the tomb of the official Hemaka. The earliest papyri with writing on them were account books of King Neferirkare of the Fifth Dynasty, about 2400 B.C.E.

The Egyptians did not leave us written instructions for transforming the papyrus plant into a writing surface. Reconstruction of its manufacture is based on a tomb painting from the Eighteenth Dynasty; on the papyri themselves; on the description

Table 2. Egyptian Chronology

Kingdom	Dynasty	Dates
Early Dynastic	I	3100–2890 B.C.E.
	II	2890–2686
Old Kingdom	III	2686–2613
	IV	2613–2494
	V	2494–2345
	VI	2345–2180
First Intermediate Period	VII–X	2180–2040
Middle Kingdom	XI	2040–1991
	XII	1991–1786
Second Intermediate Period	XIII–XVII	1786–1580
New Kingdom	XVIII	1580–1320
Amarna Period		1400–1300
Ikhnaton, Tutankhamon	XIX	1320–1200
	XX	1200–1080
End of New Kingdom	XXI–XXV	1080–664
Saite	XXVI	664–525
Persian Period	XXVII–XXX	525–332
Greco-Roman Period		
Ptolemaic		332–30
Roman		30 B.C.E.–395 C.E.

of its production by Pliny the Elder (23–79 C.E.) in his *Natural History*; and on recent attempts to reproduce the material, particularly those of Hassan Ragab of Cairo and Ignace Hendriks of the University of Groningen, the Netherlands. Harvesting of papyrus probably was done during the seasons that the Nile did not flood, either when the waters were receding (October to February), or during the drought (February to June; pl. 80). As soon as the papyrus stalks, which grew from 9 feet to 18 feet (3 meters to 6 meters) tall, were cut and collected by workers in small boats, the leafy and flowery heads were removed and the stalks were tied into bundles. Enough roots were left in the water for new growth. The stalks were delivered to another worker, who stripped off the outer rind and cut the stems into pieces about 16 inches (40 cm) long (pl. 81). According to Pliny, the center part of the stem made the best papyrus. The fresh stem, triangular in section, was sliced lengthwise into very thin strips with a knife or needle (fig. 12a). Narrow strips of pith were laid side by side on a board, with very slight overlapping. Next, a layer was placed on top, at right angles to the bottom layer (fig. 12b). The sheet then was pounded gently with a mallet or pressed to bind the two layers together. The natural sap in the fresh plant enabled the layers to adhere to each other, although Pliny claimed that Nile water glued the sheet. According to Dr. Hendriks's experiments and his interpretation of Pliny, instead of cutting individual strips that would get progressively narrower because the stalk was triangular, the papyrus maker cut the whole stalk lengthwise with a needle, working inward around the triangle (fig. 13). This resulted in one wide pith sheet, temporarily bumpy only at the corner turnings. It was placed atop a similar sheet at right angles, then pressed; pounding removed the corner lumps. Dr. Hendriks interpreted Pliny's comment about the best papyrus coming from the middle as meaning the best whole sheet was taken from the midsection of the stalk, not that the best strips came from the innermost pith. It is always possible that at different times or at different factories there were different methods of manufacture.

Pl. 80. Harvesting papyrus. Wall painting in the tomb of the priest Puremre. Thebes, XVIII Dynasty, ca. 1400 B.C.E. Copy in the Metropolitan Museum of Art, 30.4.10. Courtesy of Metropolitan Museum of Art, New York

Pl. 81. Slitting the papyrus stalk. Wall painting in the tomb of the priest Puremre. Thebes, XVIII Dynasty, ca. 1400 B.C.E. Copy in the Metropolitan Museum of Art, 30.4.10. Courtesy of the Metropolitan Museum of Art, New York

Once formed, the sheet was set to dry in the sun, which also must have bleached it white. It was further smoothed and burnished with a stone or shell. From illustrations, we know that newly manufactured papyrus was white and flexible. In time it became brittle and discolored to shades ranging from pale yellow to red-brown and dark brown. When Egyptian painters wanted to depict an ancient scroll, they rendered it in yellow.

The papyrus manufacturer glued the sheets with a starch paste into rolls of twenty sheets. The average length of a sheet during the Middle Kingdom was 15 to 16½

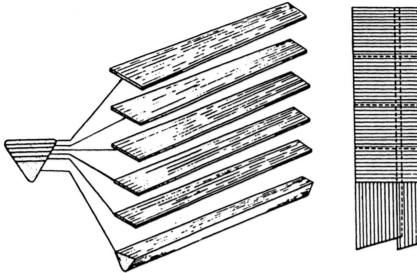

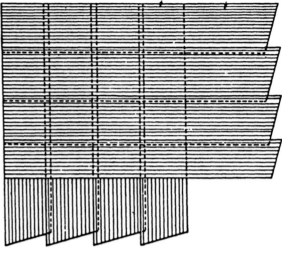

a. Strips get narrower, bottom section discarded

b. Horizontal layer on top, strips overlapping slightly

Fig. 12. Manufacture of papyrus according to Hassan Ragab

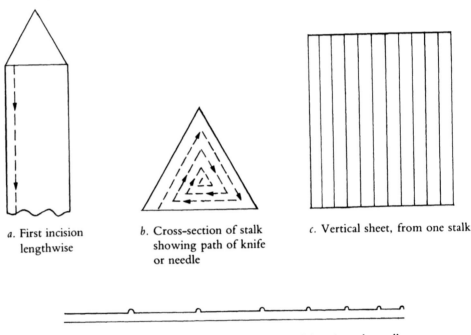

a. First incision
lengthwise

b. Cross-section of stalk
showing path of knife
or needle

c. Vertical sheet, from one stalk

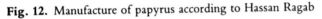

d. Lumps in the sheet caused by the corners of the triangular stalk
as the sheet is flattened

Fig. 13. Cutting of papyrus to make sheets, according to Ignace Hendriks.
Courtesy of Zeitschrift für Papyrologie und Epigraphik

inches (38 to 42 cm); in the New Kingdom, 6¼ to 8 inches (16 to 20 cm); eight was
never more than 18½ inches (47 cm) and seldom that high. The scribe received the
roll ready-made. Sheets could be added or cut off to adjust the length of the roll. The
Egyptians did not provide wooden handles for their scrolls (Jews usually did and
Romans occasionally did). Rarely, a tightly rolled papyrus was attached as a stick.

Papyrus was so finely wrought before the Eighteenth Dynasty, so thin (one-tenth of a millimeter) and translucent, that it is difficult to distinguish between the horizontal and vertical sides. Even today, although the ancient fibers are visible, it is difficult to see individual strips in many sheets, which may prove that Dr. Hendriks's reconstruction of the dynastic Egyptian method is correct for at least some of the papyri. Eventually the horizontal side was given a smoother finish for writing. The joins between the sheets, too, were barely visible in the best-made rolls. The high quality of early dynastic papyrus was never matched again; late dynastic papyrus, however, was still better than that of Hellenistic and Roman Egypt, and the latter superior to the Islamic product.

It is assumed that papyrus manufacture was a pharaonic monopoly, since later it was controlled by the Ptolemies and still later by Egypt's Roman, Byzantine, and Islamic rulers. Its production and export must have brought good income for the government at all times, although the exact price, affordability, and availability of papyrus varied. In the Hellenistic and Roman periods, the cost of a blank roll matched or exceeded an ordinary worker's average daily wages, but the common laborer would not have purchased papyrus so it didn't matter whether he could afford it. If he could write at all, he would have used the cheaper writing materials: ostraca (potsherds), animal bones, or limestone. At times papyrus seems to have been used quite lavishly for commercial and government documents, for trivia as well as for literature. To a middle-class Egyptian villager and certainly to a Roman gentleman, papyrus must have been an incidental expense. Government clerks did not have to worry about the cost of the papyrus they consumed.

Prodigious amounts of papyrus must have been manufactured by the time of the New Kingdom. It was called *twfy* in Egyptian, or *ppr,* meaning "of the king." The latter is closer to the Greek and Latin name for the material and, of course, the ancestor to our "paper." The largest papyrus scroll to be found is the Harris Papyrus in the British Museum (Cat. no. 10053), 133 feet long (40.5 m) and 16¾ inches wide (42.5 cm), composed of seventy-nine sheets. It was written in hieratic script ca. 1164 B.C.E., extolling the reign of Ramses III, and was illustrated with three large pictures that have hieroglyphic captions.

Other Materials

The ancient Egyptians carved and painted all over their funerary monuments and temples, and even on linen mummy wrappings. Ostraca and limestone flakes served for everyday jottings and as scratch paper of schoolboys and artists. Wooden tablets, some of them whitewashed, also received ink writings. The form of the wooden tablet with a handle, which goes back to the Twelfth Dynasty, continued into the Hellenistic and Roman periods, not only as the everyday writing surface (the *tabella*) but as the handled inscription panel on monuments, the *tabula ansata* (see pl. 7–9, p. 7–9). In the Islamic world the schoolboy's tablet looked the same (see pl. 10, p. 9), and the *tabula ansata* served as a decorative device in the carpet pages and headings of Qur'ān (pl. 228, 229, p. 269, 270). Animal skins as writing material were a luxury in Egypt; only a few royal documents and temple ritual texts were written on leather. Rolls of skin were mentioned in the Fourth Dynasty. The earliest preserved are a possible Fourth Dynasty fragment in the Egyptian National Museum, Cairo; a Twelfth Dynasty roll in Berlin; and a hieratic text in the British Museum (pl. 82). Leather must have been more popular in Mesopotamia, where the papyrus would have had to be imported. The leather of the Arsham and other Aramaic letters and fragments found in Egypt are assumed to have originated in Persia. Similarly, cuneiform clay tablets found at El-Amarna (diplomatic correspondence received in Egypt in the first half of the fourteenth century B.C.E.), were written in Mesopotamia, Anatolia, Syria, Palestine, and Cyprus. Some were endorsed in ink in hieratic by their recipients (pl. 44, p. 38). Sometimes the scribes of El-Amarna copied the letters they sent abroad onto clay tablets.

The scribe wrote with a thin reed (*Juncus maritimus*) that was first cut aslant at the tip and then loosened up by beating or chewing, turning it into a brush more than a pen (pl. 83, 84). This stylus was between 6¼ and 10 inches (16 and 25 cm) long. Unlike the Mesopotamian reed stylus, Egyptian pens of all periods have

Pl. 82. Leather roll from Egypt, with hieratic script. Ca. 1580 B.C.E. British Museum Department of Egyptian Antiquities, No. 10250, col. 1 and part of col. 2. Courtesy of the British Museum

Pl. 83. Ordinary scribe's writing implements: pen-brushes, palettes (one with ink depressions), and water pot. Thebes, El Assisif, XVII–XVIII Dynasty, sixteenth century B.C.E. Metropolitan Museum of Art Museum Excavations, 1915–1916, No. 16.10.299. Courtesy of the Metropolitan Museum of Art, New York

Pl. 84. Writing implements from King Tutankhamon's tomb: palettes with pen-brushes, pen holder, and papyrus burnisher. Thebes, Valley of the Kings, XVIII Dynasty, fourteenth century B.C.E. Metropolitan Museum of Art, photo by the Egyptian Expedition. Courtesy of the Metropolitan Museum of Art, New York

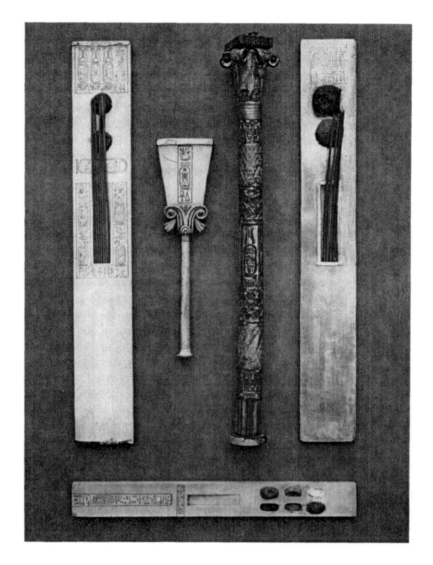

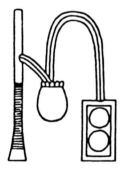

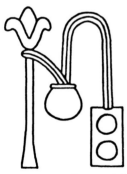

Fig. 14. Two forms of the hieroglyph for scribe. The earlier sign, *above*, shows reed pencase and bag; the later sign, *below*, shows a wooden pencase and water jar

survived. From a study of Egyptian documents of the sixth century B.C.E., some scholars believe that the reed with a cut nib was already in use at that time. More certainly, it was after Alexander the Great's conquest that the Egyptians adopted the Greek hollow-reed pen (*Phragmites aegyptiaca*), with its squared-off, split nib. Other scholars claim that in Hellenistic times the nibbed reed initially was used only for Greek script and not for hieroglyphics. The kind of brush-reed employed in dynastic times and the way it was prepared determined the cursive forms of hieratic and demotic script.

The scribe always had several pens in reserve as he wrote, either in the palette, in a pencase, or behind his ear. Thin reeds were stored in a large, hollow reed or in a long, tubular pencase made of wood and capped at times by a lid resembling a stylized palm tree. Pens also were kept in the slot of the scribe's long, flat wooden or ivory palette. The long palette, at least 10 inches (25 cm) in length, replaced the shorter one that can be seen in illustrations painted before the end of the Fifth Dynasty. The hieroglyph for "scribe," *s-sh,* shows the old, short palette (fig. 14). The palette always had two circular depressions that held small cakes of red ochre and black ink.

Black carbon ink was made by scraping soot from cooking pots, mixing it with a weak solution of gum (*Acacia arabica*) and allowing it to dry in the small, round cakes that were pasted to the palette. Ochre is a natural compound of clay and iron oxide. Either mortar and pestle were used for grinding ink and colors, or a small stone was used to grind the color in the depressed center of a larger rectangular stone. Powdered pigment could be carried in small bags. At times a tassle or rag was attached to the palette for erasing mistakes. A small water jar or bowl made of faience, the turquoise, glasslike ceramic that was a specialty of Egyptian craftsmen, was kept on hand to dissolve ink as it was needed; earlier a shell had been used. The scribe had to dip his brush-pen quite often; he could write only five to nine hieroglyphic characters with each dip.

Found in the tomb of Tutankhamon, along with pens and a decorated palette, was a pencase of the same type as the ordinary scribe's container but more luxuriously finished with painted ivory and chased gold, inlaid with carnelian, obsidian, and blue and green glass (pl. 84). With it was an ivory papyrus burnisher capped with gold leaf. (Similar burnishers made of wood were far more practical, and undoubtedly were part of the scribe's standard equipment.) Scraps of fine sandstone for erasing were contained in a small leather bag along with the other writing implements in the young king's tomb. As with all of the splendid objects found, the writing implements were of much finer manufacture than those used by the ordinary scribe. Not that Tut would have used them even if he did rise from the dead—it was a compliment to consider the dead king a scribe.

Egyptians used seals for stamping, as did all Near Eastern cultures, but they were seldom in the cylindrical form familiar in Mesopotamia. The popular type was an oval in the shape of a beetle, or scarab, made of faience (pl. 85). At times these were made in molds and pierced for threading. Scarabs were used as good-luck charms as well as seals. The text was written, or "printed" if mold-made, on the flat underside of the beetle. Eighteenth Dynasty scarabs frequently have valuable historical references on them, such as an allusion to an event or a eulogy to a king. Scarabs from the reign of Ramses II traveled as far as Mt. Ebal in Samaria and Cyprus. As with coins, it is possible to date archaeological sites by means of scarabs.

SCROLLS

The scroll was reinforced at the beginning with an extra piece of papyrus 2 to 3½ inches (5 to 9 cm) wide pasted to it. This served as protection for the outside of the rolled-up scroll at the place where it would be handled most often. Sometimes there was a sheet at the end as well. The scribe left wide top and bottom margins to allow for handling or for the eventual wearing away of the edges, or simply as a frame to the text. (The margin is a basic element of book design, found in Mesopotamian literary clay tablets as well.) The scribe usually wrote hieroglyphics in vertical rows from the right side of the roll to the left, until horizontal writing became popular.

Pl. 85. Scarab of the royal scribe Iahmes. Faience set in gold. New Kingdom, XVIII Dynasty ca. 1550–1300 B.C.E. Louvre, Département des Antiquités Egyptiennes, AE/N 2082. Courtesy of Réunion des Musées Nationaux

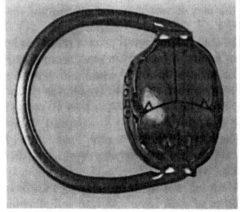

In vertical hieroglyphic writing, each column was a sentence. The columns were separated by vertical lines in scrolls as well as in wall paintings. Hieroglyphic Books of the Dead and other religious texts generally were written from left to right in vertical rows, but one can even find scrolls with some signs written in reverse so that the profiles and figures in vertical rows face each other. Symmetry and balance were prime aesthetic considerations. The scribes wrote over the joins in factory-prepared scrolls; the sheets were always stepped downhill to prevent the scribe's brush-pen from smearing ink or catching at the juncture of two sheets. When the scribe added his own sheets to make a longer scroll, however, he was not as adept in gluing as the specialist in the papyrus factory, and so he had to avoid these joins as he wrote.

Literary texts were written on the inner side of the roll only, but the lines of text do not always follow the horizontal fibers of the papyrus, as one would expect from the natural lines in the surface. (Perhaps they were not as apparent then as they are now.) At times guidelines were drawn. Even in papyrus made today, the ink "takes" smoothly and naturally, without the coat of sizing necessary in papermaking. Ink, while it was still wet, could be erased easily with a damp rag or by licking the finger and rubbing it out. If the mistake was too great or the ink too dry, and if erasing sandstone was unavailable or unsuccessful, the scribe had to cut out the error and paste a new piece of papyrus to the spot. Mistakes at times were corrected by later readers who wrote above or below the line or in the margins.

When papyrus was scarce, the reverse sides of old scrolls were used for ordinary texts, particularly account books. All of the document's writing could be erased on both sides by scraping and the papyrus reused. This sort of recycling became more common as papyrus became more expensive or scarce. In commercial documents, red ink often was used to distinguish between two sets of items, but in literary texts red was used for headings or the ending of a section, for vertical lines between rows of script, or for the opening words or title of the book. It was here that the tradition of rubrics began. Red and black ink, tastefully combined, still present a bold visual effect.

TITLES AND COLOPHONS

The title of the book, a summary of its contents, or the opening words, were at times written on the reverse side or at the outside of the scroll's beginning, with the name of the author ("made by") immediately after it. As scrolls generally lost their edges first, few titles have come down to us. Fewer authors were identified. Sometimes, however, lists of titles were written on the walls of temples or pyramids, though the books themselves have not survived. Small deeds and other documents at times were provided with titles. One Book of the Dead was entitled "Book of the Coming into the Day of Osiris Gatheseshen, daughter of Menkheperre." Long texts were sometimes divided by chapter numbers, marked by *ht,* "house." The text sometimes ended abruptly with "it comes" or "it comes well" or "in peace." Other endings appear to be more like the traditional colophon: "It is completed from its beginning to its end as it was found written, having been copied, revised, compared and verified, sign by sign." Or, "It has come to a good ending in Thebes, the place of truth." Occasionally there was a sign on the outside of the scroll to prevent the reader from unrolling it upside down.

Scrolls were stored in ceramic jars, wicker baskets, wooden boxes, and chests. A few of these had labels; one chest had an illustration on it that may have reflected the subject of the scroll that once was inside. Another had a title on it, *Book of the Sycamore and the Olive,* and an *ex libris* on a faience tag. Cylindrical book containers seen in Theban tomb paintings of the Eighteenth Dynasty resemble the later *tik,* the Torah case used by Jews living in Near Eastern countries (pl. 86). A flat-topped portable case appears in a painting in the tomb of Ramose, made during the reign of Amenhotep III (pl. 87). Some of the Egyptian scroll cases had cords or straps for carrying them, or a handle on the side if the case was of leather. A chest identical to

Pl. 86. Scribe doing field work, showing scroll chests and portable case. Detail from Thebes tomb painting. XVIII Dynasty, ca. 1500–1300 B.C.E. Courtesy of the Egyptian Museum, Cairo

Pl. 87. Chests and portable scroll case carried by mourners. Painting from the tomb of Ramose, Thebes, XVIII Dynasty (ca. 1500–1300 B.C.E.). Courtesy of the Egyptian Museum, Cairo

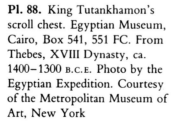

Pl. 88. King Tutankhamon's scroll chest. Egyptian Museum, Cairo, Box 541, 551 FC. From Thebes, XVIII Dynasty, ca. 1400–1300 B.C.E. Photo by the Egyptian Expedition. Courtesy of the Metropolitan Museum of Art, New York

the ones carried by the servants or mourners who bear the deceased's personal and household effects, depicted in Eighteenth Dynasty paintings such as those in the tombs of Ramose and Menna, was found in Tutankhamon's tomb (pl. 88). The checkerboard scroll cases in the paintings mentioned above are decorated with inlay squares that appear to be the same colors as those on the scroll chest found in Tutankhamon's tomb. A statue of Osiris now in the Metropolitan Museum of Art in New York also served as a receptacle for a scroll.

LITERATURE

The earliest literature of Egypt's Old Kingdom was carved on the walls of tombs. It consisted of lists of offerings of food, fabrics, and ointments by the kings' officials. Prayers came next, along with lists of the accomplishments of the deceased and his titles. These lists were standardized by the Fifth Dynasty, and from the Sixth Dynasty, there evolved autobiographical idealized self-portraiture, a literary form that was to continue for the next two thousand years. When these catalogs of morally perfect virtues or maxims were written down on papyrus, they were entitled *Instructions in Wisdom,* or simply *Instructions.* Their authorship was attributed to particular princes or viziers. Recopied during the Middle and New Kingdoms, they became popular middle-class literature. Many other literary forms were added in the Middle Kingdom, considered to be the classical age of Egyptian belles lettres. Religious hymns and secular songs were composed. Writers became aware of social evils, and lamentations, prophecies, and admonitions were added to the *Instructions.* It was in this period that the narrative of the shipwrecked sailor, *The Story of Sinuhe,* was written as well as *The Eloquent Peasant,* a tale of how a lowly peasant seeks justice by appealing higher and higher up the Egyptian social pyramid. Other short stories were of both a realistic and an imaginary nature. Ballads known as *Harpers' Songs* praised death and the afterlife. Three styles of writing continued in popularity into later centuries: prose, poetry, and an intermediate style that reflected oration and rhetoric. Some of this literature has come down to us in multiple copies written in tombs and on stelae (upright stone slabs) but some has survived only in single copies written on papyrus.

When the New Kingdom was established and there was contact with the outside world, the Egyptian empire broadened her intellectual horizons. Many Egyptian scribes were bilingual, especially in the Amarna period when Akkadian was the international diplomatic language. Literature of the Twentieth Dynasty included hymns, autobiographies, records of installations of viziers, historical inscriptions, narrative poems, tales, and some lyrics. One of the most famous works is the *Report of Wenamon,* which told of the author's mission to purchase timber in the Phoenician port of Byblos during the reign of Ramses XI (ca. 1090–1080 B.C.E.). It is from this report that we learn that Egypt exported papyrus. Wenamon's report, written on papyrus, was typical of administrative documents: its lines were vertical with signs written from top to bottom. A *Harper's Song* from the New Kingdom reflected the writer's doubts about the afterlife, and recommended making the best of this life. As this book was placed in a tomb, its message seems inappropriate.

During Egypt's late dynasties when at intervals she lost her independence, literature nevertheless flourished from time to time. Literary scribes looked back to the classics of the Middle Kingdom for linguistic models, and revived Old and New Kingdom inscriptions, royal and historical accounts of victories, decrees, and hymns. Along with the continuation of these classics, tales and *Instructions* were written in demotic, the script that appeared in the Saite Dynasty. Greek script and literature were introduced with the Ptolemies who ruled after Alexander the Great's conquest, and Egypt's culture was permanently Hellenized.

In addition to Egyptian belles lettres, other works have been preserved: astronomical and astrological texts, calendars, magic spells, and medical lore. Egyptian science and medicine were practical, not theoretical, and the Greeks were impressed with Egyptian medical knowledge. No law codes such as the ones written in Mesopotamia have been discovered, but court proceedings were recorded and stelae served as history books.

The literary work of the ancient Egyptians best known to modern readers is their Book of the Dead (pl. 89; see also pl. 1, p. 1). "Book of the Dead" is not the name the Egyptians gave to this class of compositions; they entitled them *Pert em Hru,* "Coming Forth by Day," because they did indeed foresee a living world after death. During the Old Kingdom, some of these chapters were written on the walls of the royal pyramid tombs. Books of the Dead continued to be written in burial chambers in the Middle Kingdom and also to be inscribed on coffins and stelae, and in the New Kingdom they appeared on papyrus scrolls (see pl. 1, p. 1). By that time they were commissioned by high court officials, temple priests, and wives or daughters of priests who led the temple choir. Later, common folk were able to acquire Books of the Dead, and scribes made stock copies with blank spaces left for the purchaser to fill in his or her own name. Relatives of the deceased provided the same service when it was they who purchased the ready-made Book of the Dead.

A Book of the Dead is not one book but many versions and chapters in different combinations. Altogether there were about 192 chapters or compositions, but fewer than that number appear in any one roll. The order also varied. Some are composed of descriptions of the ceremonies that preceded burial; some have prayers and spells, confessions, and proclamations of innocence to be recited by priests and relatives on behalf of the deceased; some portray his or her existence in the next world, the trials and dangers of the world beyond the grave; and some give instructions on how he or she should proceed in the netherworld.

ILLUSTRATIONS

Although Books of the Dead appear to have been made carefully, and some were illustrated beautifully, they are full of scribal errors. In the finest of them, *The Papyrus of Ani* (preserved in the British Museum and assigned to the Eighteenth or early Nineteenth Dynasty), one chapter was written twice. Sometimes historians have attempted to equate the beauty of the book's illustrations with the number of inaccuracies in textual transmission, that is, they claim that the more beautiful the book, the greater the number of mistakes. But throughout book history this has not been the case. The patron who could afford the best illustrations could also afford the best and most accurate scribe. Mistakes were, and still are, an aspect of human nature, and appear in the best of books.

Pl. 89. Weighing of the Soul, from the Papyrus of Ani (Book of the Dead). Priest of Thoth duly records the proceedings. Early XIX Dynasty, ca. 1300 B.C.E. British Museum, Department of Egyptian Antiquities, No. 10470/3. Courtesy of the British Museum

Illustrations were repeated from scroll to scroll and from wall to wall, in the case of tomb-painted Books of the Dead, with variations in detail and obvious differences in artistic competence. A definite Book of the Dead iconography can be discerned and analyzed by art historians. Favorite scenes included the carrying of the funereal furniture and other domestic objects (pl. 87), the professional female mourners, the voyage of the funeral boat carrying the bier to the land of the dead, the ceremony of the opening of the mouth after mummification (see pl. 1, p. 1), the psychostasis or weighing of the soul (pl. 89), the deceased in the heavenly fields, the deceased bowing to a god (pl. 90) or being led to one by his priest (pl. 91), the Bennu bird who was symbolic of rebirth, assemblies of the gods or priests wearing god-masks with an offering table set before them, and the deceased being presented to Osiris by Horus. At times the illustrations were drawn before the text was written, and the scribe was not always successful in fitting the appropriate text into the space left for him by the artist. Some texts do not pertain to the adjoining pictures at all.

Pl. 90. Book of the Dead of Here Ubkhet. Here Ubkhet presents herself to Osiris. Papyrus. Deir el-Bahri, XXI Dynasty, ca. 1000 B.C.E. Courtesy of the Egyptian Museum, Cairo

Pl. 91. Book of the Dead of Lady Anhai. Anhai is led by a priest of the god Herunetchstef. Papyrus, XX Dynasty, ca. 1100 B.C.E. British Museum, Department of Egyptian Antiquities, No. 10472/2. Courtesy of the British Museum

Scrolls other than Books of the Dead were illustrated, such as fables and satirical literature. The oldest extant is the *Ramesseum Dramatic Papyrus,* a coronation festival play written at the end of the Middle Kingdom (pl. 92). It displays satirical illustrations, with animals appearing as humans. Its style differs radically from official Egyptian art. Of course, one may consider all of the paintings and relief sculptures in tombs and temples as book illustrations when they are accompanied by texts, especially when they follow the same layout as a scroll open to one section. Undoubtedly scrolls served as models for tomb paintings and reliefs. The paints, made from earth pigments, have remained on the papyrus where the surface was not damaged in any way, almost with the same freshness as in the tomb paintings, although somewhat deeper in tone. Stone monuments with historical information frequently had illustrations at the top, reminiscent of Mesopotamian monuments such as the Code of Hammurabi.

SCRIBES

The earliest scribe portraits appear on several wooden panels found in a tomb in Saqqara; they show Hesire, a court official of the Fourth Dynasty (pl. 78, p. 83). In them he holds his scribal implements. Other portraits from the same period and from the Fifth Dynasty depict the scribe's tools slung over his shoulder, with the palette falling forward on his chest and the ink bag and brush case balancing it on his back. Some scribes liked to have themselves depicted with the god of writing, Thoth, usually in his baboon form (pl. 79, p. 83). Most of the popular sculptured scribe portraits of the Fifth Dynasty, which were commissioned by administrators, show the official seated cross-legged with the scroll resting on his tightly stretched kilt, at times with a pen behind his ear (pl. 93, 94). This iconography was repeated scores of times in later centuries; generals, too, wanted to appear as writers (pl. 18, p. 13). This was not the scribe at work; he was posing for his portrait. Incidentally, today this may look like a very uncomfortable writing position, but for cultures accustomed to sitting this way, it was a natural one. Some Yemenite Hebrew scribes still sit cross-legged, writing on parchment held on their laps. The Egyptian scribe sculptures were idealized *Ka* portraits that embodied the spirit of the deceased and were intended for burial with him. What better way could an official show his status than to depict himself as a scribe? More realistic in terms of how the scribe wrote are the three-dimensional painted wooden models, stone relief sculptures, and wall paintings on plaster found in tombs portraying scenes of the day-to-day life that would continue in the afterworld (pl. 86). These reliefs and paintings show a more practical writing position. In several of them, the scribe sits with one knee raised, supporting a writing board that rests on his forearm, with the same elbow resting on his knee. This certainly looks more comfortable than the cross-legged position, but still not as easy as writing at a table. In a wall painting of the Nineteenth Dynasty in the grave of Teji, secretary of Pharaoh Merneptah (son of Ramses II), a group of five scribes, depicted twice, sit on high stools at individual desks. In other illustrations, the scribe sits on the ground with a tablet propped up before him on a case. In a three-dimensional model of the inspection of cattle from the tomb of Meket-Re at Thebes (now in the Egyptian Museum, Cairo), four scribes sit on a covered porch with writing slabs before them. Sometimes the scribe at work in the field is seen standing, with the support board on his outstretched left arm, writing with his right hand. How the scribe coped with a long scroll is not seen because the writers depicted were clerks, not literary scribes, doing their fieldwork. They were there to make sure the harvest was properly recorded for tax purposes. A single sheet of papyrus seems to rest on the board, or they were writing directly on the whitewashed boards. At times we see the scribes carrying a writing kit that has a single sheet of papyrus attached to one end of a cord with a short palette on the other end. In a relief in the tomb of Kaninisut in Giza from the Fifth Dynasty (now in the Kunsthistorisches Museum in Vienna), oval palettes dangle from the writing boards

Pl. 92. Satirical papyrus. XIX–XX Dynasty, ca. 1200–1100 B.C.E. British Museum, Department of Egyptian Antiquities, Pap. 10016. Courtesy of the British Museum

Pl. 93. Seated scribe. Saqqara, Old Kingdom, early V Dynasty, ca. 2475 B.C.E. Painted limestone. Egyptian Museum JE 30272 = CG 36. Courtesy of the Egyptian Museum, Cairo

of industrious scribes, which would indicate that only a single page of papyrus rested on the writing tablet. In wall paintings of the Eighteenth Dynasty, the scribe at times has servants carrying chests that contained his implements and additional scrolls. The chest has an inclined lid, which may have been used as a sort of desk, although the inlaid decorations such as those on the chest found in Tutankhamon's tomb would have discouraged practical use unless a smooth tablet were placed over it (pl. 88). In many of these genre illustrations of scribes at work, there are usually from two to five scribes, an indication of a clerk-heavy bureaucracy in second-millennium B.C.E. Egypt. These were the fellows who didn't care about the cost of papyrus.

Pl. 94. The scribe Nykure, official of the king's granary. Giza or Saqqara, V Dynasty, ca. 2475–2345 B.C.E. Red granite, painted details. Metropolitan Museum of Art, Rogers Fund, 1948, No. 48.67. Courtesy of the Metropolitan Museum of Art, New York

Schools for scribes, along with manuals of instruction, date back to the Middle Kingdom. By the New Kingdom, scribes learned their art either from a teacher in his own home, or at official or court schools. At school the student practiced by copying model letters, speeches, and compositions on the virtues of leading the life of a scribe as opposed to that of a peasant, farmer, or soldier. The scribe then duplicated books on mathematics and geography, and wrote out place names in Egypt and abroad. He copied praises for his teacher, or advice from his teacher against dissipation. Writing from dictation was also stressed, but consistent orthography was not expected. Although students were beaten for laziness, they do not seem to have been punished at all for the numerous mistakes they made. School was the key to the bureaucratic door; if a boy attended a court school with princes, his chances for advancement were all the greater. Unlike in Mesopotamia, where potential scribes came from families of the already successful classes, in Egypt the scribe's origin could have been a lowly one. Such was the case of the scribe Amenhotep (Huy) of the late Twenty-eighth Dynasty. His parents were commoners, but through his scribehood he eventually rose to the position of steward to Pharaoh Amenhotep III and became a major landowner.

One school text that admonishes "Be a scribe" did not emphasize the material benefits of scribeship but rather the opportunity for immortality: "Man decays, his corpse is dust, all his kin have perished; but a book makes him remembered through the mouth of its reciter."

It is assumed that traditions of bookmaking continued without interruption from the time of the late Egyptian dynasties into the Hellenistic period. Hellenism revitalized a declining literary society. Some traditions of Egyptian scrollmaking survived in the Hellenistic scroll and eventually were to be found in the medieval codex and printed book: columns of text on a sheet or scroll opening, linear framing of the text or margins, protective endsheets, headings and titles, colophons, rubrics, illustrations of literary themes, even the name for our major writing surface. The Egyptian scroll contributed much to the later history of the book, of the Near East, and of the West.

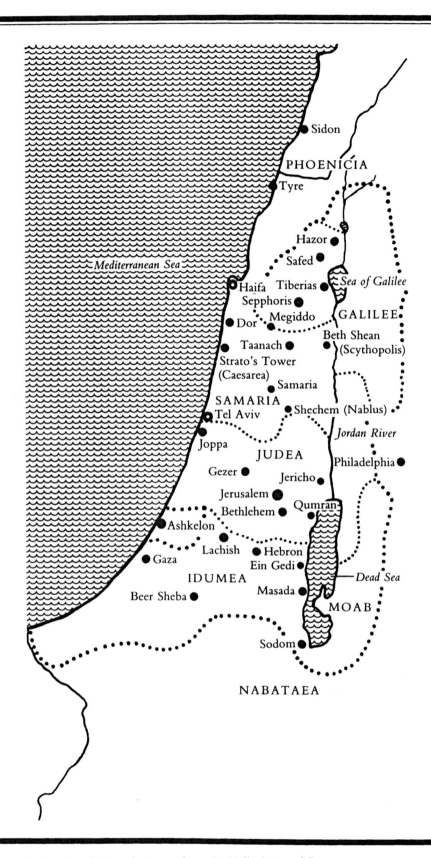

Ancient Israel. Boundaries are from the Hellenistic and Roman periods. Open circles are modern cities.

CHAPTER 5

The Hebrew Book

riting is traditional, the alphabet is traditional, and books themselves are traditional in form. The most traditional book of all is the Torah (teaching) scroll, called the Pentateuch in Greek, which comprises the Five Books of Moses (pl. 95). It is the first of the three major divisions of the Hebrew Bible (referred to as Scripture or, by non-Jews, as the Old Testament), the other two being Prophets and Hagiographa (Writings), with twenty-four books in all. The Torah is the basis of the Jewish religion. So central is it to Judaism that many believe it was this book, with its constant reading, study, and interpretation, that kept the Jewish people together as a nation during their many exiles from their own land. The Torah is still read in the synagogue three times a week. Other books of the Bible are read during the synagogue service as well, and much of the prayer book is based on biblical passages, particularly Psalms. No book of any other culture has survived with the same physical form and textual stability for so long a time as has the Jewish Torah. Nor does the book of any other culture have religious strictures as to its layout, the kind of materials that should be used for making it, and how these materials should be prepared.

The second most important book to the Jewish religion is the Talmud (study or learning), which is often referred to as Oral Torah because it existed for so many centuries before it finally was written down; not until the late fourth and fifth centuries C.E. were its editions first published in Palestine and Babylonia, respectively. It is considered by religious Jews to have the same authority as the Written Torah. The Talmud consists of two parts: the Mishna (repetition), which is divided into six orders and further divided into tractates, and the Gemara (completion), discussions and elaborations on the Mishna. The Talmud was the attempt to harmonize the laws found in the Torah with the realities of everyday life in the postbiblical period. Written in the Aramaic language, and probably always in a

Pl. 95. Torah scroll, open to the Song of the Sea (Exodus 15:1–22). Courtesy HaTzvi Yisrael Synagogue, Jerusalem

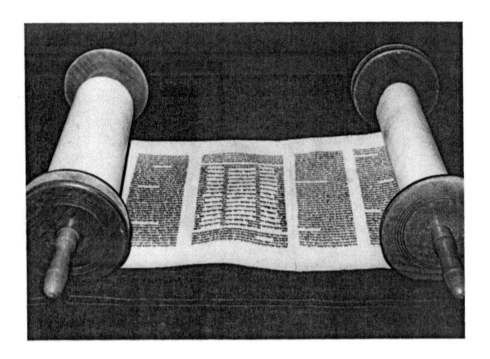

codex (the codex was already the common form of book when the Talmud finally was published), it includes divergent opinions of the rabbis and their academies on Jewish law, digressions on almost all conceivable subjects, and *midrash,* legends. Commentaries on the Talmud were written later, and these continue to be printed with its editions.

It may seem ironic that the scroll form of the book for the Torah and its methods of manufacture remained so stable when the people who made and preserved it were so mobile. In Mesopotamia, materials for the book remained the same because they came from the earth, even though the people who used these books spoke different languages. In Egypt, language, script, and the form of the book remained even more stable. Jews, unlike other Near Eastern peoples, lived in dispersion longer than they lived in their own land, and, insofar as their religion would permit, had to make some adjustments to the materials available for bookmaking in their various places of residence. Concerning the Torah, although there were slight adaptations when Jews moved from place to place (such as the replacement of early Semitic script with Aramaic script, the replacement of leather with parchment, and the replacement of the reed pen with the quill), the ancient form of the book—the scroll—persisted. The reasons for this stability were the subject matter of the book, its holiness, and its centrality to the preservation of the culture.

Because the rules for making a Torah scroll were followed so closely for so many centuries, we are able to reconstruct Hebrew scrolls and the way they were made for the ages that have left us little or no material evidence. Reconstruction of the Hebrew book in biblical times is accomplished by observing how the Torah is made today, by studying references to writing and books in the Bible, by looking at the books of neighboring ancient cultures in Mesopotamia and Egypt, and by reading the rules for Torah-making found in various parts of the Talmud.

Surviving Hebrew books from postbiblical times, too, shed light on practices of non-Jewish bookmakers in times where evidence for the latter is lacking. At times, the fragmentary nature of what has come down to us leads to uncertainty as to the identity of the innovator—the Hebrew, the Greek, or the Latin scribe. For example, word spacing and justification of margins appear in Hebrew scrolls and codices before these features are found regularly in Greek and Latin books. The fine, almost white leather of some of the Dead Sea Scrolls that resembles parchment dates from a time before the earliest extant parchment codices. We do not have the material evidence for other cultures' use of such parchmentlike leather on a large scale at the beginning of the Christian era, yet it is assumed that writing on thin animal skin was universal in western Asia from late Hellenistic and Roman republican and early imperial times. In the Islamic era, the earliest dated manuscript with illuminations is a Hebrew codex, but it is assumed that Qur'ān illumination of the same time, the late ninth and tenth centuries, was identical and may have preceded Jewish illumination.

HISTORY

To give a biblical framework to Hebrew books, one can say that the alphabet was invented shortly after the time of the patriarch Abraham. But according to a Jewish legend, writing and its implements were among the ten special acts of creation by God which took place on the sixth day, just before the Sabbath. Another legend has it that the alphabet was invented by Moses for the specific purpose of writing down the Torah he received on Mt. Sinai.

The earliest evidence for the Hebrews as a distinct group, the Hapiru (or Apiru), has been found in Egypt in a papyrus document from the time of Ramses II and on a hieroglyphic stele of Seti I from Beth Shean in Israel, both from the early thirteenth century B.C.E. *Israel* was incised in hieroglyphics on the Merneptah stele later in the same century. Table 3 provides an overview of Jewish history.

The Exodus from Egypt of the Israelites, the descendants of the sons of the patriarch Jacob, is usually dated to the time of Merneptah's reign, ca. 1220 B.C.E.; the conquest of Canaan and the biblical period of the judges and early prophets are dated from the thirteenth century B.C.E. until the monarchy was established by Saul, ca. 1020. The united Israelite kingdom was expanded by King David (1004–965). Architecture and culture flourished during the rule of David's son Solomon, but by the time Solomon died in 928, the kingdom had split in two. It was at this time that reading and writing apparently became universal. In the divided kingdom, Israel was in the north where ten of the tribes had settled, with its capital at Samaria (Nablus), and Judea was in the south where the tribes of Judah and Benjamin had settled, with its capital at Jerusalem. The weaker Israelite kingdom in the north fell prey to Assyria in 722 B.C.E. and its inhabitants were deported. The Samaritans, among the few who remained, may have intermixed with foreign peoples resettled by the Assyrians, for resettlement of populations was customary for Assyrian and Babylonian conquerors. The Samaritans retained the old Semitic alphabet and accepted the Torah but not the other two parts of the Bible. Judea was invaded by the Assyrians and the town of Lachish conquered (this was recorded on the picture-book walls of the palace at Nineveh), but Jerusalem did not fall to outside forces until the Babylonian conquest in 586 B.C.E., when the Temple built by King Solomon was destroyed. The exiled Judeans, resettled in Babylonia, did not lose their identity as their northern Israelite neighbors had ("the ten lost tribes"), and many returned to their homeland under the decree of Cyrus of Persia when Persia conquered Babylonia. These Judeans, or Jews as they were now called, came back in groups from the 520s until well into the fifth century B.C.E. It was at that time that Aramaic all but replaced the older Hebrew script; Aramaic had become the official language of the Achaemenid empire and it was natural for Jews, who always spoke the language of their host country when living in exile, to adopt the similar script of their Mesopotamian host country. In the middle of the fifth century, the Temple in Jerusalem was restored under the leadership of Ezra "the Scribe" (pl. 96) and Nehemiah, although its more sumptuous reconstruction did not take place until the time of Herod (37 B.C.E.–4 C.E.). Some Jews must have remained in Babylonia (Iraq) and were joined by Jews from later exiles. The Babylonian Jewish community

Table 3. Chronology of Jewish History

Period	Dates
Biblical Period	1800–586 B.C.E.
The Patriarchs (Abraham, Isaac, Jacob)	18th cent.
Exodus from Egypt	1220
Judean Monarchy	1020–586
King David	1004–965
King Solomon	965–928
Assyrian Conquest of Northern Kingdom (Israel)	722
Babylonian Conquest of Judea	586
Second Temple Period	538 B.C.E.–70 C.E.
Persian Period	
Edict of Cyrus and the First Return to Judea	538 B.C.E.
Return of Jews to Judea and leadership of Ezra	458–398
Hellenistic-Roman Period	332 B.C.E.–70 C.E.
Conquest of Alexander the Great	332 B.C.E
Seleucid Rule ("Era of Documents")	312
Hasmoneans	167
Conquest by Rome	63
Destruction of the Second Temple	70 C.E.
Talmudic Period	100–499 C.E.
Revolt of Bar Kokhba	132–135
Redaction of Mishna	ca. 200–250
Jerusalem Talmud	ca. 350–399
Babylonian Talmud	ca. 450–499
Gaonim	589–1038
Crusader Period	
First Crusade	1096
Saladin's Capture of Jerusalem	1187
Rabbi Moses ben Maimon (Maimonides)	1136–1204
Commentary on Mishna	1168
Mishna Torah	1180
Guide for the Perplexed	1190
Rise of European Jewry	900–1500
Golden Age in Spain	
Expulsions and forced conversions	
Making and illuminating of manuscripts	
Flowering of Hebrew literature	
Rabbinic-Legal Works	
Rabbi Solomon ben Isaac (Rashi)	d. 1105
Moses de Leon [Moses ben Shem Tov] (*Zohar*, mystical work)	1286
Jacob ben-Asher (*Arba'a Turim*)	1340
Joseph Albo (*Sefer Hakkarim*)	1425
First dated Hebrew printed book	1475
Expulsion from Spain	1492

was sizable, scholarly, and productive well into the Islamic period, until the eleventh century C.E., when the Seljuk Turks overcame the area.

In the fifth century B.C.E. there was also a Jewish military colony in Egypt on the island of Elephantine near Aswan, established by Persia to guard its western

Pl. 96. Ezra the Scribe, from the synagogue at Dura Europos. First third of the third century C.E. Courtesy of Dura Europos Collection, Yale University Art Gallery

frontier. From this garrison comes an important group of papyrus documents written in Aramaic script (pl. 97, 98). The Persian king also appointed a governor for Judea, but in reality Judea was a theocracy for the next three hundred years, ruled by descendants of the Jewish high priest. Although the Jews did not oppose Alexander the Great's conquest in 332 B.C.E., to their dismay, Jewish religious and political independence was denied by his successors. The Land of Israel, or Eretz Yisrael, including Judea, passed back and forth between the warring Seleucid rulers of Syria and the Ptolemies of Egypt; it was also invaded by the Parthians from Persia. One successful Jewish revolt against the Hellenistic Syrian regime led by Judah Maccabees, from a provincial priestly family, in the mid-second century B.C.E. reestablished the monarchy with the Maccabees' own Hasmonean dynasty. All this time, a thriving old Jewish community in Alexandria had so assimilated into Egyptian Hellenistic culture that by the early third century B.C.E. it needed a Greek translation of the Torah because Hebrew no longer was understood. According to the often-repeated story told in the *Letter of Aristeas* (written in the late second century B.C.E.), seventy-two scholars invited by Ptolemy sat in separate rooms to render the Torah in Greek and, miraculously, all translations were identical! Hence the name *Septuagint* for the Greek edition of the Bible.

Finally, in her conquest of the Near East, Rome took Judea in 63 B.C.E. Judea revolted against Rome in 60 C.E., which eventually led to the destruction of the Second Temple in 70 C.E. In 132–135 C.E., the fierce Jewish revolt led by Bar Kokhba was also suppressed. With the Roman conquest, Jerusalem's Jews moved north to the Galilee and the Golan Heights or left for communities in the Diaspora

Pl. 97. Marriage contract of Tamut. Papyrus, tied and sealed. Elephantine Island, Aswan, Egypt, July 3, 449 B.C.E. Brooklyn Museum, gift of the Estate of Charles Edwin Wilbour. Courtesy of the Brooklyn Museum

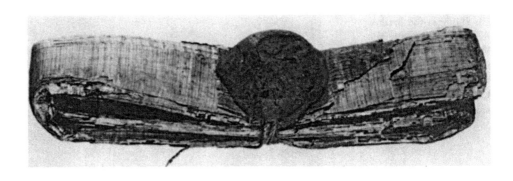

Pl. 98. Marriage contract of Tamut. Aramaic on papyrus. Infrared photo. Elephantine Island, Aswan, Egypt, July 3, 449 B.C.E. Brooklyn Museum, gift of the Estate of Charles Edwin Wilbour. Courtesy of the Brooklyn Museum

which had already been established in earlier periods: in Babylonia, especially around the area that is now Baghdad, and in Alexandria, Egypt. Jews also established themselves in new settlements of the Roman and Byzantine empires, from North Africa to Italy and Spain, and from Cologne to Constantinople. A sizable remnant of Jews remained in the Galilee and Golan Heights, where they continued to live according to the biblical laws as interpreted by the heads of the rabbinical academies, called *halakha* (the way). It is these interpretations that are found in the Jerusalem and Babylonian editions of the Talmud.

The rules for the preparation and writing of the Torah scrolls can be found in various parts of the Talmud, such as the tractate *Menahot* (Meal Offerings), but most of them are concentrated in its external tractates, *Soferim* (Scribes) and *Sefer Torah* (Book of Teaching), which were compiled by the end of the eighth century C.E. As with the rest of the Talmud, these laws had been handed down by word of mouth for centuries before they were published. We will see that correct editions of the Bible were also of concern to scholars and grammarians who lived in Palestine; the early-tenth-century Tiberian scholar Aaron Ben-Asher was considered the highest textual authority for model codices by later generations, including today's Bible scholars.

World Jewry in early medieval times was organized under the secular leadership of an Exilarch, who claimed descent from King David, and under the spiritual and legal guidance of the Gaon, who lived in Babylonia. From the eleventh to the thirteenth centuries, when the Caliphate was invaded by Seljuk Turks and then by Mongols, the center of Jewish economic, religious, cultural, and scholarly life shifted from the Near East to Europe. But Egypt still retained a vibrant, middle-class Jewish community, receiving many immigrants from other Islamic countries. In late-twelfth-century al-Fustat (Old Cairo) lived Rabbi Moses ben Maimon (Maimonides), who was not only Saladin's doctor but a leading Jewish scholar, recognized as a *halakhic* authority in his own time, as he is today. His writings were among the major books to be copied in Europe in the Middle Ages. Individual local rabbis in Germany and Spain were also sought for their legal decisions. Northern France was considered part of the German, or Ashkenazi, orbit, Southern France part of the Spanish, or Sefardi, realm. All of these rabbis based their opinions, *responsa,* which were answers to specific religious questions, on the Talmud and on the decisions of the Gaonim. Contemporary Jewry is still classified into the two major divisions that existed in medieval times: Ashkenazim, the descendants of the Europeans, and Sefardim, the descendants of the Jews exiled from Spain in 1492 who settled in Holland, Italy, and the Ottoman Empire, along with the others who continued to live in Islamic countries until the State of Israel was established in 1948. Slight differences can be discerned in the script, writing surface, and the way the codex was made in medieval Ashkenazi and Sefardi communities, and in the manner in which Torah scrolls are made today.

The Geniza

Much of the evidence for medieval Jewish history of the Near East comes from the geniza, a phenomenon of Jewish religious practice, which has its parallel in Islam. A Torah that was damaged, or one that was rejected as ritually unfit because the letters had worn off or because there were too many mistakes in it, was never destroyed. It had to be "hidden away" or buried. The practice of burial extended to any work with God's name in it, whether it was a prayer book or the records of the rabbinical court or a business or personal letter. The burial ground, or the place where holy documents were stored while awaiting burial, was called a *geniza* (treasure house). One geniza, attached to the Ezra Synagogue in Fustat (Old Cairo), became famous because it was the storage place for some two hundred thousand literary, biblical, talmudic, musical, legal, and personal records and correspondence, written from the ninth century to the middle of the nineteenth century, when it was discovered by Western scholars. Fustat was not the final resting place for the Cairo Geniza documents, however. The majority of the manuscripts are now in Cambridge University Library; others are in libraries in London, New York, and Leningrad, and in private and public collections the world over. From the wealth of Cairo

Geniza documents, most of which were written on paper in the Arabic language but in Hebrew script, the late Shelomo Dov Goitein and other scholars have reconstructed the nature of everyday life in the Mediterranean world, especially from the tenth to the thirteenth centuries. When one considers how much our knowledge of ancient books is based on what has been found in Egypt, one may think of that country as a giant geniza, with perhaps more secrets to reveal in the future.

Many Hebrew manuscripts were destroyed in anti-Jewish outbreaks in medieval Europe as well as in the autos-da-fé of the Inquisition and the Holocaust of our own century. Those that did survive are now in public and private libraries, mostly in Europe but also in the United States and Israel. A few still come up for auction. Two of the largest collections are in the Vatican and in the public library in Leningrad. It is from these scattered collections, seldom found in the countries where the manuscripts were made, that we have our evidence for the medieval Hebrew codex. Because Torah and other scrolls are not signed or dated, a medieval date cannot be assigned to any with certainty.

MATERIALS

Papyrus, and Other Surfaces

For ancient times, evidence for books other than the Torah, for the Torah itself, and for the techniques of preparing scrolls, remains slim. This is due to climatic conditions in Israel and the possible deliberate destruction by hiding or burying all nonofficial versions of the Torah in biblical and postbiblical times. Three official copies of the Torah were kept in the Temple in Jerusalem. These three were not altogether perfect; in them were thirteen recognized errors called "emendations of the scribes," which no future scribe had the authority to change. It is assumed that the earliest scrolls were written on papyrus, the material used by the Egyptians and other neighbors of the Israelites and Judeans in biblical times. The name of papyrus, *neyyar* (the Assyrian *niyaru*), can be found in the Talmud; it later became the word for paper. The papyrus plant, *gomeh*, is mentioned in the Bible (Exod. 2:3, Isa. 18:2), but the finished "paper" product is not. Although the early-eleventh-century *Report of Wenamon* mentioned the export of papyrus from Egypt, none has been found in Israel from this period. The earliest found thus far from ancient Israel is a palimpsest, a scraped and reused sheet found in a cave at Wadi Murabba'at near the Dead Sea, whose bottom layer of text is supposed by scholars to be from the mid-seventh century B.C.E. Papyrus also has been found embedded in clay-seal impressions from the sixth century B.C.E., which means the seals were fixed to papyri documents that have since disintegrated. Several papyri have been found from the Hellenistic and Roman periods, from the driest areas around the Dead Sea and from the Negev, where the desert has almost the same potential for preservation as Egypt.

Ivory was also the surface for occasional inscriptions. An ivory pomegranate with the inscription "Belonging to the Temple of the Lord, holy to the priests," recently acquired by the Israel Museum, is believed to be from the mid-eighth century B.C.E. In 1979, two tiny silver scrolls from the late seventh or sixth century B.C.E. were discovered in Jerusalem in an excavation on the slopes of the Hinnom Valley (the biblical Gehenna, pl. 99, 100). By 1986, enough of both of the silver scrolls had been restored to enable scholars to fill in the missing words and realize that the priestly benediction was written on them (Num. 6:24–26, pl. 101, 102). These are the earliest fragments of biblical text found until now. In both the ivory pomegranate and the silver scrolls, the name of God, YHVH (the tetragrammaton), appears.

There are several biblical references to seals and signet rings (Gen. 38:18–26 and 41:42, I Kings 21:8, and Esther 8:8) as well as many extant seals or their impressions on clay from the time of the Israelite and Judean monarchies (pl. 101, 102). They were made of semiprecious stones such as jasper and onyx, or of limestone, bone,

Pl. 99. Silver scroll with priestly benediction, the smaller of two. Transcription includes missing letters as reconstructed by Ada Yardeni. Semitic (Hebrew) script. Ketef Hinnom, Jerusalem, late seventh century B.C.E. Courtesy of the Israel Antiquities Authority, Jerusalem

ivory, faience, or glass, with a lesser number of copper, silver, and gold seals. Some were oval and pierced so they could be strung, as were Egyptian scarabs; some were set into rings. The owners of these seals were often officials of Judean or Israelite kings. The biblical names Jezebel and Jeremiah (pl. 102) also have been found on seals, and the bulla, or seal impression, of Jeremiah's scribe Baruch has been found. Seals were especially popular in the eighth and sixth centuries B.C.E.; some were ornamented with animal figures along with the owner's name. A large number of bullae were found in Jerusalem's City of David, from the time of the Judean monarchy.

The earliest Hebrew writing, from the fifteenth and fourteenth centuries B.C.E., has been found on metal (the bronze Lachish dagger) and on pottery (Lachish bowls) inscribed with their owners' names, and on the Izbet Sarta ostracon with its

Pl. 101. Seal of Shafat. Amazonite set in a gold ring. Eighth century B.C.E. Israel Museum No. 71.70.220. Courtesy of the Israel Museum, Jerusalem

Pl. 100. Unrolling one of the silver scrolls from Ketef Hinnom. Courtesy of the Laboratories of the Israel Museum, Jerusalem

Pl. 102. Seal with the name Jeremiah. Eighth century B.C.E. Carnelian. Collection of Teddy Kolleck. Photo courtesy of the Israel Museum, Jerusalem

practice-sheet abecedary (see pl. 50, p. 51, and fig. 11, p. 54). The latter reveals that script was already being taught in a systematic way in the twelfth century B.C.E. The simplicity of the alphabet probably obviated the necessity of turning to a professional scribe for all writing services from the time of the Israelite and Judean kingdoms until the last revolt against Rome (tenth century B.C.E.–second century C.E.). By the tenth century B.C.E., royal records were kept and people connected with the court certainly were literate. By the time of the major prophets (the late eighth century B.C.E.), legal transactions were written and children were taught to read and write. The adult population was commanded to write the Shema ("Hear, O Israel," Deut. 6:4–9) on the doorposts and gates of their homes (the mezuza), and to bind boxes containing these words on head and arm (the tefillin; pl. 103). The

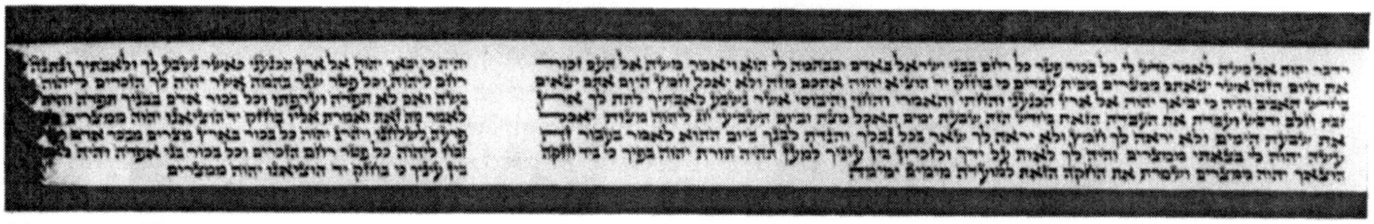

Pl. 103. Tefillin. Exodus 13:1–17. Ashkenazi (*Stam*) script. Izzy Pludwinski, scribe. Jerusalem, 1985. Photo: Patrick J. Young

Pl. 104. Lachish Letter. Cursive Semitic (Hebrew) script on an ostracon, 589–587 B.C.E. British Museum Department of Western Asiatic Antiquities, No. 125702. Courtesy of the British Museum

rules concerning the form tefillin and mezuzot should take and on what kind of animal skin they should be written were as specific as the rules for writing the Torah. These laws were recorded in external talmudic tractates, *Tefillin* and *Mezuza*.

The kind of clay used in Mesopotamia for tablets was not present in Israel's soil, nor was Israel's unfired clay suitable for alphabetic writing. Baked clay, in the form of ostraca, was the cheapest practical writing surface (pl. 104). Its universal use as the scratch paper of the ancient world has already been attested to; in ancient Israel broken pottery was used for receipts, lists, invoices, tax records, petitions, and orders for military supplies. The Lachish Letters, written on ostraca ca. 589–587 B.C.E., just before the Babylonian conquest of this important Judean town, were believed by Yigael Yadin to be preliminary drafts of correspondence written in Lachish itself. The letters actually dispatched would have been on papyrus and, therefore, lost. Ostraca also may have been the surface for the first biblical poetry, proverbs, and prophecies until they were copied in their final editions onto scrolls made of papyrus and later on leather. Inscribed stones were set up in public places for the teachings of Moses (Josh. 8:32). Israelite leaders must have followed the Egyptian practice of plastering surfaces before writing with ink (Deut. 27:2–4), an appropriate coating for arid Egypt but not for the Land of Israel, where a few good rains would wash away these documents. Wooden diptychs must have been used as well (pl. 68, p. 69). These seem to be the "pieces of wood" on which Ezekiel was commanded to write (Ezek. 37:15–20). Ezekiel prophesied in Babylonia, and perhaps these wooden surfaces were like Assyrian wax tablets familiar in the twelfth and eighth centuries B.C.E. (see pl. 67, p. 69). The prophet also drew a plan of Jerusalem on a clay brick, as one would have done in Mesopotamia (Ezek. 4:1). Some of the more unusual writing materials mentioned in the Talmud were olive, carob, and cabbage leaves, and bull's horn.

Leather and Parchment

Some scholars believe that leather was a writing surface in the biblical period, but the evidence we have for its use comes from the Dead Sea Scrolls. Leather is made by tanning the hides of animals with the tannic acid of gall nuts, which retards rotting and makes the hides impervious to water. Parchment is made by a process of soaking the skin in lime-water, stretching, and further liming and scraping (see Chapter 9). The exact date of the change from leather to parchment as a writing surface (and who was responsible for this change) is uncertain. There may have been a technological innovation in western Asia in late Hellenistic times, and another in the Byzantine Empire in the fourth century C.E. The difference in appearance of white leather and parchment is slight: leather usually is thicker. The scribe writes on the hair side only because the flesh side has not been processed fully. Jewish scribes, particularly in the Near East, continued to use leather for the Torah into modern times but to a lesser extent than parchment.

Torah scrolls, tefillin, and mezuzot must be written on the skins of *kasher* animals, those permissible for eating, although the animal does not have to be slaughtered according to Jewish ritual methods. Sacred texts are written on one side only, as was the practice for all quality scrolls in ancient times. The skins of calves, sheep, and goats were those traditionally used, depending on the area in which the scrolls were made. Deer and gazelle skin also could be prepared but were not as practical as animals bred for meat, which would provide a steady supply of pelts. Talmudic and rabbinic literature distinguished between three types of prepared hides that were permissible for writing the sacred texts, irrespective of the *kasher* animals used. The surfaces described in the Talmud do not fit into the classifications of skins we use today, that is, leather, parchment, or vellum. The three talmudic types of skin are *hippa*, *diftera*, and *matza*. *Hippa* was a hide cured with salt only; *diftera* was treated with salt, flour, and other vegetable substances. (The term comes from the Greek for hides, *diphterai*. The early medieval Hebrew codex was sometimes called a *diftar*, and the word is still used today, along with *daftar*, by Jews from Iraq, for a notebook.) The third type, *matza* (unleavened), was not treated. *Gewil* and *kelaf* are also mentioned in *Soferim*. *Gewil* is what would be called today whole-hide leather, containing both epidermal and dermal layers. When *gewil* was used, the Torah could be written on the hair side only. *Kelaf* (from *klf*, "to peel") was the inner skin parchment, with the outer and inner surfaces split or scraped off. The scribe was allowed to write on the flesh side of *kelaf.* *Klaf* has remained the modern Hebrew term for parchment, and scribes still find it easier to write on the flesh side because it provides the proper resistance to the quill. *Duxustus,* a talmudic term from Greek, was the innermost layer of split skin, next to the flesh. (Exactly how this splitting was done is still a matter of conjecture.) Only the outer side received writing, and *duxustus* could be the surface only for a mezuza, not for a Torah. *Gewil* and *duxustus* seem to refer to the layers of the skin and not to the processes of manufacture or treatment of the hide. *Kelaf* refers to a layer and a process, *diftera* originally to a process. The skins of most of the Dead Sea Scrolls are leather, light brown or yellowish in color. The finest scrolls are almost white. The skins of the Dead Sea Scrolls are not as thin as medieval parchment, but are much whiter and finer than what we think of as leather (the tan color we associate with leather is not its natural color, but a dye). The thinnest of the scrolls, only .004 mm thick, were used for tefillin. The Dead Sea Scrolls are believed to have been treated with salt and flour to remove the hair, and tanned with gall-nut liquid that was lightly brushed on or sprinkled over both surfaces of the skin. They therefore would be classified as both *gewil* and *diftera.*

Preparation of medieval parchment differed among Ashkenazim (German Jews), Sefardim (Spanish Jews), and Near Eastern Jews (called Eastern or Oriental in Hebrew). The process usually followed the practices of non-Jewish parchment makers in a given region. Because there are no dated Torah scrolls, we must rely on dated codices for this evidence. In Ashkenazi manuscripts, at times both hair and flesh sides were so thoroughly scraped that one can hardly distinguish between the two; at other times the parchment has almost a suedelike texture on one side, and the difference between the sides is obvious. Medieval Sefardi parchment is at times very thin, and it is easy to discern hair side from flesh side because the flesh side is whiter. Hair holes are obvious on most sheets. The hair and flesh sides of parchment prepared in the Near East resemble each other because of the glassy sizing used on both sides. Long before printing, paper was common in the Near East, where its manufacture was introduced centuries before it reached Europe (see Chapter 12). Paper was used in Yemen for Bible codices but never for scrolls, and for nonbiblical Hebrew manuscripts in countries bordering the Mediterranean. Today the differences between Ashkenazi and Sefardi parchment are rapidly disappearing, as scribes prefer uterine calf vellum (*shlil*) over the heavier goatskin for Torah scrolls. Some Yemenite parchment is still brushed with a coat of cooked zinc white to provide a white surface for script. Size made from the remnants of parchment processing or other ingredients is used on goatskin and calfskin when the surface is porous. There are several parchment factories in Israel today. They make parchment by methods similar to those of the Middle Ages (see pl. 170–172, p. 211), but where it is possible to use machines for part of the processing, these usually have been introduced: giant washing drums, electric hair- and flesh-removing cylinder presses, and electric sanders and finishers.

Tools

Although papyrus and animal skins are not named as writing surfaces in the Bible, there are many references to scrolls and books in the Psalms and Prophets, especially to *megillat sefer,* a "roll of the book." There are also references to the use of pens and other implements, such as the scribe's knife or penknife, used for sharpening reeds, for correcting mistakes by scraping, and for cutting papyrus to the size required. The scribe's palette was called *qeset (hasofrim),* from the Egyptian *gsti.* A metal stylus (*heret*) is mentioned in Job 19:24, made of iron and lead and used for engraving books on stone; in Jeremiah 17:1 an iron pen with a flint or adamant nib was used for engraving a tablet. A metal instrument of this type was found at Megiddo, from ca. 1800–1650 B.C.E., and one from 1000 B.C.E. was found at Ashur, one of the capitals of the Assyrian empire. An Egyptian-style ivory pen case from the time of Ramses II was found at Megiddo. The hollow, hard reed pen was called a *qolmos* in talmudic times, from the Greek *calamus*. The reeds used for writing on the ostraca of the Lachish Letters were cut so that the nib was broad, but not split. The Egyptian brush-pen was not suitable for alphabetic script. During the Middle Ages, Jewish scribes of the Near East and Spain continued to use the reed pen (pl. 105), which Sefardim still use today (the best reed pens now are imported into Israel from Japan). Ashkenazi scribes switched to the quill in the Middle Ages; goose feathers were used then, turkey feathers today.

In ancient times, ink was composed of soot and water mixed with gum of balsam. This ink could be washed off easily, as we know from the trial of a woman suspected of adultery—the words of her accusation were scraped off the document, mixed with water, and given to her to drink (Num. 5:11–29). What really happened to her when she drank those words? The thought of it was supposed to extract her

Pl. 105. Sefardi scribe's implements. Jerusalem, late nineteenth century. Courtesy of the Old Yishuv Court Museum, Jewish Quarter, Jerusalem

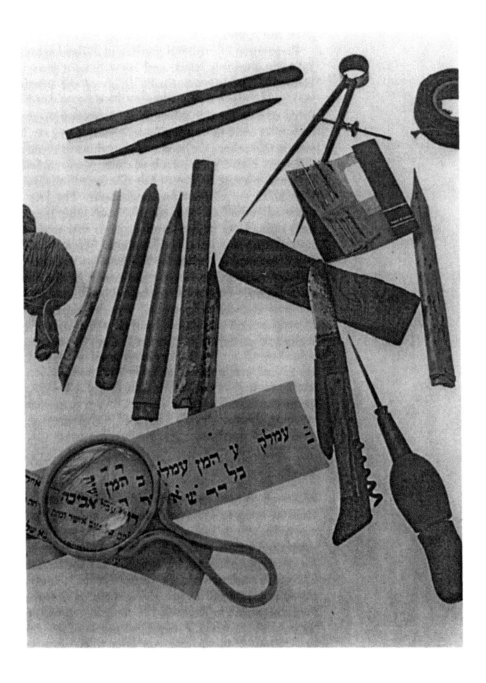

confession. The ink of the Lachish Letters was a mixture of carbon and iron. Most of the Dead Sea Scrolls were written with carbon ink (powdered charcoal), but the ink of the *Genesis Apocryphon* and a few other manuscripts show some metallic content. When there was an attempt to introduce vitriol (metallic sulfate) ink officially in the second century C.E., certain rabbis, who considered its use a pagan practice, objected, but eventually it was allowed. The ink of Ashkenazi codices of the Middle Ages is very dark brown, almost black; the ink of Sefardi codices looks brown today, indicating a metallic ingredient in its recipe. Today, scribes' ink is made from tree sap, gall nuts, and bronze and copper sulfate. More exact individual recipes are still kept secret by some scribes and inkmakers.

While carbon inks can be washed away, metallic inks could be erased only by scraping. The scribes were well aware of mistakes and ink blots that could be made while writing, and there were many instructions and opinions in the Talmud as to how letters and words should be erased and rewritten in making a Torah scroll. A completely erased sheet, or palimpsest, could not be used in a Torah scroll. Palimpsests, we shall see, were common in Greek, Roman, and early medieval bookmaking. It is interesting to note that so important was writing to Jewish culture that one of the most devastating curses, still common today, is "may his name be erased." A similar curse was used against Amalek, who attacked the Israelites in the wilderness after the Exodus from Egypt (Exod. 17:14): "I will utterly erase the memory of Amalek."

The Hebrew scribe carried his writing implements in his sash (Ezek. 9:2–3, 11), as did his Mesopotamian counterpart, but we do not know in what position he sat and wrote in biblical times. After the second century B.C.E., the Essene scribes at Qumran near the Dead Sea evidently sat on benches, writing at tables. For the Middle Ages, we can assume that the scribe's tools looked like those of his non-Jewish counterpart and that he wrote at a desk, probably in his own home, isolated for concentration. In more recent centuries the pen case and other tools of the Jewish scribe in the Near East were similar to those of the Muslim scribe.

In the Middle Ages, an awl was used for ruling the guidelines of the codex; usually the indentations made on the top sheet could be seen on those underneath. Sefardi scribes ruled two sheets at a time on the hair side of the parchment. Lead point was used for guidelines at times, but this was not the lead of today's pencil, which is graphite. Near Eastern scribes used a frame strung with parallel cords as a guide for drawing the lines of the whole sheet, called a *mastara*. The frame was placed under the sheet to be ruled. When a finger was pressed on the sheet the length of the cord beneath it, the taut string left an indented line. This method is still used for paper documents, particularly by Samaritans. Today the parchment factory will frequently provide the scribe with mechanically ruled parchment for Torahs and other purposes. If the scribe today draws the guidelines himself, he does so with awl and ruler. In the Torah, two vertical guidelines are drawn to contain the columns, and forty-three horizontal guidelines are drawn for the forty-two lines of text; an extra unused line is always left below the last text line of the Torah column. The guidelines are for the top horizontal strokes of the letters, as Hebrew letters, unlike Latin script, hang from the guidelines. Occasionally a scribe wrote between the lines; scribes of Ashkenazi codices usually wrote between the two ruled lines.

THE MAKING OF A TORAH SCROLL

Before the scribe sits down to write, he prepares himself spiritually for the task by reciting a declaration in which he dedicates his work to a holy purpose. Today's parchment maker does the same. A similar declaration is made each time the scribe writes the tetragrammaton, YHVH. The entire Torah scroll is written only on the flesh side in 248 to 252 columns, with two or three columns to each parchment sheet. The sheets are not sewn together until the work is completed. The Torah always must be copied from a model, called a *tikkun*, never from memory. Words are well spaced, as they were in ancient times, unlike those on ancient Greek and Latin manuscripts. There is no punctuation as we know it, but spaces the width of nine letters are left between sections. A few letters are dotted, and scattered within the Torah there are eleven enlarged and six miniature letters and a set of backward letter *nuns* ⌶ that bracket two sentences (Num. 10:35–36). The enlarged letter *bet* ⊐ which is the first word of Genesis (*Bereshit*), can be looked upon as a proto-capital letter. There are midrashic (legendary) explanations for all of these graphic peculiarities. The two poems of the Torah, the Song of the Sea (Exod. 15:1–19) and the Song of Moses (Deut. 32:1–44), are written in the form of "bricks," that is, in vertical columns with a space between the verses, similar to Greek hemistitches (fig. 15).

Because of the possibility of smearing after dipping the pen in ink, there was a rule in *Sefer Torah* that when writing the name of God the scribe must dip the pen before the last letter of the preceding word. Mistakes are scraped off with a knife or razor and the spot can be repumiced and written upon once again; if the spot is too worn out it may be cut out and replaced by a patch. Too many of these corrections will render the Torah invalid for synagogue use, and it must be put in a geniza. Because God's name may never be erased, if a mistake is made in writing the name, the whole sheet is set aside and a new one begun.

When the work is complete, the sheets are sewn together, first in groups of four, from the blank reverse side. Parchment patches may be glued on the back of the joins for reinforcement. The sinews used for sewing the sheets, as with the parchment itself, come only from *kasher* animals. Some sixty-two skins are used to make up a Torah scroll, which means it is very long, so each end is attached to a strong wooden roller around which the parchment is wound. A blank sheet is used at each end to wind around the rollers. In this way the Torah was unlike Egyptian scrolls, which lacked rollers, and unlike Greek and most Roman scrolls, which had only one baton if there were any. We know Torah scrolls had two rollers even in the Roman period from depictions of them on coins and on later gilded glass. The scroll held by Ezra in the wall painting of the synagogue at Dura Europos has no handles (pl. 96). Perhaps he was reading a book of the Prophets, the *Navi* or *haftara*, and it is the covered Torah that is seen at his side. Handles on rollers are still made of wood and ivory. In Ashkenazi Torahs, disks or double disks afford the rolled scroll additional stability. Sefardi rollers are fixed to the case, or *tik*, which supports the scrolls within.

Other books of the Bible besides the Torah which are read in the synagogue continue to be written in roll form: *Megillat (Scroll of) Esther*, and the other four books comprising the "Five Scrolls": Song of Songs, Ruth, Lamentations, and Ecclesiastes. Each is read on the holiday associated with the contents of the book:

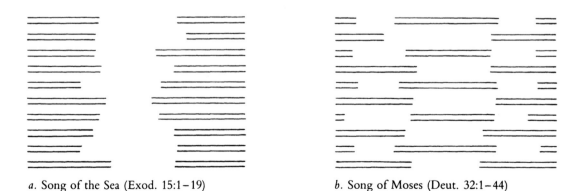

a. Song of the Sea (Exod. 15:1–19)   *b.* Song of Moses (Deut. 32:1–44)

Fig. 15. "Brick" patterns for songs in the Torah

Purim, Passover, Pentecost, the Ninth of Av (when both Temples in Jerusalem were destroyed), and Tabernacles. Because the contents of these scrolls are much shorter than those of the Torah, they are fixed to only one roller; sometimes they lack rollers. The individual books of the Prophets (*Navi*) are written in separate scrolls, each attached to a single roller and read from the scroll in some Ashkenazi and Sefardi synagogues. Less common is the *haftara* (conclusion), a double-handled scroll with all of the prophetic readings written out in the order of their annual cycle. These prophetical *haftarot,* recited after the weekly or holiday Torah portion is read, more often are chanted from a large volume because it has been printed with the vowels, accents, and cantillation signs. This way the *haftara* reader does not have to be as well-practiced as the Torah reader, who reads an unvocalized text. One may assume that in ancient times each book of the Bible had its own scroll, except possibly for the short ones, which we combined, such as the "Five Scrolls" and the "Twelve (Minor) Prophets." For the earliest known codices from the Near East, from the late ninth to the eleventh centuries, one rarely finds a one-volume Bible. Usually each of the three major divisions made up one volume, written with very large script and having three columns per page. An individual *parasha* or weekly Torah reading also could be written separately in minicodex form.

SCRIBES

The root of the word for scribe, *sfr,* means "to count," which may indicate a bookkeeping function in the time of the Judean and Israelite monarchies, in addition to scribal skills. Even though children and adults could read, there seems to have been a professional class of scribes. At that time the professional scribe was attached to the palace or the Temple in Jerusalem, or he worked as a secretary for the rich, or he wrote up legal documents or correspondence for townspeople. The leader of the revolt against Rome in the early second century c.e., Bar Kokhba, had several scribes in his employ. The status of some scribes was high; there was a special office for them in both palace and Temple, and the position was frequently hereditary. Several scribes are known by name in the Bible. Baruch, Jeremiah's scribe, was also his friend and disciple. Ezra the Scribe was the spiritual leader of the Jews when they returned to Judea from the Babylonian captivity. "Scribe," then, could be a metaphor for leader as it was for scholar.

Fathers taught their children to read and write. The scribe always learned his art from a master scribe. In the biblical period, the arrangement was familylike, even when there was no blood relationship. It seems that, even when it was prestigious, ordinary scribehood was always a low-earning profession. In the Talmud, there is one opinion that a scribe should not be paid too high a fee lest he become rich and abandon the profession. The copyist of the talmudic period was called a *lavlar,* from the Latin *librarius.* In medieval Egypt, the Bible scribe earned far more than the scribe with a lesser talent whose work was secretarial. In Europe, *lavlar* came to mean an ordinary scribe, although at times a scribe with a good hand in modesty called himself a *lavlar.* (See Chapter 9 for more information on the medieval scribe.) The Torah scribe today is called a *sofer stam, stam* being the acronym of *sifre* (books of) Torah, tefillin, and mezuzot. Nowadays, the Torah scribe usually learns in classes with either a Sefardi or Ashkenazi teacher; in Israel it is a four-month intensive course. After training, there is a rigorous examination on all of the laws concerning the making of a Torah. The scribal student pays for the course, or it is subsidized, but he can get a return on the cost of his training by writing one *Megillat Esther,* about $500. A Torah scroll will cost between $18,000–$40,000, and may take up to a year to write. A *ketubah,* the marriage contract, costs, in addition to the parchment, about $50 to $150, more if decorated. An eighteenth-century decorated *ketubah* from Italy will bring at least $40,000 at auction today. A *ketubah* does not have to be written by a *sofer stam,* and many are written by calligraphers, both men and women.

BOOKS OTHER THAN THE TORAH

Ancient Documents

The fifth century B.C.E. collection of Aramaic legal documents on papyrus from the Jewish military colony at Elephantine have been mentioned previously (see p. 104–5 and pl. 97, 98). These and all other inscriptions on sherds and occasional clay tablets are incidental as literature when compared to the Bible but they are important for social and economic history. Aramaic papyri dated 375–335 B.C.E. were found in caves at Wadi Daliya, twelve miles northwest of Jericho; they probably belonged to people fleeing from the Hellenistic army during the time of the Samaritan revolt. Coins, which were minted by Judean governments since the time of Persian hegemony, are another source of inscriptions. Besides these, there are only a few inscriptions (on ostraca and seals from the Phoenician coast) until the time of the Dead Sea Scrolls (second century B.C.E. to the second century C.E.).

The Dead Sea Scrolls include the earliest group of biblical texts on animal skins as well as other Hebrew writings, Apocrypha, apocalyptic works, rules for the sect, and biblical commentaries. They come from the caves on the northwest shore of the Dead Sea and were first discovered in 1947 (although some may have been found earlier and their source not revealed), and now number some eight hundred in all. Mystery and intrigue surrounded their acquisition. Most of the Dead Sea Scrolls are believed to have been written by the Essenes, a monkish group who separated themselves from the mainstream of Judaism about the middle of the second century B.C.E. to live at Qumran, where their scriptorium, with clay tables, benches, and one bronze and two clay inkwells were found (pl. 106). The tannery for processing skins may have been a little over a mile away. This Dead Sea sect's manuscripts are primarily biblical (all books except Esther) and most are fragmentary, with the Isaiah scroll being the most complete (see pl. 4, p. 3). The Isaiah scroll is 22 feet (6.71 m) long but may have been 30 feet (9.15 m) long when it was written. Other famous scrolls are a commentary on Habbakuk; the rules of the order, called *Manual of Discipline;* an apocalyptic work, *The War of the Sons of Light and the Sons of Darkness;* and the *Temple Scroll* (pl. 107, 108). The latter, published by Yigael Yadin, was the longest scroll to be found, at 28 feet 2 ½ inches (8.6 m). It was written in the mid-first century C.E., but its text originally was compiled around 125 to 100 B.C.E. The Temple Scroll contains ritual laws, statutes for the king and army, and a detailed description of how the Temple in Jerusalem should be rebuilt. The leather on which it was written was very carefully processed and extremely thin, only about one-tenth of a millimeter thick, as thin as the finest Egyptian papyrus. As in most of the Dead Sea Scrolls, a blank end-sheet was attached when the scroll was sewn together. The scribe drew guidelines, both horizontal ones from which the letters

Pl. 106. Inkwells from the Roman period. Israel, first century B.C.E./C.E. *Left to right:* bronze, Beth Shean; clay, Qumran; wood, Qumran; clay, with handle, Jerusalem. Courtesy of the Israel Antiquities Authority, exhibited at Israel Museum, Jerusalem. Photo: David Harris

Pl. 107. The Temple Scroll. One of the Dead Sea Scrolls. Qumran, mid-first century C.E. Ink on leather. Courtesy of the Shrine of the Book, Israel Museum, Jerusalem

Pl. 108. Statutes of the King from the Temple Scroll. Text similar to Deuteronomy 17:14–16. Qumran, mid-first century C.E. Ink on leather. Courtesy of the Shrine of the Book, Israel Museum, Jerusalem

hung, and vertical ones to contain the columns of text. Although the scribe did not make the left-hand margin 100 percent straight, as Jewish scribes were to do in later codices and Torah scrolls, there is much more of an attempt to justify the margin than there was in Greek and Latin scrolls. The Jewish scribe was ahead of his non-Jewish counterpart in that he left spaces between words, something we now take for granted, but which the ancient reader did not. Some of the Dead Sea Scrolls were wrapped in linen, and the Isaiah scroll was enclosed in a ceramic jar with a lid.

The Dead Sea Scrolls were written in the Aramaic script, also known as "Square Hebrew," but called *Ashuri* in the Talmud. It is similar enough to modern printed Hebrew to be read with ease, and displays the finial forms of modern Hebrew script (*khaf, mem, nun, peh,* and *zade*). In some Dead Sea Scrolls the name of God, YHVH, was written in the old script. Early Semitic script was revived for coins minted in Jerusalem from the fourth century B.C.E. and throughout the Second Temple Period (with one exception), and during the periods of the first (66–73 C.E.) and second (132–135 C.E.) Jewish revolts against Rome (see pl. 54, p. 53). Other than a few sporadic revivals of the old Hebrew script in the third century B.C.E., only the Samaritans retained it. It is still found in their Torah scrolls and printed in the title of their contemporary magazine, *Alef Bet.*

Caves around the Dead Sea were used as hideouts during the revolt of Bar Kokhba against Rome. Among the finds from Wadi Murabba'at and Nahal Hever were fragments of biblical literature in Hebrew, tefillin, administrative and personal documents in Aramaic and Greek, and letters written in Hebrew by scribes for Bar Kokhba himself. The books and documents from the region of the Dead Sea were written on leather and, more rarely, on papyrus but there is also a copper scroll (two rolls of copper) that listed treasures and their hiding places. To date, more than half of the Dead Sea Scrolls have been published.

No Hebrew Bible codices dating from the mid-second to the ninth or tenth centuries C.E. have come to light as yet, but there are scattered papyrus documents and fragments in Hebrew and Aramaic. Parts of books also were written in mosaics. Several synagogues built in the Galilee, Golan, and other areas of Palestine where there were large Jewish communities during the Byzantine period had inscriptions, some of them quite lengthy. The pavement of the sixth-century synagogue of Ein Gedi near the Dead Sea lists the names of biblical figures, the months, the signs of the zodiac (but with no pictures of them, as there were in other synagogues of the time), the synagogue's benefactors, and a curse against those who would reveal the secrets of the town (perfume manufacture), all written in Hebrew and Aramaic (pl. 109). Another synagogue, at Rechov in the Beth Shean valley, built in the sixth or seventh century C.E., has whole passages of the Talmud written in tesserae, the stone bits that make up mosaics (pl. 110). Why would Jews write books in mosaics? Perhaps they wanted a permanent double record, realizing the destructibility of papyrus and leather (or parchment, assuming they were using it). One must not forget that the antifigural style—iconoclasm—in religious art, which took hold in Byzantium, in Islamic lands and in England and Ireland from the seventh to the ninth centuries, expressed itself earlier in Palestine. Moreover, script was always an accepted form of art in Judaism.

Mosaic decoration of Byzantine-period synagogues may reveal something about book design at that time because their geometric patterns, organized into rectangular units, are similar to the earliest Bible codices' carpet pages, the full-page decorations that resemble oriental carpets. Some of the imagery—the ark that housed the Torah, the menorah (seven-branched candelabrum), and other vessels made for Israelite sanctuary in the wilderness are very much like ninth-to-twelfth-century frontispiece illustrations in Hebrew codices. We see in synagogue mosaics, such as the ones in Hammath Tiberias, Beth Alpha, and Beth Shean, that a tapestry separated the Torah ark from the congregation (pl. 111); so too the carpet page of the book separated the reader from the Bible codex. A poem describing the Bible as sanctuary can be found

Pl. 109. Mosaic floor inscription. Synagogue at Ein Gedi, Israel, sixth century C.E. Exhibited at the Israel Museum. Courtesy of the Israel Antiquities Authority, Jerusalem

in an early medieval codex from the Levant, and architectural decoration was common and natural in Hebrew manuscript illumination because many of the terms for parts of the book were architectonic. Illustrations of architectural elements can be seen as a visual pun, telling the reader that the Bible was God's dwelling place. (The pun exists in Greek and Latin as well: tables, chapters, capitals, thesaurus, and codex itself.)

DEVELOPMENT OF THE HEBREW CODEX: THE MIDDLE AGES

The Masoretes

The period of scant or lacking book evidence, the second to the late ninth and tenth centuries, was a crucial one for the development of the Hebrew codex and for the Christian parchment codex as well. But during that time the Hebrew Bible text was preserved and must have been recopied constantly. Along with the development of

Pl. 110. Mosaic floor inscription. Synagogue at Rechov, Beth Shean Valley, Israel, fifth–seventh century C.E. Oldest copy of some of the religious laws found in the Palestinian Talmud. Courtesy of the Israel Antiquities Authority, Jerusalem

Pl. 111. Mosaic floor of synagogue at Beth Shean. Detail of ark and tapestry. Sixth century C.E. Courtesy of the Israel Antiquities Authority, Jerusalem

the Hebrew Bible codex came the development of vowel and cantillation signs for Hebrew script.

Ancient Hebrew script, and its later development, Square Hebrew or Aramaic, is consonantal and originally lacked vowel signs, as we saw in inscriptions and ostraca of the biblical period. Nor was there vocalization in the Dead Sea Scrolls. Torah scrolls today are still unvocalized. In reading the Torah, correct vowel pronunciation always was preserved orally. If the written vowel system was developed at a specific time during these seven centuries, we have no evidence for it as yet. But by the late ninth and early tenth centuries C.E., the time of the first dated Hebrew codices, a completely developed system of notation for vowels, accents, and cantillation for the Bible existed. Vocalization never was inserted in the Torah or *Navi* scrolls read in the synagogue but, because there were no rules in the Talmud for writing codices, vowels and other markings could appear in a Pentateuch or Bible in codex format. The scribes who specialized in formulating and preserving this vocalization system, known to have been working in the eighth and ninth centuries in Palestine, called themselves *Ba'alei Masora*, "traditionalists," today called Masoretes. They did more than record vowel notations and punctuation; they continued the practice of the scribes mentioned in the Talmud who counted each and every word and letter of the Bible (*sofer*, "count"). They noted how many words and sentences were in each book; they marked the middle word of each book, and recorded details such as how many times and where each word was repeated in exactly the same form. They made lists of identical groups of words and wrote these lists and other footnotes in the margins of Bible codices, and they appended masoretic treatises to the end of the book. The work of the earlier Masoretes—even if they were not so called in talmudic times—may have been inspired by that of Greek scribes, who counted and recorded the number of lines in their scrolls. Masoretic lists were the first Hebrew biblical concordances. The early Masoretes were motivated by a compulsion to keep account of every biblical word; it was a way of ensuring that no mistake would be made and no word lost. Although masoretic notations may differ from one medieval Bible codex to another from the tenth through the fifteenth centuries, the consonantal text itself is remarkably consistent and error free. There may have been many generations of Masoretes and Bible codex scribes before the earliest dated biblical codex, the Moshe Ben-Asher Codex of 894/5 (pl. 112). This codex may have been written a century after its

Pl. 112. Moshe Ben-Asher Codex of the Prophets. Text page (p. 20), showing Masora. Tiberias, 894/5 C.E., according to its colophon, but probably later. Courtesy of the Karaite Synagogue, Cairo. Photo: Morrie Camhi

colophon declares, and therefore may be a copy of one with the earlier date. There are other masoretic Bibles with colophons from the tenth century and later. Textual study similar to the Masora occupied the scholars of Syriac versions of the Bible and other peoples of the Near East, such as the Indians, Greeks, and Arabs, who also were concerned with the science of language in their own literature, either for religious or philosophical reasons.

Among the most famous and respected of the Masoretes were the Ben-Ashers, a family of scribe-grammarians who traced the activity of their ancestors to the early eighth century. Another Masorete was Ben-Naftali, but his work is known only through later lists comparing Ben-Asher and Ben-Naftali variations. Moshe Ben-Asher wrote his codex (or the one on which the extant codex was modeled or its colophon copied) for a patron in Jerusalem. It is a codex of the Prophets, preserved by the Karaite community in Cairo. Aaron Ben-Asher, the son of Moshe, was the last and most important of these Masoretes. The Bibles he wrote and vocalized were used as model codices for Torah scrolls and as models for Bible codices of the Middle Ages written in Egypt and in Europe. They have served as models for modern printed editions as well. The contemporary edition of the Hebrew Bible is called the Masoretic Text because it is based on an Aaron Ben-Asher edition of the Bible, either the one called the Leningrad Codex now in the Leningrad Public Library (Codex B19ᵃ, an authentic copy of Aaron Ben-Asher's masoretic system, written in 1008–1009 C.E.), or the Aleppo Codex, written about 910 C.E. and vocalized by Aaron Ben-Asher himself, now in Jerusalem (its Pentateuch has been lost). The consonantal texts of these masoretic codices, where they can be compared, are very close to some of the Dead Sea Scrolls, and testify to the accuracy of Jewish scribes.

The Medieval Codex

The medieval Hebrew codex, like its parchment, was prepared for writing in a manner similar to that of the manuscripts in the countries in which Jews resided (see Chapters 9 and 11). When a scribe moved from one country to another, his scribal hand remained the same but the parchment and codex were prepared according to the methods of his new home.

In writing the Bible codex in the Middle Ages, one scribe usually wrote the consonantal text, then the *nakdan,* or punctuation specialist, pointed and vocalized it, and then the *masran* wrote in the Masora in the margins in much smaller letters. The *masran* was a masorator, a copyist, as opposed to the Masorete, the scholar who had originally compiled and systematized the Masora. If there is a colophon for a codex in which the medieval scribe accomplished all three of these specialized tasks, the scribe took pride in recording that he wrote it, vocalized it, and masorated it.

Different script styles developed in the Middle Ages due to the difference in pens and the influence of non-Hebrew scripts written in the area in which the scribe was trained (fig. 16). Medieval Hebrew scripts are classified broadly as Oriental (the hand of Near Eastern scribes; pl. 112, 117, p. 131), Sefardi (Iberia, Provence, and North Africa; pl. 113), and Ashkenazi (Germany and northern France; pl. 114). There are also Italian, Byzantine, and Yemenite styles. Sefardi script is rounded and relatively unshaded, written with a reed pen. Ashkenazi script is sharp, angular, and shaded, more like Gothic script, with contrasts between the thick and thin strokes of the letters (shading), written with a quill. These scripts have semicursive and cursive variations as well. The book hand of each group is universally legible; semicursive and cursive scripts are more difficult to read by those accustomed to another style.

The relative lack of mistakes in Hebrew Bible codices as compared to Latin and Greek manuscripts has been noted by many. This was because of the training and attitude of the scribe toward the task of writing a Torah, for which he prepared

Pl. 113. "Damascus Keter (Crown)." Carpet page of a Sefardi Bible Codex, with micrography. Burgos, 1260. JNUL Heb 4° 790, f. 428r. Courtesy of the Jewish National and University Library, Jerusalem

Pl. 114. Ashkenazi Pentateuch. Jonah and the fish drawn in micrography. Germany, latter half of the thirteenth century. British Library Department of Oriental Manuscripts and Printed Books, Add. 21160, f. 292r. Courtesy of the British Library

himself ritually. He was forbidden to add or subtract a single letter, and copied even what he knew to be a mistake, repeating it as it was written. The codex allowed the scribe more latitude because there were no talmudic limitations on this form of book. Correct spellings and pronunciations could be written in the margins (these corrections, too, were long-established traditions, and part of the Masora). Nevertheless, the Hebrew codex was a conservative entity. The early Hebrew codex looked very much like a scroll in its layout of three columns per page, six across the opening, with margins and spacing between words and columns. The early medieval Bible scribe was hesitant to elongate the horizontal bars of letters in order to justify margins because this was discouraged in Torah scrolls (five letters were permitted), but later codex scribes did so. More popular were graphic fillers—strokes or letters or partial letters—inserted at the end of a line to justify the left edge of each column.

Medieval Scribes

Torah scrolls never have colophons but it is assumed that medieval Torah scribes were also scribes of codices and that they were better paid than secretarial scribes who wrote commercial documents, rabbinical court records, and personal corre-

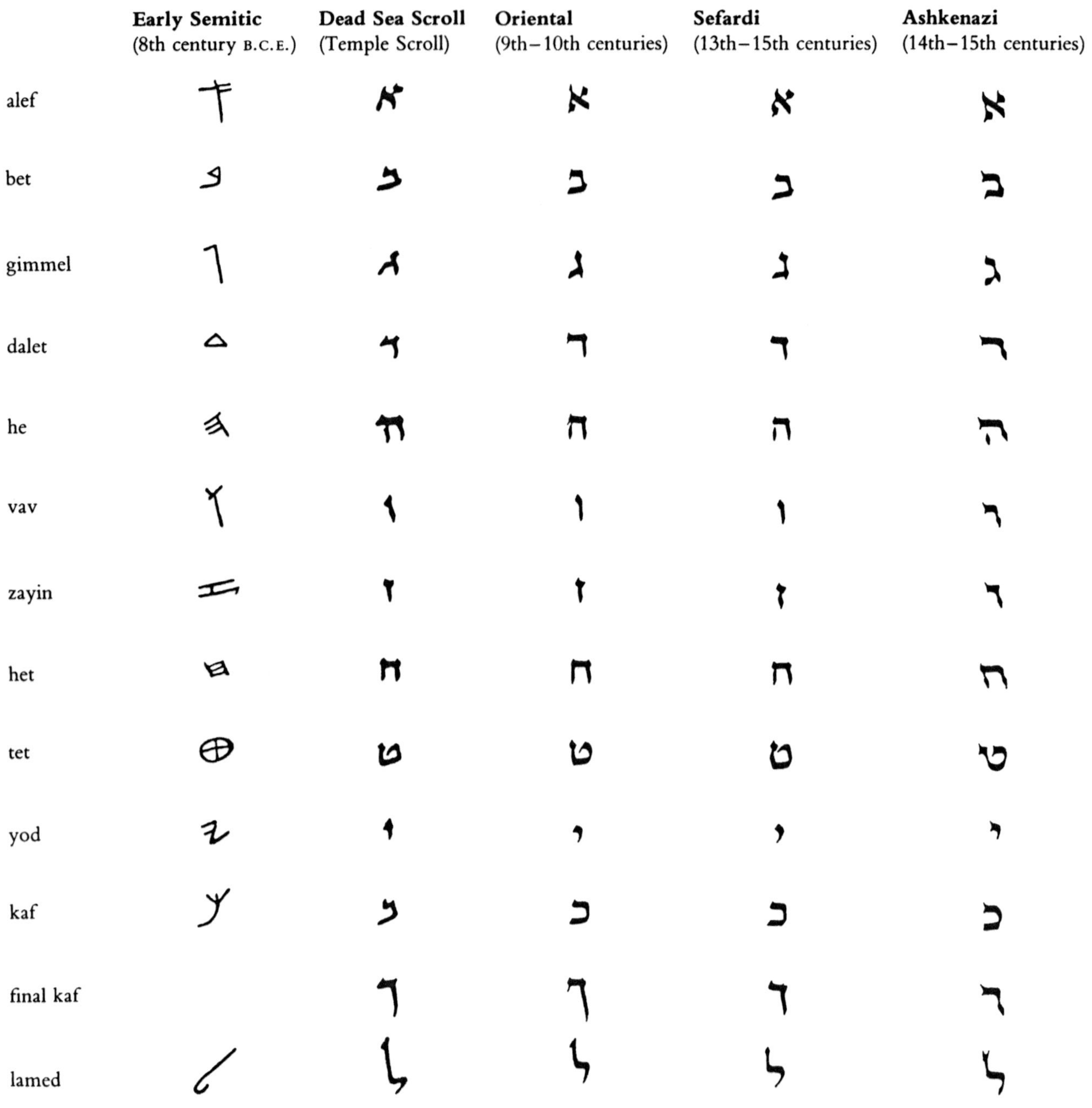

	Early Semitic (8th century B.C.E.)	Dead Sea Scroll (Temple Scroll)	Oriental (9th–10th centuries)	Sefardi (13th–15th centuries)	Ashkenazi (14th–15th centuries)
alef	ⴲ	א	א	א	א
bet	ⵄ	ב	ב	ב	ב
gimmel	ⵗ	א	א	ג	ג
dalet	△	ⴷ	ד	ד	ד
he	ⵥ	ⴶ	ה	ה	ה
vav	Y	ⴼ	ו	ו	ו
zayin	ⵣ	ⴹ	ז	ז	ז
het	ⵦ	ח	ח	ח	ח
tet	⊕	ט	ט	ט	ט
yod	ⵝ	ⴺ	י	י	י
kaf	Y	ⴽ	כ	כ	כ
final kaf		ך	ך	ך	ך
lamed	ⵢ	ל	ל	ל	ל

Fig. 16. Styles of Hebrew script

spondence. In the Near East, a medieval scribe could earn about three gold dinars for a book like the Moshe Ben-Asher Prophet Codex, 571 large text pages. The average monthly income of a lower-middle-class family at that time was two dinars. The dinar could pay one's poll tax or purchase a garment. Sometimes the scribe was paid in clothing rather than in currency. Materials were usually provided by the patron; if the scribe advanced his own capital for supplies, his fee could be much higher. A

	Early Semitic (8th century B.C.E.)	Dead Sea Scroll (Temple Scroll)	Oriental (9th–10th centuries)	Sefardi (13th–15th centuries)	Ashkenazi (14th–15th centuries)
mem	ﭏ	ﬦ	מ	מ	מ
final mem		ﬦ	ﬦ	ﬦ	ﬦ
nun	ﭏ	נ	נ	נ	נ
final nun		ן	ן	ן	ן
samech	ﬧ	ﬢ	ס	ס	ס
ayin	o	ﬣ	ﬣ	ﬣ	ﬣ
peh	ﬧ	ﬤ	פ	פ	פ
final peh (feh)		ﬥ	ﬥ	ﬥ	ﬥ
zade	ﬦ	ﬧ	ﬧ	ﬧ	צ
final zade		ﬨ	﬩	﬩	﬩
qof	ﭏ	ﭏ	ק	ק	ק
resh	ﭏ	ﭏ	ר	ר	ר
shin	ﭏ	﬩	ש	ש	ש
tav	×	ﬨ	ﬨ	ת	ת

patron sometimes gave a deposit for a promised codex. The cost of a Hebrew codex in medieval Europe has been estimated as the equivalent of a month's support for an individual, but it could take a few months to write it. The scribe was sometimes invited to live at the home of the patron who commissioned the book and who provided writing materials in addition to supporting the scribe. Unlike his monastic counterpart, the Hebrew scribe did not write in a scriptorium, nor were quires distributed to several scribes at one time to manufacture a book quickly. However, several scribes could have written one manuscript; ten is the highest recorded number. These could have been written in the house of study, the *beth midrash* or *yeshiva*, or they could have been written by students of a master scribe, or by the scribe's children. Usually the scribe wrote at home. Medieval Jewish scribes were not always professional copyists. It is known from manuscripts with colophons that one-third of them were written by learned persons who wrote books for their own study. By profession they were doctors, goldsmiths, seal makers, cantors, butchers, teachers, and students. A scribe could write between six and sixteen pages a day, and perhaps wrote for six or seven hours a day in a five- or six-day workweek, excluding holidays. If he had another job, the scribe naturally spent fewer hours on his codex, and it took him longer to complete it. It was considered a virtue for the scribe to copy his master's hand as closely as possible.

Because the Torah must be written by one who dons tefillin, the profession was limited to men, but a few women scribes from the Middle Ages are known, and fifteen are known from the Renaissance to modern times. One thirteenth-century European scribe who wrote several books, Paula bat (daughter of) Abraham, came from a family of scribes, as did the Yemenite Miriam bat Benayah.

Colophons

The colophon in the codex usually reveals the scribe's name and that of his father and perhaps his grandfather, the name of the *nakdan* and *masran* if different, the name of the patron or the fact that the scribe wrote the codex for himself, and the city and date of writing. Of about 50,000 Hebrew manuscripts that have survived until modern times, there are some 2,800 with colophons bearing dates earlier than 1540. It has been estimated that a million Hebrew manuscripts were written by that date.

The colophon of the Moshe Ben-Asher Codex is typical of those written in the Near East in the Middle Ages:

> I, Moshe Ben-Asher have written this codex of the Scripture according to my judgment "as the very good hand of my God was upon me" (Nehemiah 2:8), "very clearly" (Deut. 26:8) in the city of Ma'azya Teveriah (Tiberias), "the renowned city" (Ezekiel 26:17). . . . May it please our Creator to illuminate our eyes and enlighten our hearts by His Torah, that we may learn and teach and act "with a perfect heart and a willing mind" (I Chronicles 28:9) and for the whole of Israel. Amen. It was written in the year 827 after the destruction of the Second Temple . . .[1]

Alongside Moshe Ben-Asher's colophon is an additional note of warning, reminiscent of the old Mesopotamian colophons:

> Whoever alters a word of this codex . . . or erases one letter or rips off one leaf . . . may he have neither pardon nor forgiveness, neither "let him behold the beauty of the Lord" (Psalms 27:4), nor "let him see the good that is reserved for those who fear Him" (Jeremiah 29:32). He shall be like a woman in impurity and like a leprous man who has to be locked up so that his limbs may be crushed, the pride of his power broken, "his flesh be consumed away that it cannot be seen and his bones corrode to unsightliness" (Job 33:21). Amen . . .[2]

Dating of Manuscripts

Manuscripts written in the medieval Near East were dated either from the time of the Second Temple's destruction, which was miscalculated by two years to be 68 C.E., or according to the "Era of Dating of Documents" (*Shtarot*), the Seleucid Era, 312 B.C.E. In Europe, from the twelfth century, dating followed the calculations of Jewish historiographers as to when the world was created, assumed to be 3761 B.C.E. Thus the Year of Creation 5243 would be 1482–83; 5751 would be 1990/91. The

Jewish year, a lunar one, begins in the fall, and every few years an extra month is intercalated to coordinate it with the solar calendar. There are seven of these leap years in a nineteen-year cycle. If the month is not recorded in the colophon, the date is transcribed as the two years of the Gregorian calendar that it spans.

ADORNMENT AND ILLUMINATION OF HEBREW MANUSCRIPTS

The Torah Scroll

The covering of the Torah in Ashkenazi and Sefardi communities differs, which may indicate that there were multiple ways of protecting it in antiquity. We have already seen that some of the Dead Sea Scrolls were wrapped in linen and encased in clay jars (see pl. 4, p. 3). In the Ezra portrait at the Dura Europos synagogue, we see a fabric covering over what appears to be a Torah in a stand (pl. 96, p. 105). The Sefardim of Islamic countries keep the Torah in a metal or wood cylindrical case called a *tik* (pl. 115). It opens down the center and stands upright on the reading table in the synagogue. The open case is held up to show the congregation the Torah before it is read. As noted in Chapter 4, the *tik*'s shape is remarkably like that of the receptacle carried by the Egyptian scribe in the Eighteenth Dynasty (see pl. 86, 87, p. 92). Some Sefardi communities cover the *tik* with a fabric mantle that opens in the front or drape it with scarves.

The Jews of Europe and their descendants—Ashkenazim—covered the Torah scroll with a fabric case only, which slips over the top, made today of silk or velvet or other fine materials (pl. 116). When the Ashkenazi Torah is read, it lies flat and

Pl. 115. Sefardi Torah. *Tik* (case) Persia, 1873. *Rimonim* (finials) Persia, nineteenth century. Courtesy of the Israel Museum, Jerusalem. Photo: David Harris

Pl. 116. Ashkenazi Torah scroll and adornments. Mantle from Germany, 1749; *rimonim* (finials) Germany, early nineteenth century; *yad* (pointer) Nuremburg, early seventeenth century; silver *tas* (breastplate) Germany, early eighteenth century; ark curtain Glogow (Poland), 1795. Courtesy of the Israel Museum, Jerusalem. Photo: David Harris

uncovered on the reading stand, although its mantle is used temporarily between readings of the sections as a cover. Lifting the two-handled Ashkenazi Torah above the head for the congregation to see after it is read takes a good deal of strength and balance, especially at the beginning or end of the yearly reading cycle in the fall when one roller is almost empty and the other full. If the Torah is dropped, the congregants who witness it must fast for forty days (not nights!). Before the Torah is dressed again with its mantle, Ashkenazim sometimes wind around it a *wimpel,* a long, narrow, cloth binder painted or embroidered with decorations and inscriptions, which had been made for wrapping a baby during his circumcision and afterwards donated to the synagogue.

Since the Middle Ages, both Sefardim and Ashkenazim have adorned the Torah with silver accessories: crowns at the top and finials on the scroll handles, called *rimonim* (pomegranates), sometimes with bells attached. Ashkenazim also hang a shield called a *tas* on the Torah, an ornamental breastplate that indicates which Torah is to be used on festive occasions when there are readings from two or three different scrolls. (To save time, someone has rolled each Torah to the assigned reading before the service begins.)

Because of its holiness, the Torah's parchment and letters are never touched by the bare hand; a pointer is used to keep the place. Pointers, in the past few centuries at least, have a small hand at the tip with an extended index finger. When the reader touches his own finger to the place he is going to read to kiss it before reciting the benediction, he covers his hand with his prayer shawl. Conservation of the book is built into religious practice.

The Medieval Codex

Decoration of the Torah scroll itself, as opposed to its ornamental handles, crowns, finials, and coverings, was forbidden. A Torah with the tetragrammaton YHVH written in gold letters in the time of Ptolemy II Philadelphus (285–247 B.C.E.) was ordered by the rabbis to be hidden away in a geniza, unfit for synagogue use. But by the Middle Ages, Bible codices were illuminated and sometimes prayer books and rabbinic literature were illustrated. While a few rabbis in Germany disapproved of decorating prayer books on the grounds that it was a distraction to worship, the practice nevertheless was popular among those who could afford to commission an illuminated Bible or liturgical book.

Illumination in Hebrew manuscripts reflected the style of the host country in which Jews resided. There were two reasons for this. First, the artists were not always Jewish. Patrons at times contracted with non-Jewish workshops for illustrations in Hebrew manuscripts. The lack of colophons sometimes leaves the art historian in doubt as to the religion of the artist. But there is proof that many of the artists were Jewish, even when the illustrators or decorators did not leave colophons, because instructions were written to the illustrator in Hebrew and because the artist obviously was familiar with the rituals depicted. The other reason for the resemblance of Jewish illustration and decoration to non-Jewish illuminations is that Jews were well integrated into the societies in which they lived, not socially or religiously, but certainly economically and culturally. They always spoke the vernacular of the country in which they resided, although they frequently wrote it with the Hebrew alphabet, which gave rise to Judeo-Arabic (the language of the Cairo Geniza documents), Judeo-Spanish (Ladino, Spanolit, or Castilliano), Judeo-Portuguese, Judeo-German (Yiddish), and Judeo-Persian.

In Islamic countries and in Spain, where artists were not so rigidly organized into religious confraternities (guilds) that Jews could not learn a craft, many Jews were artisans, craftspersons, and artists. Spain in particular depended on Islamic and Jewish artists; Jewish goldsmiths and silversmiths of Spain often worked for the Church. That they were aware of the book arts of their host countries is obvious from the similarity of style in Jewish manuscript illustrations to both Islamic and European styles, and to Christian iconography in Europe, and to secular iconography and geometric, nonfigurative Qur'ān decoration in Arabic manuscripts. Jews also were bookbinders in late medieval Spain and Germany for non-Hebrew as well as Hebrew books. And so we find in France, Spain, Germany, and Italy, Jewish artists decorating, illuminating, and illustrating in the style of their contemporaries. But at times in Spain and Germany, style in Hebrew manuscripts lags about fifty to one hundred years. There are not enough Hebrew illuminated manuscripts from France to generalize on the style gap, and in Italy non-Jewish workshops executed most of the illuminations.

In the Islamic Near East, particularly in Palestine and in Egypt from the tenth through the twelfth centuries, complete Hebrew Bibles or one of the three major divisions were decorated with carpet pages of geometric or vegetal designs, similar to Qur'āns (pl. 117, 118, and 228, 229, p. 269, 270). These elaborate pages of abstract patterns came at the end of the Hebrew codex, along with decorated masoretic treatises. In the Near East, colophons containing the name of the scribe and the patron at times received special embellishment. Because the ornaments and designs are so frequently integrated with Hebrew script, it is assumed that the

Pl. 117. *Shelah Lekha* (Num. 13–16), a weekly Torah reading in small codex format. *a.* Text pages, f. 3v and 4r. *b.* colophon (Isaac ben Abraham Ha-Levi) and carpet page with ansa. Egypt, 1106/7. JNUL Heb. 8° 2238. Courtesy of the Jewish National and University Library, Jerusalem

Pl. 118. Finispiece carpet page of figured *masora* from The Leningrad Codex. Bible written by the scribe Samuel ben Jacob in Egypt, 1009 C.E. State Public Library, Leningrad, Firkovitch B19ᵃ, f. 475r.

illuminators were Jewish. The beginning or end of sections or books of the Bible was occasionally marked with decorations similar to *sura* (division) headings of Qur'āns. The Moshe Ben-Asher Prophet Codex of 894/5 was also one of the earliest dated Hebrew illuminated Bibles, even if it is later than the date of its colophon. It displays at least one carpet page at the beginning and twelve more at the end (the book is no longer bound, so it is uncertain whether there were more frontispiece carpet pages). Some of the blue and gold ornaments painted in early codices were combined with minute script called micrography (pl. 118). Human and animal forms were avoided by Jewish artists in Muslim countries just as they were in the holy book of Islam. But a few early tenth-century Bibles depicted in stylized form architectural motifs or the menora and other ritual implements made for the tabernacle, as described in Exodus, chapters 25–27. These themes in masoretic Bibles were familiar from the synagogues of Palestine, which were still in use after the Islamic conquest of the seventh century. Or these themes may have been copied from earlier codices of which no examples have survived. In Egypt, children's alphabet books were decorated, as were small books of one weekly Torah reading, perhaps meant as gift books for a boy's *bar mitzvah* at age thirteen (pl. 117). Marriage documents, *ketubot,* were also decorated in Egypt from the twelfth century with architectural as well as geometric motifs. In Yemen, Bibles, especially the Pentateuch and an accompanying grammatical treatise, were embellished from the

Pl. 119. Menorah and Vessels of the Sanctuary. Duke of Sussex Catalan Bible. Catalonia, third quarter of the fourteenth century. British Library, Department of Oriental Manuscripts and Printed Books, Add. 15250, f. 3v and 4r. Courtesy of the British Library

fourteenth through the sixteenth centuries. The central rosette in a micrographic carpet page was the most popular motif, similar to the cover design on South Arabian Muslim bookbindings of the same period. In one Yemenite Hebrew manuscript fish were drawn, another has birds. Both are rare for Near Eastern Hebrew manuscripts. Perhaps Jews illustrated secular literature as well in the Near East, such as translations of Arabic classics and the Hebrew literature they inspired. The iconography found in illustrated Arabic literature from Syria sometimes appears in Hebrew manuscripts in Spain.

As European Jewish communities became more successful economically, their manuscripts were richly illuminated in the manner of their Christian neighbors. In Spain, from the mid-thirteenth century to the expulsion of the Jews in 1492, Hebrew Bibles exhibited Islamic-influenced geometric carpet pages, which were placed at the beginning, at the end, and in between the major divisions of Pentateuch, Prophets, and Writings. In Bibles of the thirteenth century from Toledo and Burgos, ornamental carpet pages framed by text were similar to the architectural decoration found in the synagogues of Castile, where geometric designs were surrounded by Hebrew inscriptions (see pl. 113). The similarity of architectural and book decoration is reminiscent of the earlier period in Palestine, where the book-sanctuary pun had been present. Book ornamentation was by no means exclusively abstract in Spain; flowers, birds, and sometimes figurative illustrations related to the text appeared in several magnificent Sefardi Hebrew Bible codices. The menora and vessels of the tabernacle were also popular as a double-page frontispiece to Pentateuchs and Bibles made in Catalonia and Provence (pl. 119). But the kind of biblical narrative cycles that occupied several pages, such as those found in illustrated Latin manuscripts from France, do not appear in Sefardi Bibles. Instead, these scenes, particularly from Genesis and Exodus, were illustrated in the *haggada,* the ritual book that recounts the Exodus from Egypt and is read in Jewish homes on the eve of Passover (pl. 120). Illustrated *haggadot* were especially popular in

Pl. 120. Scenes from Exodus. The Golden Haggada. Barcelona, ca. 1320. British Library, Department of Oriental Manuscripts and Printed Books, Add. 27210, f. 10v. Courtesy of the British Library

Catalonia in the fourteenth century. The iconogaphy and style of many *haggada* illustrations originate in the typical French psalter of the mid-thifteenth century, such as the St. Louis Psalter (see pl. 217, p. 255), or in picture-book Bibles, such as the Pierpont Morgan Old Testament. Mixed with this art from France were stylistic elements from the illuminated manuscripts of Italy and Spain. The decoration of *ketubot,* which had been practiced in Egypt, continued in Spain, but the few surviving examples are not as lavish as marriage documents were to become in Italy from the days of the seventeenth century.

In the latter part of the fifteenth century, there was one workshop in Lisbon producing illuminated Hebrew manuscripts in a sumptuous style as well as a Jewish bookbindery tooling morocco bindings in Mudéjar (Hispano-moresque) style. There is also a late medieval treatise on manuscript illumination written in Judeo-Portuguese. With the exile of the Jews from Spain and Portugal, most of the owners of manuscripts took their books with them to their new countries of residence: Italy, Holland, and lands throughout the Ottoman Empire. Scribes, artists, and bookbinders all went their separate ways. There already had been a tradition of richly illuminated manuscripts in Italy in the late medieval styles of various cities in which Jews lived, even before exiles from Spain joined their co-religionists. Legal works, such as the codes of Maimonides and other rabbinic scholars, were also illuminated in Spain and Italy. Sometimes a book written in Spain or Portugal later was decorated or bound in Italy or another country. As noted previously, in Italy, workshops illuminating Hebrew manuscripts were headed by non-Jews.

Some Sefardi Bible illuminators left colophons, but there are none in *haggadot*. In Germany, a few Jewish artists' colophons appear in a variety of manuscripts. Lack of a colophon in any of these groups does not necessarily indicate a non-Jewish artist. In only a few instances did the scribe also serve as the artist. One Jewish scribe-illuminator, Joel ben Simon, who traveled between Germany and Northern Italy, wrote and at times decorated eleven known manuscripts (pl. 121).

In northern France and Germany in the Gothic age, Hebrew manuscript decoration included more animal and human figures than there were in the codices of Spain. Initial-word panels, the equivalent of decorated and Romanesque historiated initials of Latin Bibles, received elaborate ornamentation, often with the same delightful grotesques one finds in Romanesque manuscripts. Because Hebrew did not undergo the development of capital and small letters, it seemed logical for the scribe to emphasize the first word, which at times was the title as well. Festival prayer books were illuminated more often for Ashkenazim than for Sefardim. Ashkenazi *haggadot* were enhanced in the margins or at the bottom of the page with biblical scenes pertaining to the written text on a specific page. They were not based on Christian iconography, as they were in Spain. Also popular in both Ashkenazi and Sefardi *haggadot* were scenes of preparations for the Passover festival, such as baking *matza,* the unleavened bread, or housecleaning, and the celebration of the *seder,* the ritual meal at which the *haggada* is read (pl. 121). These genre illustrations give us a picture of Jewish costume and customs in medieval Europe.

With the invention of printing, Hebrew manuscript illumination declined, although there was a revival in the seventeenth and, especially, the eighteenth centuries of illustrated *haggadot* in folk-art style in Germany (Bohemia) and

Pl. 121. The Murphy Haggada. Written (Ashkenazi script) and illustrated by Joel ben Simon in Northern Italy, mid-fifteenth century. JNUL 4° 6130, f. 18v. Courtesy of the Jewish National and University Library, Jerusalem

Austria-Hungary. It also became the custom to draw, paint, and engrave illustrations in *Megillot Esther* in Italy, Germany, and Holland (pl. 122). Sometimes the iconographic sources of these eighteenth-century manuscript *haggadot* and *megillot* were illustrations in printed *haggadot,* or woodcuts and engravings in non-Jewish Bibles. Calligraphers and artists today still make *haggadot* by hand, either as manuscripts or as limited edition artists' books.

The most consistent, charming, and original aspect of decoration in Hebrew manuscripts is micrography. Micrography is the art of minute Hebrew script, drawn at first as geometric shapes and later figured into animate forms. From the time of the Moshe Ben-Asher Codex in the late ninth or tenth century, micrography was the most traditional kind of medieval Hebrew Bible decoration (pl. 112). As with Jewish manuscript illumination itself, the shapes delineated by script followed the style of illumination of the age and the host country—geometric, vegetal, and architectural in the Islamic world and Spain; symbolic and figurative in Europe, both in Sefarad and Ashkenaz, with grotesques even more popular than humans in the latter. The pictures drawn with micrographic text seldom were related to the biblical text on the pages in which they were placed, although there are a few exceptions to this in Spain, France, and Germany (see pl. 114). At first, in the Bibles of the Near East, the text used to shape the figures was the Masora (see pl. 112, 118). It was written in margins and at the end in the external carpet pages. *Ketubot* from Egypt were also embellished with micrography. Psalms then became the favored text for the Bible's external carpet page designs in Egypt, Yemen, and Spain. Prayer books were seldom decorated in Spain, but there is a unique *mahzor* (a festival book of liturgical poetry for the New Year) from fourteenth-century Barcelona, with twenty-three preliminary pages and margins illustrated micrographically with heraldic, Islamic, Christian, and Jewish themes, drawn with Psalms, in minute semicursive script (pl. 123).

Scribes continued to use micrography when they decorated *ketubot* in Italy from the early seventeenth century to the present. Small gift books of prayers for special occasions were micrographed, as were single parchment or paper sheets of script-pictures that could be hung in the home. Some were displayed on the eastern wall of the house or synagogue to indicate the direction of prayer. From the nineteenth century, inexpensive lithographed micrographic pictures of biblical scenes and

Pl. 122. Megilla (Esther Scroll). Raphael Montalto, scribe. Holland, seventeenth century. New York Public Library, Heb. Ms. 2. Courtesy of the New York Public Library, Spencer Collection

Pl. 123. Catalan Mahzor. One of twenty-three frontispiece pages with Psalms written in Sefardi semicursive script. Barcelona, second quarter of the fourteenth century. JNUL 8° 6527, f. 4r. Courtesy of the Jewish National and University Library, Jerusalem

heroes, scholars, literary figures, rabbis, statesmen, and philanthropists served as a sort of pop art. Non-Jews, especially European kings, were also portrayed with texts related to their accomplishments. Contemporary Hebrew scribes and calligraphers still practice this traditional Jewish art in written form.

The Hebrew codex changed little during the Middle Ages, developing according to book design and manufacture in the area in which the Jewish scribe resided. If he moved of his own free will or because of forced emigration, he adopted the codicological practices of his new home while continuing to write in the hand he had mastered. Chapter and verse divisions in Latin Bibles eventually found their way into Hebrew Bibles in the Renaissance. All the while, the Torah scribe continued to follow the same talmudic rules as did his ancestors for preparing synagogue scrolls. While the Hebrew book had little direct impact on the medieval European codex, except perhaps on leather-cut German bookbindings in the fifteenth century, its predecessor, the scroll, may have had some influence on the Mediterranean book of late Hellenistic, Roman, and Byzantine days. In those early days, all literature was written on scrolls, and at present we are not certain if the Dead Sea Scrolls reflect universal practices. Or, were these scrolls unique in their time, and did they influence the scrolls of the Mediterranean world? Scholars of the past sometimes accounted for the change from roll to codex in the early years of Christianity as the deliberate Christian break with the Jewish scroll tradition.

Notes

1. Leila R. Avrin, *The Illuminations in the Moshe Ben-Asher Codex of 895* c.e., Ph.D. diss. (Ann Arbor: Univ. of Michigan, 1974), 11–12.
2. Ibid.

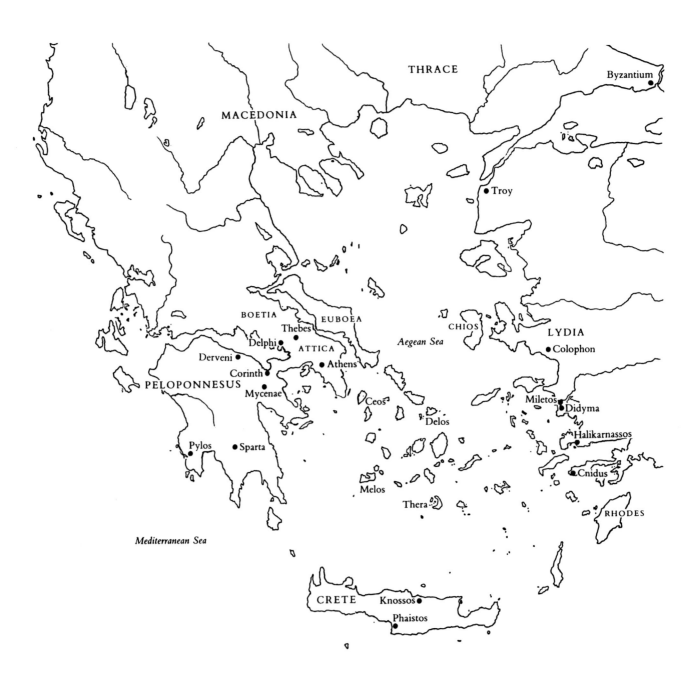

THRACE

MACEDONIA

Byzantium

Troy

BOETIA

EUBOEA

Thebes

CHIOS

LYDIA

Delphi

ATTICA

Aegean Sea

Colophon

Derveni

Corinth

Athens

Miletos

Didyma

PELOPONNESUS

Mycenae

Ceos

Halikarnassos

Delos

Pylos

Sparta

Melos

Cnidus

Thera

RHODES

Mediterranean Sea

CRETE

Knossos

Phaistos

The Ancient Greek World

CHAPTER 6

The Greek and Hellenistic Book

HISTORY AND EVIDENCE FOR THE BOOK

J ust as Greek script came from the outside world, so did the major materials for making books. Ironically, but not illogically, while her literature endured, most classic Greek books did not. This is precisely because the materials for book production were imported; the geographic factors that allowed papyrus to grow and the climatic factors that preserved it were in Egypt, not Greece. And so it is not surprising that what was preserved of Greek books and documents from ancient times should have been found in Egypt. Greek literature written in books also was preserved in other places and in later ages.

In forms of literary expression, the Greek contribution to Western civilization was more varied than that of any other ancient culture. Epics, lyric poetry, drama, oratory, law, politics, philosophy, history, geography, natural history, travel, and scientific description all have come down to us only because someone later took the trouble to copy and recopy them. No one doubts that Greeks of the fifth century B.C.E. (the classical period) read books, yet none of these is left for us to examine. Two recent papyri finds come from the ancient Greek mainland: the first is a carbonized papyrus from the late fourth century found in a Macedonian tomb in Derveni, near Salonika, and is a prose commentary on an Orphic religious poem written in a good calligraphic hand in regular columns. The second is a small, damaged roll found in a tomb in Athens in 1981 and believed to be ca. 450–400 B.C.E. Before these discoveries, the oldest known fragment was from Abu Sir (Memphis), Egypt; it is part of a poem, *Persae,* by Timotheus, from the late fourth century B.C.E. The evidence for most Greek books in Egypt comes from the third century B.C.E. on—the Hellenistic period, after Alexander the Great's conquest, when Greek was the official language. (Table 4 provides an overview of important events and individuals in Greek history.) But the greatest number of books and documents are from the Roman, Early Christian, and Byzantine periods, when

Table 4. Chronology of the Greek World

Period	Dates
End of the Bronze Age	1200 B.C.E.
Protogeometric Period (Pottery)	1100–900
Dorian Invasions	
Migrations	
Geometric Period (Age of Homer)	900–750
Archaic Period (Age of Colonization)	750–500
Athens	
Laws of Draco	621
Solon (expansion of trade and economy)	ca. 600–550
Black-Figure Pottery	620–530
Red-Figure Pottery	530–400
Classical Period	ca. 499–400
Greco-Persian Wars	ended 489
Rebuilding of the Acropolis	from 480 B.C.E.
Development of Greek Tragedy	480–450
Age of Pericles	461–429
First Peloponnesian Wars	430–404
Spartan Domination of Greece	404–371
Theban Domination	371–360
Athenian Writers	
Aeschylus	525–455
Sophocles	497–405
Euripides	480–406
Aristophanes	446–385
Herodotus	485–425
Thucydides	460–400
Socrates	469–399
Plato	427–347
Aristotle	384–322
Rise of Macedonia	359–336
Philip II	382–336
Alexander the Great	336–323
Hellenistic Age	323–30
Hellenistic Writers	
Theophrastus	372?–287
Menander	342?–291
Didymus	80–10

educated Egyptians continued to read and write Greek. Unlike Hebrew books that were preserved through deliberate burial or by hiding in caves, preservation of these Greek papyri was accidental: they were found in excavations of graveyards and garbage dumps. Archival material was saved deliberately, although it is doubtful that clerks ever went back to read what they filed away. The greatest treasure house for the modern scholar of ancient Greek manuscripts was at Oxyrhynchus, a town 125 miles south of Cairo, where papyri were unintentionally mummified by refuse heaps. Excavations were carried out from 1896 to 1906 by Arthur S. Hunt and Bernard P. Grenfell of Oxford, about eight years after Greek manuscripts found by villagers started showing up on the antiquities market. Thus was launched the field of papyrology, the study of ancient literature and the daily life of ordinary readers by means of literary scrolls and nonliterary documents, birth and death notices, marriage contracts, correspondence, and official records. Manuscripts came from cemeteries of other towns of the Fayyum, for when embalmers ran out of linen, they wrapped mummies in papyri that had been thrown away or sold for recycling by government administrators who cleaned out their offices. In addition to the material evidence that comes almost exclusively from Egypt, one must turn to Greek literary sources to see what Greek writers themselves occasionally said about books and readers, to later Byzantine Greek manuscripts that were copies of older works, to Greek sculpture and vase painting of the classical and Hellenistic periods, and to Roman books and wall paintings in Hellenistic style in order to reconstruct the appearance of the Hellenistic book (pl. 124). From these later sources and visual and literary references it must be supposed that classical Greek books were similar. As

Pl. 124. School scenes on a red-figure kylix, painted by Duris. Cervetari, Etruria, 500–480 B.C.E. *a.* A man holds a scroll, with words written in direction contradictory to actual practice. A capsa for scrolls is behind him. *b.* A man writes on a wax tablet; a scroll and tablet are left, above. Antikenmuseum, Berlin, F 2285. Courtesy of Antikenmuseum Berlin, Staatliche Museen Preussischer Kulturbesitz. Photo: Ingrid Geske-Heiden

with the reconstruction of Hebrew books, it is hypothesized that because methods of making books, like script, are traditional, later books reflect earlier practices.

In Greek literature there are sometimes allusions to reading and writing, but not as many as we would hope for and not as many as there were in Roman literature, possibly because writing and books were taken for granted and calligraphy was not yet considered an art. From these meager references we know that although drama and poetry may first have been written down for performance only in the seventh and sixth centuries, by the fifth century there was an Athenian audience who wanted to read plays and other books. From the vast amount, variety, and quality of Greek literature, it is assumed that general literacy was higher in Greece than it was in Mesopotamia and Egypt—at least for its citizens, which did not include slaves, women, and children. The amount of graffiti written in sixth-century Athens also shows that writing was common there. Private letters were written to all parts of Greece and even as far away as the Russian shore of the Black Sea. In law courts, magistrates and secretaries and probably jurors could read and write. The plaintiff submitted his case in writing, and witnesses' testimony likewise had to be written, although professional scribes could have been hired for this purpose. By the fourth century B.C.E., there were written business contracts and ledgers, wills, correspondence, and memoranda. From literary references, today's scholars speak of multiple copies of books and even of a book trade in fifth-century Athens—there seems to have been a special section of the marketplace for selling books. Xenophon, in the late fifth century B.C.E., mentions the export of books from Athens to the area of the Black Sea; by 300 B.C.E., book fairs were held there. Although oral traditions, dialogues, and discussions were essential to Greek education, elementary schools in Athens are assumed to have had book collections, and Plato's Academy, founded in 387 B.C.E., and Aristotle's Lyceum, founded in 335, must have had libraries. Even if they did not, the notes students took recording the works and teachings of their masters—the Sophists—became the books of the future.

MATERIALS

In Solon's day (594 B.C.E.), laws were written publicly on "notice boards." These could have been made of bronze, stone, or painted wood; statutes written on stone were found in Chois from the first half of the sixth century B.C.E. Solon had revised the laws of Draco of 621, which could have been published on similar surfaces. Stelae, or stone slabs, were also inscribed at Athens and set up in public places such as the Acropolis; on them were decrees, treaties, laws, or sentences against lawbreakers (pl. 125). There were funeral stelae as well. One does not see as many inscriptions on the stone buildings of classical Greece as one sees on the later monuments of Rome. Possibly this is because Greek script at that time was not yet perfected, and was not on the same aesthetic level as her architecture and sculpture. Perhaps the Greeks did not yet consider writing to be an art. At the Sanctuary of Apollo at Delphi, built in the last quarter of the sixth century, the polygonal limestone blocks were engraved at a later date with manumission records (see pl. 60, p. 58). The inscribed monument was not as important to the Greeks as it was to become to the Romans. Another kind of stone writing, but writing *with* stones as opposed to writing *in* stone, came in the late classical and Hellenistic periods, when illustrations in the pebble mosaics of Macedonia displayed name labels similar to those on pottery. Mosaics were found at Olynthus (ca. 400 B.C.E.) and at Pella (first half of the third century B.C.E.).

Fine Attica clay also provided two types of writing surfaces for Athenians and other Greeks: painted pottery and ostraca. Writing is often found on black-figure ware, popular from 620 to 520 B.C.E. and often later. From 530, red-figure pottery, also inscribed, was made and exported as well. Greek writing on pottery reads in either direction, depending on the pottery painter's aesthetic sense. Vases show various inscriptions rendered in an amateurish hand: some are the names of gods and

Pl. 125. Laws against tyranny. Decreed to ensure against absolute power. Greek Capitals inscribed in stone, with no word-spacing. Athens, 336 B.C.E. Courtesy of the Agora Excavations, American School of Classical Studies at Athens

heroes depicted thereon, some describe the subject (a sort of title to the work), some are the names of objects or animals. Sometimes the painter explained what the figure was doing or about to do, at other times a person's speech comes out of his mouth in comic-strip fashion. At times there is praise for a youth named on the vase; sometimes the painter greeted the person who picked up the vase. At times the letters have no meaning; this is a phenomenon seen again in the late Middle Ages in the lustreware of Spain, on which meaningless Latin and Arabic inscriptions were written, and in Islamic countries where Arabic letters on crafted objects are so elongated and distorted that decipherment is impossible unless one already knows the repeated formulas. Pseudo-writing existed in all ages, either because the script the artist used was foreign to him or because he was illiterate but liked the idea of written decoration. Letters and marks perhaps used in transactions are sometimes found on the underside or feet of Greek vases, and signatures are also found there or on the handle or rim; these generally were painted before firing. Signatures are rare, but when they do appear, from the second half of the sixth century and the early fifth, they are the names of the potter or painter. At times the same artist fashioned and decorated the vase: "_____ made and painted it." Did scribes sign their works in the same way? Unfortunately we have no Greek scribal signatures until well into the period of Byzantine codices.

As in the rest of the Mediterranean world, an important everyday writing surface in Athens was the ostracon, the recycled broken pot. One use for sherds was for banishing unwanted leaders. This custom was introduced by Cliesthenes, one of the founders of Athenian democracy, toward the end of the sixth century B.C.E. In late winter, when the Athenian assembly thought it necessary, each citizen wrote down on an ostracon the name of the politician he wanted to see leave Attica. Hence our word "ostracize." To get rid of someone for ten years, six thousand of these negative write-in votes were needed (there were about thirty thousand citizens in Athens in 500 B.C.E.). Collections of ostraca actually have been excavated. In one instance 190 ostraca were found on a slope of the Acropolis with "Themistocles" written on them in fourteen different handwritings, which means that citizens either hired scribes to write the name for them, or that the invitations to leave town were prepared by members of an anti-Themistocles political party.

Only a few wax tablets with Greek inscriptions have survived (pl. 126, 127). But wax tablets with their triangular-headed metal styli attached to the outer side of a board can be seen on Greek vase paintings, so they must have been well known (pl. 128, 129). Thongs, drawn through holes, fastened the boards on their inner edges; on the outer edge an additional tie could keep the two closed. In Greek the tablet was called a *diptychon* (pl.: *diptycha*). If there were three boards, they were known as *triptycha*; more, *polyptyca*. They were used for letter-writing, documents, spontaneous notations, and schoolwork. *Diptycha*, used by the Etruscans as well, remained in vogue in Rome, where the Greek name for them continued to be used into the Middle Ages. Whitewashed tablets apparently were common as well. Greeks wrote on tablets with a *stilus*, a pointed instrument made of iron and flattened at the other end for erasures (pl. 135 and 141, p. 151 and 166).

Coins of silver, gold, and bronze, with alloys, were another surface for writing. The Lydians of Anatolia were the first to introduce coinage to the world in about 630 B.C.E. A century later coins were government certified and, as minting became more popular, mainland Greeks spread the practice throughout the Mediterranean world. Athens minted her first coins between 520 and 510 B.C.E. Silver coins of Attica, more in circulation than gold, were brought to a high degree of aesthetic perfection by the early fifth century B.C.E. Many bore inscriptions: the name of a city, a ruler, or a god or goddess. Philip II of Macedonia inscribed his gold coin with his name. Coins were made by stamping, or by hammering cast blanks of metal in a bronze die. Thus coins were the Greek equivalent of printing two millennia before Gutenberg. All nations subsequent to the Greeks minted coins with inscriptions.

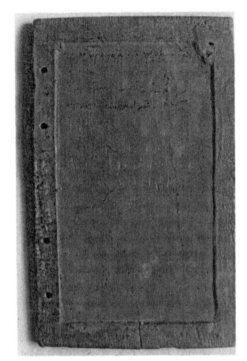

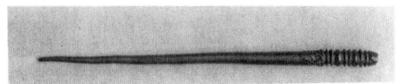

Pl. 127. Stylus for writing on a wax tablet. Egypt, 332–30 B.C.E. Gold. Metropolitan Museum of Art, Carnarvon Collection, gift of Edward S. Harkness, 1926, 26.7.1361. Courtesy of the Metropolitan Museum of Art, New York

Pl. 126. Tablet used by child learning to write. Wood covered with wax. Egypt, first centuries C.E. Wax on wood. Metropolitan Museum of Art, Rogers Fund, 1914, 14.2.4b. Courtesy of the Metropolitan Museum of Art, New York

Pl. 128. Two women, one carries a wax tablet. Red-figure Greek kylix, fifth century B.C.E. Metropolitan Museum of Art, Rogers Fund, 1906, 06.1021.167. Courtesy of the Metropolitan Museum of Art, New York

From the earliest days of Greece, writing appeared on other metals, such as bronze weapons and utensils. The Greeks also used seals made of ivory or stone. Gems, too, were inscribed at times in Greece and Rome.

Papyrus

According to Herodotus (*The Persian Wars* 5:58), the Greeks used papyrus as their primary writing material once the Phoenician alphabet was introduced. He noted that the Ionians wrote on the hides of sheep and goats, as was common among barbarians in his own day. (A barbarian originally was one who did not speak Greek, but undoubtedly the name carried a pejorative connotation.) Papyrus could have been introduced first to the Greek islands, but not used regularly, as early as the

Pl. 129. Youth and teacher, with wax tablet above. Greek red-figure skyphos, Euaichme painter, ca. 470 B.C.E. Metropolitan Museum of Art, Rogers Fund, 1941, 41.162.5. Courtesy of the Metropolitan Museum of Art, New York

Pl. 129. Youth and teacher, with wax tablet above. Greek red-figure skyphos, Euaichme painter, ca. 470 B.C.E. Metropolitan Museum of Art, Rogers Fund, 1941, 41.162.5. Courtesy of the Metropolitan Museum of Art, New York

tenth or ninth century B.C.E., when the Phoenicians first introduced the alphabet. We already know from Wenamon's report that Egypt exported papyrus through Byblos in the early eleventh century B.C.E. But because it was not until after 750 B.C.E. that Greek expansion, trade, and colonization flourished, the late eighth century B.C.E. would be a more realistic date for the first practical use of papyrus on a large scale in the Greek world. Papyrus was known to be one of the important Mediterranean trade items in the seventh century, and it must have been quite common in Greece by the early sixth century. The Greeks who had established their own colonies in Egypt by the seventh century naturally wrote on papyrus.

The name of the Phoenician port town of Byblos (Gubla in Phoenician, later Gebal) is thought to be the origin of the Greek word for the papyrus reed, *biblion,* and for book, *biblos.* Our *Bible* and *bibliography* and the French *bibliothèque* are derived from these Greek words. We shall see that many other book-related materials take their name from their port of trade. Perhaps these modern terms are from the town's name, or perhaps the Egyptian *ppr* sounded like *bbl* to the Greek ear. Papyrus, both leaf and sheet, was also called *chartes* in Greek, which became the term *charta* in Latin.

Hellenistic and Roman papyrus was thicker and not as perfectly formed as it had been in earlier dynastic Egypt, and in general the Greek scroll was shorter and smaller than its Egyptian ancestor. This may have been for practical reasons; certainly each Greek and Latin literary roll had more frequent use than Books of the Dead or panegyric papyri. After all, the Hellenistic scroll maker, who fabricated the whole scroll before selling it to scribes, libraries, or publishers, had to consider his customers. The Hellenistic scroll was usually 17 feet to 30 feet (5 m to 10 m) long, although it could have measured up to 35 feet. The individual sheet was 9 inches to 15 inches (23 cm to 38 cm) wide (across) and 8 inches or 9 inches (20 cm to 23 cm) long, but a few are 12 inches to 13 inches (30 cm to 33 cm). Scrolls with poetry were about 5 inches (13 cm) long (top-to-bottom); 2-inch (5-cm) scrolls were used for epigrams. The average-sized scroll was long enough for writing one play, or two or three short books of Homer's works. The division of the *Iliad* and *Odyssey* into "books" may have been determined originally by the scroll's standard length. The papyrus manufacturer continued to paste sheets into ready-made rolls of twenty sheets in Roman times, no matter what the ultimate purpose of the papyrus would be, with joins overlapping about ½ inch (1 cm to 2 cm), running downhill as did the scrolls of dynastic Egypt so that the scribe's nib would not get caught. In Hellenistic times the Ptolemaic court controlled the manufacture and trade of papyrus. They marked the beginning of each scroll with their *protocol,* a practice that continued in the papyrus trade in the Byzantine Empire (but not in the Roman, as far as we know) into the Islamic period, when there were bilingual protocols in Greek and Arabic. The term *protocol* is still with us today in diplomatic and medical practice.

Tools

The Greeks introduced an innovation in their pen for writing on papyrus. Instead of the thin Egyptian rush, they used a hard, thicker reed pen, *Phragmites aegyptiaca,* which they called Καλαμος (pl. 130). The end of the *calamus* was trimmed with a knife and its nib split. In this way, an even flow of ink was assured. It is always possible that the Phoenicians, when they introduced writing, also introduced the sharpened pen, which was much more suitable for alphabetic script than was the dynastic Egyptian reed-brush. (Some scholars believe that the hard reed was introduced into Egypt in the sixth century B.C.E.) These hard reeds eventually were imported into Greece from Egypt, or from Cnidus in southwest Asia.

Greek ink was ground lamp black, gum, and water, the same as the Egyptian recipe. The Greeks may also have used cuttlefish (sepia) ink, a brown secretion of that octopuslike sea creature, which is still used today as a natural food dye in the Aegean and for gourmet cooking in the United States (pl. 131). (It is comforting to know that drinking ink is harmless—for all of those women who were suspected of adultery and had to "drink the water of bitterness," and even for the prophet Ezekiel and the apocalyptic St. John, who were book eaters.) Both of these inks could be erased with water.

Among the scribe's other tools were his knife, for trimming pen and papyrus; pumice, for smoothing the papyrus before writing or after erasing and for pen sharpening; and a sponge for erasing. The lead disk or wheel for marking off equal spaces for ruling guidelines was probably not introduced until medieval times. Traces of guidelines have disappeared from most ancient manuscripts. Greek scribes could use the horizontal fibers of the papyrus as guidelines, but did not always do so.

Pl. 130. Reed pens. Egypt, from the Coptic monastery of Epiphanios, Thebes, first centuries C.E. Metropolitan Museum of Art, Museum Excavations, 1913–1914, 14.1.259, 14.1.260. Courtesy of the Metropolitan Museum of Art, New York

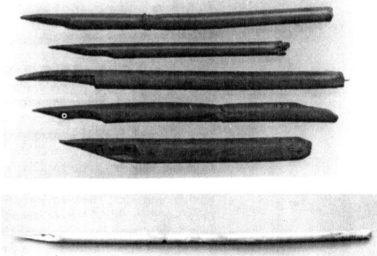

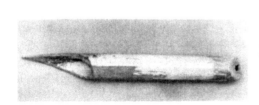

Pl. 131. Cuttlefish, painted on an amphora. The source of sepia ink. Crete, ca. 1500 B.C.E. Courtesy of the Heraklion Museum, Crete

THE WRITING OF A SCROLL

Scholars have determined how the Greek scroll was made on the basis of finds from Hellenistic and Roman Egypt (pl. 132). The width of the column, called *selis* in Greek and *pagina* in Latin, was not uniform for prose; it was about 3 to 3½ inches (7.6 cm to 9 cm) wide, and included sixteen to twenty-five letters. Alexandrian scholars seem to have standardized the column width to 2 to 4 inches (5 cm to 10.1 cm), including the margins. In poetry the column was determined by the length of the line; the unit of measurement was the *stichos,* or hexameter—fifteen or sixteen syllables. There were two or three columns to the sheet, and columns of writing ran over the joins. There could have been twenty-five to forty-five lines per column, sometimes twenty-three in smaller scrolls. When scrolls with text were depicted on Greek classical vases, and later in Hellenistic and Roman art, the open scroll did not show columns at all, but this seems to be an artistic convention, not based on reality (pl. 124a). Similarly incorrect in painting and sculpture, letters and script often run parallel to the rolled sides of the scroll, rather than across it, the way text, in fact, was written. The fourth-century B.C.E. papyrus from Derveni shows writing in columns, the way it always would be in later scrolls. Margins between columns were very small, and at the top and bottom there were usually margins of 1½ inches to 2 inches (4 cm to 5 cm). In Hellenistic scrolls, no attempt was made to justify the right-hand margin; much later the size of the letters was sometimes adjusted to even the margin. Words could be divided at the end of the line for the same purpose. No spaces appear between words. The carvers of Greek and Latin lapidary inscriptions often separated words with dots, as did Semitic stone engravers in an earlier age, but Greek manuscript scribes did not seem to feel this was necessary. Letters were evenly spaced in the book hand, but words ran on and on, except where there was an important break in subject matter. It may seem strange to modern readers that Greek and Latin readers put up with the lack of word spacing for so long. This has been explained by some as a simple matter of aesthetics: The scribe considered spaces between words disturbing to the artistry of majuscule script. Others explain it thus: because people read aloud, the reciter was already familiar with the text and did not require the aid of word spacing to understand the author's verbal flow.

There was no systematic punctuation in the earliest known Greek manuscripts, although some accent marks were used here and there by Alexandrian scholars as an

Pl. 132. Orations of Hyperides. British Museum, Papyrus 115, col. 27–34. Second century C.E. Courtesy of the British Museum

aid in reading continuous script. The most common from the fourth century B.C.E. were the *paragraphos,* a horizontal stroke indicating a change of speakers in drama or a sharp break in prose, usually placed below the start of the first line after the break; and the *dicolon* (:), originally three vertical dots, later reduced to two. A dot at the top (˙), was the equivalent of our period; at midpoint (·), a comma; and at the bottom (.), a semicolon. Sometimes names in a text were dotted above their letters. When a word was dotted, it could be a proofreader's correcting mark, either meaning "delete" or referring to a marginal note. An apostrophe could appear between double consonants or after the final consonant of a foreign (Semitic) word. At the end of a passage the scribe at times prolonged the final stroke of a letter. Columns were rarely numbered, but sometimes each hundred verses were marked, a practice that still exists in the printing of poetry and drama. If the book was meant to be illustrated, the scribe left space for it, according to those who have reconstructed the appearance of ancient manuscripts (pl. 133). The entire question of illustrated Hellenistic literature and scientific works is a hypothetical one, based on Hellenistic and Roman mosaics and painting, and extant late antique codices or fragments (see Chapter 10).

The scroll was sometimes treated with saffron or cedar oil to preserve it or to keep out moths and worms, which dyed it a yellowish color. Sometimes the edges of the papyrus sheets were colored black—a forerunner of fore-edge gilding, not only for aesthetic enhancement but to keep out dust. Some rolls conveniently had a handle, called an *omphalos* in Greek, *umbillicus* in Latin, made of folded papyrus, a reed, ivory, or wood, or gilded wood for a deluxe edition, especially for poetry. When a Greek official or commercial letter was rolled up for mailing, a fiber was drawn from the outside and wrapped around it; then it was sealed with clay. Correspondence and documents were at times folded, which eventually damaged the papyrus. Scrolls, especially fine ones, were covered with fabric; later they had colored leather wrappers fastened with colored strings, and were stored in buckets or covered cases, or on shelves, as they were later in Rome.

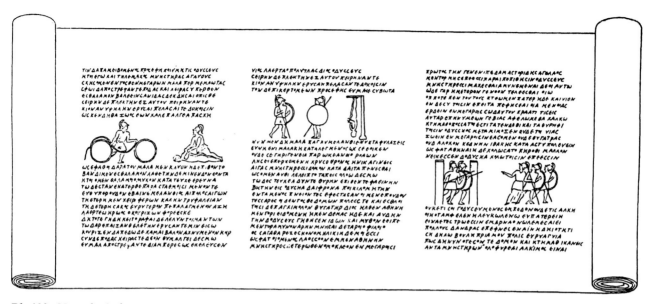

Pl. 133. Hypothetical reconstruction of an *Odyssey* scroll from the third century B.C.E. Reproduced from Kurt Weitzmann, *Illustration in Roll and Codex.* Courtesy of Princeton University Press

The scroll was usually reinforced at the beginning and end with extra papyrus, later with parchment. The title may have been written at the opening or at the end, but too many beginnings and ends of scrolls are missing to tell if this was the common practice. As far as we know, the title at times was on the outside of the roll, opposite the opening. A leather tag called a *syllibos* in Greek, sometimes dyed red, was hung from the middle of the lower edge of the scroll (see pl. 138, p. 161). This tag included minimal information and identification: the owner's name; the total number of columns, *stichoi*, or lines of the book; and, at times, its price. The information on this *syllibos* (*titulus*, or *index* in Latin) could also appear at the end of the scroll as part of the colophon (or *superscriptiones*), or at the beginning, in the *protocol*. The book's name was not always like our modern title, that is, the subject of the work. Homer did not call his books *Iliad* and *Odyssey*. (But in Rome, Virgil did entitle his work *Aeneid*.) Authors like Herodotus and Thucydides described the contents at the beginning of their books. This custom continued in the printed book and was popular in nineteenth-century English novels, and is still with us at times, when the chapter is summarized at its head.

When the Greek writer ran out of fresh papyrus, he washed off the carbon ink from an old manuscript, turned the sheet on its side, and wrote over it at a 90° angle from the erased script. In late antiquity, as papyrus became scarce or expensive, these palimpsests (Greek for "rubbed over") were common. Many old Greek and Latin texts have come to light by reading the bottom layer of the rewritten sheet, especially with the help of ultraviolet or infrared light and photography (pl. 134). The world's record for palimpsests is held by the Codex Arabicus in St. Catherine's monastery in the Sinai desert, with five layers of writing: one in Greek, two in Syriac, and two in Arabic. The term *palimpsestos* was taken over by the Romans, and refers to scraped and reused parchment as well.

READERS AND SCRIBES

We know that there were elementary schools in fifth-century Athens, and we even know something of how students were taught to read. Even if the average Athenian citizen could not read well, he at least knew the alphabet. The richer the citizen, the better the education. Slaves were at times taught to read and write. At school, reading and writing were taught together; the instructor wrote out the letters for students to copy and learn. Syllables were taught after the individual letters were mastered: two-, three-, then four-letter syllables. Lines of poetry came next.

Pl. 134. Palimpsest. Lower text in Greek Uncials, Matthew 2:13–16; later text, upside down, in Greek cursive minuscules, ca. fourteenth century, possibly the theological orations of Gregory of Nazianzus. Trinity College Library, Ms. 32 (Gregory 035), f. 3r. Courtesy of the Board of Trinity College, Dublin

Students were taught to read aloud, and learned music and gymnastics as well as literature. The real purpose of Athenian education was to train the sons of citizens, from age six to fourteen, to have a sound mind and sound body, so that at age eighteen they would in turn become good citizens. From sculpture and vase paintings we know that girls were taught to read and write. They undoubtedly were taught at home by tutors and not in the schools attended by boys. The woman who could read was exceptional; seldom was she encouraged to learn more than she would need for operating her household. After a young man's military service, at about age twenty, higher education was undertaken by the Sophists, paid professors of wisdom. At times Sophists came from foreign countries and were much in demand. They trained Athenians in public speaking (rhetoric—the art of persuasion through oratory) for success in political life. The Sophists and their students were responsible for creating a need for literary works to be copied.

Whether there was training for scribehood in Athens, either for the purpose of reproducing literary texts or for government service, is unknown. Was there a separate training program in calligraphy for students of a certain age group or for students with a fine hand? Were all boys taught the Greek equivalent of the Palmer method and only those whose handwriting did not deteriorate grew up to be literary copyists? Were favored slaves singled out to be future scribes? Did a student learning with a Sophist do scribal work to earn his own tuition when his parents couldn't afford it? Were scribes apprenticed to master scribes? Was a scribe merely an educated drudge who couldn't make it as politician? As yet, nothing is known or can be reconstructed of the careers of classical Greek and Hellenistic literary scribes. In Hellenistic times they undoubtedly worked for authors, teachers, publishers or booksellers, and libraries. Argument still rages among those scholars who care, and the issue may never be resolved, whether Hellenistic scribes in Alexandria wrote from dictation or copied from an exemplar, as did medieval scribes. Some historians have imagined a large scriptorium with a master dictating to the assembled scribes so that a multiple-copy edition could be published. This debate centers around the plethora of mistakes made by Alexandrian scribes. Were they mistakes of the eye, and therefore the scribe copied a text, or mistakes of the ear, and therefore many scribes wrote from dictation to produce multiple copies?

We are not certain, either, how the early Greek scribe sat as he wrote; most portraits are of readers rather than writers. Even when a writer is depicted, he or she is usually posing after the work was completed. After 400 B.C.E., scribes may have had a table or desk, but holding the long prepared scroll open as they wrote, even

Pl. 135. Greek writer with wax tablet and stylus. Sixth century B.C.E. Louvre, Départment des Antiquités Grecques et Romaines, CA 684. Courtesy of the Louvre

Pl. 136. Parian marble funeral relief of a girl, reading. "Avita, who lived ten years and two months, Hail." Unknown provenance, ca. first century B.C.E. British Museum, Department of Greek and Roman Antiquities, *BM Catalogue of Sculpture,* 649 (GIBM 1127). Courtesy of the British Museum

with weights at the sides, could not have been very efficient. At times in Byzantine manuscripts the scribe is represented as standing, holding tablets and stylus, or seated, with tablets on his knees or with a scroll stretched across his lap. But by this time the scribe no longer was writing scrolls, so we must assume the drawing was made with artistic license. Many medieval artists depicted codex writers incorrectly, as if the already bound book were being written, and we know that this was not the procedure. The earliest Greek scribe portrait is presumed to be a terra cotta statue in the Louvre, dated sixth century B.C.E. (pl. 135). If he is a scribe, he must be writing a scratch copy on his wax tablet. In an Athenian relief from the Roman period, now in the British Museum, a woman sits on a backless stool next to a stand with an open scroll on it. She seems to be reading (pl. 136). If ancient Greek scribes really wrote with complete scrolls on their laps, they must have suffered from backache, unless they were trained from an early age.

COLOPHONS

The note found at the end of the scroll eventually was called *colophon,* believed to mean "summit" or "finishing stroke" in Greek, although no one is sure of the term's origin and it may not have been used until the Renaissance. It has been attributed to Erasmus. (Colophon was the name of a town off the coast of Asia Minor.) No Hellenistic colophon with a scribe's name has yet come to light. The major purpose of the Greek colophon in the Hellenistic and Roman periods seems to have been to prove the authenticity of the text copied, not only for its own validity but to emphasize the authority and quality of the text that served as its model. The archives or library or temple in which the original was housed was identified. Jewish authors and scribes in the Hellenistic period and early Christian writers at times used this postscript of verification in their writings as well. For example, in some editions of the Septuagint's book of Esther there is a note that reads:

> In the fourth year of the reign of Ptolemy and Cleopatra (78–77 B.C.E.), Dositheus, who said he was a priest, and Levitas, and Ptolemy his son, deposited the preceding "Letter of Purim," which they said really exists and has been translated by Lysimachus [son of] Ptolemy, [a member] of the Jerusalem community.[1]

Some Hellenistic scribes and Greek-writing scribes of the Roman and Byzantine periods, in their colophons, counted the lines that they wrote, for poetry at first (stichometry) and then for prose as well, and recorded the total. The practice originated as an assurance to the reader or the purchaser of the scroll that the text was copied properly and in its entirety. But line-counting also served a more practical purpose—it determined the scribe's fee for transcribing the book. A comparable practice is still maintained by many printers today, who provide their typesetters with a keyboard and computer terminal at home, remunerating them for their keystroke output. This custom should not seem strange to any author who has been paid by the word or even by the keystroke after an article has been edited and typeset. The computer now does this counting for printer and publisher. In Byzantine times, the Greek scribe's pay was also fixed by the quality of his script. Notaries of legal documents received the lowest pay, while literary scribes using the most beautiful calligraphy were paid the best. During Diocletian's reign (245–316 C.E.), the rates were twenty-five denari per one hundred lines for the finest script, twenty for intermediate quality, ten for a notary's hand. A few colophons also recorded the price of the book. In colophons of medieval Greek Christian manuscripts, the scribe left his name, his patron's name, the date he began or completed the work, and at times the date of the original text from which he copied. He sometimes cautioned the future copyist to write carefully and make corrections judiciously.

Sometimes it is assumed that the colophon came at the end of the text rather than at the beginning because the reader did not usually rewind the scroll for the next reader's convenience. When provided at the end, the author, title, or information on the scroll's contents would be available to the next reader immediately. Only then, if he thought it worth his while, would the reader rewind the scroll to the beginning.

The ancient reader of Greek was inconvenienced in several ways. Holding the scroll open as one read and simultaneously rerolling the scroll in one's left hand, required exceptional coordination. Looking up an exact quotation in a different scroll was totally discouraging. If the scroll fell to the floor, retrieving it was a nuisance, much worse if it ripped. Unless the reader was familiar with the text, the absence of word spacing and punctuation slowed comprehension. When the reader found the scroll with the end of the story first, he or she had to reroll it before having the pleasure of reading the book. No wonder that when readers finished the scroll, they did not rewind it for the next person!

LITERATURE

The Greek book buyer had more to choose from than did any other literate person of the ancient world. Imagine all the tragedies and comedies of classical Greece (some three hundred plays) as well as the writings of historians, philosophers, poets, and orators that Athenian citizens could take off the shelves of their personal libraries, or read in the city library—the *museion* (Latin *museum*). Or imagine what a scholar, who could not afford to buy everything he wanted to read or consult, could see in the library of Alexandria, which was said to have housed seven hundred thousand volumes. Even if one book filled four or five rolls (*volumen* in Latin, from *volver*, to roll), or if Alexandrians exaggerated their library's size, it was still a large collection. The Great Books of the age were Homer's works and, from third-

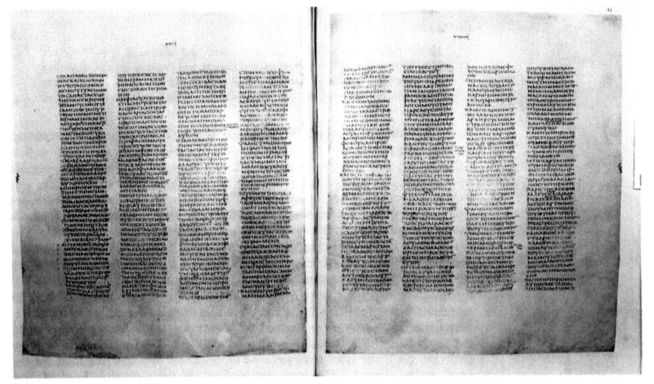

Pl. 137. The Codex Sinaiticus. One of the earliest Greek Bible manuscripts (the Septuagint, and part of the New Testament). Parchment, fourth–fifth century C.E. British Library, Add. 43725, f. 243v and 244r. Courtesy of the British Library

century B.C.E. Egypt and later, the Old Testament in its Greek translation—the Septuagint. The Septuagint not only served the needs of the large Jewish community in Alexandria but was later used by Egypt's Greek-speaking Christian community. Scriptural tales may have been popular among non-Jewish Greek readers even before the Christian era. Some scholars believe that biblical stories may even have been illustrated in Alexandria (see Chapter 10).

The most beautiful extant early Bible in Greek, containing Old and New Testaments, is the Codex Sinaiticus, written in the late fourth century C.E. (pl. 137). Three scribes worked on it; two of them were poor spellers. (It is hard to imagine the Bible being dictated to them!) This codex gives us an early Byzantine example of the Hellenistic type of colophon. The proofreader left a note at the end of II Esdras (Ezra) and Esther that the book was corrected according to a manuscript written by Pamphilus, who used Origen's edition. This would imply that Pamphilus signed his manuscript. The Codex Sinaiticus was in St. Catherine's monastery at Mt. Sinai until 1844 when German Bible scholar Constantine von Tischendorf took a part of it, which he gave to the Leipzig library. In 1859 he took as much of the remaining manuscript as he could find, which he presented to the czar of Russia. Tischendorf reported to the world that the leaves of this precious manuscript were being burned when he saved the first part, and that he removed the larger part for study with the permission of the monastery's prior. The Soviet Union sold the Codex Sinaiticus to the British Museum in 1933 for £100,000, a true bargain price when compared to a 1983 auction record of $11.7 million for a twelfth-century manuscript, even considering inflation. The Codex Sinaiticus today is on display at the British Library where its label perpetuates the legend that the manuscript was saved from destruction by Tischendorf's timely arrival. The monks at St. Catherine's know otherwise. During restoration of the monastery in the late 1950s, Tischendorf's original 1859 letter was found in which he promised to return the "borrowed" codex after he completed his study. The letter and its English translation now hang on the library wall at the monastery. The tale of the

Codex Sinaiticus is but one of many that demonstrate how manuscripts sometimes change owners.

Greek literature continued to be copied in both the Roman and Byzantine empires. More of it has been preserved from Byzantium because Greek continued to be the spoken language there, and because the Byzantine court continued to patronize secular as well as religious literature. Educated Romans were bilingual during the period of the late republic and early empire, and some Greek literature was translated into Latin, but little of it was preserved in medieval Europe. Before the twelfth century, only a fourth-century translation of Plato's *Timaeus* and Boethius's version of some of Aristotle's works on logic were known in the West. But during the twelfth century the number of translations from Greek increased. Greek literature became popular in the West again only with the Renaissance, when Byzantine scholars fleeing from the conquering Ottoman Turks found an audience for Greek learning in Italy. In an earlier age the Arabs, too, had appreciated and translated Greek mathematics, medicine, philosophy, and science, and some Greek works reached medieval Europe through Hebrew intermediaries and translations accomplished in Spain.

HELLENISM AND THE BOOK

Athens had scorned Philip II, his son Alexander the Great, and the Macedonians, whom Athenians considered semibarbarians. But Alexander, whose teacher was Aristotle, always had a soft spot in his heart for Athens. Alexander was thoughtful enough to send back to his teacher examples of the local flora and fauna of conquered lands. Alexander's ambition for world conquest was not solely for the purpose of spreading Hellenic ways, but he and his heirs did much to introduce Greek culture to the peoples they subdued. The Greek language in its Hellenistic form, the *koine* or *dialektos,* became the international diplomatic language from the late fourth century B.C.E. to the sixth century C.E. (much longer of course in the eastern Roman Empire). In this way, Greek served as had Akkadian in the second millennium B.C.E. and Aramaic in the first, until Alexander the Great's victories. The Hellenistic empire was much larger than any previous Near Eastern realm, extending from the western Mediterranean to central Asia. One could find a Greek identity as far away as Afghanistan, where Delphic maxims were copied. Even for lands not conquered by Alexander, trade with India and the Far East was established, with mutual religious and artistic influences.

The Hellenistic *gymnasia* of the cities in the rival empires carved out by Alexander's generals, from Alexandria to Babylon, were modeled on Greek education. These schools inculcated Greek physical and intellectual values in upper-middle-class youth. Greek schools in Egypt taught athletics, music, mathematics, and language. School texts included maxims, fables, little stories of the lives of famous persons, and some history. Boys started school at age five, and girls were also admitted to elementary schools. Advanced studies took place from ages twelve to fifteen. These students continued to learn language and history, and also composition, mythology, genealogy, and rhetoric. (In the Byzantine Middle Ages, the function of the school was to train civil servants.) For the reader of Greek, new authors were added to the classical reading list: the philosopher and natural scientist Theophrastus, and writers of comedy such as Menander. Encyclopedic works, descriptive works on botany and zoology, and texts of mathematics and medicine also were written. So were romantic novels. Some copies of books were written in an amateur hand; some are believed to be scholars' personal copies because they are the most accurate textually, and some were luxury editions. An author had no copyright on a book. The only motivation for publishing was to ensure that a correct copy of the work circulated, rather than a distorted, pirated edition. But once the book appeared on papyrus, it was virtually an invitation for publishers to market their own editions of the original. Authorized works naturally were of higher prestige than nonauthorized ones and brought higher prices, especially if they were autographed by the author. In Hellenistic times, a book cost two to four drachmas. That could be anywhere from one to six days' wages for an unskilled laborer (who would not be buying books even if he could read). A luxury edition or an antique book could cost up to 750 drachmas. Old books could be faked by burying them in grain. "Antiquing" books seems to have been a phenomenon of the trade from the time of Egyptian papyri to today's sophisticated forgeries.

Hellenistic rulers had chanceries to draft decrees and laws and to keep records. Each ministry as well as the military and the local governor must have had its own secretaries and archivists as well. We get a glimpse of these from what has survived and been excavated in Egypt. Because Greek was the official language there, even the most minor officials were literate. As with all governments, bureaucracy only gets heavier, and from the second century on, the Egyptian variety became less and less efficient.

Pergamum, on the Caicus River in northwest Asia Minor, not far from the coast of the Aegean Sea, became the second cultural capital of the Hellenistic world because her rulers, the Attalids, who were related to Alexander's successor Lysimachus, were patrons of learning and the arts. The Pergamenes, like the Alexandrines, preserved and promoted Greek culture, but were hated by the mainland Greeks for their consistent alliance with Rome. Apparently Pergamene scribes and those who employed them were more interested in copying and teaching philosophical works than were their counterparts in Alexandria. Other Greek cultural centers arose or persisted in Hellenistic times where books undoubtedly were published: Rhodes, Antioch, and Athens.

PARCHMENT

The name *parchment,* or *charta pergamena* as the new material was called in Latin, came from its city of trade. The name exists in Greek as well. Pliny told the story (*Natural History,* 13:21), quoting Marcus Varro (116–27 B.C.E.), that competition existed between Ptolemy V Epiphanes, ruler of Egypt from 205–185 B.C.E. and Eumenes II, King of Pergamum from 197–159 B.C.E., as to whose library was the greater. Ptolemy halted the export of papyrus to Pergamum and thus forced the people of Eumenes' capital to invent the substitute material. It is doubtful that Pliny's and Varro's tale is true (Pliny also believed that papyrus was invented in Alexander the Great's time, and that there was no Egypt in Homer's day, so there could not have been papyrus at such an early date!). In Pergamum, hides were imported from the region of the Black Sea and made into *pergamena,* parchment. Pergamum gave the product its name in the same way that other book materials acquired their names—the color "sinopia" from Sinope, and "morocco" and "cordoba" from those well-known North African and Spanish centers of leather production.

Among the documents found at Dura Europos (a border town between the Roman and Parthian empires destroyed and thereby preserved in its own rubble in 245 C.E.), there were several works written on a leatherlike material. A few of these are believed to be from as early as the second century B.C.E. They have been called parchment, although these fragmentary writing surfaces do not seem to be any closer to the early medieval product than are the Dead Sea Scrolls. Because the Dura manuscripts are damaged, it is difficult to ascertain the material; an Aramaic fragment now in the Bibliothèque Nationale (Suppl. grec 1354–2 IV) is congealed and looks almost like plastic, if it were not for the hair holes. We do not know if Eumenes' animal skins were similar to medieval parchment or to the *gewil* of the Dead Sea Scrolls, or if the names *pergamena* or the Latin *membrana* were used for the earlier leather and then transferred to true parchment at a date as yet undetermined from lack of evidence. Several translators and scholars of the twentieth century have confused the issue by calling all ancient animal skin parchment or even vellum, no matter what process was used to prepare the hide for writing.

The refinement of animal skin into parchment could have come at any time or place in western Asia or southern Europe where animal husbandry flourished and where leather had already been used as a writing material: Mesopotamia, northern Greece, Persia, Palestine, or Pergamum. For Egypt there would have been no motivation to refine leather to the whiteness or thinness of parchment when papyrus was still plentiful and cheap to manufacture, and where leather rarely was used for scrolls. But in Asia, where the importation of papyrus must have been costly, it took some ingenuity and experimentation to realize that goatskin, calfskin, or sheepskin could be treated and worked in a manner different from the long-known tanning procedure, in which the hide was treated with liquid derived from oak galls. In medieval European parchment making, after soaking hides in quicklime to remove the hair or wool, the skins could be stretched, scraped, and treated with chalk—powdered limestone—throughout the soaking and stretching and scraping stages, resulting in a thin, white writing surface (see Chapter 9). As yet, there is no proof that the Pergamene parchment makers knew of the lime-assisted process. The impact of *pergamena,* whatever its process of manufacture may have been, on the Mediterranean book may not have been noticed until Roman and Christian times, and so tradition attributed its invention to Eumenes.

The manual labor required to make both papyrus and parchment was considerable, and the popularity of either depended on the availability of labor and raw materials, consumer demand for the product, price, long tradition, and even its prestige. Early Christian writers in Rome and then in Byzantium may have preferred parchment at first simply because of its availability and not because of its low cost or the association of papyrus with pagan literature. By the fourth century, the Church could not have helped but notice that parchment endured much longer than papyrus. By that time, the material had grown in prestige because the Church had gained in status, and because the Church already was beginning to serve as both publisher and patron.

Note

1. Elias J. Bickerman, "The Colophon of the Greek Book of Esther," *Journal of Biblical Literature* 63 (1944): 362.

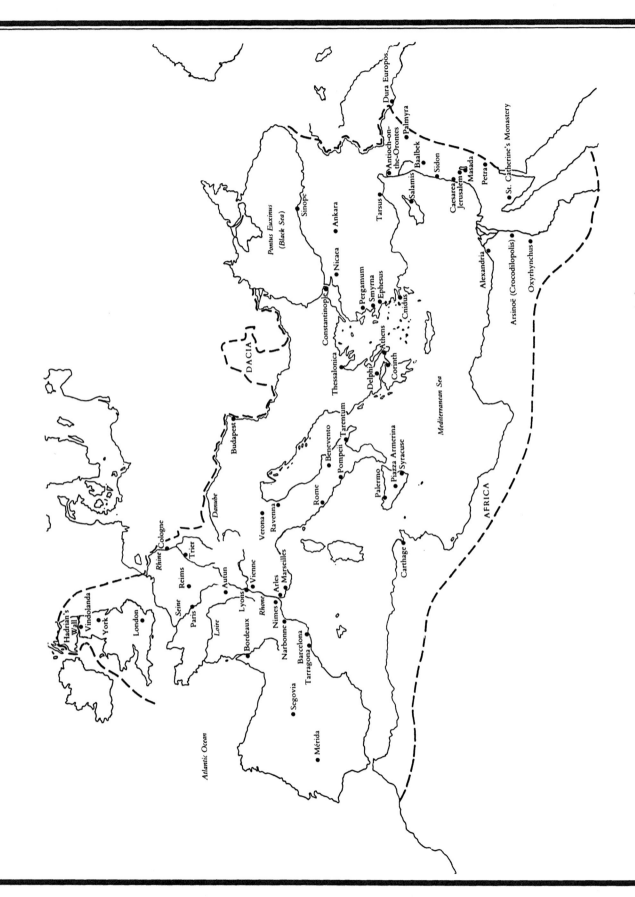

The Hellenistic and Roman World. The boundary lines encircle the Roman Empire in the second century C.E.

CHAPTER 7

The Roman Book

HISTORY AND LITERATURE

Roman books continued many of the traditions of the Hellenistic world, but eventually bookmakers modified the design and utilized the new Pergamene material, and thereby changed the course of book history. There are many more references in Roman literature to the making and selling of books than there had been in Hellenistic writings. Pliny the Elder was a major contributor to our knowledge but not always a reliable one, for he mixed observation with folklore.

The world that Rome ruled was even larger than the empire left by Alexander the Great, even if the latter had not been divided. One would then expect the form and subject matter of Roman script and books to have had a much wider influence. This is true for the European world of writing and books. Whereas the Greek language and Hellenism continued to predominate in much of the Near East, the western Roman Empire, even after successive barbarian invasions, remained Latin in its language, script, and literature. The Latin tongue gave birth to Romance languages, the Latin script to monumental and manuscript Roman hands and later to Roman typography. Script in books developed into minuscule letters, while the capitals on Roman monuments inspired duplication in Italian Renaissance calligraphy and printing. Although it was the pagan Roman Empire that gave Europe and eventually the New World its basic script, it was the Roman Catholic Church that shaped it. This is why the peoples who converted to Catholicism write with Latin script, and those who were converted by Byzantine monks write with adaptations of Greek script. The Church also gave Europe and Byzantium the parchment codex, but, like writing, it did not give books to everyone. Education was in the hands of the Church, primarily in the monastery. The ordinary person had almost no opportunity to learn to read or write, and would not have had many opportunities to see books.

From the beginning of her history, Rome seemed to have loved the law, more so than any other subject that could be written down. While admiring Greek literature and, for the most part, imitating its forms and style, Rome never proved to be as original as her predecessors in literary forms or thoughts. Some writers have remained important to Western culture: Virgil, Ovid, Martial, Horace, Pliny the Elder and the Younger, Seneca, and others. But law seems to have been the consuming passion. In the middle of the fifth century B.C.E., the first written law code was inscribed on bronze tablets set up in the Roman Forum—the "Law of the Twelve Tables." These remained so basic that, even in the first century B.C.E., schoolchildren still committed them to memory. Today only fragmentary copies remain. Laws proliferated with each government—republic and imperial—although by the second century C.E. it was the emperor's laws rather than the senate's which were to be heeded. Romans drafted laws by committees; they wrote laws of warfare, treaties, legal textbooks, religious laws. Historical annals as well as myth and legend were important to Romans, beginning with tales of Rome's foundation. As told by Virgil, Rome was first established after wanderings and hardships by the Trojan Aeneas in the twelfth century B.C.E. Other legends claim Romulus (d. 717) as the founder of the village on the Palatine, one of the seven hills of Rome. After they first conquered and then joined forces with the Sabines, the Latins in turn were vanquished by the Etruscans, who ruled over what was transformed into a true city in the seventh and sixth centuries B.C.E. The Etruscans' most lasting gift to Rome was the alphabet—if not the shapes of the letters, which the Romans could have derived from a western Greek version, then probably their names.

Rome grew in military strength, first conquering the rest of Italy and then challenging the other great powers of her day. By the end of the second century B.C.E., she encompassed most of the Hellenized world and then some. Spain became a province in 197 B.C.E. Carthage (Phoenicia's one-time colony that became a major power in the Mediterranean), Africa, Macedonia and the Achaean League, Sardinia, and Corsica were incorporated by Rome by 146 B.C.E. The empire of Pergamum, whose kings traditionally had been allies of Rome, became her Asian province when Attalus III died with no heirs. Britain was added in 43 C.E. Table 5 provides an overview of periods, emperors, and writers in Roman history.

Each province Rome conquered and each colony she founded was given its own written constitution, which was relatively uniform throughout the empire but allowed for local variations. The provincial governor, appointed annually by the Roman senate and later by the emperor, was the chief administrator, fiscal secretary, and head of the supreme court of justice. While the coffers of Rome expanded with the wealth of lands it conquered, the cities who had sided with Rome were accorded tax breaks and other privileges of citizenship, and maintained a certain amount of independence in running their own affairs. As the Roman world grew and her armies became more loyal to their generals than to the city-state, republican Rome found herself unable to control her vast territories. The machinery of the emperors proved to be more effective. During the early empire, the government was well centralized at Rome.

The first emperor, Augustus, established a new institution which eventually changed the character of the empire—the Equestrian Order. Admirably democratic in its time because it gave former noncitizens and commoners the opportunity to advance politically and socially, it ultimately was one of the factors contributing to Rome's downfall.

New literary forms appeared in imperial times: the satire of Lucilius; tragedy and comedy by Plautus and Terence; oratorical and historical writings by Cicero, Julius Caesar, and Sallust; and the philosophy of Lucretius. But for the most part Roman literature was a sterile imitation of the Greek. The Golden Age of Roman imperial literature came during the reign of Augustus, when the emperor's friend Maecenas was a major sponsor; his name has become a metaphor for patronage. Even when literature was Roman in subject matter, Greek classical style was imitated. This can be seen in the works of Virgil, Horace, and Livy. Along with other spoils taken back to late republican and imperial Rome were books, especially from Athenian and other Greek private libraries. Captives at times were educated and sometimes professional Greeks displayed scribal talents. They often proved their ability to teach the much-admired Greek language, script, and literature to children of Roman citizens. Roman education, like art and literature, was Hellenic in character for a few centuries. Literate slaves also served as a work force for publishers (near-free scribal labor—they did have to feed them).

There are few extant Roman inscriptions from before the first century B.C.E. For the physical remains of Roman books in the early empire we are fortunate to have a source other than Egypt: the towns engulfed by the eruption of Mt. Vesuvius in 79 C.E. The towns that the lava, ash, and mud preserved, especially the thriving middle-class town of Pompeii but also the suburban villa communities of Herculaneum, Boscoreale, and Boscotrecase, have yielded evidence of daily life, wall paintings of intelligentsia posing as readers, and books themselves (pl. 138, 139). The oldest Latin literary text, *Carmen de Bello Actiaco*, was found at Herculaneum. From the remains of Pompeii, urban Roman history of the first centuries B.C.E. and C.E. lies before us. Commerce, industry, construction, the economy, religious life, art, and leisure activities of its citizens were all frozen in time by the hot lava. Inscriptions of names, election posters, and graffiti tell us about trade associations, politics, and trivia. Wall paintings show us illustrations of classical Greek and Roman literature and religious rituals as well as pictures of writing materials and implements, books and their readers, even a child reader.

Pl. 138. Magistrate and his wife holding scroll and codex. Wall painting from Pompeii, before 79 C.E. National Archeological Museum. Courtesy of Museo Archeologico Nazionale, Naples. Photo: Art Resource, New York

Pl. 139. Portrait of a lady who poses with codex. Wall painting from Pompeii, before 79 C.E. National Archeological Museum. Courtesy of Museo Archeologico Nazionale, Naples. Photo: Art Resource, New York

Table 5. Chronology of the Roman World

Period	Date
Early Republic	6th c. B.C.E.–264 B.C.E.
Expansion in Italy	485–265 B.C.E.
Middle Republic	264–133 B.C.E.
Punic Wars (against Carthage)	
Late Republic	133–31 B.C.E.
Early Empire	31 B.C.E.–193 C.E.
Late Empire	193–235 C.E.
Military anarchy, disintegration	235–270
Recovery	270–337
Constantine the Great	324–337
Fall of the Western Roman Empire	395–500
Emperors	
Augustus	27 B.C.E.–14 C.E. (Golden Age of Literature)
Tiberius	14–37
Gaius (Caligula)	37–41
Claudius I	41–54
Nero	54–68
Vespasian	69–79
Titus	79–81
Domitian	81–96 (Silver Age)
Trajan	98–117
Hadrian	117–138
Marcus Aurelius	161–180
Commudus	180–192
Septimius Severus	193–211
Caracalla	211–217
Illyrian Emperors	270–284
Diocletian	284–305
Constantine	324–337
Julian	361–363
Valentinian	364–375 (Brother Valens in Eastern Roman Empire)
Theodosius I	379–395 (Made Christianity the official state religion)
Justinian	527–565 (Eastern Roman Empire)

One papyrus library of scrolls was found in the 1750s at the "Villa of the Papyri" in Herculaneum, a town which was engulfed by oozing mud rather than by the volcanic ash that took Pompeii. Some thousand works on papyrus were excavated there. Many manuscripts of this villa were carbonized beyond restoration, but many were decipherable. Nearly all of them were in Greek, with only a few in Latin. The charred remains were broken off bit by bit, held up to the light, and copied, because their opaque, shiny black ink stood out against the black carbon surface that once had been papyrus. Before examining the scrolls, scholars anticipated revealing the reading habits of these suburban Romans. To their disappointment most of the carbonized library proved to house the works of a minor Epicurean philosopher, Philodemus, a teacher of Virgil, and his school. Philodemus, who came from Gadara in Palestine, was a friend of the wealthy Lucius Calpurnius Piso (Julius Caesar's father-in-law), and the villa is assumed to have belonged to him. Perhaps

	Date
Authors	
Plautus	254–184 B.C.E.
Terence	195–159
Lucilius	ca. 180–ca. 102
Cicero	106–43
Julius Caesar	100–44
Lucretius	99–55
Sallust	86–34
Catullus	84–54
Virgil	70–19
Horace	65–8
Livy	ca. 59 B.C.E.–17 C.E.
Martial	ca. 40–104 C.E.
Ovid	43 B.C.E.–17 C.E.
Seneca	4 B.C.E.–65 C.E.
Plutarch	ca. 48–122 C.E.
Tacitus	55–116
Pliny the Elder	23–79
Pliny the Younger	61/62–ca. 112
Juvenal	67–after 127
Dioscorides	40–90
Ptolemy	127–151
Galen	129–199
Donatus	fl. 353
Origen	186–254
Eusebius	ca. 264–340
St. Gregory of Nazianzus	329–389
St. Basil	ca. 330–379
St. Jerome	340–420
Pamphilus	d. 309
St. Augustine	d. 340

the philosopher Philodemus, who also wrote erotic, sexist poetry, had been a guest. (The Villa of the Papyri is the one whose reconstructed plan was copied for the J. Paul Getty Museum in Malibu, California. In 1987, archaeologists returned to dig at the Villa of the Papyri, an extremely difficult site to excavate because of the nearly impenetrable mud layer, which now has a rocklike layer on top of it from a 1631 eruption.) Piso is believed to have gone back, as some successful Pompeiian homeowners did, to recover objects from his villa, but he experienced the same frustration as the eighteenth-century archaeologists. Some scholars feel the Greek Epicurean collection is only a small part of the library, and there are many Roman works as yet to be uncovered. Among the finds was a group of wax-tablet deeds and tax receipts, 127 of them in one box, most of them triptychs. Of the other eighteenth-century finds, there still remain to be deciphered about eight hundred scrolls, most of which are now in the National Library at Naples. A few are on exhibit at the National Archaeological Museum. In the 1820s, eighteen documents were sent to England in exchange for kangaroos for King Ferdinand IV's zoo.

MATERIALS

Papyrus

Papyrus scrolls continued to be read, with the same inconvenience of Hellenistic days, until they were almost completely abandoned at the end of the third century C.E. Much of the book terminology we use today is based on Latin, some of which was borrowed from Greek and transferred from scrolls to codices when the change in format occurred.

Pliny and other Roman writers noted the various grades of papyrus available, which were named according to their quality, strength, size, and whiteness. There were ten grades in all, from *chartae regiae* (*charta* from the Greek), the best (later called *Augustus*) to second-best *Livia,* in honor of Augustus' wife, down to the coarse *emporetica* (from the Greek for "merchant")—merchants' papyrus, used as wrapping paper. Each grade also had a specific width for the individual sheet, measured in digits (about 1½ inches, or 4 cm); the best was thirteen digits, the cheapest, six digits. The names of the grades changed with the emperor, or at times were designated by the location of the factories, for example, *Amphitheatrica,* nine digits wide, was named for the factory at the amphitheater in Alexandria. These official sizes of papyri do not always correspond with the sizes of scrolls found. Pliny tells us that if the imported papyrus was not good enough, it could be improved upon by the workshop of Fannius and upgraded to first quality. Emperor Claudius I did not like the transparency of Augustan papyrus, so he ordered its manufacturers to make the vertical layer thicker. Twenty sheets still made up the roll in the first century C.E. Enormous amounts of papyrus were consumed by Roman administrative offices. In Egypt, in the third century C.E., 434 rolls were used in one month. In Dura Europos, archives filled ten rooms.

The Romans called the inside of the scroll *recto* (meaning the proper side or ruled), the outside or back, *verso* (*verso folium* meant turned leaf). In the beginning only the shinier recto side was used, as in Egyptian dynastic and Hellenistic practice. An *opistographus,* a scroll or document written on both sides, was considered inferior, because literary scrolls were not planned with writing on the verso. When the form of the book changed from scroll to codex and both sides of the surface were used, recto came to mean the first page, the right-hand side of the book's opening, and verso was the overleaf, without the connotation of right or wrong side. Those who study medieval manuscripts still use these terms today for enumerating leaves, as opposed to using page numbers, for example, f. 1r, f. 2v, and so forth.

The elder Pliny noted that papyrus did not last more than two hundred years, and that was considered rare; Galen claimed three hundred years. Pliny also noted that in the time of Tiberius, when there was a papyrus shortage, the senate appointed supervisors to oversee its distribution so as not to upset life. This shows not only how dependent the government was on the material but that it did not occur to them to substitute parchment. Although with time papyrus proved to be less durable than parchment, it seems to have had a higher status in imperial Rome. Parchment (*membrana*) was considered coarse and common, as it may very well have been when it was first imported or manufactured there. Pagan scribes and publishers were the major buyers of papyrus; Jews were restricted religiously to using animal hides. In Rome, Christian writers may have used parchment because they did not have easy access to papyrus; in Egypt, where there was a good supply, Christians did use papyrus for their codices.

In Rome, when the scroll rods (*umbillici*) made of ebony, ivory, and gold had projecting handles, called *bullae* or *cornua,* the latter term was used interchangeably with *umbillici.* (*Cornua* is from the Hebrew *qeren,* the horn of an animal.) Few rollers

Pl. 140. Etruscan stylus. Bronze. Antikenmuseum, Berlin, Inv. Misc. 7265. Courtesy of Antikenmuseum Berlin, Staatliche Museen Preussischer Kulturbesitz. Photo: Julia Tietz-Glagow

from Hellenistic and Roman times have survived. Scrolls were stored in an open or covered box or case, called a *capsa* or *scrinium* (the latter portable), or they were laid on open shelves or in wall cases with pigeon-hole dividers, called *nidi* (birds' nests). Portable cases were made of leather, wood, or metal; some of them were decorated. Leather mantles were called *paenula,* from the Greek word for cloak.

Tools and Other Writing Surfaces

Descriptions and comments made by Roman and early Christian writers, scrolls and fragments of them, tablets, actual writing implements (pl. 140), Pompeiian and other wall paintings preserved by Vesuvius, and evidence from Egypt's Roman period all add to our information on tools and writing surfaces other than papyrus. Stone was a major writing surface. Workshops undertook the responsibility for designing the script and layout and for carving inscriptions in Greek and Latin. They advertised these services. Model books apparently were used for standard inscriptions. One large papyrus cartoon (the full-size working drawing) with monumental-sized Rustic Capitals was found in Egypt. Inscriptions were colored in, usually with red pigment, occasionally with gold. From the fourth century, one calligrapher of inscriptions is identified by name—Furius Dionysius Filocalus.

Exactly when did the Romans write on the inner bark of trees? Did they ever make paperlike sheets by beating the inner bark, as did the Mayans of Central America? The Romans must have seen or used this surface some time in their early history, because "bark" is the meaning of *liber,* which came to mean "book." Pliny the Elder (*Natural History,* 13:21) said that, before papyrus, people used to write on tree barks, *arborum libris.* Cicero and Virgil both used *liber* with this meaning; other writers used it for "treatise" or a "book-in-series." *Liber* was the basis of the Latin words for "bookseller" and "scribe" in republican days, then for the "scribe" alone, *librarius,* whether slave or freedman. Cicero called the bookcase *librarium.* Eventually *liber* became the French *livre* (book) and *librairie* (bookstore) and the English "library." Trees could not suffice for long as a writing surface in a literate urban culture with such a complex government structure, but the name persisted. Linen was also mentioned as a writing surface, *libri lintei.* Stone, bronze, and wood were the three major surfaces for official documents of the republic and early empire.

Pliny informs us that folding tablets made of lead were used for official documents and sheets of linen were used for personal ones, along with the ever-popular wax tablets: *diptycha, triptycha,* and *polyptycha.* A nine-board (eighteen-page) wax tablet was found in Egypt. The small tablet with one or two triangular handles, the *tabella ansata,* was common enough in Rome to have inspired its depiction as a frame for inscriptions on larger monuments. (The *ansa* lives on as the name of the Italian news agency.) Ordinary diptychs were used for correspondence, dictation, and writers' first drafts (pl. 141). Extremely thin wooden tablets made of birch or alder wood, some thinner than .25 millimeter, of several panels folded face-to-face, were found at Vindolanda in England, where there was a Roman fortress in the late first and early second centuries c.e. Ink was used for writing. The Mediterranean equivalent, made of lime wood, was not mentioned until the middle of the third century.

Some *tabellae* without handles were quite luxurious, their outer boards covered with gold or silver or made of carved ivory (see pl. 142, 143). Holes were drilled in the ivory tablets so that thongs could be strung to fasten them, or they could be held together with clasps. Ivory tablets were used to commemorate special events, such as a wedding, or were given as gifts to friends when a high official was installed, especially in Constantinople where diptychs were distributed by consuls from the fifth century, until that office was eliminated by Justinian in 541. Consular diptychs would have double portraits of the consul himself or simply a decorated inscription with his name. Other luxury ivory diptychs show the poet and muse (pl. 17, p. 12),

Pl. 141. Roman administrator, with tablet. So-called altar of Domitius Ahenobarbus. Marble. Rome, ca. 100 B.C.E. Louvre, Départment des Antiquités Grecques et Romaines. Courtesy of the Louvre

Pl. 142. Ivory Codex. Diptych of the Consul Justin, with medallions of Christ, the Emperor Justinian, and the Empress Theodora. Constantinople, 540. Courtesy of Früh-christlich-Byzantinische Sammlung, Staatliche Museen Preussischer Kulturbesitz, Berlin-Dahlem

Pl. 143. Diptych of Boethius, an ivory codex. Rome, 487. Commissioned by Nario Manlio Boethius, father of the philosopher Boethius. Museo Civica, Brescia, Avori Inv. n. 5. Courtesy of Museo Civica, Brescia

Pl. 144. Inside of Diptych of Boethius: Miniatures of the Raising of Lazarus (*left*), and Sts. Jerome, Gregory, and Augustine (*right*). Underneath, bishops' and other believers' names. Early liturgical use of a consular diptych; ca. seventh–ninth century. Courtesy of Museo Civica, Brescia

poet and audience, mythological figures, or, when their owners were Christians, subjects from the Gospel. Luxury diptychs that survived into the Middle Ages were reused in several ways. Lists of martyrs could be written in the wax or incised in the ivory of the inside panel where wax had once been (pl. 144). Some of these *diptycha* had sheets of liturgical music pasted to them and were carried in Church processions. Some became the decorative panels of book covers.

In imperial times, when a soldier was honorably discharged from the army, he was awarded his diploma on a bronze *diptychon*. If he was not already a citizen, army service enabled him to become one. He was entitled to join the Equestrian Order, without having to be a member of a "good family." The bronze discharge diploma was inscribed with an extract from a longer document of privileges granted former soldiers, which had been posted on a public building or at the Roman Forum. It provided a land grant and allowed him to contract a legal marriage. These awards were a way of attracting men to army service once the draft was disbanded. *Diploma* (the term originally a Greek one), besides being military discharge certificates, were also letters of introduction issued to travelers by a Roman governor to facilitate the safe journey of the bearer, according to Cicero's usage of the term. Mosaics, coins and medals, pottery, and gems were also surfaces for inscriptions from time to time in the Roman Empire.

The stylus (*stilus* in Latin, from Greek) for writing on wax *tabellae* or *pugillares* (that which can be grasped with the fist), was at times made of ivory. More frequently it was of bronze and other metals, sometimes with a cast figure on one end for embellishment. If there was no figure, the end was flattened to serve as an eraser. Metal pens also may have been used in the beginning of Rome's history, but apparently were given up in favor of the Greek split hard-reed pen for writing on papyrus. Scrolls could be carried in the portable *scrinium*. The scribe's other equipment included a ruler and a single or double inkwell—one for red and one for black. Ink (*atramentum*) was mixed with gum and water, as before. Pliny affirmed (*Natural History,* 13:20) that the best gum came from Egyptian acacia, that it was far better than almond, cherry, or plum, and that it cost three denarii a pound. The wood of pitch pine or resin was sometimes burned for making black ink, but soot also was collected from the furnaces of factories and baths. At times soot was mixed with calcinated wine lees. Another source of ink was the brown secretion of the cuttlefish, *sepia* (Latin, from the Greek term; the name of both the sea creature and the ink). Compressed sticks of ink and colors were kept in small bags. When mistakes were made, or if the scribe wanted to turn an old manuscript into a palimpsest, the ink was washed off with vinegar, scraped, and rubbed again with pumice and chalk so that all traces of the old script would vanish as far as the naked eye could discern. The Roman writers Catullus, Cicero, and Plutarch all told of the practice of making *palimpsesti* on papyrus and wax tablets; the Talmud forbade their use in Torah scrolls, and in 692 C.E. the Council of Trullo issued a canon condemning the use of Bible manuscripts as palimpsests. But the latter practice seems to have continued. Of some 250 New Testament manuscripts from that period, one-fifth are the bottom layer of palimpsests. Erasing on stone was accomplished with the chisel, and was done when Romans wanted to forget about an unpopular emperor's reign. Ordinary mistakes in stone were often ignored; one simply did not color in the letters.

No illustrated literary rolls from Roman antiquity have been preserved, if they existed at all. But scholars, particularly Kurt Weitzmann, have made hypothetical reconstructions on the basis of literary and mythological themes illustrated on Greek pottery and depicted in Roman mosaics and wall paintings from the towns around Vesuvius (see pl. 133, p. 149). Virgil's portrait was known to have been drawn and painted in his works published in Rome, and he appears between two muses on a Tunisian mosaic (pl. 145, 146). Scientific and didactic treatises required explanatory figures; the earliest fragment of a work on geometry with diagrams comes from the first century B.C.E. Narratives of the Hebrew Bible lent themselves to depiction as well; the extensive illustrated cycles of scriptural subjects in the earliest known illuminated Christian Bible codices indicate that there may have been prototype scrolls illustrating stories from the Septuagint. Historical picture scrolls with no text were also a Roman phenomenon. We have seen previously that Assyrian kings published visual narratives of their triumphs on palace walls (see pl. 66, p. 67). So, too, the Column of Trajan in the Roman Forum recorded the emperor's earlier victory over the Dacians in a stone relief scroll that winds around the column twenty-three times. But no text ran along with the scroll. If a Roman wanted to read about it, the library was right there overlooking Trajan's Column. The later column of Marcus Aurelius (180–190 C.E.) similarly showed his conquests in scroll form. The style of some of these scenes, with masses of soldiers in battle, is similar to that found in one of the earliest extant codices, the Ambrosian Iliad.

PUBLISHERS, SCRIBES, AND READERS

Orators and writers seemed to have had scribes who followed them around taking dictation. Julius Caesar had seven scribes. When Vesuvius erupted and Pliny the Elder took a boat to rescue friends and to get a closer look at the volcano that was to take his life, he had someone along with him to write down his observations.

Pl. 145. Mosaic portrait of Virgil flanked by Muses of Epic and Tragedy. Sousse, Tunisia, second–third century C.E. Courtesy of Musée du Bardo, Le Bardo, Tunisia

Pl. 146. Virgil with scroll and capsa, from the Virgilius Romanus. Rustic Capital script. Fifth century. Vatican Library, cod. lat. 3867, between the fifth and sixth Eclogue. Courtesy of Biblioteca Apostolica Vaticana, Vatican City

(Pliny the Younger did not accompany his uncle on this final mission because he was busy finishing some other writing task the latter had assigned to him.) For classical Greece one can imagine a possible book trade, for Hellenistic Egypt, "trade copies" (the none-too-correct books), but for late republican and early imperial Rome, one can speak confidently of publishing as big business. At first, both scribes and booksellers were called *librari*. *Scribae* originally meant all persons who wrote for their livelihood, but in middle and later imperial times, when copyists came to be called *librari*, *scribae* became the term for personal secretaries of individuals or for public servants who worked for magistrates. *Scribae* were free citizens who could be accountants or archivists for the Senate, or work for financial, military, or municipal administrators. They were members of *scribae questorii*, which was divided into different branches. Some of these scribes were *apparitores*, secretaries of the senate. Although theoretically they had an annual appointment, they usually kept their jobs for life.

Publishers and booksellers also were called *bibliopola*, from the Greek root for papyrus and book. We do not know at what point *bibliopolae* had to start paying copyists for their labors; certainly it must have driven up the cost of producing a scroll. As with Hellenistic production methods, it has also not been determined if Roman literary scribes copied a text that was before them, or if someone dictated to a group of them to bring forth many copies simultaneously. Trade copies of Latin books issued by publishers were filled with mistakes, like their Greek counterparts.

Literary scribes wrote in the formal book hand, but government *scribae* wrote in documentary and cursive scripts. Punctuation was present at times, but still was not standardized; readers complained that they didn't know where a sentence began and ended. In early Latin manuscripts, sometimes words were distinguished from one another by dots as they had been on lapidary inscriptions, but later Latin scribes gave up this considerate practice, possibly under Greek influence.

Several prominent Latin writers, like scribes, originally were captives from other provinces. One such captive was Terence, master of comedy. He is believed to have written out copies of his own works for distribution. But after his time, authors did not act as their own scribes. The vast amount of literary production in all parts of the Roman Empire in both Greek and Latin—history, drama, epics, poetry, philosophy, science, practical agriculture, grammar, and law—implies an active profession of publishers and booksellers. Several publishers from the first century C.E. are known by name: Q. Pollius Valerianus, Tryphon, Vicus Sandeliarius, Atrectus, Secundus, and the Sosii Brothers. The publisher Dorus was mentioned by Seneca, and Polybius was his own publisher. Cicero's publisher was Titus Pomponius Atticus; he came from a higher class family than the ordinary Roman publisher and bookseller. As with the Hellenistic book, there was no copyright, not even for the publisher, and the author received no royalties. He depended on the generosity of a patron to finance the publication of his book. For this sponsorship, the patron received a dedication from the author. Once an authorized copy left his hands, it was open to plagiarism and piracy, just like ·Greek writing in Hellenistic times.

In the late fourth and early fifth centuries C.E., manuscripts were produced by the literary circle of the Symmachi, the followers of Symmachus (ca. 340–402), one of the greatest orators of his time (Symmachus held a high state position at one time and was proconsul in Africa and consul in Rome). The Symmachi were staunch supporters of pagan literature in a growing Christian environment. In the manuscripts they copied, there would sometimes be a colophon with the names of a copyist and a corrector, and the place of writing. There are more extant Latin colophons than Greek ones, but they do not appear until the fourth century. The colophon was very short, with the reviser's or corrector's name being the most prominent because he was a scholar and was considered from a literary point of view to be the most authoritative figure in book production after the author. Place or date or both were also given at times: *Ego Torquatus Gennadius emendaui feliciter.* ("I, Torquatus Gennadius, have corrected it successfully.")

In Cicero's day, the first century B.C.E., bookstores were located in the Roman Forum. Authors sometimes came to these shops to recite their works, and readers as well as writers came to browse, gossip, and buy. Even provincial towns like Brindisi, Ilerda (Lérida, Spain), Carthage, Lyons, and Reims had bookshops, anxious to keep up with what was being read in the capital. Both new and secondhand books were sold, more of the latter as the empire declined. Advertisements and book lists were posted on pillars or circulated. Not all readers had their heads in the books of Virgil, Pliny, or Julius Caesar; Romans wrote and read grade B and X-rated books as well. There were many private libraries and about twenty-eight public ones in Rome by the fourth century; the largest one in the Forum housed Greek and Latin collections, shelved separately. Children were taught to read and write, not to become scribes but to grow up to become "intelligent readers." Most families of means had a library in their suburban villas and in Rome, whether they read their books or not.

Because Rome admired Greek culture so much in the first centuries after conquest of the Hellenistic kingdoms, the government had no objection to the continuation of Greek language and script in the eastern provinces and in Egypt. And so these areas were never Latinized as were the European provinces. Political and religious distinctions between the two parts of the empire became more exaggerated as time went on, but differences in language, script, and culture were a basis for the eventual division, which was hastened by Constantine's establishment of the "new Rome" at Byzantium in the fourth century.

EDUCATION

As Rome expanded her empire and an increasing number of persons became eligible for citizenship, it was necessary to educate them. In the second century C.E., soldiers became citizens as soon as they enlisted. In the days of the late republic and early empire, Greek was considered a necessity by Rome's educated citizens. Because of this, much Greek vocabulary, including terms of book production, entered Latin. Greek slaves or freedmen were tutors to the children of citizens, probably at home, while students received their Roman education at schools (pl. 147). Girls were educated in Rome, more so than they had been in Greece, and their status at

Pl. 147. Roman school in Gaul. Sandstone relief. Neumagen, ca. 200 C.E. Courtesy of Rheinisches Landesmuseum, Trier. Photo: H. Thörnig

maturity accordingly was higher. Undoubtedly they were taught at home. In addition to the Greek libraries and literate slaves that came with the spoils of conquest, Greek teaching methods were adopted. A Roman boy's schooling began at age seven. First he was taught to read and recite the letters, in all combinations; syllables came next, then words. Literature was introduced when he was eleven. Rhetoric, oratory, poetry, and philosophy were cultivated.

The Equestrian Order, introduced by the Emperor Augustus and standardized by later emperors, allowed provincials and foreigners, barbarians and slaves to climb the social, economic, and political ladder. As a reward, usually for army service, the status of Equine was bestowed by the emperor on those he felt were deserving of it. The Equestrian Order provided a nonaristocratic or senate-approved pool from which the emperor could draw civil servants or imperial advisers, and even provincial governors. Judea, for example, was an Equestrian province, and Pliny the Elder was an Equine who had both a military and administrative career under Vespasian. The senate, virtually stripped of its legislative powers in the second century, became less and less important in conducting the affairs of empire, and its aristocratic members withdrew to their enormous landed estates. Italy itself eventually declined in importance in the imperial scheme. It had been these aristocrats who were the promoters of Greek-based education and, with their absence from Rome as a book-buying public, publishing and selling waned.

The upwardly mobile Equines may have admired Greek literature in the beginning but, as time went on, new generations of them were not the readers that earlier Roman citizens had been. Greek was not helpful on the European front. The high standards set by Greek literature for early Roman writers no longer were part of the cultural consciousness in the late empire. There were fewer authors, fewer books, and hardly any trade to speak of for Greek or Latin works. Aristocrats, however, still valued education, even in the fourth and fifth centuries, and there were still schools in Rome, Milan, Athens, Antioch, Alexandria, Bordeaux, and Carthage, where rhetoric and literature of the past continued to be studied. Newer writers in Greek were read: Ptolemy in mathematics, astronomy, and geography; Dioscorides in the field of pharmacology; Galen in medicine. Some of the best writings of the late empire were historical in nature, including biographies of the emperors.

Meanwhile, the body of Christian literature was growing, from the apologists of the second century to political-historical writers such as Eusebius of Caesarea in the fourth century. Preachers and commentators, such as St. Basil of Caesarea, St. Gregory of Nazianzus, and St. John Chrysostom of Antioch, wrote and were being read in the eastern empire. In the western empire, St. Jerome's Vulgate, the Latin translation of the Old and New Testaments, became the standard version for medieval Europe. St. Augustine, theologian and author, was another favorite of the Roman Catholic west.

In the beginning, the Roman army was the main force behind the spread of the Latin language and script throughout the western empire, especially on the Iberian peninsula and in Gaul, and in the Danube area that is now Romania. Latin was not only the official language of local government but also the *lingua franca*. If the common people clung to their former languages, or were bilingual, they generally did not write their barbarian tongues, because few of them wrote at all, and eventually the spoken languages died out (except for the Basque, Catalan, and Welsh regions, where native tongues persisted). The *writing* of Latin was therefore of key importance in its preservation as a *spoken* language. Eventually this phenomenon gave us Romance languages.

When barbarian invaders established their own kingdoms at the expense of the Roman Empire in the fifth century—the Visigoths in Spain and southern France and the Franks in Gaul—Latin still remained the language and script of administration. The Church reinforced the use of Latin by the preservation of its own literature and liturgy in that language. Education was soon to be almost exclusively in the hands of the Church (the exceptions being Jews and Muslims), as was bookmaking. Once Christianity became the official and only legitimate religion of the empire under Theodosius (395), the Church, now wealthier, became full-scale consumers of parchment and the makers of parchment codices, which gained in prestige along with the Church. Christians had used parchment before Christianity was tolerated, but in those early days it was second choice, evidently considered inferior to papyrus by publishers and their non-Christian patrons.

When literacy, book production, and the Roman economy declined with new waves of barbarians in the sixth century, any remaining sellers of new books in Rome must have closed shop. For a few centuries used books only seem to have been available, and rare books fetched high prices. Old books at times were forged for the rare book market; one way of aging them was to bury them in the ground. Plundered manuscripts from Italian monasteries, and whatever remained of great private and public collections, became available to ecclesiastical and royal shoppers from the monasteries of England and the Carolingian court.

FROM SCROLL TO CODEX

The major change in the structure of the book, from scroll to codex, occurred at the end of the first Christian century. Whereas earlier cultures in Mesopotamia, Greece, and Etruria from time to time used luxury or ordinary wax tablets, Romans wrote on *pugillares* or codices regularly, for personal letters, dispatches, schoolwork, authors' first drafts, diplomas, notices, documents, and especially for legal matters (hence our legal "codes" and "codicils"). Polyptychs, fastened together like our three-ring notebooks, numbered up to ten tablets. For convenience, in the first centuries B.C.E. and C.E., *membranae* sometimes substituted for wood panels. There is no Greek precursor for the Latin *membranae; dipthera* simply meant "hides" until the meaning was extended to notebooks. Martial said *membrana* was used for classical literature as well, but we have no examples from such an early date. Quintillian (ca. 30–100 C.E.) mentioned that students used *membranae* for lecture notes. The first person to do this probably did not think himself an innovative book designer. We do not have examples from this date to tell us whether *membrana* was made in the manner of the parchment we know from the Middle Ages, or whether it was like the thin leather of the Dead Sea Scrolls. But scholars such as C. H. Roberts and T. C. Skeat consider ca. 100 C.E. as the date for the first parchment codex.

The Roman Empire had a well-developed postal system. Officers at the far frontiers of the empire, where there were either wars to fight or defensive measures required to repel advancing barbarians, needed to be in constant communication with central command. Civil servants also were sent out to administer these areas, and governors had to keep in touch with the emperors who appointed them. Trajan, for example, corresponded with Pliny the Younger when the latter was governor of Bithynia. Although papyrus was shipped to all parts of the empire, it may not have been quite so accessible at the northern and western borders. The postal service undoubtedly discouraged cumbersome wooden tablets (what bureaucrat could limit himself to a one-*diptycha* report?), so one may surmise that *membranae,* thin animal skins, leather, or parchment began to replace wooden *tabellae* even in the first century B.C.E. Many scholars are now of this opinion.

The first reference to the codex as the form of a book was made by Martial. Parchment codices were particularly suited to the traveling missionaries of the early Church, but pagan writers also commented on their portability, noting that fragile papyrus scrolls should be left in the library. The codex also could be concealed more easily than a scroll, when necessary. In addition, it was far easier to find a quotation by consulting an Old Testament codex than to search for the exact wording of a proof-text in a cumbersome scroll. Another advantage of the parchment book was that both sides of the sheet could be written on without difficulty and without prejudice against the author or publisher for being cheap.

The earliest Christian Bible codices that have been preserved come from Egypt, sixteen of them on papyrus. Seven were of the New Testament, but there were also parts of the Pentateuch, Isaiah, and Psalms, the favorite scriptural books of early Christians. These were not written in the scribe's formal book hand known later from monastic scriptoria, but in a neat documentary script. Undoubtedly they were made for the use of the Egyptian Christian community by its own members. Papyrus codices were prepared with their quires gathered first for binding, then they were written upon, just as papyrus scrolls had been premanufactured. The exact number of lines per page was not always planned in advance for the whole codex, as they were to be in later codices. The missionary activity of St. Mark, who may have written his Gospel in codex form, and the influence of the Roman Church on Egypt have been suggested as the reasons for the early introduction of codices into the community there. From second-century Egypt, all of the surviving Christian works are codices, while non-Christian codices represent only 2 percent of the manuscripts found. This statistic has led to the conclusion that pagan works continued, due to their conservatism, to be written on scrolls.

The structure of the papyrus codex often differed from that of its parchment counterpart. In the gathering of papyrus leaves, sheet was placed within sheet. There could be two to eighteen leaves per gathering, but a quire of ten to twelve leaves was the most common. (One codex has a gathering of fifty-six sheets, or 112 leaves.) In the parchment codex, the sheet was folded, usually once, but if the skin was large or the manuscript very small, it could be cut in half and then folded again. There was usually one column per page in the papyrus codex, which gives it the appearance of a modern book. Some early codices display numbered pages, but pagination, like the one-column layout, was dropped by the Middle Ages. In planning the papyrus book, the manufacturer arranged the leaves so that recto faced recto, and verso faced verso. The medieval scribe had the same aesthetic sense when he matched the hair side of the parchment to hair side, flesh side to flesh side.

Papyrus was not as suitable a material as parchment for the bound codex, because folding and sewing weakened it just where it needed to be the strongest—at the spine. After many years, those papyrus codices fortunate enough to have withstood time and the elements had to be reinforced at the spine with parchment. As the quality of papyrus and its production and export from Egypt declined in the early centuries of Christianity, so did the scroll production. The nature of the materials, then—papyrus and parchment—had much to do with the form the book ultimately took. Folding papyrus made it brittle, so the scroll form was better suited to it. Sewing ruined it. Parchment could not be pasted easily and permanently, but sewing suited it, especially in the fold, and did not weaken the material if the book was bound properly. The parchment scroll was quite heavy, as we know from Hebrew Torah scrolls. A scroll written on both sides was neither practical nor aesthetically pleasing. Far more text could be written on a codex of approximately the same size as the bulkier scroll.

Even though Christian scribes did not consider the roll a proper form of book, they still clung to earlier traditions of layout. Although some of the first books display one column per page, the finest early and nearly complete Bible codices extant today (from the fourth and fifth centuries) were planned with three or four columns per page (see pl. 5, p. 4, and pl. 137, p. 154). When one opens an early Christian or Byzantine luxury manuscript, such as the Codex Sinaiticus, one sees eight columns across two pages, which gives the impression of an open scroll. Another Greek Bible manuscript, the Codex Vaticanus, of the middle or late fourth century, was written in three columns per page. The earliest Hebrew Bible codices from the tenth to the twelfth centuries show three columns per page. Later the number was reduced to two in both Hebrew and Latin European Bibles. Today the two-column tradition still exists in Bibles, dictionaries, and encyclopedias. The latter are frequently paginated by column rather than by page for quick reference. Was the two-column layout retained because the narrow column is easier for the eye to scan? Today's book designer may rationalize it in this way, but an underlying reason is that tradition always dictated that a Bible and a dictionary should be in two columns.

The parchment codex is often considered a Christian innovation, associated with the city of Rome where St. Mark wrote his Gospel. This location is emphasized by both C. H. Roberts and Paul Needham. In the early years of Christianity it was the professional scribes and publishers in Rome who had access to papyrus scrolls. Christians would not have been using their services or buying their pagan books because they were not interested in the subject matter. Some historians have asserted that Christians could not afford the expensive papyrus, but C. H. Roberts points out that we have no information on the relative cost of *membrana* and papyrus. Christianity was illegal and Christians were often persecuted, and missionaries kept a low profile. In recording their own literature they were left to their own devices, and therefore they could have been more practical and, in the end, more creative makers of books. Parchment notebooks (*dipthera*; we have already seen that the Greek term passed into Hebrew and Aramaic) used by Jews and new Christians therefore were the models for Gospel books and writings of the early Church fathers.

So while book evolution from roll to codex and from papyrus surface to parchment began in the first centuries B.C.E. and C.E., and the popularity of the parchment codex grew steadily in the second and third centuries C.E., the parchment codex as *the* form of luxury manuscript was not firmly established until the fourth century C.E. Constantine the Great, in 331, ordered fifty Bibles to be written on fine parchment by professional scribes for the churches of Constantinople, according to Eusebius in his *Life of Constantine*. St. Jerome reported that books of the decayed and damaged libraries of Origen and Pamphilus were recopied onto vellum. And an edict of the emperor Valentinian in 372 noted that scribes wrote codices for libraries. It must be remembered that when we speak of *membranae,* parchment, and vellum in the early Christian and Byzantine periods, we are uncertain of their manufacture. We do not know whether the hide was still treated with tannin, as leather is, or whether lime was used in its manufacture, as it was in European parchment after the eighth century. But unlike leather, both sides of the sheet were used.

Papyrus did not disappear altogether from the European continent. A few literary works were written on it in the sixth century, and it was still used for official documents by the Merovingian kings of France in the sixth century, for deeds in France in the seventh century, and for commercial documents in Ravenna between the fifth and tenth centuries. It apparently was in daily use in the papal chancery until the middle of the eleventh century. The last papal bull written on papyrus was dated 1057, but there are even later references to the use of papyrus in the pope's chancery. All the while in the Near East, papyrus remained the standard writing material, especially in Egypt, where it was the surface for official documents, business accounts, and correspondence well into the Islamic period, until paper began to replace it in the late eighth century.

While we must thank the Romans for our codex form of book, it was the Christian Church that provided the magic combination of parchment and codex to make the medieval book in Europe and Byzantium the vehicle of knowledge and the object of beauty it was to become.

Latin Script

All formal alphabets of antiquity were majuscule, or big letter, alphabets. Now we call them capitals or uppercase letters. Small letters, or minuscules, now termed lowercase, developed in the Middle Ages. We call them uppercase and lowercase letters because in typesetters' cases the capitals were housed in the compartments above, the small letters below. Even though few typesetters still assemble letters from cases into composing sticks, the terms uppercase and lowercase have remained. The term *capitals* comes from the monuments on which Roman inscriptions were carved, although the words were not necessarily written on that architectural component.

Latin script on monuments is closely related to the book hand at the beginning of Latin bookmaking, during the late days of the Republic and early days of the Roman Empire, and at the end of manuscript making, when the introduction of printing fixed Roman letters in their typographic form. There were further developments in calligraphy after the Renaissance, sometimes in conjunction with typography, sometimes for the sake of handwriting alone. The study of script in monuments is called epigraphy; the study of script in manuscripts is called paleography. Table 6 lists the major script styles and the dates of popular use.

CAPITALS

Square Capitals

Roman script at its finest can be seen in the famous inscription at the base of the Column of Trajan in the Roman Forum, dedicated in 114 c.e. (pl. 148). Do these letters appear to be perfect to us because there is some objective standard of beauty in script, or is it because our eyes are accustomed to seeing them as printed capitals in our books? It is no accident that these letters are identical to our bookface capitals;

Table 6. Script Styles and Dates of Popular Use

Script Style	Period
Square Capitals	ca. 1–500
Rustic Capitals	ca. 1–500
Uncials	ca. 300–900
Semi-Uncials	ca. 400–900
Hiberno-Saxon	ca. 680–850
Caroline Minuscule	783–1000
Gothic	ca. 1150–1500
Bastarda	ca. 1200–1500
Humanistic	ca. 1400–
Cursive Humanistic (Italic)	ca. 1400–
Copperplate	ca. 1600–
Foundational	1916

when the first printers of Italy and the best of twentieth-century typographers sought models, they were inspired by the monuments of imperial Rome. Nor is it an accident that the letters were flawless in their own day. Stone carving was a highly developed craft in Rome, as emperors wished to immortalize their deeds and declare the glory of the empire. All facets of the inscription were planned and executed with the goals of clarity, legibility, and balance. When the legend on the Column of Trajan is read from below, all of the letters appear to be the same size, but a photograph taken directly opposite shows that the size of the letters gradually diminishes from the top to the bottom rows, from 5⅓ inches (13.5 cm) on the uppermost line to 3⅝ inches (9.2 cm) below. The letters are perfectly rounded and shaded. Some scholars and calligraphers believe that in order to achieve the appearance of shading, the letters were planned, before the stone was chiseled, by painting them with a brush or double pen, which would account for the graceful

Pl. 148. Roman Square Capitals on a monument. Column of Trajan. Roman Forum, dedicated 114 C.E. Photo from cast in the Victoria and Albert Museum, London. Courtesy of the Victoria and Albert Museum, London

thick and thin lines of the curved letters (*C, G, O*, and *Q*,), and the bowls of the *B, D*, and *P*. In calligraphic and typographic terminology, *shading* means the contrast of thick and thin strokes of the letter. If a brush or broad-nibbed reed were used for planning the design, it was held at a slight slant, which would account for the thinnest part of the *O* being slightly off center. Rounded letters are not natural to stone carving, which has led some to the conclusion that Roman capitals must have been perfected first in manuscript books, and then copied by the monuments' designers. We lack evidence for this theory, however. The beauty of the best Roman inscriptions lies in the perfect balance of discipline and freedom. While most of the letters appear to have been worked out geometrically with ruler and compass, other letters show the spontaneity of an artist's hand, unregulated by measurements or theories.

Attempts have been made by contemporary calligraphers and paleographers to reconstruct the ductus of the late antique and medieval scribe, that is, the direction and order of the strokes of each letter. But there is no consensus for any of the script styles. The tradition of handing down a style from master to pupil was broken at various times in history. At critical stages both in the Middle Ages and in modern times scribes had to teach themselves anew how to write a script that had ceased to be in practical use, drawing on what they saw in old manuscripts.

The edges of stone-carved letters would have been left rough by the chisel if not for the final vertical and horizontal finishing strokes. These are called *serifs*, from the seventeenth-century Dutch word *schreef* (stroke). The first serifs to be found in Roman inscriptions are from the early second century B.C.E., but by that time they were already in existence in Greek lapidary inscriptions. By the first century B.C.E., serifs were common in Latin monuments. These two aspects of Roman Capitals, serifs and the shading of letters, were to become important aspects of type design. In imperial Latin inscriptions, words were not spaced but were separated by dots. When carved, the dots looked like triangles ▼ ▲ ; a few resembled inverted commas ◣ , and in the first century C.E. a small leaf appeared as a divider ◆. This inspired Italian Renaissance printers (pl. 162, p. 195), and the leaf as a divider and paragraph mark is still found in modern fine printing (pl. 149). The *J, U*, and *W* did not exist in monumental Square Capitals.

Square Capitals, or *Capitalis Quadrata*, called majuscules, also gave their name to the first formal book hand (pl. 150, fig. 17). The dates of their use are usually given as 1–500 C.E., although the earliest Latin manuscripts and fragments to display this handsome script can be dated only to the third, fourth, and fifth centuries. Greek capitals can be found much earlier in papyri from Egypt but without serifs. In general, Greek script underwent the same development in styles as did Latin, except that it lacked Half-Uncials. It is natural that Roman capitals would look slightly different when written with a reed pen, the *calamus*, on papyrus and parchment from the way they appeared when incised on stone, even if the letters originally were copied from stone inscriptions. The contrast between the thick and thin strokes of the letters is more exaggerated on the softer writing surface. The vertical and major diagonal strokes, such as those in the *M, N*, and *V*, are emphasized. Serifs are also slightly flourished in manuscripts, even though they are very thin. The letters *F* and *L* rise slightly above the top line, and at times the substroke of the *V* and the tail of the *Q* extend slightly below the lower line. The horizontal bar of the *A* is exceptionally thin, at times nonexistent. A page or a new subject may begin with an enlarged letter, a rudimentary initial. Dots between words are dispensed with most of the time, but spaces have not yet taken their place. The scribe wrote Square Capitals very slowly, holding the nib of the pen parallel to two guidelines. Majuscules took up a great deal of space, and were reserved for the finest of manuscripts; Virgil's work was considered worthy of Square Capitals. The most notable of these manuscripts is the late-fourth-century Codex Augusteus (see pl. 150). Part of this manuscript is in the Vatican Library (lat. 3256), another part in the

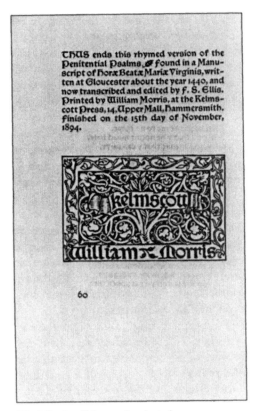

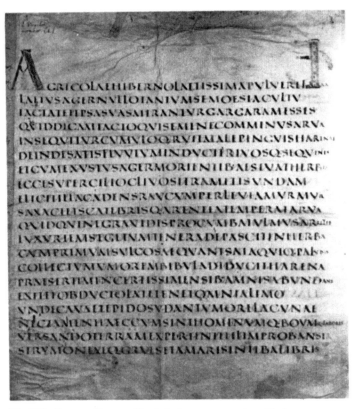

Pl. 149. Leaf decoration in private press book. From the colophon of William Morris. *Penitential Psalms* (London: Kelmscott Press, 1894). Courtesy of the Jewish National and University Library, Jerusalem

Pl. 150. Roman Square Capitals in a manuscript. Codex Augusteus. 375–400 C.E. Staatsbibliothek, Berlin, Ms. lat. fol. 416, f. 1v. Courtesy of the Staatsbibliothek Preussischer Kulturbesitz, Berlin

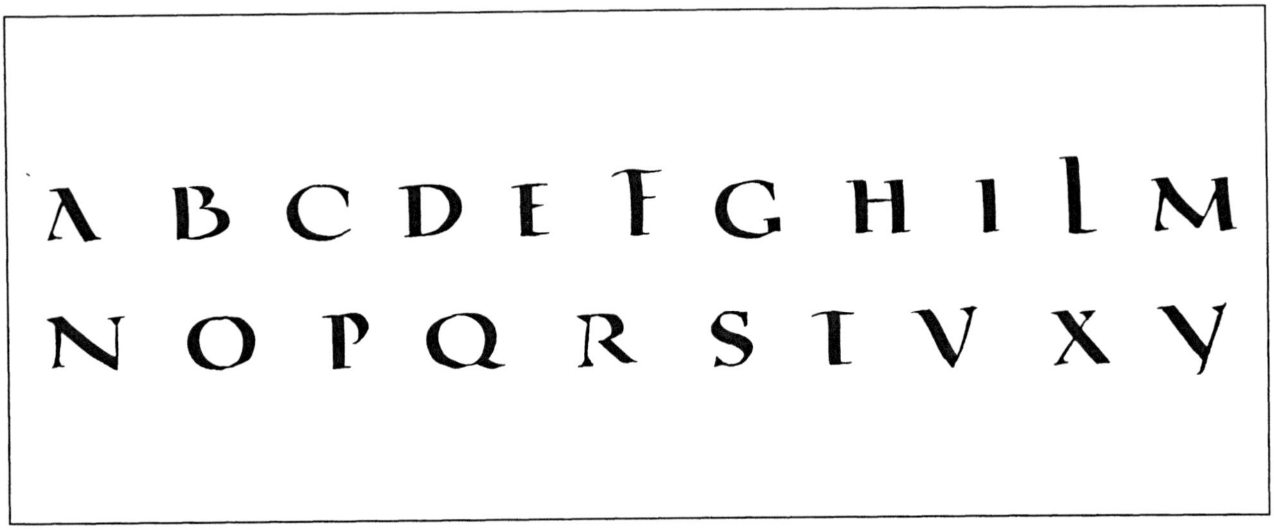

A B C D E F G H I L M
N O P Q R S T V X Y

Fig. 17. Square Capital script

Berlin Staatsbibliothek (lat. fol. 416). As in monumental capitals, the thin strokes of the *O, C,* and *Q* are slightly off center, so that the page exhibits a diagonal aspect that subtly leads the eye from top left to bottom right.

Rustic Capitals

At the same time that Square Capitals were written on monuments and in codices, scribes and designers of inscriptions also used a more compact script, Rustic Capitals (1–500 C.E.) (pl. 151, fig. 18). The stone monuments of the Iberian peninsula and the Near East usually display Rustic Capitals. When compared to Square Capitals, vertical compression of the letters is obvious; this was somewhat of a stone and parchment saver. Diagonal strokes that had been straight were curved, such as the A, X, and V; the latter looked almost like a U. The G, O, and Q became more elliptical. In addition to being used on monuments throughout the empire, Rustic Capitals also served for less formal public notices and advertisements. Because of its use in public documents, the script is sometimes called *Scripta Actuaria*. Even in lapidary inscriptions, Rustic Capitals give the impression that the letters were influenced by pen and ink on papyrus or parchment. They may look as if they were executed hastily because of the exaggeration of the thicker strokes and serifs, often with flourishes of the pen, but by no means did the scribe of Rustic Capitals write fast. The upper and lower horizontal bars of letters, such as those of the E, F, I, L, and T, are treated as if they were serifs, so there is often a uniformly flourished line running along top and bottom. The scribe held the pen with the nib at a 45° angle to the base line. The crossbar of A is lacking. Depending on the individual scribe,

Pl. 151. Rustic Capitals on a monument. Museo Nazionale Romano Inv. nr. 384, CIL 2042,e. Rome, 59–60 C.E. Marble tablet. Reproduced from Arthur E. and Joyce S. Gordon, *Album of Dated Latin Inscriptions.* Courtesy of University of California Press, Berkeley

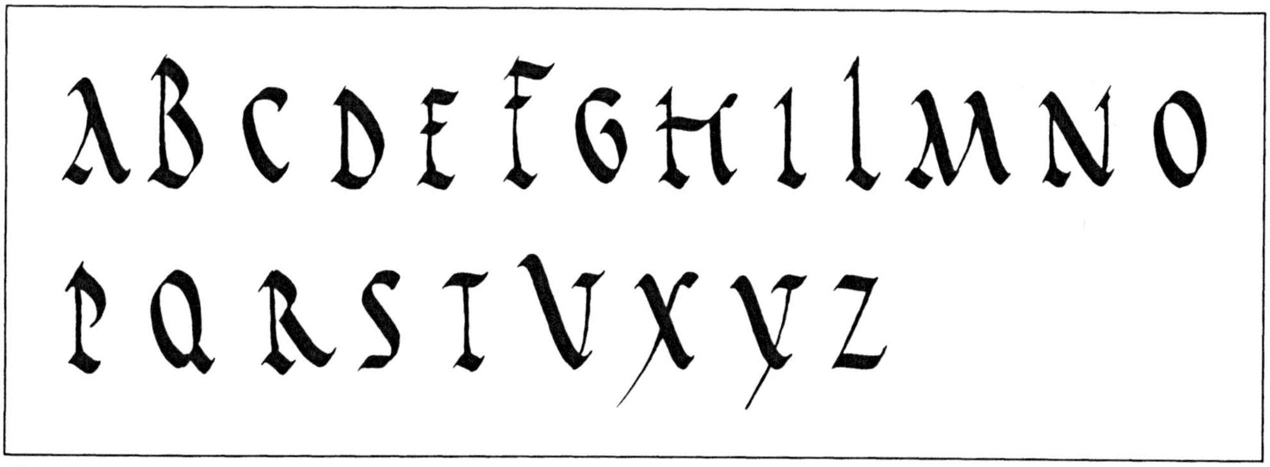

Fig. 18. Rustic Capitals

a few letters rose above the top line: the *B, E, P,* and *Y.* These strokes are called ascenders. A few, called descenders, sink below the base line, such as in the last vertical stroke of the *N* and *V.* There are fragments of about twenty Virgil manuscripts written in Rustic Capitals, and four almost complete Virgil codices. The most famous are two in the Vatican Library, lat. 3225 and 3867 (see pl. 146). Other deluxe editions were written in Rustic Capitals, the Bembinus Terence (Vatican lat. 3226) among them. Only two known Christian manuscripts, one by Prudentius and one by Sedulius, were written in Rustic Capitals. We know of no Bibles written in either Square or Rustic book hands in the time of the Roman Empire, perhaps because early Church scribes associated both scripts with pagan literature and considered them improper.

Square and Rustic Capitals went out of style by the sixth century but were revived in Carolingian times, when scribes looked to the authority of the older alphabets for titles, headings, and the beginnings of chapters. The first Carolingian scribes to write capitals had to teach themselves the old scripts and, after mastering them, taught these styles to the next generation of scribes with no apparent prejudice against using them in Bibles.

CURSIVE SCRIPTS

Literate Romans, as the Greeks before them, did not usually write as scribes did, in the formal book hand. Most people wrote their correspondence and family or public documents on wax tablets or papyrus in their own everyday, or cursive, script. Running script, where letters were joined as a time-saver, was based on majuscules but it introduced many individual variations that all but defy classification. Cursive script is a real challenge to the paleographer and papyrologist, who may spend months deciphering the handwriting of a single fragment. Cursive script did have its effect on later book hands that developed from Roman Capitals. It is in cursive scripts of the first three centuries of Christianity that most of our small letters or minuscules had their source. By writing rapidly and by not lifting the pen from the surface, the writer unconsciously left off parts of letters. That is what happened to the *B, D, H,* and *R:* Β b D ð H h R r. Strokes also were automatically extended, as in the *G, P,* and *Q:* G g P p Q q. In this way, exaggerated ascenders and descenders ultimately determined the form of minuscule letters. Changes were gradual and did not affect formal scripts immediately. Mixing of capital letters with what would eventually become book-hand minuscule is seen first in wax tablets and in nonliterary and chancery documents in the kingdoms that arose from the disintegrating Roman Empire. Word spacing, too, is to be found in cursive writing before it was adopted by the book hand.

Abbreviations and ligatures began with early Christian formal manuscripts. One ligature that persisted throughout the Middle Ages was the joining of the *N* and *T,* N̄ used occasionally at the end of the line. Early Christian manuscripts, first Greek and then Latin, contracted the name of Christ, the *nomina sacra* (holy name), omitting the vowels, a practice derived from the Hebrew Bible, where the Deity's name was written YHVH. In Greek, θ̄C̄ was used for θεός, K̄C̄ for κύριος (Lord), X̄C̄ for χριστός. Christ's monogram, ✱ or X̄P̄, was combined with the latter to become X̄P̄C̄. When these were adopted by the Roman church, the Greek *C* was changed to the Latin *S,* and θ̄C̄ became D̄S̄ (Deus), X̄P̄C̄ became X̄P̄S̄, and Ī̄H̄C̄ (a combination of Ī̄C̄ and Ī̄H̄ in Greek) became Ī̄H̄S̄.

UNCIALS

Uncials may be looked upon as rounded Square Capitals; the edges were curved naturally as the scribe wrote with a flexible reed or quill pen (*penna*=feather; pl. 152, 153). By the end of the third century and beginning of the fourth, when Christianity became the official religion of the Roman Empire, Church scribes devised their own script for Bible manuscripts and for writings of the Church fathers, which they used

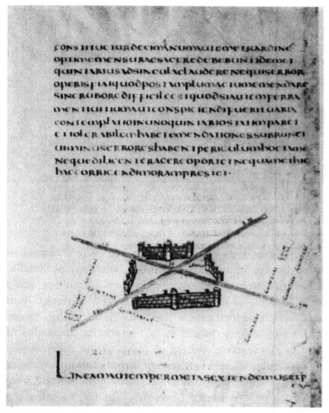

Pl. 152. Uncials. *Corpus Agrimensorum Romanorum*, a collection of treatises by Roman land surveyors. Sixth century. Herzog August Bibliothek, Cod. Guelf. 36.23 Aug. fol, f. 55v. Courtesy of Herzog August Bibliothek, Wolfenbüttel

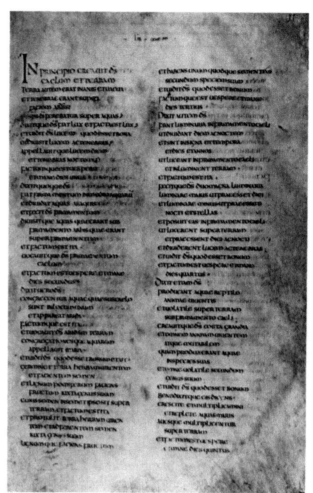

Pl. 153. Uncials. Codex Amiatinus. Wearmouth-Jarrow, England, early eighth century. Laurentian Library Florence, Amiat. 1, f. 11r. Courtesy of the Biblioteca Laurenziana, Florence

until the ninth century. Although there are examples of serifed Greek Uncials in second-century C.E. papyri, and lapidary examples of Uncial script in the third century C.E., and although several individual letters appeared in Uncial form even in the first century C.E. (the *D, E, H,* and *M*), the moment of the script's formalization is unknown. By 400, Uncials were there, fully developed. The fathers of the Church, or the masters of monastic scriptoria, or perhaps an individual creative scribe must have sought a majestic hand, as formal as Roman Capitals, that would be distinct from the handwriting of pagan manuscripts. St. Jerome (ca. 340–420) was the first to call them Uncials, although the name was not attached to this specific script style until the eighteenth century. *Uncia* was the Roman inch, and St. Jerome considered these "inch-high" letters wasteful, especially when written in gold and silver ink on purple parchment. In reality, the largest of the letters on Uncial manuscripts is ⅝ of an inch. It is sometimes called ADEM script, because it can be recognized easily by the design of these four letters: ⲁ δ ∈ ꟽ (fig. 19). The *M* looks as if it were written with one sweep of the pen, without lifting it off the vellum, as if dropping the serifs saved time. Speed could not have been the scribe's objective in forming these handsome letters; rather it was the formalization of certain aspects of cursive script and the earlier Square Capitals. A few letters began

Fig. 19. Uncials

to look like our modern small letters, particularly the *H* and *Q*. The є started to close up into the *e*, but not completely, and the loop of the λ heralded our small *a*. In some manuscripts, ascenders on the *d, h,* and *l* and descenders on the *f, p,* and *q* are more exaggerated than on others. A few punctuation marks appeared with Uncial script, but it was still very much a *scriptio continua*. Some scribes wrote Uncials more ornately than others, adding flourishes to the letters. Examples of artificial Uncials can be found in manuscripts written in England and Germany.

There are some four hundred extant Greek and Latin Uncial manuscripts from the fourth to the eighth centuries. Most of them are Bibles, among them the Codex Amiatinus of the early eighth century, now in the Laurentian Library, Florence; the Vercelli Gospels in the Capitulary Archives, Vercelli (southern Italy) of ca. 371 C.E.; and the Greek Codex Sinaiticus (pl. 137, p. 154). Several pagan Latin authors were preserved in Uncials—Cicero, Livy, and Pliny among them—and there is one poem by Ovid. Like Roman Square Capitals, Uncials did not go out of style completely at 800 C.E.; in Carolingian times they served as headings in manuscripts using more "modern" scripts. The spread of Christianity throughout western Europe in the fifth and sixth centuries guaranteed the diffusion of Uncial and Half-Uncial script as the major monastic hands, as missionaries brought manuscripts with them when they founded new monasteries, and perhaps even brought the scribes to reproduce the manuscripts and teach new scribes how to write in the old style. Although majesty and clarity in reading were the aims of the scribe, it must be remembered that codices were not for the ordinary person to read. Unlike the days of the Roman Republic and early Empire, literacy was almost exclusively limited to the monastery in the early Middle Ages.

MINUSCULES

Half-Uncials

All of the scripts seen thus far—Square Capitals, Rustic Capitals, and Uncials—are majuscule alphabets. The first minuscule script was Half-Uncials (pl. 154). It appeared in the fifth century and thrived in the sixth. Half-Uncials were no more half the size of Uncials than Uncials were inch-high letters. If we were to compare the smallest Uncials with the largest Half-Uncials, we would find some Half-Uncials larger than Uncials. But Half-Uncials could be written more rapidly, and more words could be written per page. Cursive script and documentary hands influenced Half-Uncial, or Semi-Uncial, script more than they did Uncials. Half-Uncials mixed Uncials with cursive script into this new formal hand. As with Uncials, Half-Uncials were written with the reed or quill pen with its nib parallel to the baseline, but instead of being written between two wide guidelines, Half-Uncials were formed between four lines (theoretically if not actually):

Pl. 154. Half-Uncials.
Augustine, *Epistula*.
Sixth century. Bamberg
State Library Msc. Pat.
1.87, f. 79v. Courtesy of
Staatsbibliothek,
Bamberg

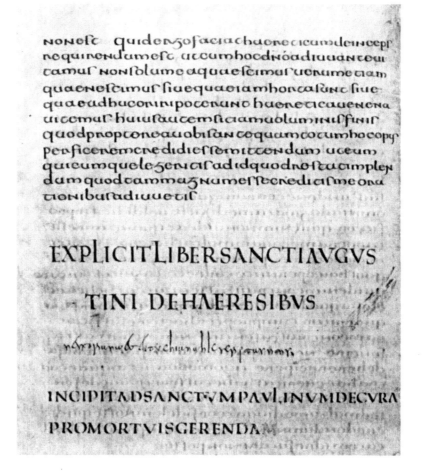

Half-Uncials can be identified by the ascending *b, d, h,* and *l* and the descending *f, g, p,* and *q.* The *E* now is completely closed, in most manuscripts, when compared to Uncials; the *A* looks like a closed modern cursive *a;* and the *M* has an initial vertical stroke like that of the modern printed *m.* Nearly every letter resembles later minuscule scripts and modern lowercase typography, except for the *N* ℕ *T* Τ (fig. 20). Ligatures were employed to a greater extent in Half-Uncials than in Uncials; prominent among them was the et ligature which developed into the & for *et,* still in use, and the abbreviation ę as a substitute for *ae.*

Just as St. Augustine and other missionaries of the late sixth century reintroduced Roman book script into England, English missionaries took their scripts to Germany, where they thrived in new monasteries. About 160 Half-Uncial manuscripts have come down to us, most of them ecclesiastical. Most famous of them is a Hilary manuscript, Vatican Basiliacanus D.182, written ca. 510, and a St. Augustine manuscript in Bamberg, Staatsbibliothek B. IV. 21.

National Hands

Each monastery developed its own variations on Uncials and Half-Uncials, with influences from cursive, charter, and documentary hands of their own provinces. These are often referred to as National Hands, although the concept of nations as such did not yet exist. These scripts were the graphic equivalents of Romance languages, which developed naturally with the decline of the Roman Empire. This does not mean that National Hands were used to write these languages; they were

Fig. 20. Semi-Uncials (Half-Uncials)

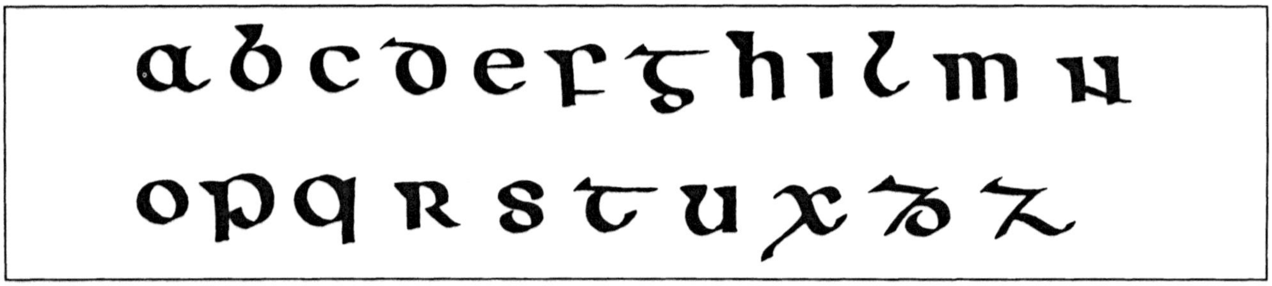

Fig. 21. Insular "National Hand"

used to write Latin in monasteries, and they developed from all of the existing Latin scripts: Capitals, Uncials, and Half-Uncials.

The most admired of National Hands was the Insular script, called Insular Majuscules, Irish Half-Uncials, or Insular Semi-Uncials (fig. 21). Unlike continental Semi-Uncials, the script was majuscule in size, although the shapes of the individual letters resembled the first minuscule writing, brought to Ireland by St. Patrick in the fifth century. It can be identified easily by its clarity and elegance, by the thickening of the serifs and the tops of the ascenders into a wedge shape, and by the curve in some of the vertical strokes, especially the *B* and *L*. The *A, D, R,* and *S* appear in both Uncial and Half-Uncial forms, and sometimes the *N* took on an unusual shape **u**. Initial letters frequently were surrounded by dots, resembling a late Antique metalwork technique. As in many other National Hands, the initial letter became an object of decoration. The outstanding example of Insular script is in the Book of Kells, in Trinity College Library, Dublin (pl. 155). Irish monks took this script to the monasteries they founded on the continent in the seventh century: Luxeuil in France, Bobbio in Italy, and St. Gall in Switzerland. They introduced it into England, Scotland, and Northumbria, notably at Lindisfarne in the late seventh and early eighth centuries. The Lindisfarne Gospels in the British Library displays Insular Half-Uncials.

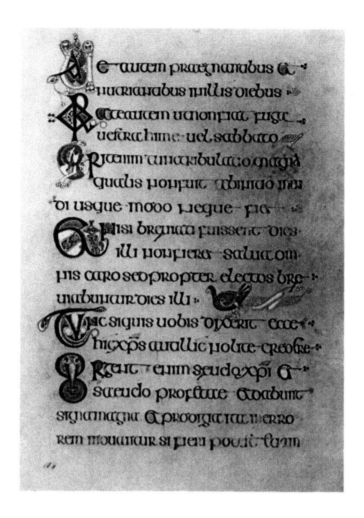

Other National Hands that appeared in the seventh century were Visigothic script in Spain (pl. 156), also called *Littera Toletana* (Toledo), at its best in the tenth century; various Merovingian hands in France, among them Luxeuil in the seventh and eighth centuries and Corbie (which was influenced by Luxeuil) in the eighth and ninth centuries; Northern Italian hands; and Beneventan in Southern Italy, between 700 and 1200. Word spacing occurred in some National Hands, especially in England and Ireland, but it was not yet the rule. A page of these national scripts was often strikingly ornamental, but usually lacked the more practical legibility of Insular script. National Hands retained all of the local abbreviations and ligatures. Luxeuil script of the early eighth century probably was the most exaggerated and artificial of all the National Hands, in spite of the monastery having been founded by Irish monks under St. Colombanus.

Irish scribes wrote minuscules as well, especially for glosses between the lines of their majuscule Bibles. This minuscule script, too, displayed the wedge-shaped serifs, but was written with the pen held on the diagonal. It is sometimes referred to as a pointed hand, as opposed to the rounded hand of Semi-Uncials, for the letters are long and narrow. Local cursive elements were introduced, as in other National Hands. The earliest examples date from the eighth century. The Book of Armagh in Trinity College Library, written in 807 and containing the New Testament and the Confessions of St. Patrick, is the most famous of Irish minuscule books. A version of this script was used for writing Anglo-Saxon until the twelfth century, and Gaelic until the present day. A look at the Irish pound note will show both Irish

majuscule and minuscule hands. One letter from the Insular minuscule, the *uu,* became part of the modern alphabet, although some attribute the *W*'s origin to the Anglo-Saxon *wen* or claim it to be an invention of eleventh-century Norman scribes.

Caroline Minuscule

The next medieval book hand, Caroline Minuscule, or *Littera Gallica* or *Scriptura Francisca* as it was called in the Middle Ages, was a reaction not against Uncials, the preceding formal script, but against the cursive, ornamental character of the Semi-Uncial–derived National Hands that prevailed in the seventh and eighth centuries. Yet this refined hand actually may have been modeled on one or more of these less prestigious scripts. Its certain origin is still disputed; some say it came from

Luxeuil; others say it came from the manuscripts of German or English monasteries. It later was named in honor of Charlemagne, who encouraged and sponsored the renaissance of classical Roman art and learning along with Latin secular literature. The earliest Caroline Minuscule appeared in the dedication of the Gospel Book of Charlemagne written by the Frankish scribe Godescalc (the remainder of which was written in Uncials), and in the Ada Gospels. The Godescalc Gospels (pl. 157), now in the Bibliothèque Nationale, Paris, was written before 783, and the Ada Gospels, in the Stadtbibliothek, Trier, before 785. Just before that time, in 781, Charlemagne had met the English scholar Alcuin (ca. 735–807), head of the cathedral school at York. Alcuin was invited to direct the educational system of the monasteries in Charlemagne's empire. As abbot of St. Martin at Tours from 796 until his death, Alcuin was responsible for the production of many manuscripts that exhibit Caroline Minuscule. For many years, therefore, tradition held that Alcuin introduced this clear, neat minuscule into court and monastic scriptoria. He was no more the creator of the Caroline Minuscule than was Charlemagne, who could barely write. Just as with Eumenes and parchment, and T'sai Lun and paper, he who has a big name and promotes gets historical credit for the invention, while the silent monk who plods away receives his reward in heaven.

Caroline Minuscule was used in Bibles first, but soon was adopted for all religious books, then for secular and pagan literary works and legal documents. One principle of Carolingian script was to eliminate the cursive and to limit the length of the ascenders and descenders (fig. 22), which had become unnaturally elongated in

Pl. 157. Early Caroline Minuscule. Godescalc Gospels. Court school of Charlemagne, 781–783. Bibliothèque Nationale, Nouv. Acq. lat. 1203. Courtesy of the Bibliothèque Nationale, Paris

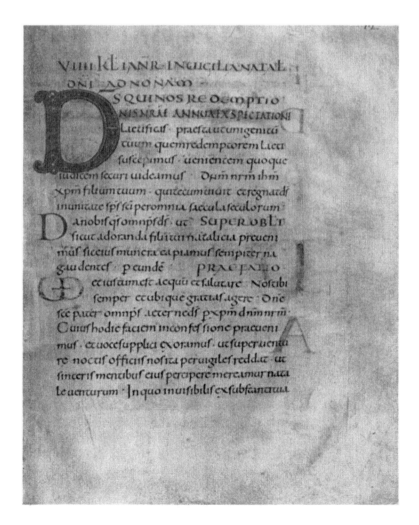

a b c d e f g h i l m n

o p q r f t u x

Fig. 22. Carolingian

National Hands. Now the extended vertical stroke of the letter would be the height of its body, starting at the curve in the letters *b, d,* and *p.* The *N* now appears as a small *n,* and the *g* looks less like the 5 that it did in Half-Uncials and more like the modern *g.* Early Caroline Minuscule *a*'s were open, but they eventually closed up to look like our printed *a.* For the sake of clarity, Caroline Minuscule employed fewer ligatures than did the National Hands, but these did not disappear altogether. The & for *et* and the *ę* for *ae* remained, as did Ń, but *ᴕ* was also used, and *st* appeared as *ſt , ct* as *ct* . The script looks almost identical to today's bookface type, except that it was written with a quill whose nib was slanted in relation to the baseline.

Other reforms were associated with this legible, practical hand. Punctuation and spacing of words and sentences were now employed systematically. Contractions, ligatures, and abbreviations were standardized. Many Carolingian and Ottonian manuscripts displayed a similar script program: First, titles and book headings were written in Roman Capitals. Next, Rustic Capitals were used for *Incipits* (here begins) and tables. Then Uncials were used for chapter headings, tables of contents, and the first line of new chapters; after that, Half-Uncials were used for prefaces and for the second line of the text. Majuscules opened sentences. This hierarchy of old scripts showed the conservatism of the Carolingian scribe, or of the original master scribe who created this system and programmed a prototype. It demonstrated a need both to innovate and to honor the older, established scripts. This system was the origin of our tradition of initial-word and proper-name capitalization, and shows us why large and small letters are a permanent feature of modern European scripts but are lacking in Semitic scripts, which did not undergo the same medieval scribal development. By the eleventh century, capitalization of initial and important words began; it became more common in the thirteenth century, and was fixed in the sixteenth. The spread of Caroline Minuscule as an authoritative script in the ninth century throughout France, Germany, and Northern Italy guaranteed its success internationally. In England, it was popular from the late tenth century. Many Carolingian manuscripts were copied in the Renaissance, among them Alcuin's revision of St. Jerome's Vulgate, classical Latin literature, and, to a lesser extent, Latin translations of Greek works.

Not every Carolingian manuscript was written in the fashionable minuscule. Some scribes were eclectic, not just in their use of old scripts for headings and initial lines and letters but at times for an entire manuscript (pl. 158). A beautiful codex made about 830 at Hautvillers, near Reims, was written in Rustic Capitals—the Utrecht Psalter, named after the University library in which it is now preserved (see pl. 208, 209, p. 248). Psalm headings were written in Uncials in red ink and, although there are dots for punctuating the three-column, unjustified text, there is no word spacing. This manuscript, and many others, were made under the direction of Ebo, Archbishop of Reims (foster brother and schoolmate of Louis the Pious), who served as imperial librarian as well. In the days when Ebo was in court favor, he established a country villa at Hautvillers for archbishops, which housed a scriptorium that made sumptuous manuscripts and whose style was to influence European book art for many years.

GOTHIC SCRIPT

Caroline Minuscule remained the international script through the eleventh century. In the beginning it was well spaced, but gradually word and letter spacing were reduced, and the letters became more compressed and angular. Hairline flourishes and other artificial variations attached themselves to the letters, and by the end of the twelfth century the new Protogothic style took over (pl. 159). Said to have first

Pl. 158. Rustic script on centaur, Caroline Minuscule below. Aratus Ms., British Library Harley Ms. 647, f. 12. Courtesy of the British Library

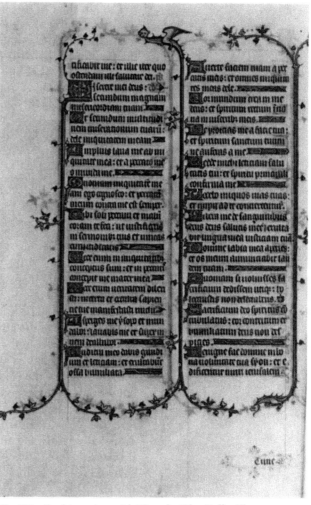

Pl. 159. Gothic script with Versals. The Belleville Breviary. Paris, 1323. Bibliothèque Nationale, Ms. lat. 10484, f. 24v. Courtesy of the Bibliothèque Nationale, Paris

Fig. 23. Gothic

appeared at St. Gall, it spread to Germany, France, and England. As the script became more compressed and the nib was cut wider, the letters assumed a blacker and more angular aspect (fig. 23). Eventually the individuality of each letter was obscured by the total pattern of words, lines, and the text block.

Certain rules of writing were common to Gothic script all over Europe. The *D* was written like the Uncial ᚦ; *s* at the end of a word was written like the *s* that resembled a figure eight, and at the beginning and middle of the word it looked like the *f* without a crossbar ſ. That *f*-like *s* was carried over into printing and was still to be found occasionally in nineteenth-century English books. There was hardly a curve to be seen in Gothic; verticals, straight lines, and diagonals were emphasized. Perpendicular main strokes were thick, with hairline substrokes. Corners were sharp and angular; ascenders and descenders became shorter. The script was basically a minuscule alphabet. In early Gothic, large letters of older alphabets, especially Uncials, were used as capital letters. These were called Versals, and were often colored red or blue and surrounded by pen flourishes. As time went on, enlarged Gothic letters served as capitals, but there was little uniformity in the majuscule chosen for this purpose.

Bastarda

A more cursive form of Gothic script was written after 1200, especially in manuscripts intended for university study, for government and commercial documents, and eventually for vernacular literature. Scholars wrote their own works in this hand. It was called Bastarda (lowborn). The term *lettre bâtarde* was used in an inventory of the library of Charles V (1337–1381) of France's library. Bastarda was written faster and appeared more angular than standard Gothic but gave the impression of a lighter touch (pl. 160).

By the end of the Middle Ages, scribes were not always attached to monasteries but worked in the growing towns. They were mostly not as tradition-bound as the earliest monastic scribes had been, and their handwritings show a greater variety than the more standard scripts of their predecessors. With the growth first of cathedral schools and then universities, there were more scribes and manuscripts than ever before. Students hired scribes to write textbooks for them, and may even have served as scribes themselves to earn extra money during their university studies.

Because letters were so similar to each other in Gothic, certain scribal practices led to features of the modern alphabet. In the twelfth century *ij,* already in use at times,

Pl. 160. Bastarda script. Grand Chroniques de Hainault. Simon Nockart presents the book to Philip the Good of Burgundy. Burgundy, 1448. Bibliothèque Royale, Ms. 9242, v. 1, f. 1r. Courtesy of Bibliothèque Royale Albert 1ᵉʳ, Brussels

began to replace the *ii* because the double *i* appeared to be identical to the *u*. The Uncial *J* already had been used as an initial letter *I* without any phonetic distinction. In the thirteenth century the letter *v*, which had looked like *u* in Uncials, Semi-Uncials, and Caroline Minuscule, came to be written as a *v* at the beginning of a word but remained a *u* in the middle. There was no differentiation of the two into consonant and vowel until the sixteenth century. Scribes writing Gothic scripts and Bastarda also began marking the *i* with a slanted stroke above it *í* to distinguish it from the nearby *m, n,* and *u;* this led to our dotted *i*'s.

Gothic script was predominant for three centuries, until about 1500. It was at its best in thirteenth-century France, and it lingered on in Germany and Northern Europe. Its verticality and ornamentality were in harmony with the pointed arches, angularity, and verticality of the Gothic cathedral. It has been called Black Letter, Textura, *lettre de forme* (in fifteenth-century France), or simply Gothic, the name of the period of art history in which it was popular. The term *Gothic* had been a pejorative designation coined by Italian humanists for the "barbaric" architecture of the North. Gothic script was also called *Fractura* in the Middle Ages, a name that continued to be used for a specific German typeface it inspired. The Italians had their own variety of Gothic, with fatter, more rounded letters, called Rotunda. Those who thought the script to be beautiful, even if not very legible, did indeed invoke Gothic art and architecture as its kin.

HUMANISTIC SCRIPT

The humanists of the Italian Renaissance saw nothing spiritual in Gothic script. Instead they turned to Caroline Minuscule manuscripts of the tenth and eleventh centuries for their Humanistic models (pl. 161). When they revived the works of Latin authors of the past in the late fourteenth and early fifteenth centuries, they considered the hand in which the original codices were written to be the clearest and most beautiful to be seen. One of the first to use this new Humanistic script was Petrarch (1304–1374), who discovered and purchased a greatly admired tenth-century minuscule manuscript in his youth. Many others emulated him in his admiration, among them Coluccio Salutati (1330–1406), chancellor of Florence; Niccolò de' Niccoli (1363–1437), who wrote with three versions of Humanistic script; and the professional scribe and secretary Poggio Bracciolini (1380–1459), who was an officer in the papal curia and eventually became chancellor of Florence. By the time of Poggio's death, Humanistic replaced Gothic cursive as the standard script for the classics. Although Poggio's own cursive was a combination of Gothic and Humanistic, his formal Humanistic hand was used as a model by most Italian calligraphers, and eventually by printers (pl. 162).

Humanistic scribes wrote with the quill. They attempted to eliminate most of the abbreviations and ligatures found in earlier scripts. Humanistic script at times looks so much like Caroline Minuscule one must frequently look for other codicological evidence to distinguish between the writing of one period and another, such as the size of the script, the number of lines per page, spacing, vellum, or the text of the manuscript. Humanistic script is more delicate than Carolingian, more even and regular, with letters more closely spaced, and with less differentiation between thick and thin strokes (fig. 24). A cursive Humanistic (fig. 25) was employed by scholars

Pl. 161. Humanistic script. Giannozo Manetti, *De Dignitate et Excellentia Hominis.* Written by Ciriagio. Florence, 1454. British Library, Harley Ms. 2593, f. 68r. Courtesy of the British Library

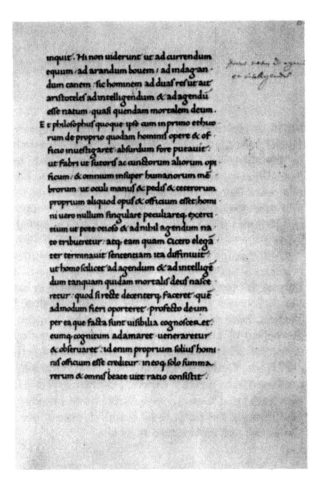

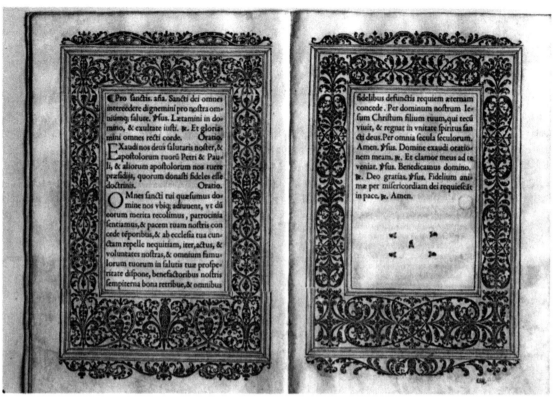

Pl. 162. Roman typography in a sixteenth-century printed Book of Hours (Paris: Simon de Colines, 1543). Courtesy of the Metropolitan Museum of Art, New York

and scribes working in government offices (pl. 163, 164). The version used in the papal curia and displaying more flourishing brushstrokes was called *Littera Cancellaresca.* This script was recommended as a general hand by chancery scribe Ludovico degli Arrighi in his manual on handwriting, *Operina,* printed in 1522. This and his other work, *Il Modo de Temperare le Penne* (1523), are still followed by calligraphers. Early printers such as Aldus Manutius used the Humanistic cursive as a model for typography, which came to be called Italics.

Humanist scribes and artists were also concerned with the forms of capital letters, and some of them designed very decorative majuscules (fig. 26). But the old Roman inscriptions provided the best models for Renaissance architectural inscriptions, for engraved coins and medals and, eventually, for printed books. Artists, mathematicians, and printers became preoccupied with the concept of perfect proportions of Roman Capitals; this became the subject of treatises in Italy, France, and Germany. The first of these essays was by the antiquarian scholar-printer Felice Feliciano of Verona (1432–ca. 1479) who, in 1463, applied compass, ruler, and geometric principles to the inscriptions he collected. Other constructed alphabets were devised by Damianus Moyllus (Damiano da Moyle of Parma), ca. 1483, and the Franciscan Lucas (de Burgo) Paciolus (1509). More famous were the treatises by Leonardo da Vinci, who was a friend of Paciolus; French printer and engraver Geofroy Tory (ca. 1480–1533); and German artist Albrecht Dürer (1471–1528), all of whom were influenced by Paciolus, who had imposed on capital letters contrived proportions that combined Euclidian geometry with the human figure.

When printing began in the 1450s, printers looked to the handwriting of the scribes in the area for models on which to base typography, and they often employed scribes as type designers. Gothic became the standard typeface in Germany and for some time in other parts of Europe as well. But when German printers went to Italy, they chose Humanistic typefaces so that their books would be read by the local population. Eventually Humanistic, or Roman, typefaces triumphed, due as much to their inherent clarity and beauty as to the influence of

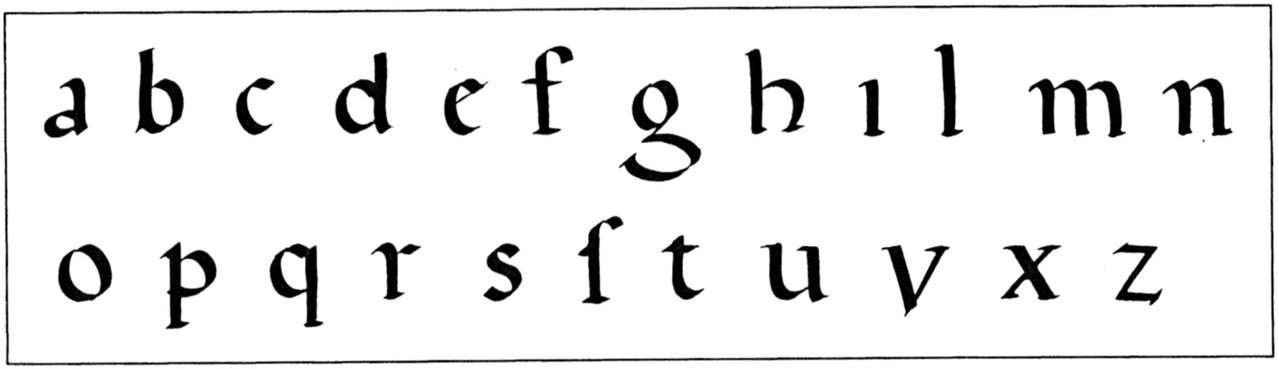

a b c d e f g h i l m n
o p q r s ſ t u v x z

Fig. 24. Humanistic

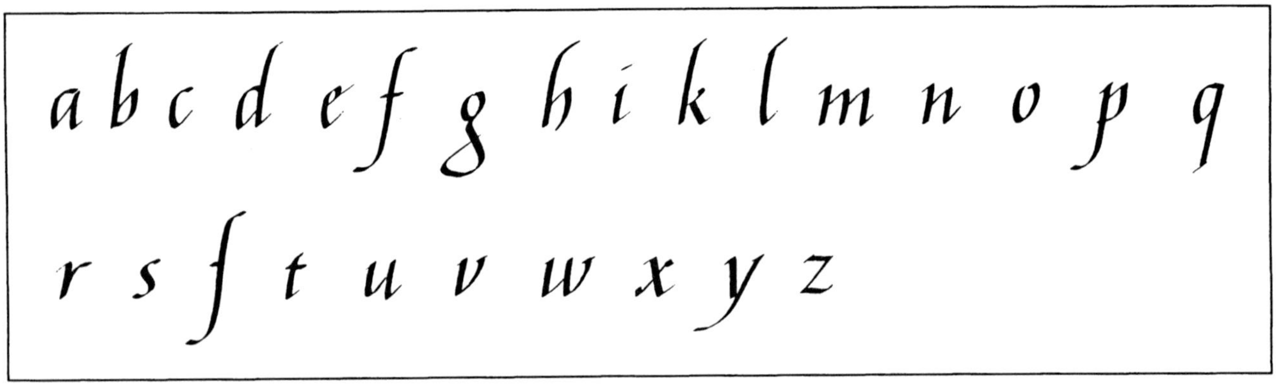

a b c d e f g h i k l m n o p q
r s ſ t u v w x y z

Fig. 25. Cursive Humanistic (Italic)

Fig. 26. Filigree initials, based on Tagliente. After Alexander Nesbitt, *History and Technique of Lettering*. Courtesy of Dover Press

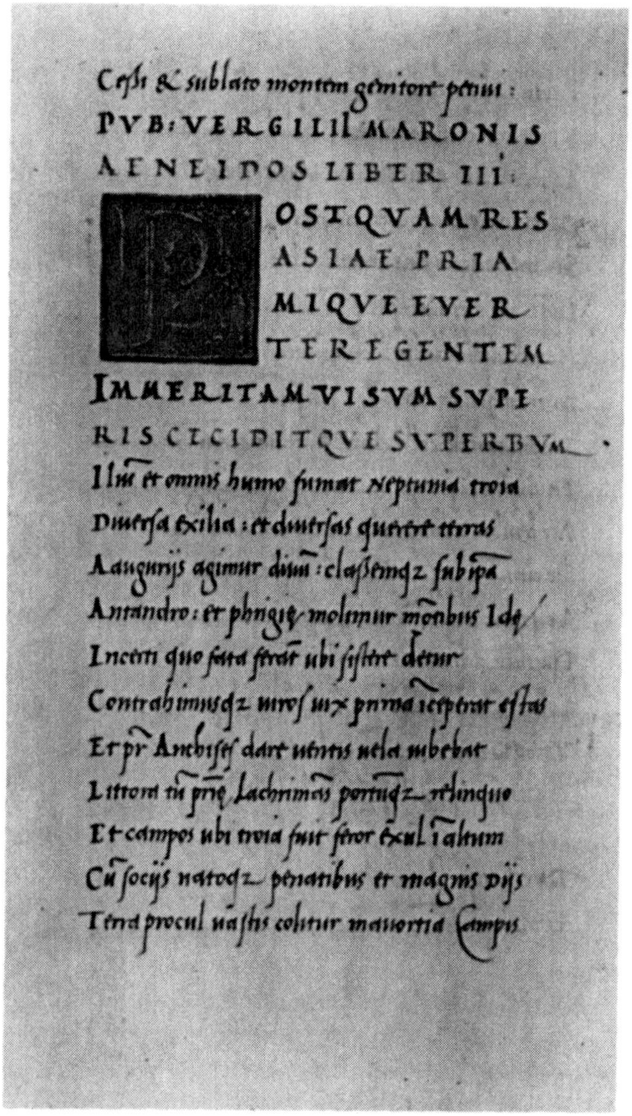

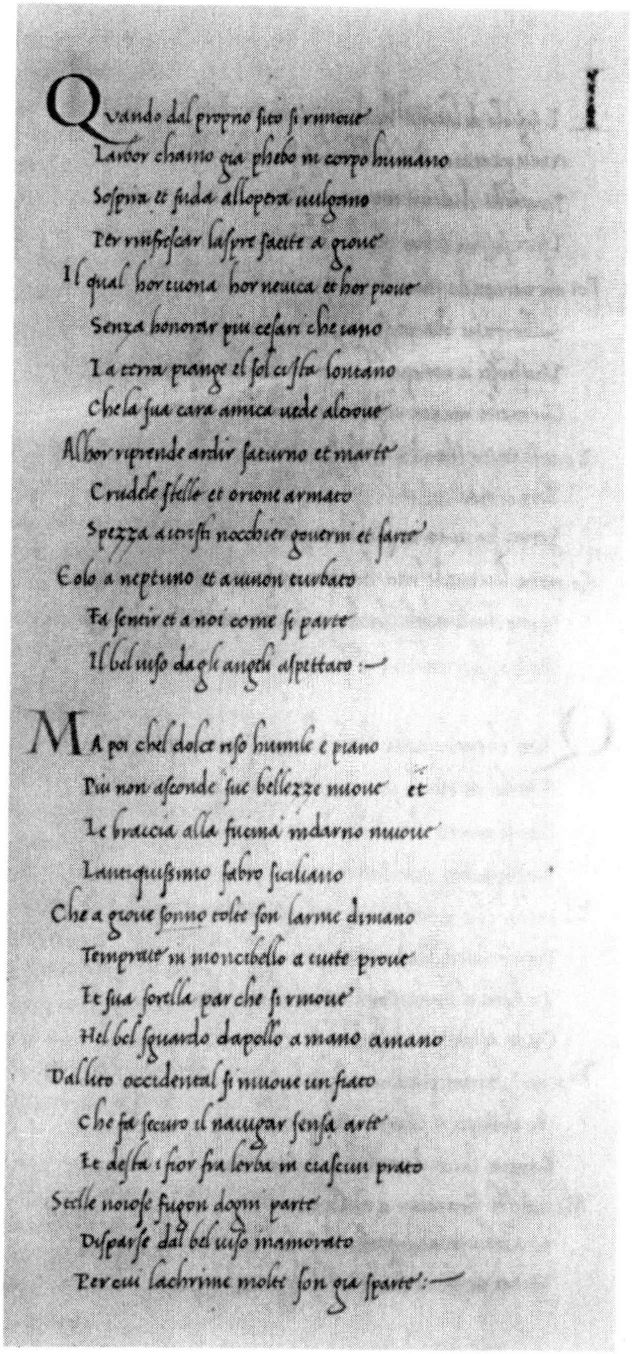

Pl. 163. Humanistic Italic script, with heading in Rustic Capitals. Virgil, *Aenead*. Ca. 1500. British Library, Add. Ms. 11355, f. 118v. Courtesy of the British Library

Pl. 164. Humanistic Italic script. Petrarch, *Sonetti e Canzoni*. Rome, ca. 1500. Pierpont Morgan Library, M.474, f. 18r. Courtesy of the Pierpont Morgan Library, New York

printers and typographers working in Italy: Nicholas Jenson, Aldus Manutius, and Francesco Griffo.

As one surveys the variations on the Roman letter created and adapted throughout the Middle Ages and Renaissance, one sees that each script style was based on an earlier prototype. No scribe was a radical. The scribe who was an innovator or reformer of script assiduously studied the existing written forms in the codex he copied, and looked upon it as a revered model to follow, to individualize according to the needs of the reader and his own capabilities and aesthetics, or to improve upon or beautify in his own eyes. This description of medieval Latin script styles has been oversimplified for the sake of classification. As universal as a script was, individual scribes still had their own personal styles. Given a codex written by several scribes, scholars now can identify the different hands.

Stanley Morison (1889–1967), one of the twentieth century's greatest type designers and historians of script, believed that script styles from the sixth century B.C.E. until modern times reflected the political situation in the larger realm in which the inscription designer and the scribe worked. In his classic *Politics and Script,* Morison expressed the opinion that in the ages when there was no strong central government, handwriting was freer; in ages of more powerful empires, writing was more disciplined.

CALLIGRAPHY AFTER THE INVENTION OF PRINTING

The story of Latin calligraphy does not end with the invention of printing. But with its introduction, writing a book by hand was no longer a necessity and comparatively few manuscript books were made and illuminated in the sixteenth century. Calligraphy became a skill to cultivate for display, such as on correspondence, official documents, and commemorative certificates, for theoretical speculation, and, later, for commercial purposes. Manuals of calligraphy were at times like the treatises on the perfect proportions of letters; at other times they were simply copybooks for aspiring calligraphers. Handwriting books became an important genre from the sixteenth through the eighteenth centuries in Italy, Spain, Germany, Holland, Belgium, France, and England. The first masters to write manuals of importance were Italian: Sigismondo Fanti of Ferrara (active 1514–1535); and Giovantonio Tagliente (active 1491–1541, see fig. 26, p. 196), instructor to the doge's chancery in Venice, whose engraved book included sample scripts in Hebrew and Arabic. Giovanbattista Palatino (active 1538–1575) reprinted his manual, which displayed a highly compressed and angular script, three times in Rome between 1540 and 1566. Gianfrancesco Cresci (active 1552–1572), a Vatican scribe, published writing books in 1560 and 1570.

In the sixteenth century, manuals were printed with woodblocks, which meant that in order for the letter to print black, it had to be cut in relief. This was accomplished not by the calligrapher but by a woodblock cutter, just as the practice had been for woodcut illustrations. In one copybook, written by the Nuremberg printer Wolfgang Fugger in 1553, the letters were cut in relief on soft metal (pl. 165). It was unnatural to reproduce calligraphy by a relief technique; it often modified the shapes of the letters, particularly the ascenders, which became wider and curved at the top. Inking the woodblock with such thin letters was also difficult. The more accurate way to reproduce handwriting was to cut the letters intaglio, into the block, as in engraving, and to ink the entire block lightly so that white letters appeared on a black ground when it was printed. Several alphabets were printed in this manner.

Copperplate Script

Although the technique of copperplate engraving was known for about a century, the earliest copybook to be printed from copper plates was published around 1574 by Giulantonio Hercolani of Bologna. The intaglio method reproduced the lines of the pen with greater accuracy than the relief method, and could display all the flourishes of the pen (pl. 166). Many calligraphers who reprinted their manuals by copperplate, from 1600 on, sought the effects that were created by the burin on copper rather than the look of the pen on parchment or paper. Some calligraphers even made a game of drawing endless pen flourishes into the shapes of objects and figures. Italics were best suited to copperplate, and although manual writers usually gave samples of other styles, they promoted Baroque Italics over Roman Capitals,

Pl. 165. Figured calligraphy. From Wolfgang Fugger's handwriting manual, *Ein Nutzlich und Wolgegrundt Formular Manncherly Schöner Schriefften* (Nuremberg, 1553). Courtesy of Staatsbibliothek, Bamberg

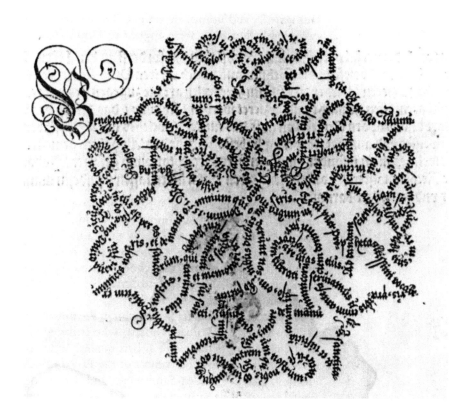

Pl. 166. Copperplate. George Bickham, *The Universal Penman* (London, 1733–1734). Victoria and Albert Museum, L526/1939. Courtesy of the Victoria and Albert Museum, London

Education strikes in with Philosophy in many lessons; teaches us not to be over-joy'd in Prosperity, nor too much dejected in Adversity; not to be dissolute in our Pleasures, nor in our Anger to be transported to a Fury that is Brutal. Wxyz

Humanistic, and minuscule scripts. The exception to this was in Germany, where calligraphic flourishes were applied to Gothic-based scripts. After more than two centuries of copperplate, however, writers lost all touch with the medieval letter.

Handwriting and Penmanship

As time went on, cursives became more and more exaggerated, possibly because calligraphers and engravers did not want their work to look like book typography. In Paris, calligrapher Louis Barbédor (ca. 1589–1670) wrote with a cursive whose words as well as letters were connected in a manner known as *ronde,* which he published in his manual in 1647. In England the script was called Round Hand.

English writing masters, apparently persons of high status because of the demand for their services by the commercial world, were lovers of cursive Italics and pen flourishes. To their writing skills they added stenography (the art of shorthand writing) and bookkeeping. Some writing masters established their own schools, such as "Hand and Pen," the school of John Ayres (active 1680–1705), a master of the Round Hand. This practical script became the mainstay of nineteenth-century American penmanship.

Handwriting was at its lowest ebb in the nineteenth century. Even artists such as William Blake and William Morris, who believed in the handmade book as a work of art, used scripts that were at best quaint. William Morris did not live to see the revival of calligraphy, but others of the Private Press Movement—C. H. St. John Hornby, T. J. Cobden-Sanderson, and Count Harry Kessler—commissioned capital letters to be written or block printed by Edward Johnston and his students.

America's nineteenth-century calligraphers took a practical view of the art and desired to teach a clear hand for commercial purposes. Platt Roger Spencer (1800–1864), who grew up in Ohio, developed his own sloping, angular style while still in his teens, then taught at the school he opened on his farm. His sons and a nephew continued his message by establishing the Spencerian Colleges of Penmanship and Business, which influenced American script for much of the nineteenth century. Then, in Iowa in 1894, Austin M. Palmer, who had been selling writing books and accessories, founded a corporation to promote a handwriting that would be both legible and written with ease and speed, based on five strokes of the pen. The Palmer method was taught in the United States, Latin America, and parts of Canada for the next fifty years. Although Palmer's script has been criticized as "vapid commercial cursives," it is nevertheless a greater pleasure to read a letter written by someone who is now between sixty-five and eighty years old, rigidly disciplined in the Palmer method in elementary school, than to read an exam written by many American university students aged thirty and under, because penmanship is no longer considered a serious subject of study in grade schools. It is ironic that as penmanship has declined as an academic subject, calligraphy has risen as a profession and avocation. Every sizable city in the United States now has a flourishing calligraphy society; the number of classes and workshops on calligraphy and illuminating grows annually, and books and journals devoted to the practice and history of handwriting have proliferated. This renaissance in modern calligraphy owes its existence to Edward Johnston.

Edward Johnston and the Revival of Calligraphy

Edward Johnston (1872–1944) was born into a family that can only be described as Dickensian: a grandmother with a cause (the abolition of slavery), an unemployed father who used up most of his own inheritance, a bedridden mother, and an overbearing aunt who ran the household. The Johnstons moved frequently, from Scotland to East Anglia to Uruguay and back to England. Edward was brought up with no formal schooling. When he was seventeen, his parents noticed his artistic inclinations and gave him a book about illuminating manuscripts, which he immediately put to good use. After his mother's death and his father's remarriage, Edward first considered medicine, but after a few months at Edinbourgh University's Preparatory Institute, the aunts and uncles who looked out for his welfare realized he was not healthy enough for such a career. Relatives had commissioned him to write out some passages and verses, and so Johnston was encouraged to pursue art. Calligraphy, as a profession, did not exist at that time. William Morris had dabbled in it, and architect Henry Colinshaw did calligraphy and illuminating as a hobby. Colinshaw introduced Johnston to the architect W. R. Lethaby, one of the founders, with William Morris, of the Arts and Crafts Movement. In 1899, Lethaby, after commissioning Johnston to "do a parchment," arranged for him to introduce the first course in calligraphy in modern times in the new London Central School of Arts and Crafts, of which Lethaby was principal. (Rudolf von Larisch and Rudolf Koch later opened calligraphy schools in Austria.)

The manuscripts of the British Museum and E. M. Thompson's *Greek and Latin Palaeography* were Edward Johnston's teachers; his mentors were Lethaby, who always encouraged him, and Sydney Cockerell, book artist and William Morris's former secretary. At the Arts and Crafts Exhibition Society in 1899, Johnston exhibited a marriage service he had written out for a relative, a children's book, and a Pater Noster. The calligrapher's first principles of readability, beauty, and character stayed with him all of his life.

A member of Johnston's first class was architect and book illustrator Eric Gill, who wrote, "The first time I saw him writing and saw the writing that came as he wrote, I had that thrill and tremble of heart which otherwise I can only remember having had . . . at a view of the North Transept at Chartres. . . . I did not know such beauties could exist. I was struck, as by lightning, as by a sort of enlightenment."[1] Gill became Johnston's roommate until the latter married, and they remained close friends for many years. Other early students were Noel Rooke, Florence Klingsford, (William) Graily Hewitt, and Irene Wellington Bass. Edward Johnston also taught at the Camberwell School of Art, and in 1901 initiated the calligraphy courses of the Royal College of Art. He was a natural teacher and his classes were always full. Teaching exhausted him. When he was forced to miss classes at the Royal College of Art because of ill health, he was sorely missed. In the words of one of the assistants who taught in his absence, Violet Hawkes, "Our teaching is simply mundane, but you teach out of eternity and infinity. We instruct but you inspire."[2] Of his classes, Noel Rooke commented, "He related his subject to everything in heaven and earth."[3]

Another of his fine students was Anna Simons (1871–1951), who came to England because women were not admitted to art schools in Prussia at that time. When she returned to her native country, she translated Johnston's book into German and was instrumental in spreading his methods. During Johnston's brief stay in Germany, Anna Simons acted as translator for his blackboard lectures. His influence in Germany was considerable, particularly on the movement to adopt Roman typography there and in the adoption of sans serif types.

T. J. Cobden-Sanderson was among Johnston's students at the time he established The Doves Press with Emery Walker, who had been Morris's type designer. Johnston executed the handsome initial letters for several Doves Press books, and also designed initials that were carried out in woodcut by Gill and Rooke.

Johnston's handwriting seemed to move in stages, from the Half-Uncial to Carolingian to a more compressed Gothic, then to a sixteenth-century Italic, which he called his "heavy Italic." He later added his own versions of Versals and Roman Capitals. Between 1916 and 1919 he perfected his own Foundational script (pl. 167) based on a late Carolingian script he found in a tenth-century manuscript written in Winchester. It became one of the standard scripts for all calligraphers of the future to master. At the height of his career, just as he started to go blind, his handwriting achieved a freedom and life it never before had embodied.

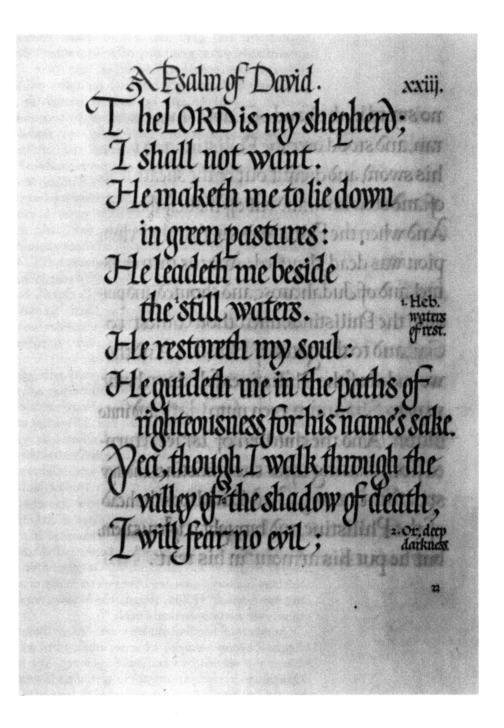

Johnston was a person of poor health and limited energy, with an inability to get himself moving in the morning, attributed by his biographer-daughter to a thyroid condition. He could spend most of the day taking his bath and reading the paper, then spend the whole night in conversation with a friend. Guilt at not accomplishing required work would prevent him from taking vacations, and when he did take a holiday, he brought his work along with him. Said his daughter, "It really seemed that a nervous compulsion to work was induced in him by fear of being prevented from doing so."[4] With all of his commissions, it took a hard and fast deadline to bring out the best in him at the very last moment.

Johnston was cajoled by art and music patron Count Harry Kessler, who had established his Cranach Presse in Weimar in 1913, into designing, contrary to his policy, an Italic (only the lowercase was completed) and a black-letter type (scattered during World War I and not completed until 1930). Another principle of Johnston's was to forbid reproduction of his work; when he finally allowed a commissioned handwritten diploma to be engraved, it took five years to do so. He could not come to terms with the concept that a designer could design for industry, because he felt design should never be separated from the making of the object. A major commission for Johnston came from the London Underground, for its logo and its block-letter alphabet. These seemingly simple letters became the basis for England's road signs, and later the model for sans serif alphabets used on the Continent and eventually in the United States, including Monotype's Gill Sans.

It took three and one-half years for Johnston to write his *Writing & Illuminating, & Lettering* (John Hogg, 1903), frequently reprinted and still a classic in its field. Fortunately his publisher was very patient while Johnston taught himself all of the contents of the book, the prerequisite for passing this knowledge along to others. He worked on its revision for many years; the unfinished second edition was later revised by Heather Child and published by Lund Humphries as *Formal Penmanship*.

Edward Johnston's influence on modern calligraphy, through his work, his book, and his teaching, was profound. It is fortunate that we have Priscilla Johnston's biography of her father, because in it we see the life of a single calligrapher before us. How happy would we be if we could similarly glimpse at the lives of the individual medieval scribes who created Half-Uncials, Caroline Minuscules, and Gothic script.

Notes

1. Priscilla Johnston, *Edward Johnston* (London: Faber & Faber [1959]), 100–101.
2. Johnston, *Edward Johnston*, 263.
3. Johnston, *Edward Johnston*, 264.
4. Johnston, *Edward Johnston*, 246.

Manuscript-making Centers of Europe

CHAPTER 9

Codices Manu Scripti: Books Written by Hand

THE MONASTERY AND LITERARY TRADITION

The book of the European Middle Ages was the parchment codex, and the making of the book was the accomplishment of the monastery. Although reading and writing existed to some degree outside the monastery, it was within its walls that most manuscripts were written, bound, and illuminated, at least until the thirteenth century (pl. 168). From the time of the breakup of the Roman Empire, it was the Church in general, and the monastery in particular, that was responsible for the preservation and transmission of literary traditions. As the barbarian invaders became firmly established, towns that had existed in the empire declined. Ordinary people sought the protection offered by rich landowners in exchange for their continuing services. Peasants were granted a plot of land on the lord's manor, to be planted and harvested both for self-support and for contribution to the manor's economy. In the time that remained after working their own farms, peasants served their lords in whatever personal capacity was demanded of them. The local lord, in turn, pledged himself to the noble higher up the socioeconomic ladder in return for the land he had been allocated. This civil, financial, and military system—feudalism—was the basis of medieval society until the end of the Crusades. The greatest landowner was the Church, which had been granted tax-free status by the Roman Empire once Christianity became the official religion. In the Middle Ages the Church was often the recipient of bequests, in addition to being supported by both peasants and nobility. The Church provided education as well as all services, such as they were. Former barbarian kings, whose tribes followed them in their conversion to Christianity, remained illiterate until after Charlemagne's day. The Holy Roman Emperor himself could not read. According to Charlemagne's biographer Einhard, the Emperor kept a tablet under his pillow so that he could practice lettering, but, having begun this activity late in life, he had no success.

Table 7. Chronology of the Medieval World

	Date
Kingdoms	
Ostrogoths in Italy	489–554
Lombards invade Italy	568
Visigothic Kingdom in Spain	466–711
Frankish Kingdom	481–752
Book Persons	
St. Irenaeus	ca. 130–200
Boethius	475–524
Cassiodorus	485–575
St. Patrick in Ireland	432
St. Columbanus	543–615
Isidore of Seville	ca. 560–636
Benedict Biscop	ca. 640–709
Aldhelm	639–703
Ceolfrith	642–716
The Venerable Bede	673–735
Alcuin of York	735–807?
Royal Book Collectors	**Reign**
Carolingian Empire	
Charlemagne as King of Franks	768–814
Charlemagne as Holy Roman Emperor	800–814
Louis the Pious	814–840
Charles the Bald as King	843–877
Charles the Bald as Emperor	875–877
Disintegration of Carolingian Empire	814–887
England	
Alfred the Great	871–899
Saxon Empire	
Otto I (936–73), Otto II (973–83, m. Theophanu 972), Otto III (983–1022)	936–1002
Henry II (1002–24), III (1039–56), IV (1056–1106)	1002–1106
France	
Philip II (Augustus) m. Ingeborg	1180–1223
Louis IX (St. Louis)	1226–1270
Philip IV (the Fair)	1285–1314
Charles IV (m. Jeanne d'Evreux in 1325)	1322–1328
Charles V (the Wise)	1364–1380
Duc de Berry	d. 1416
Renaissance Collectors	
Louis XII	1498–1515
François I	1515–1547
Henri II	1547–1559
Charles IX	1560–1574

Alcuin tutored Charlemagne in other subjects: rhetoric, dialectics, and astronomy. The emperor was a great patron of the arts and of education. He established palace, state-sponsored, abbey, and cathedral schools. His palace housed a library, whose catalog is extant. Charlemagne's descendants and later European emperors fared better with their education.

Pl. 168. Monk/bookmakers. Ambrosius Manuscript. *Clockwise:* Bookbinding, parchment making, writing on wax tablet, quill cutting. Readers at top and bottom. Third quarter of the twelfth century. Bamberg, Msc. Patr. 5, f. 1r. Courtesy of Staatsbibliothek, Bamberg

The only way a layman could obtain an education was to study with one of the religious orders, whose brethren were in charge of preparing men for the priesthood, because one aspect of the potential priest's training was to learn to read and write. These acolytes were granted certain privileges, such as exemption from military service. Many of them never became priests at all, providing instead a pool of labor for the chanceries of rulers—the civil service. It was not at all necessary to educate peasants, whose way of life did not allow time for leisure reading. The Bible was taught by the local priest with the help of the visual imagery of frescoes and sculpture. Nor did the Church see any value in educating women, even in most convents. There were a few scribe-nuns, but the convent was not a manuscript production center to the same degree as the monastic scriptorium. Nuns were recruited from the aristocracy, the sector of medieval society in which one would expect to find the only readers and writers. Because Jews and Muslims lived outside the European Christian sociopolitical system, they fared better with their education, and were as literate as their coreligionists in the Near East.

So few works of Antiquity have come down to us through the Latin West that it is a miracle any nonbiblical manuscripts survived at all in Europe. It was not that the abbots before the Carolingian Renaissance deliberately suppressed classical learning; they simply did not care enough about it to read it or have it copied. When found, the parchment on which a pagan text was written provided handy material for a palimpsest. Only a few classical works were copied anew in Northumbria in the eighth century. The existence of ancient texts in the medieval world was due to the accidental survival of books originally from pagan libraries as well as to the conscious efforts of three sixth-century individuals. Two of these men were officials at the court of the Ostrogothic emperor Theodoric: Boethius and Cassiodorus. Both men were imbued with classical learning. The Roman philosopher and statesman Boethius had planned to translate all of Plato and Aristotle into Latin. While that plan did not materialize, his writings on the seven liberal arts influenced the organization of knowledge in the Middle Ages. Cassiodorus, whose intention to establish a university in Rome was thwarted, firmly believed that classical learning should be transmitted along with Christian texts. He collected manuscripts and in his own monastery of Vivarium, founded around 540 in the south of Italy, he initiated the copying of manuscripts of all kinds, including Latin translations from Greek. A few manuscripts from the library of Cassiodorus were recopied in later periods. He also collated the Vulgate of St. Jerome, of which nine copies were made, one of them known as the Codex Grandior, a key model codex. This was the prototype for an important manuscript written in England in the early eighth century, the Codex Amiatinus (pl. 169).

The third promoter of reading and, by inference, copying of manuscripts was St. Benedict, who founded Western monasticism at Monte Cassino in 529 and whose rule became the monastic ideal. He set aside a period each day for reading, and by doing so he established the ecclesiastical educational system and the mechanism for transmitting written works. While he never advocated intellectual pursuits neither did he forbid them, thus leaving the monastic door open to scribes and educators of the later Middle Ages.

Pl. 169. Ezra the Scribe. Codex Amiatinus. Wearmouth-Jarrow, England, early eighth century. Laurentian Library, Florence, Ms. Amiatinus 1, f. 5r. 13¾ × 9¾" (350 × 248 mm). Courtesy of Biblioteca Laurenziana, Florence

Between the sixth century and the middle of the eighth century, virtually all classical texts ceased to be copied, surviving until today only as palimpsests. After the decline of Rome, Ireland and then England became the important centers of culture. One assumes that St. Patrick brought books to Ireland. The first major literary figure in England, who had a great impact in mainland Europe, was St. Columbanus, who established the monasteries of Luxeuil in Burgundy (590) and Bobbio in northern Italy (614). His pupil Gallus founded St. Gall in Switzerland in 613. Meanwhile, Anglo-Saxon Christian culture was initiated in 597 by St. Augustine, sent by Pope Gregory the Great. In the same period another Irishman, St. Columba, founded the monastery of Iona, whose daughter monastery was Zindisfarne. A century later Benedict Biscop (ca. 628–689) founded Wearmouth and Jarrow, twin monasteries. He made six trips to Italy, presumably bringing back manuscripts for copying. The Codex Amiatinus (Florence, Laurentian Library, Cod. Amiat. 1) was one copy of the Codex Grandior. A chain of scholars in England, from Benedict Biscop to Abbots Ceolfrith, Aldhelm, and Bede, all demonstrated a command of Latin classical authors. Alcuin, in a poem praising York, described the partial contents of its monastic library, which housed pagan as well as Christian literature.

The Carolingian revival, under Alcuin's administration, ensured the survival of the little that remained of Latin literature. In the monasteries of Charlemagne's empire, classical learning was kept alive through copying, even if these manuscripts were not actually studied. The cathedral schools, some of which were established along with monastic schools in Charlemagne's time, were later to take upon themselves the responsibility for education and for transmitting classical tradition, which comprised the seven liberal arts: arithmetic, geometry, music, astronomy, grammar, rhetoric, and logic. While the purpose of the monastic school was to train candidates for priestly orders, the purpose of the cathedral school was to train secular clergy. The secular clergy, in turn, became the educators. But because cathedrals were located in growing urban centers in England, France, Spain, and Italy, they attracted many laypersons. A former peasant who moved to town had a chance to be educated. Cathedral schools flourished in what is known as the Twelfth-Century Renaissance. In Italy, even Monte Cassino, in the late eleventh and early twelfth centuries, enjoyed a revival of the works of classical and Christian authors. The universities of the thirteenth century carried on classical textual transmission, adding to it philosophical, legal, and local vernacular literature. The influx of works and translations from the Byzantine and Islamic worlds was a boon to university studies.

The chain of transmission in medieval Europe was always a fragile one, with the works of many Latin and a few Greek authors in translation existing only in single copies. Western monastic libraries were diminutive when compared with those of the Byzantine and Muslim empires. Reichenau, which possessed one of the largest libraries in Europe in the eighth and ninth centuries, could boast of only 415 manuscripts. Most *editions de luxe* of these libraries were Bible codices, and it is these that will be examined for their miniatures (see Chapter 10).

After two centuries of Crusades, from the late eleventh to the late thirteenth centuries, Europe was the cultural beneficiary of contacts with the Byzantine and Muslim empires. The Crusades had emptied the purses of many feudal lords and nobles who had sold freedom to their peasants and granted charters to towns in order to raise capital. Peasants flocked to the growing towns, and as freedmen they could engage in trade or in the newly flourishing crafts. Because agricultural methods improved at about the same time, their presence on the farms was not missed. Luxury goods, such as metalwork, ceramics, silks, and other textiles, that once had been imported from Byzantium and Islamic lands now could be made locally. Artisans banded together into guilds and businesspeople governed in cities with their own elected officials. Cathedrals were built not only to glorify God but to express the newfound wealth and economic strength of the cities. Schools, at first attached to cathedrals in the twelfth century (Chartres being the most famous in France), became independent in the thirteenth century, as guilds of lecturers and students formed universities. To serve the growing number of students and readers, new methods of publishing books came into being. Learning passed from the religious domain to the secular, and at times the brightest monks were sent to the universities to study.

MATERIALS

Just as paleography is the study of scripts, codicology, a newer discipline, is the study of all aspects of making the medieval codex: parchment and its method of manufacture; other materials used and the tools used to prepare them; the gathering of leaves into quires; the pricking and ruling for guidelines and columns; the use of catchwords, graphic signs, justification and other techniques of the scribe; the layout of the text; and the manuscript's modes of decoration. Different materials and methods of preparing and writing the manuscript reveal the place and date of the book's creation as much as does its script.

Parchment

Parchment manufacture is a variation on leather making. The essential difference is that, in parchment making, the skin is stretched and scraped and limed instead of being treated with tannins. Medieval methods are known from treatises written in the eighth and later centuries, from occasional pictures drawn or painted in manuscripts, and from twentieth-century investigation, particularly by Ronald Reed of the University of Leeds. The process was much the same all over Europe, with slight variations from time to time and place to place. The similarity of parchment manufacture in contemporary England and Israel, two major sources today, indicates a single basic European method, with local and individual recipes. The occupation was necessary but not particularly desirable; a parchment factory smells like a slaughterhouse. It was built outside the monastery and town in the direction opposite that of the prevailing winds for good reason. The animal hides came from the monastery's own stock, were donated by local herders, or were purchased in town.

The skin of the newly slaughtered animal, whether sheep, calf, or goat, was sent immediately to the parchment maker. If not, it could be preserved by pickling in salt. The early winter may have been the best time for this activity for practical reasons: livestock owners would not have to feed their herds over the winter, and the population would have a sufficient supply of cured meat for the season. The skin was soaked in a bath of lime and water for three to ten days to dehair it. Then excess fat and flesh were cut and scraped off. Soaking was accomplished in a wood-lined or stone pit in the Middle Ages. Wooden poles were used from time to time to turn the pelts. Paddle wheels in a stone or concrete tub are sometimes used today for the same purpose and could have been used in the past as well. The best limewater was that which had been used for a previous soaking of skins; it permitted a more gradual, even treatment. This soaking loosened most of the hair or wool. Pelts were washed and returned to a cleaner lime liquid for a few more days. Another ingredient used in parchment manufacture, known from the leather industry, was dog dung, whose bacteria and pancreatic juices assisted in breaking down skin fibers and fat. The alternation of lime-soaking, dehairing, and washing, and any additional treatments that may have been guarded secrets, varied from one parchment maker to the other. At this point, the skins could be dried and stored, and redampened when it was time to process them further.

The wet, rubbery pelt was then stretched onto a wooden rectangular or (less commonly) circular frame (pl. 170). The skin had to be stretched gradually as it dried, to counteract natural shrinkage, so it was attached to the frame with ropes

Pl. 170. Contemporary parchment making: fastening the hide to the frame. Courtesy of the Gallandauer Parchment Factory, Jerusalem

Pl. 171. Parchment making: scraping the parchment. Courtesy of Gallandauer Parchment Factory, Jerusalem

Pl. 172. Parchment making: finished sheets. Courtesy of Gallandauer Parchment Factory, Jerusalem

fixed to wooden, keylike pegs that were tightened slowly. While it was taut, the skin was scraped with an ax- or crescent-shaped knife, called a *lunellarium* in the fifteenth century (pl. 171). The moon-shaped scraping blade used today has two handles, each grasped with one hand. A paste made of ashes, lime, and water was rubbed on the stretched pelt to remove excess oils and to provide resistance to the scraper, or powdered gesso (gypsum), chalk, pumice, or quicklime were thrown on it as it was scraped over and over again until the desired thinness and smoothness were achieved on both sides. The slow drying process (pl. 172) was always controlled by the parchment maker. As the pelt air-dried after scraping, still on the frame, it was chalked or pumiced further. Alternatively, freshly whipped egg whites (glair), varnish, size, or linseed oil was applied, depending on the desired finish. The scribe, too, usually had a pumice stone, powdered chalk, or pounce at hand to further enable the sheet to accept ink (see pl. 178, p. 222).

The supervisors of parchment production for the monastery were called *fratres pergamentarii.* Parchment was not made at the monastery exclusively. Monks bought commercially prepared parchment in the city (pl. 173). We also read of scribe-nuns who were granted permission to go to town to buy vellum.

A codex is usually described as having leaves of parchment or vellum. What is the difference between the two? There is still no agreement on the proper terminology and the exact distinction between parchment and vellum. Vellum is literally "veal skin" or calf skin (*vitulus*), but skins were so well processed in the Middle Ages that few hazard a guess today at the original animal whose hide was used. Some scholars define parchment as the skin of the adult animal—cow (which would produce an enormous sheet), sheep, or goat, eight to twelve months old—and vellum as the skin of the younger animal—calf, lamb, or kid, four to six weeks old. Others claim that salt was used for preparing parchment but not vellum, the softer product. Still others say that vellum, as opposed to parchment, is a sheet that does not show any hair holes. To be on the safe side in describing a sheet, it is best to call the heavier, glossier product parchment and the finer, softer variety vellum, and not to expect uniformity and consistency in catalog descriptions.

Pl. 173. Craftsman sells parchment to a monk. Lunellarium at bottom of sewing frame. Hamburg, 1255. Royal Library, Copenhagen, Ms. 4, 2° II, f. 183r. Courtesy of Det Kongelige Bibliotek, Copenhagen

The problem of definition does not end here, for there was a more delicate material that appeared in the late Middle Ages, especially in France, called uterine vellum or *abortivum, pergamena vitulina,* or *pergamina virginea.* This is known to have come from the skin of aborted or stillborn calves. On medieval uterine vellum, Daniel V. Thompson remarked, "I should be inclined to think that animal husbandry must have been in a very precarious condition if enough calves were stillborn in the thirteenth century to provide all the pages which pass for 'uterine vellum.' "[1] But this soft fetal product is still manufactured by parchment makers and is very much in demand. In today's abbatoirs of South American countries, there are some forty aborted calves per hour whose pelts are sold to parchment makers.

The size of the sheet depended on how the parchment manufacturer made the best use of the available skin. He tried not to waste any of it. The bits and pieces of skin and the leftover shavings and scrapings were boiled up into a gelatin, called size. Parchment could be dipped in size, or the size could be brushed on, to provide an even coat for the whole sheet. Size could also be used as a binding medium by the manuscript's illuminator, to fix pigments and gold to parchment.

The source of parchment at any given time and place in Europe depended on the local population's meat-eating habits. It is believed that goatskin was a major source until the tenth century (and continued to be in later centuries around Bologna), and that in the eleventh and twelfth centuries sheep provided skins for most of Europe's parchment. Parisian vellum from that time and later was of sheepskin and calfskin. Goatskin parchment has an overall grayish look and sheepskin has a yellowish hue, but otherwise it is difficult to tell the difference between the two by the hair holes (grain), especially when the sheep were of the hairy rather than woolly type.

Diet and the climate where the animal was bred affected the end product; a cool, moist climate produced the best vellum. Not all of the livestock were in perfect health. Mites and insects, such as warble flies, ate holes or burrowed into the animal's skin and laid eggs there. At times scar tissue grew over the holes; these are called blind warbles. Accidents to the live animal or carelessness in manufacture also left marks and holes on the parchment, as did the manner in which the animal was slaughtered. For example, iron compounds entering the blood caused veins to show in the parchment. Veined parchment may make an interesting bookbinding today, but in the Middle Ages it never would have been acceptable for a text page. When natural or other defects appeared in the parchment, scribes and artists worked around them. In general the quality of medieval parchment and vellum was very high, especially when compared to the sixteenth-century product. Just as in the writing and decorating of the manuscript itself, quality was a more important factor than speed. It has been estimated that in the Middle Ages, some 200 to 225 hides of sheep or goats were used for the making of each Bible manuscript.

On the parchment sheet itself the hair and flesh sides can usually be discerned. The hair, or grain, side is normally darker, and tiny holes, the roots of the hair follicles, can be seen. From the time of the earliest codices, the book designer (assumed to be the scribe or his supervisor) arranged folios so that when the book was opened the two pages facing each other matched—grain opposite grain, flesh opposite flesh. This matching is called Gregory's Law, after Caspar René Gregory, the scholar who first noted this consistent practice in 1879 (see fig. 30, p. 221). In Europe, the quire, or gathering of leaves, began and ended with the hair side; in Byzantium the flesh side opened the quire. The less fatty hair side made a better surface for writing, and ink is often darker and clearer on that surface.

Ink, Gold Leaf, and Pigments

The medieval scribe wrote with a goose quill, its feathers removed. He used any one of a few kinds of ink. The first type, known since ancient times, was composed of ground soot, water, and gum arabic, except that the source of gum was the almond and plum trees rather than *Acacia arabica*. The ink varied according to the lamp providing the soot: beeswax or tallow; linseed, hempseed, or olive oil; incense; pitch; or animal oils. This rich, black carbon ink could be scraped and washed off easily, leaving hardly a trace. More common were metallic inks made from organic iron salts (iron sulfate, or green vitriol), oak galls, and gum arabic. Gall "nuts" are swellings on trees caused by gall flies or wasps laying their eggs in the tissue of the tree, which grows a covering over the spot of irritation. When the egg hatches inside, the larva grows to maturity, causing the protuberance. Oak galls provide the best tannic acid for ink. Tannic acid is soaked out of the dried gall nuts. Tannic acid alone is colorless, but when it is mixed with iron salts and oxygen, a black or gray ink results. With time, the medieval metallic inks faded to brown and even yellow. Lampblack or compressed charcoal made of soot and carbonized plant materials such as beechwood, charred twigs, or peach stones were sometimes added to the oak gall–iron sulfate recipe. The ink oxidized, or "burned into," the parchment (*incaustum,* ink) and, even where the color has faded almost completely, it can be restored by chemical means or by ultraviolet light. Unintentionally humorous are medieval recipes for pure black ink whose very ink that wrote them now has paled and nearly disappeared. Both carbon and iron-gall inks were used until the seventh or eighth centuries, after which scribes preferred the latter.

A third type of ink was made from thorns. Instructions for its preparation were written by the monk Theophilus around 1100. Thorns from the blackthorn tree were cut in the spring, before buds appeared. After several days, the bark was removed and soaked for three days. The water, which turned reddish-brown, was boiled and recombined with the bark, and the process repeated a few times. The liquid was then boiled again with wine, and left to dry in the sun in a parchment container.

When he wrote, the monastic scribe was not allowed to change what he thought to be a mistake in the text being copied. But when he noticed and corrected his own errors, he did so by scraping off the ink with a knife or a razor. When the spot was repumiced or pounced he could rewrite over it with ease. If simple pumicing was not enough, a mixture of milk, cheese, and lime softened the parchment; some concoctions included orange juice. Many were the errors the scribe did not find. The manuscript needed a good proofreading, first by a corrector, if there was one, and finally by the abbot. Corrections were made above the word or in the margins.

If the manuscript was intended to include decorations, the scribe left room for them. As instructions to the decorator, a tiny initial letter would be written in the space where a large ornamental letter would later be drawn, painted, or illuminated. The earliest printed books continued this manuscript practice. *Illumination* literally meant to brighten up with gold; it was illumination that endowed majesty and brilliance to the medieval manuscript. There were two kinds of gold used. Until the twelfth century most artists made gold paint from powder. Afterwards, gold leaf predominated. Gold leaf was made by hammering gold, usually a coin, to the thinness of a cobweb. First the piece of gold had to be rolled or beaten to a foil, then cut into smaller pieces, stacked, and beaten down again (pl. 174). In order to keep the beaten pieces of gold foil from sticking to one another, they were alternated with layers of goldbeater's skin, made from the layers of connective tissue of the *caecum* of cattle intestines, free of all fat. These fat-free sheets were necessary because gold leaf adheres to anything near it that is even slightly moist or sticky. Even breathing on gold leaf will cause it to billow, or move to the wrong place, or adhere to anything nearby.

A great deal of gold leaf could be obtained from a single coin, or, as today's illuminators and binders would express it, "a piece of gold the size of a pea can cover a warhorse." To make the gilded letter or ornament stand out and appear to be solid gold, the illuminator prepared the parchment surface with chalk or gesso, a mixture

Pl. 174. Goldbeating, from Denis Diderot, ed. *Encyclopédie, ou Dictionnaire Raisonné des Sciences, des Arts, et des Métiers* (Paris, 1751). Courtesy of the Jewish National and University Library, Jerusalem

of gypsum and plaster and thick white water-paint. Then a layer of pink or red, usually a claylike earthy substance called Armenian bole, was applied and polished. This reddish underlayer was an artist's trick for gold enhancement, known since the days of gilded mummy cases in Egypt and the mosaics of Byzantium. The illuminator then applied the binding agent: honey, sugar, size, gum arabic, glair, or even the artist's breath or saliva. The gold leaf was next transferred with a metal knife or the tip of a brush to the prepared ground. Excess gold leaf was scraped or wiped away with a gilder's rubber before it dried, to be saved and reused. After the gold dried thoroughly, it was burnished to a mirrorlike finish, usually with the smooth tooth of a carnivorous animal, such as a dog, or with hematite mounted in a wooden handle. In the late Middle Ages, burnished gold was often tooled with patterns—geometric shapes, rosettes, and fleur-de-lis—which broke up what would have been considered a monotonous metallic background into a surface on which there was a play of light and shade. From a sixteenth-century copy of a fifteenth-century treatise on illumination written in Judeo-Portuguese come the following instructions on the application of gold leaf:

> Take saffron and gum and white of egg mingled with all these things and place it on the place or letter which you wish to gild. And then take the leaf of gold, very neatly and carefully, in a house where there is no wind, and where there are no people (in order that he may not speak to anyone) and place a bandage or piece of cloth upon your mouth and your nostrils in order that you may not breathe upon the gold, which (bandage) should be tied around the head. And place it over the things mentioned and let it stand for one hour in the day time. And then take a little cotton and place it gently on this leaf. That which is to remain on the letter, let it stand, and take the rest away. As soon as you have done this, lay hand on the burnishing iron and burnish it very well with a swine's tooth.[2]

It was just as difficult to make gold-powder paint as it was to make leaf, since gold molecules stick to each other as they are ground. To powder the gold, foil or leaf had to be mixed with honey or salt, then ground, with the honey or salt washed out afterwards. It is not certain that gold dust from riverbeds was the source in the Middle Ages. Powdered gold, remixed with glair (whipped egg white) or gum, was used as ink to write texts, especially in Byzantine, Carolingian, and Ottonian manuscripts. There were various recipes for imitation gold as well. Here is one of them:

> Make a small hole in a hen's egg and take out the white only and fill the egg with quicksilver; close up the opening carefully, place it under hot dung for 40 days. Then remove the quicksilver and take 1 oz. of crystal [glass] and reduce it to a very fine powder and incorporate it with the yolk of the egg. Then with this composition smear the paper or whatever else you want and when it is dry, rub gold or silver upon it and it will remain the color of gold or silver.[3]

A codex written in gold ink was exceptionally beautiful. It did not tarnish as did silver. The book was even more luxurious when the parchment was dyed purple. Dyeing parchment purple was costly when the source of purple was murex (*Murex brandaris* or *Trunculariopsis trunculus*), a Mediterranean marine snail whose hypobranchial gland produced only a drop of dye. It is no wonder that purple was a royal color! The Phoenicians were famous for their production of this valuable purple dye in biblical times, and Julius Caesar seems to have been the first to use Tyrian purple in imperial garments. In medieval England and Europe, whelks served to dye parchment reddish, as did folium from turnsole, or archil (orchil), a dye made from the lichen *Rocella*. The medieval artist did not buy paints ready-made but manufactured or processed them from elements found in nature. In Europe, some of the raw materials for pigments were imported, such as lapis lazuli ("true ultramarine"), but it had to be reduced to powder form for pigment. Brazilwood, too, was imported. It came from Ceylon (now Sri Lanka) by way of Alexandria and Cairo where, according to the records found in the Cairo Geniza, this source of red dye was an important commercial item. In larger illuminating workshops, one specialist may have been responsible for making pigments and gold leaf for all of the illuminators and colorists. Recipes were handed down from master to apprentice, undoubtedly in guarded secrecy, but occasionally artists wrote treatises on the manufacture of pigments. These medieval handbooks (along with chemical and other analyses) are a major source of knowledge on how paints were made. Toward the end of the Middle Ages, there are a greater number of these treatises as well as model books that gave the illuminator decorative patterns to copy (pl. 175).

Some of the most popular colors were obtained in the following ways. Ochres were a mixture of oxides of iron and earth minerals. Found in nature, they provided ancient and medieval artists with yellow, orange, and red. One red ochre was called sinopia after Asia Minor's town of Sinope. Other shades could be obtained by roasting lead in the open air until it gradually turned yellow and then orange. Vermillion, the brightest red, was a heated mixture of mercury and sulfur. It may have been known in eighth-century Europe, although it did not become popular until the twelfth century, possibly with the influence of Arab technology. Other red dyes were called lakes; gum lac came from incrustations on trees produced by the larvae of the insect *Coccus lacca,* formed in a manner similar to oak galls. The sap of the East Indian shrub *Dracoena draco,* which hardened into a red-brown gum, was called dragonsblood, after the blood of the elephant and dragon mingled in mythical epic combat, according to medieval artists. Madder root, from the shrub *Rubia tinctorium,* also served as red. The original source of crimson was the red dye of an insect, *kermes* in Arabic. Imported brazilwood, *Caesalpinia,* was shaved down from blocks and reduced to a powder by scraping with glass, by filing, or by pounding. In ancient times, one source of red was the pebbles found in the River Minium in Spain (now Menjo), hence the common name for red pigment, *minium.* Some art historians, ignoring the meaning of *minutus* (small), believe that the linguistic source for "miniature" was *miniare,* to paint with red, the result of which was decorative

Pl. 175. Göttingen Model Book. Step-by-step illustrated instructions for illuminators. Some illuminations are similar to those of a copy of the Gutenberg Bible. Bastarda script. Göttingen Library, Ms. Uffenb. 51, f. 8v–9r. Courtesy of Niedersächsische Staats- und Universitätsbibliothek, Göttingen

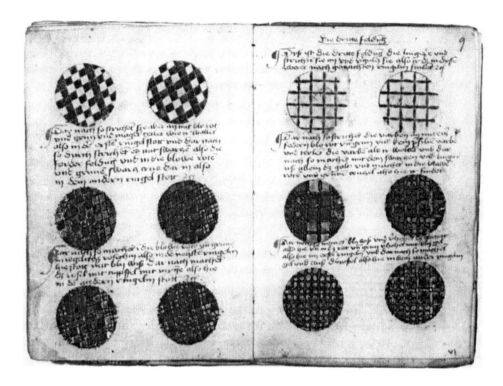

writing and drawing, the *miniatura,* from the time of Egyptian chapter headings to medieval rubrics and illustrations. The term *minium* was sometimes used interchangeably with *cinnabar* from classical times through the Middle Ages. It was native red sulfide of mercury. By the middle of the fifteenth century, the term *rubrication* came to mean illumination (from *ruber,* red) or other ornamentation in manuscripts and printed books.

Blue was as important as red to the medieval painter. In ancient times the color came from lapis lazuli. The Romans had to import it from its sole Persian source north of the Oxus River. Lapis was probably the most expensive pigment to obtain in medieval Europe. Therefore substitutes for this so-called Persian or Indian azure were made from plant substances, such as indigo (*Indigofera*), or from azurite, a copper ore. Azurite was ground up, but the finer it was ground the whiter it became. The medieval admirer of miniatures could not tell the difference between azurite and lapis. Nor could one see the lumps in the partially ground azurite that can be discerned today with a microscope. Blue also could be extracted from a weed called woad, the shrubby herb *Isatis tinctoria,* which grew broad green leaves containing a blue dye. At the time of the Roman conquest, the native Britons colored their bodies with this dye. Woad was the cause of water and air pollution in medieval England, where its cultivation and manufacture for potash and soap as well as dye brought good income to farmers. As with other colors, the pigments mentioned here were not used exclusively for illuminating manuscripts, but for dyeing cloth as well.

Green came from the gemlike mineral malachite, from earth clays, from the sap of plants such as the iris, or from the leaves of parsley and the medicinal plant rue. Verdegris (*vert de Grèce*) was an acetate of copper. It was made by hanging plates of copper over hot vinegar in a sealed pot until a crust formed on the copper. The following more precise recipes are from the Portuguese handbook quoted previously.

> Take very thin leaves of copper foil and wet them in very hot and strong vinegar, and put them in a pot leaning on its side. Smear the mouth of the pot with honey and cover it with potsherds and burial earth or manure of large animals and let it stand thirty-one days. At the end of these days take out the pot and you will find verdegris.

> Take a wide bowl and half fill it with very putrid urine and take a basin of brass, very well washed from the bottom to the top, and place it above the bowl in such a way that the urine does not come within two fingers' distance of the bottom of the basin. Let the bottom of the basin be smeared with good honey, and the basin itself be half full of the same urine. And above the basin place upside down another bowl. Above the bowl place coverings for pack mules, and pour the urine from the basin into the bowl placed at the bottom. And go to the bottom of the basin and you will find the honey which you placed on it turned into verdegris. . . . And for tempering this green, when you wish to work with it, grind it previously very thoroughly and place in it a little saffron well ground, and temper it with gum-water, for there is no devil who can take away its worth from this color.[4]

Bright yellow was orpiment, a sulfide of arsenic, but saffron and other vegetable substances also were used, as was the earth mineral *Crocus Martis,* the "saffron of Mars." White could be made from lime, from the ashes of burned bones and eggshell (especially those of birds), or from lead. The medieval maker of paints, if he was a specialist in a large workshop, suffered from their poisonous ingredients without recourse to a suit against his employer for exposure to industrial hazards. Today, painters and paint manufacturers do not make these pigments according to their medieval recipes. Reconstitution of medieval pigments has been a subject of study for art historians, book conservators, calligraphers, and illuminators, and for chemists. Tradition has left us many of the ancient and medieval names for modern colors, even when they are manufactured synthetically and purchased in tubes.

Pigments and gold were fixed to parchment with glair *(clarea),* the white of egg whipped with a wooden whip or fine twigs. After the egg white came to a froth it stood until it turned watery enough to flow from a brush or pen. Leftover egg white was preserved by storing it with a bit of red sulfide of arsenic or vinegar in the egg's shell, carefully reclosed. The other popular binding medium was size, made of parchment scrapings or of fish glue. Honey and sugar were also part of the illuminator's store, and a little saliva was always helpful. After the decorations, miniatures, and illuminations were accomplished, the manuscript was bound. Hopefully, the quires would be kept in their proper order. In the fifteenth century, rubrication and bookbinding frequently were activities of the same workshop. The gold left over from the illuminated letters could be recycled for use in gold-tooled bindings.

DESIGN AND PREPARATION OF THE CODEX

The design and layout of the codex were planned before any writing was done. The abbot was ultimately responsible for the programming of the codex, even if other monks did the actual design, or if there was an *armarius* or librarian to supervise the scriptorium, or if the manuscript at hand was to be reproduced without any changes or innovations. The rectangular parchment sheet, about 10 inches (25½ cm) high and 18 inches (46 cm) wide, was folded in half, to make two folios, or leaves—in other words, four pages. Four sheets of parchment, folded once down the center, were placed one inside the other to make up a *quaternion* (or *quaternus,* a set of four), also called a quarto (figs. 27–30). This quire *(cahier* in French), or gathering of eight leaves (that is, four folded *bifolia*), was the medieval European standard. Quires could be made up of six, ten, and twelve leaves as well. If the text was longer than the space allotted for it, a stub could be added, with one page a little wider than the

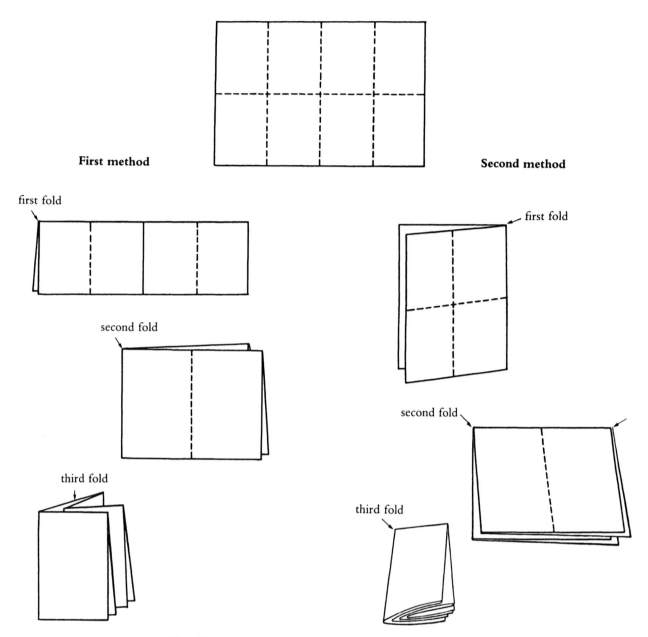

First method

Second method

first fold

second fold

third fold

first fold

second fold

third fold

Fig. 27. Two methods of folding a parchment sheet that will be cut to make the quire. After Léon Gilissen, *Prolégomènes à la Codicologie*

others so its edge could extend over the fold to be sewn with the rest of the quire by the binder. When more than one monastic scribe wrote the text, as was the common method, each worked on his own quire or quires. The quires at times were marked so they would be kept in proper order for later binding. A *q* was followed by a minuscule Roman numeral in the bottom margin of the final page of the quire, for example, q i, q ii, q iii, q iiii. The first half of the quire could also be numbered to keep its leaves together. The second half did not need to be numbered because its leaves were conjoint. Each quire could also be marked with letters. Catchwords, the first word of the following quire, were written on the final page of each quire from about the end of the eleventh century. Catchwords for pages were common in the fifteenth century and persisted in printed books until the nineteenth century. Although pages had been numbered in the very earliest codices from Egypt, the

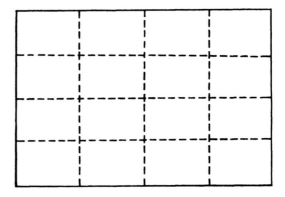

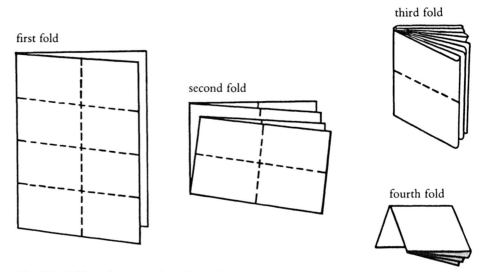

Fig. 28. Folding the paper sheet for a thirty-two-page signature in a printed book

Fig. 29. Four-sheet quire, opening with hair side, made of two sheets of parchment, folded twice

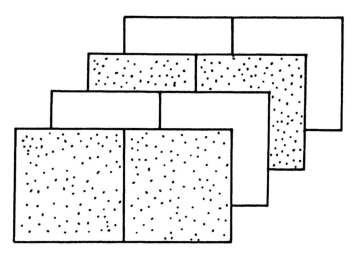

Fig. 30. Four-sheet quire, showing Gregory's Law: flesh-to-flesh, hair-to-hair sides

practice was given up, as was stichometry, the counting and recording of the number of lines (except for poetry). Consecutive numbering of pages was reintroduced in the thirteenth century, but it did not become a firmly established tradition until the sixteenth-century printed book.

Other aspects of layout familiar to us today were in existence by the thirteenth century. Running heads were used at times. Tables of contents appeared at the beginning of the book, sometimes with a summary. In scholastic commentaries, or glosses, which began in the twelfth century, commentary was written in two columns flanking the central text written in larger letters. This format was followed by early printers. Concordances of the Bible, cross-references, alphabetical glossaries, and subject indices began in the thirteenth century. In the same century the division of the Old and New Testaments into chapters and verses was finalized. Subdivisions also were created for medieval texts and revised for the few known classics. Versals, those ornamental capitals at the opening of a verse or paragraph, often in contrasting colors, were additional guides for the reader. Quotations were underlined in red.

The first task of the scribe or his assistant was to rule guidelines for the text (pl. 176). He did so by pricking the parchment at the desired intervals with an awl held against a ruler, or with a compass, or with a metal wheel with projecting spokes that ran along the surface of the parchment (pl. 177). In the late Middle Ages, these prickings were in the inner and outer margins and often could not be seen after binding, because they were embedded in the sewing of the spine in the center of the folio, and at the outer edges they were cut off when the book was trimmed. Lines were drawn through the prickings with a dry metal stylus or a dull knife, with lead point (plummet) by the eleventh or twelfth century and, more rarely from the thirteenth century, with ink. In Onsular practice, the whole quire was ruled at one time (everywhere else they were ruled before folding)—and if the scribe pressed hard enough on the first sheet of the stack of four, progressively fainter impressions remained on the other three for guidelines. Vertical rulings were also marked off to contain blocklike columns of text. Most medieval Bibles display two columns per page.

The scribe frequently began the text with *Incipit,* "here begins," and ended it with *Explicit* (*explicitus,* unrolled, a tradition from scroll times) or *Finit.* In the fifteenth century this changed to *Finis,* which is still seen in a few printed literary works. The scribe's implements were provided by the *armarius:* desk, reading frame to hold the book or quire to be copied, awl, stylus, parchment and pumice or *plana* for

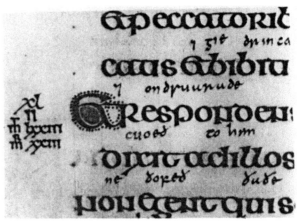

Pl. 177. Prickings for ruling lines. From the Lindisfarne Gospels. Lindisfarne, ca. 700. British Library, Ms. Cotton Nero D. IV, f. 36r. Courtesy of the British Library

Pl. 176. Scribe/monk ruling lines on his parchment. Hamburg, 1255. Royal Library, Copenhagen, Ms. 4, 2° I, f. 137v. Courtesy of Det Kongelige Bibliotek, Copenhagen

Pl. 178. One scribe/monk sharpens his quill, the other smooths parchment. Hamburg, 1255. Royal Library, Copenhagen, Ms. 4, 2° III, f. 142v. Courtesy of Det Kongelige Bibliotek, Copenhagen

smoothing it, goose quills and a knife to sharpen them or to correct mistakes (pl. 178), ink and inkpot or bull's horn, and weights to hold down the parchment as the scribe wrote. Pounce has been mentioned as a substitute for pumice in areas where there was no volcanic rock for the final smoothing of the surface before writing and painting and after scraping out smudges or errors. Pounce could be made of powdered chalk, but in England it was concocted from brewer's yeast, flour, and powdered glass, which was left to rise and then baked into loaves. Pounce powder, sold in bags, is still used today not only by calligraphers but by architects to prepare vellum before drawing (but their "vellum" is a smooth, high-quality paper).

THE SCRIBE

Several scribes sat together in the scriptorium, which usually served as the monastic library as well, or in separate cells called carrels partitioned off of a large room (pl. 179). Carrels are a tradition still seen in the modern university library, where doctoral students can isolate themselves. In the Benedictine monastery the scriptorium was over the chapter house, and carrels were at times open to the cloister walk. The scribe wrote for six hours a day, that is, all the daylight hours not

Pl. 179. Scribes at work in the scriptorium of Echternach. Gospel Book of Henry III. Early eleventh century. Universitätsbibliothek, Bremen, Ms. b.21, f. 124v. Early eleventh century. Photo courtesy of Dr. Ludwig Reichert Verlag, Wiesbaden

devoted to liturgical duties. As there was a potential danger of candles burning his efforts, he would stop work at sunset. Silence was the scriptorium rule, and the scribe made his need for additional materials known to the *armarius* by hand signals. He sometimes expressed his feelings to his fellow scribes and to posterity by writing in the margin of his quire notes such as:

"Thin ink, bad vellum, difficult text."

"The parchment is hairy."

"Thank God, it will soon be dark."

COLOPHONS

The colophons left to us by Latin scribes of the Middle Ages number into the thousands. Here are a few:

"Let the copyist be permitted to put an end to his labor."

"Now I've written the whole thing: for Christ's sake give me a drink."

"Let the reader's voice honor the writer's pen."[5]

The European writer of the colophon usually recorded his name, the date, and the place of writing. Occasionally he left a curse *(anathema)* against the unauthorized borrower or destroyer of the book, in Near Eastern fashion. Here is one from Barcelona, which may have been influenced by its Jewish or Muslim counterpart:

For him that stealeth, or borroweth and returneth not, this book from its owner, let it change into a serpent in his hand and rend him. Let him be struck with palsy, and all his members blasted. Let him languish in pain crying aloud for mercy, and let there be no surcease to his agony till he sing in dissolution. Let bookworms gnaw his entrails in token of the Worm that dieth not, and when at last he goeth to his final punishment, let the flames of Hell consume him forever.[6]

THE ARTIST

Was the scribe also the illuminator, and were they both always monks? Without colophons for most manuscripts, the question cannot be answered satisfactorily. A few scribes and illuminators left self-portraits as colophons. In the León Bible of 960, the master scribe Florentius and the painter-student Sanctio drink a toast in praise of God for the happy results of their long labors (pl. 180). There is evidence that in the early Middle Ages the monastic scriptorium occasionally hired an artist from outside the monastery to decorate the codex. But one wonders where he came from, and where he would have been trained if not in the monastery. The number of fugitives from the Byzantine iconoclastic milieu must have been limited. In twelfth-century Tuscany and England there were both monastic scribes and paid scribes and illuminators. Hildebert was a famous Bohemian scribe and artist of the twelfth century who was not a monk (pl. 181, 182). He left self-portraits, with his apprentice, in a few of the manuscripts he executed as scribe or as *pictor,* identifying his scribal or artistic role by holding either a curved pen and inkhorn, or a straight brush and bowl for pigments.

It is sometimes assumed that, in the most beautifully written and illuminated manuscripts, each scribe and artist was a specialist in his own area of expertise, particularly from Carolingian times. Yet in the Lindisfarne Gospels, an example of extremely complex design and illumination of the late seventh century, the scribe Eadfrith is believed to have been the illuminator as well. Just as today, in the Middle Ages exceptional artists were capable of developing their talents in more than one medium—script and art. Possibly within the scriptorium, talent in drawing was recognized in a particular scribe, and his skill as a miniaturist was developed (pl. 183). Later, the perfect integration of script and decoration characteristic of Romanesque and Gothic manuscripts indicates a well-planned layout, and not

Pl. 181. The scribe/monk and the lay brother Hildebert the artist (with his journeyman Everwinus) at the bottom of a page in a breviary. At the center, Gregory the Great dictates to his scribe, Peter the Deacon. Bohemia, 1136. The Royal Library–National Library of Sweden, Ms. A 144. Courtesy of the Kungliga Biblioteket, Stockholm

Pl. 180. The scribe/teacher Florentius and the student/painter Sanctio drink a toast, praising God for the happy results of their long labors. "Omega Page" from the León Bible of 960. San Isidore, León, Cod. 2, f. 515v. Courtesy of Colegiata de San Isidoro, León

Pl. 182. The distracted illuminator Hildebert and Everwinus. Inscribed in the book, "Cursed mouse for provoking my anger so often, God do away with you." Augustine, *De Civitas Dei.* Ca. 1140. Archives of the Prague Castle, Library of the Metropolitan Capital of St. Wenceslas, sig. A XXI/1, f. 153r. Courtesy of the Chancery of the President of the Czech and Slovak Federal Republic and the Archives of the Prague Castle

Pl. 183. Eadwine the scribe (not the illuminator), with pen and penknife. Eadwine Psalter (Tripartate Psalter). Canterbury, 1147. 18⅛ × 12⅞″ (460 × 327 mm). Trinity College Library, Cambridge, Ms. R.17.1, f. 283v. Courtesy of Trinity College Library, Cambridge University

execution of script and art by the same hand. Yet Matthew Paris, working in England in the middle of the thirteenth century, not only was a scribe and illuminator, but also wrote a history of St. Albans (pl. 184). By the fifteenth century, it is known with greater certainty that scribes and illuminators specialized in their own areas.

When scribes were depicted in illustrated manuscripts, they often appear to be writing in the already-bound codex. This is a medieval artistic convention, just as columnless writing and the incorrect orientation of script had been in Greek and Roman art.

WOMEN AND BOOKS

In medieval times, it was believed generally that women should not concern themselves with reading and writing, even in nunneries. In England, the Anglo-Saxon period seems to have been the only one in which nuns were known to be learned, although a work of the late twelfth century, a *Life of St. Catherine,* written in Norman-French, is attributed to the nun Clemence of Barking. Throughout the medieval period, however, women were involved in the production of books, both inside and outside nunneries, and evidence is increasingly being found for widespread female literacy. In Germany, on the other hand, there were at times nuns who were authors and scribes. In the tenth century the nun Roswitha at the Abbey of Gandersheim in Saxony, who obviously was familiar with all of the Latin authors whose works were copied in Carolingian times, wrote poetic legends

in Latin, a poem on Emperor Otto the Great, and the history of the convent. Another abbess, Gerberga, apparently knew Greek. It was at Gandersheim, founded in 852, that Otto II's educated Byzantine wife Theophanu often retreated, and sent their daughter Sophia to study at the age of four. Sophia later became Gandersheim's abbess. The abbess of Niedermannstadt, Uta, in the codex she commissioned, received a small portrait in the upper corner of a page devoted to St. Erhard celebrating mass (pl. 185), and appears in full figure dedicating the book to the Madonna and Child. The abbess Hitda of Meschede, too, is portrayed on the dedication page of her Gospels of ca. 1000–1020 (Darmstadt, Landesbibliothek, cod. 1640). Herrad of Landsberg, abbess of Odilienberg (1167–1195), compiled and illustrated the *Hortus Deliciarum* (Garden of Delights), which became a sourcebook for medieval iconography. Two of Herrad's contemporaries, St. Hildegard of Bingen (1098–1179) and St. Elizabeth of Schönau, wrote of their own visions. In the thirteenth century, the nuns of Hefta in Saxony collected, copied, and illuminated books; a few of them composed their own works as well. Some nuns received books as bequests from family members and, because they were aristocrats, may have brought books with them when they entered the convent. But libraries in nunneries were small, and usually contained service books only.

THE LATE MIDDLE AGES

Although monastic manuscript production continued after the twelfth century, the growth of the cathedral schools and then the universities created a need for many more texts than ever before. City workshops of scribes and artists began to meet this

Pl. 185. St. Erhard celebrating mass. Uta Codex.
The Abbess Uta, who
commissioned the manu-
script, is in upper right
frame. Regensburg, elev-
enth century. State
Library, Munich, Ms.
Clm. lat. 13601, f. 4r. 11
× 8³⁄₁₆″ (280 × 208 mm).
Courtesy of Bayerisches
Staatsbibliothek, Munich

demand. By the late thirteenth century in Paris (a century later in England), ateliers of scribes and illuminators were known by the name of their master artists. The city-dwelling publisher, or *stationarius*, provided manuscripts for clients, hiring and coordinating the work of scribes and illuminators. In England the Stationer's Company eventually became the printers' guild. One way of providing texts was the *pecia* system, which began in Italian and French university towns around 1200. The *stationarius* rented out authorized manuscripts by the quire to student or scholar, or to their hired scribes, for copying. For an additional fee, *pecia* copies were proofread by the stationarius for accuracy. Although none of the exemplars have been discovered, many *pecia* copies of theological, civil, and canon law books have survived from Bologna, Padua, Naples, Salamanca, Paris, Toulouse, Oxford, and other university towns. Some of the rules that universities tried to impose on the *pecia* system are extant as well.

**SOURCES OF
MANUSCRIPTS**

With so few books available in the Middle Ages, one may wonder where monasteries obtained manuscripts to copy. When a new monastery was founded, missionaries brought books with them to inaugurate the library. Intermonastic library loans were made at times, but the lending institution sometimes had difficulty in securing the return of the model codex. Sometimes the lending monastery sent a monk to supervise the copying. Enterprising abbots scoured the used-book market in Rome for old codices while such a market still existed, possibly into Carolingian times. Important churchmen, royalty, and nobility commissioned and received books as gifts. They, in turn, had copies made. In the twelfth century, the time in which cathedral schools flourished, some authors dictated their works to scribes who wrote on wax tablets for their scratch copies until the works were transferred to parchment. By the fourteenth century, authors wrote out their own commentaries and other texts, usually in a cursive hand, and these were copied and published by stationarii. University students did not take dictation. In some instances, they already had the book before them as the professor lectured. If they could not afford a *pecia* copy from the stationarius, they borrowed it from the library. In larger university towns there were guilds of stationarii, scribes, and illuminators. From the time of the Early Renaissance, monasteries were cajoled into parting with codices to enrich the libraries of noble and aristocratic manuscript collectors. By then there were many successful book dealers, who supplied the first printers with manuscripts as well.

Notes

1. Daniel V. Thompson, *The Materials and Techniques of Medieval Painting* (New York: Dover, 1956), 27.

2. David Simon Blondheim, "An Old Portuguese Work on Manuscript Illumination," *Jewish Quarterly Review* 19 (1928): 132.

3. Ronald Reed, *Ancient Skins, Parchments, and Leathers* (London, 1972), 162.

4. Blondheim, "An Old Portuguese Work," 124.

5. Falconer Madan, *Books in Manuscript: A Short Introduction to Their Study and Use,* trans. Peter Gulewich, rev. ed. (London: K. Paul, Trench, Trubner, 1920), 53–54.

6. Marc Drogin, *Anathema! Medieval Scribes and the History of Book Curses* (Totowa and Montclair, N.J.: Alanheld and Schram, 1983), 88.

CHAPTER 10

Manuscript Illumination

METHODOLOGY

Throughout the history of manuscript illumination, from late Antiquity until shortly after the invention of printing, the book designer and artist had to solve certain problems of composition and style in planning the decorations and miniatures for the codex.

In making a statement such as this, we are taking several things for granted. We assume first that there was book illustration in late Antiquity; second, that there was a specific designer for the book; and third, that the designer or artist was aware of design problems and stylistic traditions as early as Hellenistic and Roman times and into the Middle Ages. Of these three assumptions, the one for which there is least evidence is the existence of a book designer as a distinct individual. It was the scribe or illuminator or publisher-bookseller who undoubtedly devised the program for decorating the scroll or early codex. In the early Middle Ages, in monastic scriptoria, it was the abbot or an *armarius* with aesthetic inclinations. In the late Middle Ages, when guilds were involved in bookmaking, it was the *stationarius* or master craftsman in the urban workshop. Most scribes and miniaturists of the Middle Ages were not creative, and were content to copy the style and format of the manuscripts they had before them, some making adjustments to suit the age and place and, possibly, the needs of the person for whom the book was made. The codex was a conservative entity, once it was accepted, and it changed little over the centuries. Models, or prototypes, of the illustrations were respected, too, just as exemplars of texts had been.

As for the existence of book illustration in Antiquity, it is assumed that the art in Egyptian scrolls was seen by makers of books in hellenized Alexandria. The library there was reported to have housed seven hundred thousand scrolls in the time of Julius Caesar, when part or all of it was set afire. While it cannot be proven that Hellenistic book artists were aware of Books of the Dead, it is very likely that there

231

were other works the two cultures, Greek and Egyptian, shared: magical, scientific, and astronomical works; animal fables; and erotica. If we are dealing in hypothetical illuminated scrolls, we may as well assume that the Septuagint was illustrated. According to Aristeas, the name of God was written in a Torah with letters of gold (see Chapter 5). Once the Bible was translated, it provided rich narrative material for the Greek reader. It was as suitable for cycles of illustration as were Greek mythology and Homeric epics, which were subjects to be depicted on pottery and tablets as well as on painted walls and in mosaics of Hellenistic and Roman homes in Pompeii and the other towns around Mt. Vesuvius. When illumination did "appear" in the fifth and sixth centuries C.E., the major subjects were scenes from the Bible, the *Iliad* and the *Aeneid*. It can be assumed that there were other centers of manuscript production besides Alexandria. Pergamum, after all, boasted a rival library. Rome, Constantinople, and Antioch were art capitals in the early years of the Christian era, and probably had workshops where miniatures were painted.

The third hypothetical issue, that of book design and style, is imposed by the modern art historian who surveys the history of illumination according to the evidence from extant codices, with an overview of art of all periods. The illuminators themselves may have given little thought to these problems. But whether the artist knew it or not, the major problem of the book designer who needed or wanted to illustrate a text was how text and picture would fit together, or how the decoration or visual aids would be integrated with the written word. Scientific texts were accompanied by diagrams or sketches within the body of the text, alongside the written material, or in the margins. In the luxury codex, illustration could occupy the whole page.

Another aspect of the ancient book's decorative program was the portrait of the author. In the earliest manuscripts and their copies, authors appeared as busts in medallions, as standing figures (sometimes reading their works), or as seated scribes. Pliny (*Natural History* 37) said that Varro included seven hundred portraits among his books, and that these books were distributed all over the world. As for illustrations to literature, fragments show unframed pictures in columns of text at frequent intervals. There may also have been framed narrative scenes as well, for these appear in the earliest codices of Homer and Virgil. In many instances it is later copies, from the sixth century, the Carolingian age, or the Middle Byzantine period, that are believed to reflect earlier practices of artists. The "original" manuscript model, from which all copies are derived, is called a prototype, and when two manuscripts display similar depictions of a single theme, even when they were made at different places and times, it is assumed that they were derived from a single prototype. When the source of a new theme is unknown in a medieval manuscript, it is convenient to attribute that theme's origin to a lost prototype. The primary study of ancient manuscripts, both real and hypothetical prototypes, has been accomplished by Kurt Weitzmann.

In addition to the problems of how to illustrate a text and of integrating text and illustration, the artist had to decide, consciously or subconsciously, how he was to view the surface of the page. Should the picture suit the two-dimensionality of its parchment surface, or deny it in favor of three-dimensional effects, which were the legacy of Hellenistic and Roman illusionistic painting? Illusionism was the realistic style which gave a three-dimensional appearance to the picture by means of atmospheric and architectural perspective, foreshortening, and modeling of figures with light and shade, all of which changed the relative size and clarity of figures as they moved back into space. We will see that artists of the periods into which medieval illumination is divided solved these two problems—integrating text and illustration, and creating three-dimensional illusionistic space—in different ways, according to the age in which they painted, their geographic region, the style of their monastery or workshop, the prototypes they followed, and their individual skill and taste. Table 8 lists the major periods and styles of illumination and the period each was used.

The earliest extant papyrus and parchment manuscripts are studied for their own place in manuscript illumination and for what they may reveal of lost books. Fragments of literary manuscripts on papyrus scrolls, a romance from the second century C.E. and a poem about Heracles, show interspersed with text unframed drawings that carry the stories forward. This format, which was known in first-millennium Books of the Dead, continues in more sumptuous parchment manuscripts such as the Vienna Genesis of the sixth century, where frameless scenes run along the bottom of the page, and in the Carolingian masterpieces, such as the Utrecht Psalter. Other, more formal codices deliberately separate illustrations from text by framing them, as if they were wall paintings. At times a picture occupies a full page; at other times, a third or half of it with text filling the rest of the page. Table 9 lists important illuminated manuscripts and the dates they were made.

EARLY CHRISTIAN AND BYZANTINE MANUSCRIPTS

As far as is known, the earliest illustrated manuscripts were Homer's *Iliad;* Virgil's *Aeneid, Georgics,* and *Eclogues;* the comedies of Terence; a calendar known only from seventeenth-century drawings of a Carolingian copy; scientific treatises, the most popular of which in the Byzantine and later in the Islamic worlds was the herbal *De Materia Medica* by Dioscorides; the Old Testament; and the Gospels. Because so few codices have remained and the location of their execution is unknown, it is difficult to generalize on stylistic characteristics of the period or even to speak of specific workshops. Illustrations in the same manuscript will reveal their classical heritage and also point to the art of the Middle Ages. The fifth-century Vatican Virgil (Virgilius Vaticanus, Biblioteca Apoltolica Vaticana, cod. lat. 3225) is just such a manuscript. It is believed to have been made in Rome. With seventy-six folios remaining, its text, *The Aeneid, Georgics,* and *Eclogues,* was written in carefully formed Rustic Capitals. The miniatures, separated from the text by frames, look like frescoes painted in the Hellenistic illusionistic tradition, with animal and human figures rendered three-dimensionally, in light and shade. Interior scenes, such as two which depict the death of Dido, show real furniture and marbleized walls (pl. 186). Yet at times the artist, or one of several artists, disregarded perspective and true spatial relations and relative size of figures, either through lack of technical ability or because of the conscious need to economize for the sake of the miniature.

The tendency to abstraction is considered a medieval device. It is evident in the other Virgil manuscript in the Vatican Library, nicknamed the Codex Romanus or the Virgilius Romanus (cod. lat. 3867) to distinguish it from the Vatican Virgil. Dated to the fifth century, it is often called a provincial or "Eastern" manuscript because its absence of illusionistic technique implies a less sophisticated workshop.

Table 8. Major Styles of Manuscript Illumination

Style	Centuries
Early Christian and Byzantine	Fourth–Sixth
(Middle Byzantine)	Mid-ninth–Twelfth
Hiberno-Saxon (Insular, Anglo-Celtic)	Seventh–Eighth
Carolingian	Eighth–Ninth
Ottonian	Tenth–Eleventh
Romanesque	Eleventh–Twelfth
Gothic	Thirteenth–Fifteenth

Table 9. Important Illuminated Manuscripts

Manuscript	Date (c.e.)
Early Christian and Byzantine	
Ambrosian Iliad	Late 300s or early 400s
Vatican Virgil	Late 300s or early 400s
Virgilius Romanus	Late 300s or early 400s
Vienna Dioscorides (Dioscorides of Juliana Anicia)	ca. 512
Vienna Genesis	500–600
Rossano Gospels	ca. 580
Paris Psalter	ca. 900–950
Joshua Roll	ca. 900–950
Hiberno-Saxon	
Book of Durrow	ca. 680
Lindisfarne Gospels	ca. 700
Codex Amiatinus	ca. 700
Book of Kells	760–820
Carolingian	
Gospel Book of Charlemagne (Godescalc Gospels)	781–783
Ebo Gospels	Before 823
Utrecht Psalter	ca. 830
Grandval Bible	840
First Bible of Charles the Bald	846
Ottonian	
Gospel Book of Otto III	1000
Uta Codex	1015–1025
Romanesque	
Winchester Bible	1150–1200
Lambeth Bible	1150–1200
Gothic	
Ingeborg Psalter	ca. 1200
St. Louis Psalter	1256
Douce Apocalypse	1270
Breviary of Belleville	1323–1326
Hours of Jeanne d'Evreux	1325
Très Riches Heures de Duc de Berry	1413–1416
The Antiquities of the Jews	1470

In common with the Vatican Virgil are its Rustic Capitals, headings in red, and framed miniatures (except for one). But the heavily outlined figures are flat when compared to those of the Vatican Virgil and other classically influenced manuscripts. Folds of drapery (clothing) are patterns of line rather than naturally falling fabric, and highlights on figures have no relation to a single light source. In a full-page pastoral miniature from the *Georgics,* animals, shepherds, and vegetation are scattered on the surface of the page to give a tapestry or mosaic effect (pl. 187). Three-dimensional, illusionistic techniques surrender to overall design. Once again, this can be seen as a lack of technical skill or simply as disinterest in the spatial effects of the Hellenistic and Roman classical painterly style. On two folios of the Codex

Pl. 186. The death of Dido. Vatican Virgil (Virgilius Vaticanus). Rome, early fifth century. Vatican Library, cod. lat. 3225, f. 41r. 8⅝ × 7¾″ (219 × 196 mm). Courtesy of the Biblioteca Apostolica Vaticana, Vatican City

Pl. 187. Shepherds tending their flock, from the *Georgics*, Book III. Codex Romanus (Virgilius Romanus). Fifth century. Vatican Library, cod. lat. 3867, f. 44v. 13 × 12¾″ (332× 323 mm). Courtesy of the Biblioteca Apostolica Vaticana, Vatican City

Romanus there are portraits of Virgil holding his scroll (see pl. 146, p. 169). Alongside him are his writing stand and *capsa*. Although realistic portraiture cannot be expected from this manuscript, the author portrait itself represents a link in an uninterrupted tradition from Antiquity to the present-day book.

Representing the tradition of illuminated scientific manuscripts is the Vienna Dioscorides, commissioned about 512 by the Byzantine princess Juliana Anicia, granddaughter of Valentinian III (Vienna, Nationalbibliothek, cod. med. gr. 1, pl. 188-191). It contains *De Materia Medica* and other pharmacological works, such as Nicander's treatise on snakebite. It also includes a theological treatise. This sumptuous codex commences with seven full-page miniatures, a dedication page depicting the patroness, two pages of group portraits of the authors of the pharmacological treatises (seven per page), and two full-page portraits of the author Dioscorides, the first-century physician and chemist from Cilicia. In one of these portraits, Eureses, the personification of Invention, holds the mandrake root that the dog has unearthed, referring to the legend that he dies from this act (although this legend is not mentioned in the text; pl. 188). The other portrait shows Dioscorides in the studio with a theatrical-looking architectural backdrop, at the side of an artist who draws the mandrake root from life while the author reads from his codex. They are inspired by the personification of Thought, Epinoia. The dedication of a church built in 512 at Honoratae, a suburb of Constantinople, is mentioned on f. 6v, the page on which Juliana Anicia is flanked by personifications of Prudence and Magnanimity, while Gratitude of the Arts prostrates herself before the princess (pl. 189). Behind her is a cherub, holding up the dedication pages. This seemingly natural combination of pagan classical iconography and Christian subjects will become a permanent aspect of many religious manuscripts. The iconography of group portraiture, such as the assembled physicians on f. 3v, will be adopted by Christian illuminators as apostle portraits, the central seventh figure transform-

Pl. 188. Dioscorides with mandrake, inspired by Invention. Dioscorides of Juliana Anicia. Constantinople, before 512. Vienna National Library, cod. med. graec. 1., f. 4v. 15 × 13″ (380 × 330 mm). Courtesy of the Bild-Archiv der Österreichische Nationalbibliothek, Vienna

Pl. 189. Portrait of Juliana Anicia between Prudence and Magnanimity. Dioscorides of Juliana Anicia. Constantinople, before 512. Vienna National Library, cod. med. graec. 1., f. 6v. 15 × 13″ (380 × 330 mm). Courtesy of the Bild-Archiv der Österreichische Nationalbibliothek, Vienna

ing himself from Galen (in this instance) to Christ in the context of the Gospel book (pl. 190).

In the Vienna Dioscorides, the figure style is purely classical, even when furniture and settings are limited to solid colors or gold backgrounds. These are framed magnificently with elaborate borders on large parchment pages. Patron portraits, like those of authors and their accompanying personifications, became an important feature of the medieval book, the personification figure transforming itself into an evangelist in the Christian context. Within the Greek Uncial text of the Vienna Dioscorides there were 435 full-page illustrations, of which 383 have remained (pl. 191). In the earliest papyrus herbals, plants were illustrated at the top of each column describing them. In the Vienna Dioscorides, each plant has its own page. Many are rendered realistically, as if copied from nature. Some are more abstract; some include mythological figures. All painted drawings are perfectly composed. The manuscript was in the hands of several later owners who spoke different languages; this is revealed by the notes in various scripts on the plant pages: Greek Minuscule, Persian, and Hebrew. In 1569, the Vienna Dioscorides was sold to the emperor Maximilian II by the son of the physician to Sultan Suleiman II.

A few illuminated Old Testament manuscripts have survived from this age. Their narrative illustrations show so many detailed scenes that some believe there must have been multiple prototypes for Old Testament manuscripts, wall paintings, or mosaics. One partially extant manuscript is the Quedlinburg Itala of the early fifth

Pl. 190. Galen with six physicians, including Nicanor with snake. Dioscorides of Juliana Anicia. Constantinople, before 512. Vienna National Library, cod. med. graec. 1., f. 3v. 15× 13″ (380 × 330 mm). Courtesy of the Bild-Archiv der Österreichische Nationalbibliothek, Vienna

Pl. 191. The rose. Dioscorides of Juliana Anicia. Constantinople, before 512. Vienna National Library, cod. med. graec. 1., f. 282r. 15 × 13″ (380 × 330 mm). Courtesy of the Bild-Archiv der Österreichische Nationalbibliothek, Vienna

century (Berlin, Staatsbibliothek, cod. theol. lat. fol. 485), six leaves of which were used as binding material in the seventeenth-century book, found in 1865. The pages depict incidents from the books of Samuel and Kings. Folio 2r shows four scenes in sequence, with figures rendered economically but dramatically against a sketchy background similar to that of the Vatican Virgil. Two famous sixth-century manuscripts are the Cotton Genesis (British Library, Cotton Otho. B. VI), now in 150 charred fragments since the 1731 fire at Ashburnham House, and the Vienna Genesis (Vienna, Nationalbibliothek, cod. theol. gr. 31). Most of the miniatures of the Cotton Genesis are placed in the single column of Greek Uncial text, but a few occupy almost a whole page with little text. In the Vienna Genesis, the lower half of the page was reserved for continuous narrative illustrations, sometimes divided into two registers with minimal background to emphasize the handsome purple parchment (pl. 192). The text, written in Greek Uncials in silver ink, is an abbreviated version of stories from Genesis. The several artists working on the manuscript used all of the illusionistic techniques known to them, including impressionistic landscapes and foreshortening in figures, and a full repertory of classical architectural forms and personifications, including nymphs and river goddesses. The literary source of some of the illustrations, especially those of the Joseph cycle, cannot be found in the Bible but were present in Jewish legends. These pictures of Jewish legends would indicate that illustrators based their pictures on visual or literary sources outside the Bible itself, either illustrated Hebrew Bibles or the Septuagint. It is also possible that similar Christian legends had an oral or written source that has been lost.

The earliest illuminated Gospel manuscripts also display lingering classical illusionism, mixed with a reduction in spatial effects and a lack of interest in the physical reality of the human body and landscape. These stylistic aspects foreshadow the art of the Middle Ages. Christian iconography, the religious and symbolic subject matter, begins to emerge, parallel to the developments in Church mosaic art and frescoes. The Rossano Gospels (Calabria, Cathedral of Rossano) do not present a sequence of continuous narrative illustrations as did the Old Testament manuscripts (pl. 193). Illustrations grouped together in the pages preceding the Gospels depict half-figure Old Testament prophets who lean on text-blocks of their prophecies and point to the pictures above that fulfill them in the Gospel: The Good Samaritan, The Wise and Foolish Virgins, The Raising of Lazarus, Christ's Entry into Jerusalem. The Gospel text that follows is written in silver Uncials on a purple ground. The Communion of the Apostles appears along the bottom of preliminary pages f. 3v and 4r, followed by a frontispiece to the canon tables on f. 5r—a double circle of busts of the four evangelists. On f. 121r, St. Mark sits on a high-backed wicker chair, writing his Gospel on a scroll, inspired by the standing haloed figure of Hagia Sophia, Holy Wisdom (pl. 194). This Byzantine miniature plays a key role in the transformation of a pagan theme into Christian iconography. Just as the authors and poets of antiquity were inspired by their muses, the evangelists of Western manuscripts will be inspired by their symbols, according to the system worked out by St. Irenaeus: the man of St. Matthew, the lion of St. Mark, the ox of St. Luke, and the eagle of St. John. The literary origin of the evangelists' attributes was in Ezekiel's chariot vision, later repeated in the Apocalypse of St. John. These can be seen in the Ascension of the Rabbula Gospels, along with a projecting "hand of God" beneath Christ in Majesty—two other themes that are to reappear throughout the Middle Ages (pl. 195). In this Syriac manuscript (Florence, Laurentian Library, cod. Plut. I, 56), monumental human figures lose their corporeality even more than in the Rossano Gospels, and are manneristically elongated. The codex was written by the scribe Rabbula in 586 in the Monastery of St. John at Zagba, in northern Mesopotamia. Birds, animals, and lively, colorful vignettes illustrating incidents in the Gospel story, in quick-sketch style, appear

Pl. 193. Parable of the Wise and Foolish Virgins. Rossano Gospels (Codex Purpureus). Greco-Syrian(?), sixth century. Episcopal palace, Rossano, f. 4r. 12 × 10¼″ (307 × 260 mm). Courtesy of Museo Diocesano, Rossano. Reproduced from *Byzantine Painting* by André Grabar (photo Hinz, Archives SKIRA, Genève)

Pl. 194. St. Mark with Hagia Sophia. Rossano Gospels (Codex Purpureus). Greco-Syrian(?), sixth century. Episcopal palace, Rossano, f. 121r. 12 × 10¼″ (307 × 260 mm). Courtesy of Museo Diocesano, Rossano. Reproduced from Kurt Weitzmann, *Late Antique and Early Christian Book Illumination*. Courtesy of George Braziller

Pl. 195. The Ascension. Rabbula Gospels. Monastery of St. John of Zagba, Mesopotamia, 586. Laurentian Library, Cod. Plut. 1.56, f. 13v. 13¼ × 10½″ (336 × 266 mm). Courtesy of the Biblioteca Laurenziana, Florence

alongside the canon tables (pl. 196). Standing or seated Old Testament figures and evangelists appear in architectural settings. The canon tables listed the passages that were parallel in the four Gospels, according to the system of Eusebius of Caesarea (ca. 330). These canon tables became a standard subject of ornamentation in medieval New Testament codices, and were usually given an architectural framework.

From 726 to 843, during the iconoclastic period in Byzantium, illumination of sumptuous religious manuscripts ceased. In the monasteries though, where underground iconodule art continued, manuscripts such as the ninth-century Khludov Psalter (Moscow Historical Museum) continued the tradition of marginal vignettes. Psalms were an essential part of Byzantine liturgy, and continued to be the most popular Old Testament book to be illustrated in both East and West. In the Second Golden Age, or Macedonian Renaissance, Hellenistic and Roman classical subjects and style were renewed, even for biblical manuscripts. The tenth-century Paris Psalter (Paris, Bibliothèque Nationale, Ms. grec. 139), like the several manuscripts that resemble it, is a showpiece of classical illusionistic technique and themes (pl. 197, 198). The author portrait of King David with lyre is based on the Greek classical iconography of Orpheus taming the beasts. He is inspired by the figure of Melody, and the River Jordan is identified by a reclining river god. The Joshua Roll (Vatican, gr. 431), from the same period, is another example of a religious subject expressed in the classical idiom (pl. 199). It was executed in a delicate wash drawing technique of brown, blue, white, and purple, recalling antique illusionism. Eclecticism is demonstrated by the revival of the horizontal scroll form—no longer of any practical use.

Pl. 196. Canon table page. Rabbula Gospels, Syriac. Monastery of St. John of Zagba, Mesopotamia, 586. Laurentian-Library, Cod. Plut. 1.56, f. 8r. 13¼ × 10½″ (336 × 266 mm). Courtesy of the Biblioteca Laurenziana, Florence

Pl. 197. King David. Paris Psalter. Byzantium, tenth century. Bibliothèque Nationale, Ms. grec. 139, f. 1v. 14¼ × 10¼″ (360 × 260 mm). Courtesy of the Bibliothèque Nationale, Paris

Pl. 198. Crossing of the Red Sea. Paris Psalter. Byzantium, tenth century. Bibliothèque Nationale, Ms. grec. 139, f. 419v. 14¼ × 10¼″ (360 × 260 mm). Courtesy of the Bibliothèque Nationale, Paris

Pl. 199. Joshua and the emissaries of Gibeon; the sun and moon stand still. Joshua Roll. Byzantium, tenth century. Vatican Library, Ms. Palat. gr. 431. 12″ × 35′ (305 mm × 10.66 m). Courtesy of the Biblioteca Apostolica Vaticana, Vatican City

HIBERNO-SAXON

The illusionism of Byzantine painting can be seen as a denial of the two-dimensionality of the codex page. When one looks at the Hiberno-Saxon book, the surface of the parchment and the decoration upon it are in perfect harmony. The abstract, linear patterns of Gospel books, such as the Book of Durrow and the Book of Kells, and the English Lindisfarne Gospels are prime examples of two-dimensional ornament. Their pages of script, with ornamental initials, are cohesive decorative units. The interlace pattern so prominent in Hiberno-Saxon manuscripts was present in the pre-Christian art of England, to be found in the metalwork of the Sutton Hoo burial of the early seventh century C.E. It also must have been present in the Mediterranean book of early Christianity, for interlaces were popular in Coptic illumination and on early leather bindings, and in the Islamic art that was heir to Coptic style. But unlike Islamic interlaces, zoomorphic forms entered the Anglo-Celtic vocabulary of ornament. A seemingly infinite variety of ribbons, plaitwork, dots and knots, grid patterns, circles, spirals, whorls, lozenges, fretwork (interlaced angular designs), scrolls, trumpet, and step and key patterns in symmetrical and asymmetrical arrangement either cover the whole page (except for the parchment margins) or are enclosed in an enlarged initial letter.

The carpet page is another distinct feature of the Hiberno-Saxon book, so called by later art historians because of its resemblance to the all-over pattern of an oriental carpet. It too may have originated in some lost classical prototype whose descendants were also the earliest Islamic Qur'ān manuscripts and Hebrew illuminated codices. Carpet pages in the books of these cultures indicate an early medieval "International Style." The earliest carpet pages are in the Book of Durrow (Dublin, Trinity College Library, Ms. 57), written about 680 (pl. 200). Folio 1v displays a double cross. The other outstanding decorative feature of the Book of Durrow, which continues in Insular Gospel Books, is the evangelist symbol page. St. Matthew's symbol, the man, does not look like a man at all but like a checkerboard bell with projecting head and feet. Zoomorphic forms, rows of interlacing animals, appear in a carpet page facing the beginning of St. John's Gospel, on f. 192v.

The Lindisfarne Gospels, written ca. 700, also was named for the monastery in which the manuscript was written (British Library, Cotton Ms. Nero D.IV, pl. 201). It has five magnificent interlaced carpet pages based on the cross. Architectural ornamentation enhances sixteen pages of Eusebian canon tables. The evangelists themselves appear *with* their symbols rather than as symbols alone, as they did in the Book of Durrow. There is little reference to classic, realistic form in their bodies. St. Matthew resembles Ezra the Scribe in the Codex Amiatinus (see pl. 169, p. 208), a manuscript with known Mediterranean connections—the copy of Cassiodorus's Codex Grandior. There are other references in the Ezra illustration to an Italian prototype in its realistic furniture, scribal implements, and open *armarium* (book case). The Old Testament scribe is wearing the Jewish *tefillin* on his forehead. Although the iconography of the Lindisfarne Gospels' St. Matthew is similar to the

Pl. 200. Carpet Page. Book of Durrow, ca. 680. Trinity College Library, Ms. 57, f. 192v. 9⅝ × 5¾" (245 × 145 mm). Courtesy of the Board of Trinity College, Dublin

Pl. 201. St. Matthew. Lindisfarne Gospels. Lindisfarne, ca. 700. British Library, Ms. Cotton Nero D. IV, f. 25v. 13½ × 9¾" (343 × 248 mm). Courtesy of the British Library

Codex Amiatinus's Ezra, it is stylistically dissimilar. The artist ignored reality to form patterns in drapery and hair, and showed even less understanding of or interest in space than did the artist of the Codex Amiatinus.

The most splendid of the Insular group is the Book of Kells (Dublin, Trinity College Library, Ms. 58), thought possibly to have been produced in Iona just before the Viking invasion of 807 (pl. 202-204 and pl. 155, p. 187). Handsome, large Irish Half-Uncials; a profusion of decorated monograms and initial letters; a variety of abstract, zoomorphic, and stylized human forms; and exceedingly complex interlaces have rightfully inspired all who have seen this manuscript to consider it one of the finest of the Middle Ages. In addition to the decorated canon tables, of which ten out of twelve were completed, there are carpet pages based on the cross, four-evangelist symbol pages (pl. 202) and single evangelist portraits, a full-length portrait of Christ, and the Madonna and Child (pl. 203), based on a Coptic prototype, the Temptation of Christ and the Arrest of Christ. Nearly every page displays inventive decoration, executed with subtle, refined taste. The most celebrated page is that of the *Chi Rho* monogram, f. 34r, within whose profusion of microscopic interlacing ornament are scattered humans and animals: cats, mice, moths, and an otter (pl. 204). They hint at the consistent love of nature that will be seen again in the illuminated pages of Romanesque manuscripts.

Pl. 202. Symbols of the four evangelists. Book of Kells.
Iona, before 807. Trinity College Library, Ms. 58, f. 27v.
13 × 9⅞″ (330 × 250 mm). Courtesy of the Board of
Trinity College, Dublin

Pl. 203. Virgin and Child. Book of Kells. Iona, before
807. Trinity College Library, Ms. 58, f. 7v. Courtesy of
the Board of Trinity College, Dublin

**CAROLINGIAN
RENAISSANCE**

Manuscript art of the Carolingian Renaissance was a revival of classical style, that is,
classical style as it was known to the Carolingian artist. Under the influence of
Charlemagne and his successors, splendidly decorated books for monastery, school,
church, and court libraries became desirable items of acquisition. Books available in
Rome or Monte Cassino were brought to the court at Aachen or to monastic
scriptoria associated with it. New exempla were made and sent out to other centers,
such as Tours, Orléans, Salzburg, and Lyons, where their content, script, book
design, and illuminations were copied. Unlike the Hiberno-Saxon period, when
nearly all manuscripts were made for monastic use, in Carolingian times manuscript
patrons were imperial and aristocratic as well as ecclesiastical. Important churchmen
commissioned books for themselves and as gifts for their colleagues and royal and
noble friends. Emperors presented books to abbeys. All perpetuated the tradition of
the "gift book," which must have existed from the very beginning of books.

So many manuscripts were made in the Carolingian empire in comparison to
earlier periods that it is possible to discern schools of illumination. These schools are
essentially chronological, associated with individual patrons and artists who
established recognizable styles. The first is a masterpiece of the court school, the
Godescalc Gospels (Paris, Bibliothèque Nationale, Nouv. acq. lat. 1203), named for
the court scribe who wrote the lectionary (book of pericopes, or selected Gospel
readings) for Queen Hildegarde (who died in 783). The gold and silver ink on purple
parchment were obviously inspired by Byzantine manuscripts, as were certain
iconographic themes, such as the Fountain of Life (f. 3v; pl. 205). There are other
sources for the style and iconography of the Godescalc Gospels: an Italianate Christ

Pl. 204. Chi Rho page. Book of Kells. Iona, before 807. Trinity College Library, Ms. 58, f. 34r. Courtesy of the Board of Trinity College, Dublin

in Majesty (f. 3r), Hiberno-Saxon interlaces in decorative frames and initial letters (f. 4r), and flora and fauna that resemble those of Syriac manuscripts. The artist did not reconcile two- and three-dimensional picture space but combined in the same illustration flat ornament with bodily substance to figures. This undoubtedly was due to the artist's dependence on more than one model for what was one of the first Carolingian attempts to produce a luxury codex. The Godescalc Gospels then served as a prototype for other codices. In 827, Louis the Pious, Charlemagne's son, presented a Gospel book to the Abbey of St. Médard at Soissons (Paris, Bibliothèque Nationale, Ms. lat. 8850; pl. 206). The Fountain of Life was repeated with even less spatial reality than there had been in the Godescalc Gospels, in spite of the artist's attempt at drawing an architectural backdrop. Even more than the Godescalc Gospels, this codex seems to follow many models, and gives the impression that the artist has crammed in every detail he found in his sources.

The typical early Carolingian Gospel book maintained the tradition of single pages of evangelists-as-scribes, with their attributes, as well as canon table pages with architectural ornament. Themes from the Gospels also appear as vignettes on text pages. Although these scenes are small they may appear to be three-dimensional, with figures rendered in light and shade. Yet the overall effect of the page is flat and decorative. The artists of the generation after the Godescalc Gospels

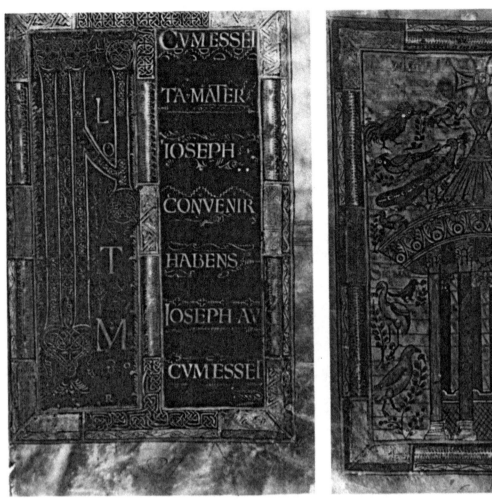

Pl. 205. The Fountain of Life and initial. Godescalc Gospels. Court School of
Charlemagne, 781–783. Bibliothèque Nationale, Nov. Acq. lat. 1203, f. 3v and 4r.
12¼ × 8¼″ (310× 210 mm). Courtesy of the Bibliothèque Nationale, Paris

were more consistent in planning the space of the individual page. Some pages show
two-dimensional ornament, especially where script is part of the layout, but on
pages where illustration is predominant, illusionistic effects were sought. Throughout early Carolingian illumination, both two- and three-dimensional decorated
pages can be found within the same manuscript.

Books other than Gospel lectionaries and complete Bibles were subjects for
illustration. Also popular were the Apocalypse; a picture poem called *De Laudibus
Santae Crucis* by Hrabanus Maurus, who was a student of Alcuin of York at Tours;
Prudentius's poems, including the *Psychomachia;* and many non-Christian classical
works such as Aratus's *Phaenomenon* (see pl. 158, p. 191), Terence's *Comedies,* and
Physiologus's second century C.E. pseudo-scientific treatise on the nature of animals.
The latter was a link in the tradition that began with Aesop's *Fables* and continued
in the Romanesque bestiary.

The next identifiable Carolingian school appears at Reims, where Louis the
Pious's foster brother and school companion, Ebo, was archbishop. At the
archbishop's abbey at Hautvillers, between Reims and Epernay, scribes and artists
created a group of manuscripts in the distinctive Reims style, which has been
compared to late-nineteenth-century Impressionism. The Ebo Gospels (Epernay,

Pl. 207. Detail from a canon table page. Ebo Gospels. Hautvillers, ca. 820. Municipal Library, Epernay, Ms. 1, f. 13v. 10¼ × 5⅞" (260 × 149 mm). Courtesy of the Bibliothèque Municipale, Epernay

Pl. 206. The Fountain of Life. Gospel Book of St. Médard. Abbey of St. Médard, Soissons, 827. Bibliothèque Nationale, Ms. lat. 8850, f. 6v. 14¼ × 10½" (362 × 267 mm). Courtesy of the Bibliothèque Nationale, Paris

Bibliothèque Municipale, Ms. 1) was made under the direction of the abbot Peter in approximately 820 (see pl. 19, p. 14). It displays magnificent pages of gold capital letters and Insular-style initials and evangelist portraits in gold-highlighted robes. Their expressionistic faces reflect nervous energy and the intensity of artistic creation. The architecture of the canon tables supports little figures who engage in everyday activities of hunting and construction of the gables on which they stand (pl. 207).

The thoroughly illusionistic effects and figure style of the Ebo Gospels are repeated in the most delightful of Carolingian manuscripts, the Utrecht Psalter, made about the same time and possibly by the same artist (Utrecht, Bibliotheek der Rijksuniversiteit, Cat. Cod. Ms. Bibl. Rhenotraiectinae, I, Ms. 32; pl. 208, 209). Its Rustic Capital text with red Uncial headings is accompanied by pen drawings that interpret the Psalms with pictures that appear to be in narrative sequence, but nearly all the illustrations are literal renditions of isolated words and phrases. The artist did not invent all of these word-images; some can be found in ninth-century Byzantine psalters and in another Carolingian psalter. From a seemingly infinite repertoire of gestures and figure groupings, graceful acrobatic poses, impressionistic draperies and landscapes, bits of vegetation, rounded hills, angels' wings, animal sketches, musical instruments, engraved pagan gems and classical buildings, columns and

Pl. 208. Opening page, with King David inspired by an angel. Utrecht Psalter. Hautvillers, ca. 820–830. Utrecht University Library, Bibl. Rhenotraiectinae, Ms. 32, f. 1v. 13¼× 10¼″ (335 × 260 mm). Courtesy of the Bibliotheek der Rijksuniversiteit, Utrecht

Pl. 209. Psalm 73 (72 in ms.). Utrecht Psalter. Hautvillers, ca. 820–830. Rustic Capital script, Uncial heading. Utrecht University Library, Bibl. Rhenotraiectinae, Ms. 32, f. 41v. 13¼ × 10¼″ (335 × 260 mm). Courtesy of the Bibliotheek der Rijksuniversiteit, Utrecht

statuary, the artist repeated motifs in varied combinations for each psalm. In doing so, he created one of the masterpieces of the Middle Ages. The Utrecht Psalter exhibits such charm, spontaneity, stylistic freshness, vivacity, and perfect draftsmanship that one wonders why art historians have expended so much effort in search of its prototypes. It *was* a prototype. It inspired many Carolingian manuscripts in its own day, and when it was brought to England about the year 1000, it was copied at least three times, and exerted a strong influence on the draftsmanship of English pre-Romanesque manuscripts. The Eadwine Psalter was one of the English copies, made at Canterbury ca. 1150 (see pl. 183, p. 226).

Reims style persisted in the next Carolingian school at Tours. In some manuscripts made there, one can easily pick out figures that look like emigrants from the Ebo Gospels and Utrecht Psalter. Although Alcuin of York's name is associated with Tours, the finer illuminated manuscripts from the Abbey of St. Martin were not made during his lifetime but during the time when Count Vivian was lay abbot (843–851), and afterwards. The artists themselves could have come from Reims after Ebo's political downfall in 833. The lavish painting in the manuscripts of Charlemagne's court—the restless, exuberant illusionistic style of Reims; the fine initial pages; the earlier Carolingian Gospels' iconography of Christ in Majesty; evangelist portraits and architectural canon tables; the interest in cameos and engraved gems as collectors' items and in bookbindings—all can be seen in Tours Bible manuscripts. Scenes from the Old and New Testaments were depicted

Pl. 211. King David and his musicians. Vivian Bible (First Bible of Charles the Bald). Tours, 846. Bibliothèque Nationale, Ms. lat. 1, f. 215v. Courtesy of the Bibliothèque Nationale, Paris

Pl. 210. Presentation of the book to Charles the Bald. Vivian Bible (First Bible of Charles the Bald). Abbey of St. Martin, Tours, ca. 846. Bibliothèque Nationale, Ms. lat. 1, f. 423r. 19½ × 14¾" (495 × 375 mm). Courtesy of the Bibliothèque Nationale, Paris

in parallel horizontal registers in two large Bibles made about 846—the Moutier-Grandval Bible (London, British Library, Add. Ms. 10546), and the Vivian Bible, also called the First Bible of Charles the Bald (Paris, Bibliothèque Nationale, Ms. lat. 1). The latter contains a dedication page (f. 423) illustrating the presentation of the Bible by Count Vivian to Charles the Bald, surrounded by an assembly of military and civilian attendants and monks (pl. 210). The resemblance of the emperor to King David surrounded by his psalm writers on f. 215v could not have been an accident (pl. 211). Even truer portraiture of the emperor can be found in the Psalter of Charles the Bald (Paris, Bibliothèque Nationale, Ms. lat. 1152), made some time between 842 and 869. Although these and later manuscripts for Charles the Bald probably were made in monasteries, they are considered court productions.

OTTONIAN

The major source for Ottonian illumination (960–1060) is found in Carolingian art, but the style and total effect as well as the types of manuscripts to be illuminated are strikingly different. At times Byzantine sources are more obvious. The name of the period is taken from three successive Saxon emperors, Otto I, II, and III. Old Testament personages and scenes all but disappeared from the iconographic repertory, just as complete Bibles and Psalters were neglected in favor of Gospel books, pericopes (Gospel readings), and the Apocalypse. Gone was the conscious desire to perpetuate the antique classical heritage in art. Manuscripts were written and illustrated in state-sponsored abbeys as in Carolingian times, but now the abbeys were at Lorsch, Fulda, Mainz, and Reichenau in the early Ottonian period and later at Regensburg, Salzburg, and Echternach. The splendor of the illuminations lay in their burnished gold backgrounds that seem to be of solid gold. Figures were usually rigid, frontal, and hieratic, their faces forbidding, with cold, wide-open eyes, whether they were enthroned emperors or Christ with evangelists or characters in Gospel scenes. Typical is St. Luke in the Gospel Book of Otto III, written about 1000 (Munich, Bayerische Staatsbibliothek, Clm. 4453; pl. 212).

So didactic is the nature of Ottonian illumination that it is not surprising to find a manuscript like the Uta Codex (Munich, Bayerische Staatsbibliothek, Cod. Lat. Clm. 13601), the subject of which is a composition by a theologian, Hartwic (see pl. 185, p. 228). His text was woven into the patterns and compartments of the illuminations meant to illustrate it, in the tradition of text-figuring that had been popular in the Carolingian Aratus and Hrabanus Maurus manuscripts. Text-figuring, or pattern poetry, can be looked upon as one way of integrating illustration with writing. It has a history of its own that began in ancient Greece. The Hebrew equivalent was micrography.

Problems of picture space do not seem to concern Ottonian illuminators. Backgrounds are flat, burnished gold leaf or bands of color, the latter inherited from Carolingian art. If the figures seem solid and three-dimensional, it is only because the prototypes the artist depended upon were thus, not because the artist was interested in plastic form. The only lasting effect of Ottonian art is the monumentality of its figures, which continues in Romanesque. It was not this world that preoccupied the Ottonian artist, but the next. Art was expressionistic and

Pl. 212. St. Luke. Gospel Book of Otto III. Reichenau, ca. 1000. State Library, Munich, Clm. 4453, f. 139v. 13 × 9⅜″ (330 × 240 mm). Courtesy of Bayerische Staatsbibliothek, Munich

didactic. The lavish book, including its gold, ivory, and jeweled binding, paid homage to Christ.

ROMANESQUE

There are more illuminated manuscripts extant from the Romanesque period than from all earlier periods. Their style is not limited to one country, which was true of earlier European illumination. While there are "national" or monastic differences among them, style has an international aspect, from southern Italy to Winchester and from Canterbury to Scandinavia. Monasteries of England and France were the Romanesque trendsetters. Style spread not because manuscripts were taken or sent out for copying but because artists began to move from one monastery to another. Stylistic and iconographic characteristics of other crafts, such as wall painting, gold and enamel work, and monumental sculpture, can be discerned in illuminations, which gives the impression that these traveling artists, laymen as well as monks, often worked in more than one medium.

In the ages preceding the Romanesque in Europe, most of the manuscripts reserved for illumination were Gospel or other books used in the Church service, seen only by the privileged patrons who commissioned them or received them as gifts. Illuminated books intended for reading, as well as secular and pagan works were the exception, even in the Carolingian Renaissance. To meet improved educational efforts in the monastery, particularly with Cluniac reforms, more manuscripts were written so that each monk could fulfill his obligation to study one book a year. Large Bibles and commentaries on them by Church fathers, theological works by medieval authors, illustrated lives of the saints, missals, and psalters became much more popular books for ornamentation. Some books were intended for the eyes of many viewers: large antiphonaries were illuminated in Italy for the whole choir to read from a distance, and Exultet rolls were painted with upside-down figures so that, as the scroll was draped over the pulpit during reading, the congregation could see the pictures. Here the vertical scroll had a definite function.

If one were to look at all the Romanesque manuscripts of France and England, one would notice two outstanding features: their grotesques and their historiated initials. Grotesques, or caprichos, are exuberant creatures that became a permanent aspect of medieval illumination. Dragons, partially human nudes, hybrid animals such as lions with dogs' heads, human-headed quadrupeds, winged beasts, dwarfs, and giants contort themselves into initial letters, perch themselves on foliage, and creep in and out of arabesquelike vines. These animate beings possibly originated in Mozarabic and Merovingian zoomorphic initials, but they reappear in Romanesque as independent, three-dimensional beings. The popularity of fables, travel literature, and the bestiary, with their descriptions of almost-familiar and weird beings, stimulated the desire to transfer grotesques to Bibles, commentaries, and patristic writings. Some see these beasties as symbolic, representing evil or a fear of the unknown in nature or the pagan element in man as opposed to the Christian. Yet it is difficult to assign specific meaning to these adorable-ugly oddities in the context of each and every page on which they appear. Whatever their purpose, if they had a purpose other than to delight the reader, they must be accepted as part of the Romanesque tradition, just as carpet pages belong to the Hiberno-Saxon tradition. The demonic was acceptable in Romanesque and Gothic sculpture and manuscripts. There was even a special kind of book known as the Devil's Bible made in the thirteenth century—it was usually very large and was assumed to have been completed in one night with the help of the devil. Such a Bible is in the Royal Library in Stockholm (A 148), written in Bohemia about 1205. The devil himself makes an appearance on f. 290r (pl. 213).

The other outstanding aspect of Romanesque is its historiated initials. The scribe left space at the head of the chapter for the illuminator, who used his imagination in creating an initial that would contain a portrait, foliage-cum-grotesque, or a picture story taken from the text itself. In this period, historiated initials were far more numerous than full-page biblical illustrations or continuous narrative bands of them. A few Carolingian manuscripts, such as the Sacramentary of Drogo, display Gospel events within initials, but it is in the twelfth century that historiated initials flourished. Historiation permitted the perfect integration of text, decoration, and illustration that typifies Romanesque manuscripts such as the Winchester and Lambeth Bibles (Winchester Cathedral Library; Lambeth Palace Library, London, Ms. 3; pl. 214, 215).

Romanesque, or Romanlike, refers to the period of the impact of Roman art on Europe after the year 1000. This is true of architecture and, to a lesser extent, of relief sculpture and frescoes. To the artists of the time, Roman usually meant Byzantine as it was known in Europe. Manuscript painting only hints at the renewed interest in the human form and space that was to develop in Gothic miniatures. Drapery, termed *wet* or *Byzantine,* clings to the figure in ornamental patterns. The body beneath the drapery is slightly more alive than it had been in Carolingian and Ottonian art, but the artist did not really observe live models. Vegetation is alive in a linear sense, not in an organic one. Backgrounds are still of solid color or burnished gold leaf.

Pl. 213. The devil summoned to assist in completing the manuscript in one night. Devil's Bible (Gigas Bible). Benedictine monastery of Podlazice, Bohemia, ca. 1220. The Royal Library–National Library of Sweden, Ms. A 148, f. 290r. 35½ × 19⅝" (900 × 500 mm). Courtesy of the Kungliga Biblioteket, Stockholm

Pl. 214. Historiated initial: Elijah and the king's messengers; chariot of fire; Elisha receives Elijah's mantle. Winchester Bible, II Kings. Early Gothic script. Winchester, 1150–1200. Winchester Cathedral, f. 23r. 23⅜ × 16½" (595 × 420 mm). Courtesy of Winchester Cathedral. Reproduced from Walter Oakeshott, *The Two Winchester Bibles.* Courtesy of Oxford University Press

Some codex traditions are dropped, some modified, and new ones are introduced. Gone are the carpet pages. Author portraits continue, frequently as part of the historiated initial. King David as author of Psalms, St. Jerome as translator of the Vulgate, prophets, and apostles are seen at the head of the books in Bibles. In the twelfth century, especially in England, Psalters began to appear as private deluxe books, often made for noblewomen or nuns, displaying a new format. The Romanesque Psalter opens with a decorated *B* for *Beatus Vir* (Happy is the man . . .), followed by the calendar and scenes from the Creation, from the life of King David, and from Christ's childhood and Passion. The cycles one would expect to find in an illustrated Bible are transferred to the Psalter, as artists of large Bibles, including Old and New Testaments and the Apocrypha, shift their decorative scheme to historiated initials. Iconography from the Romanesque Psalter will appear later in the Gothic Book of Hours.

A new iconographic theme of the Romanesque period is the Tree of Jesse, depicting Christ's ancestors from the time of King David's father. The Lambeth Bible, made at Canterbury in the latter half of the twelfth century, is one of the manuscripts that displays it. This theme, and the drawing of parallels between Old and New Testaments, will become even more popular in the Early Gothic period.

GOTHIC

The spread of Islamic science to Europe, the growth of a lay intelligentsia, and the rise of the cathedral schools and then the universities in Paris, Oxford, and Bologna contributed to an intellectual renaissance during the twelfth century, expanding the demand for books of all kinds. Textbooks, translations from Greek and Arabic, and native European vernacular literature were all produced. With the increase in books came an increase in the need to embellish secular and religious manuscripts.

The Ingeborg Psalter (Chantilly, Musée Condé, Ms. 1695) stands at the threshold of the Gothic age (pl. 216). It was decorated between 1195 and 1200 by two artists for the short-time wife of Philip II of France. It is typical of both English and Ile-de-France illuminated Psalters. Strong reds and blues with touches of green reflect the art of stained-glass windows, as does the black outlining of figures. Psalters had been decorated in many imaginative ways since Byzantine times—we have already seen the tenth-century Paris Psalter with its Old Testament thanksgiving scenes preceding the Psalms (see pl. 197, 198, p. 241), and the Utrecht Psalter with its literal ink drawings (see pl. 208, 209). (The Utrecht Psalter, or copies of it, was still a prototype for English illuminators, although biblical scenes and the Tree of Jesse were added to the English editions.) The Ingeborg Psalter typifies the popular decorated Gothic gift book. It displays full-page historiated *B,* initial letters within foliage that resemble architectural bosses and metalwork, and a cycle of illustrations on twenty-seven pages depicting New Testament subjects, including the Pentecost, the Last Judgment, and the Tree of Jesse. Tall, sculpturesque figures fill the vertical space of the picture against gold backgrounds with few references to landscape or architecture. Shaded drapery reveals plastic form but faces still resemble those of Middle Byzantine painting.

As time goes on, figures become smaller, more in proportion to their background. The Psalter made for art patron and bibliophile King Louis IX of France around the middle of the century contains seventy-eight Old Testament illustrations on facing pages, with short descriptions of the scenes at the top of the reverse side of the page (Paris, Bibliothèque Nationale, Ms. lat. 10525). Each picture, through f. 42, is framed at the corners by ivy leaves in arabesques and grotesques with intertwined heads; after that the borders change to gold arabesques on a red or blue ground, with bosses or grotesques at the corners (pl. 217). Figures are not much more realistic than those of the Ingeborg Psalter, but at times the artist seems to have enjoyed rendering the body from different angles. The interior scenes are set in Louis IX's private chapel in Paris, Ste. Chapelle, which is depicted with a stylized version of its stained-glass windows and other architectural elements. References to contemporaneous events and costume are also present in this handsome manuscript. The Israelite conquerors of the Holy Land wear Crusader battle dress, and Old Testament personages wear Jews' hats.

Tall, graceful *S*-shaped figures, and identical sweet faces with curly hair and beards are typical aspects of the St. Louis court style that continued through the latter half of the thirteenth century in stained-glass as well as in manuscripts. The Bible Moralisée was another typical French manuscript at mid-century (pl. 218). Old Testament antetypes were matched with New Testament or moralistic scenes. The book opens with the image of God as architect of the universe, an apt metaphor for a cathedral-building society.

In England in the latter half of the thirteenth century, the figures of the Douce Apocalypse, illuminated at Canterbury between 1250 and 1270, fill the picture space vertically as they did in the Ingeborg Psalter but they resemble the personages of the St. Louis Psalter, apocalyptic subject notwithstanding (pl. 219). In the Douce Apocalypse, masterful, elegant medieval pen-and-ink draftsmanship is revealed on the unfinished pages, just as it had been in the Lambeth Bible of the previous century. In these manuscripts, one sees the division of labor in the medieval painter's workshop between the illustrator and the colorist.

At the end of the thirteenth century, the Parisian illuminator Honoré was known to have headed a workshop; among his miniaturists were his daughter and son-in-law. By that time figures were more skillfully modeled and the color scheme became more subtle. Illuminators were on their way to returning to illusionism,

Pl. 216. Tree of Jesse. Ingeborg Psalter. Ile-de-France, ca. 1195–1200. Musée Condé, Chantilly, Ms. 1695, 14v. 12 × 8″ (304 × 204 mm). Courtesy of Musée Condé, Chantilly. Photo: Giraudon, Paris and Art Resource, New York

Pl. 217. Trumpets of Jericho. St. Louis Psalter. Paris, 1256. Bibliothèque Nationale, Ms. lat 10525, f. 41v. 8 × 5½″ (204 × 140 mm). Courtesy of the Bibliothèque Nationale, Paris

Pl. 219. St. John and the angel, harlot, and seven-headed beast. Douce Apocalypse. Canterbury, 1270. Bodleian Library, Ms. Douce 180, p. 71. 12¼ × 8½″ (311 × 216 mm). Courtesy of the Bodleian Library, Oxford

Pl. 218. God as the architect of the universe. Bible Moralisée. Paris, mid-thirteenth century. National Library, Vienna, Codex Vindobonensis 2554, f. 1v. 13½ × 10¼″ (344 × 260 mm). Courtesy of the Bild-Archiv der Österreichische National-bibliothek, Vienna

albeit slowly. The outstanding illuminator known by name in Paris in the early fourteenth century was Jean Pucelle who, like Honoré, was the master of a workshop and received commissions from European royal and courtly patrons. Many unsigned manuscripts from the second quarter of the fourteenth century are attributed to him, including the Book of Hours of Jeanne d'Evreux, made about 1325–28 (New York, Cloisters Collection of the Metropolitan Museum of Art, 54.1.2; pl. 220). Pucelle's "signature" of the dragonfly as well as his name appear in the Belleville Breviary of 1323–26 (Bibliothèque Nationale, Ms. lat. 10483; see pl. 159, p. 191). Like many other manuscripts of that day, the text page in the Breviary is surrounded by ivy leaves inhabited by creatures now called drolleries (formerly grotesques). Decoration begins to overwhelm the text, as the blank spaces in lines of text are filled with decorative bars; ivy leaves around the text become more elaborate; and scenes at the bottom, *bas de page,* supplement framed scenes at the head of chapters, where historiated initials are reduced in size. Some backgrounds are patterned, as was common in late-thirteenth and early-fourteenth-century illumination, while others show the influence of Italian Renaissance perspective and modeling of figures. The Book of Hours of Jeanne d'Evreux, made for the wife of Charles IV (1310–1371), is a masterpiece in grisaille painting—black and white with touches of color—a technique found in stained-glass windows. Even if it is not the "little book of orisons" illuminated by Pucelle that is mentioned in Jeanne d'Evreux's will, it is a perfect example of Pucelle's style, which unites text and decoration into an organic unit.

Pl. 220. The Annunciation. Book of Hours of Jeanne d'Evreux. Jean Pucelle, artist. Paris, 1325. Metropolitan Museum of Art, the Cloisters Collection, Purchase, 1954, 54.1.2., f. 16r. 3⅝ × 2⅜" (92 × 60 mm). Courtesy of the Metropolitan Museum of Art, New York

If one can say that there was a sublime moment in the history of European illumination when the two-dimensional vellum page and three-dimensional illusionism were in harmony and when there was perfect compatibility of script, ornament, and illustration, this was it.

The Book of Hours, a private prayer book devoted to the Virgin and divided by the eight canonical hours of the day, began to be illuminated in the second half of the thirteenth century. By the fourteenth century, the Book of Hours became a best-selling gift book. This tradition continued in fifteenth-century manuscripts and in illustrated printed books, especially in France. Different versions of prayers were written according to the wishes of the patron. Because Louis IX had been a favorite of the women in the French court, the Hours of St. Louis often were selected for reproduction. The Hours of Jeanne d'Evreux followed this version, and the life and miracles of St. Louis are illustrated after the childhood and Passion of Christ; these cycles are preceded by calendar pages. Pucelle was popular with book collectors of the French royal house, and manuscripts made a half century later often borrowed iconography from his works. The calendar pages served as prototypes for those of the Grandes Heures of the Duc de Berry (Paris, Bibliothèque Nationale, Ms. lat. 919), illuminated in 1409. The Psalters of England, contemporary to Pucelle's work, are no less remarkable than their French counterparts. Among them are the Psalter of Queen Mary (British Library, Royal Ms. 2 B. VII) and the Ormesby Psalter (Bodleian Library Douce Ms. 366).

Charles V of France (Charles the Wise) was an avid book collector, with a library of about one thousand books. Most of them were historical, scientific, and literary, and were not decorated. But he did patronize illuminators, some of whom emigrated from the Low Countries to Paris. Among his artists were Jean Bondol (Jean of Bruges) and the sculptor André Beauneveu of Valenciennes. The latter painted the king's image realistically in the Bible of Charles V in a patron portrait, in which the book is presented to the king by Jean de Vaudetar, who was responsible for its execution. Royal portraiture, the presentation of the book, and the Christ in Majesty illustration seen in the gift Bible have their sources in Carolingian illumination but the style has changed. The enthroned Christ now resembles a work of sculpture; his face is individualized, as if a real person modeled for the picture.

Charles V, as ruler of France, could not expend all of his energies on his books, even though he did read them and write notes in them. But his younger brother Jean, Duc de Berry, could devote himself full-time to art and antique collecting and traveling from one of his seventeen residences to another, taking with him some of his collectibles. His favorite book artists, among them André Beauneveu and Jacqmart de Hesdin and the Limbourg brothers, were installed in various chateaux. He must have driven them crazy when he picked up an unfinished book on which one illuminator was working to take it to his next place of residence for possible completion as well as for his own pleasure. He can be seen with his entourage in the Petit Heures (Paris, Bibliothèque Nationale, Ms. lat. 18014, f. 288v; pl. 221). Among the three hundred to four hundred manuscripts he commissioned were some twenty Books of Hours. In many of them, the decoration overwhelms the Gothic script, as if the book were made only for art and not at all for devotional use. The calendar pages of the Très Riches Heures (Chantilly, Musée Condé), begun in 1413 by the Limbourg brothers, serve as a record of aristocratic (and occasionally peasant) life at the castles of the Duke (pl. 222). The style of the Très Riches Heures is a blend of perfect realism in architecture, portraiture, and costume, with mannered elongation suited to noble subjects, brilliant colors, and mysterious atmospheric effects in the distance. The illusionism that characterized the work of the Limbourg brothers is not the direct descendant of Hellenistic and Roman illusionism by any means, but rather an aspect of the early-fifteenth-century International Gothic style, whose artistic centers were in Italy, Flanders, and France.

Pl. 221. The Duke accompanied by his mace-bearer. Petit Heures de Duc de Berry. France, late fourteenth century. Bibliothèque Nationale, Ms. lat. 18014, f. 288v. 7 × 5″ (178 × 127 mm). Courtesy of the Bibliothèque Nationale, Paris

Pl. 222. April. Très Riches Heures de Duc de Berry. France, 1413. Musée Condé, Chantilly, f. 4v. 11¼ × 8¼″ (290 × 210 mm) Courtesy of Musée Condé, Chantilly. Photo: Giraudon, Paris

When the Duke died in 1416, his Très Riches Heures had not been completed by the three brothers. Parts of it were filled in much later by Jean Colombe.

By the late fifteenth century, text and illustrations are separated more than ever before. The illusionistic picture overwhelms the text. This trend at its best is reflected in the works of Jean Fouquet—The Hours of Etienne Chevalier (Musée Condé, Chantilly), painted 1452–1456, and Josephus' *Antiquities of the Jews* (Paris, Bibiothèque Nationale, Ms. fr. 247; pl. 223). Fouquet's talents as a monumental painter are easily detected in his miniatures. Architecture and landscape are so perfectly rendered in biblical and historical scenes that if one did not see the gold frames, chapter headings, inscriptions, and ivy-leaf borders in reproductions, one would think his works were Renaissance panel paintings. If we could speak in superlatives, Fouquet's works are the most three-dimensional we have seen.

But this three-dimensionality seems to deny the parchment page itself. By the time of the mature works of Fouquet, who had learned his technique in Italy before returning to Tours around 1450, printing had already been invented and new techniques of decorating the book were coming to life. Although manuscript painting continued after printing, it is to the advantage of the history of illumination that we leave it at its finest, with the books of the Limbourg brothers and Jean Fouquet.

Pl. 223. Trumpets of Jericho. *Antiquities of the Jews.* Jean Fouquet, artist, 1470. Bibliothèque Nationale, Ms. fr. 247, f. 89. 17 × 11¾″ (430 × 300 mm). Courtesy of the Bibliothèque Nationale, Paris

The Islamic World in the Eighth Century

Indus River

Kabul

Mosul
Baghdad

Damascus
Jerusalem

Medina
Mecca

Fustat (Cairo)

Constantinople

Rome

Mediterranean Sea

Tours

Toledo
Cordoba
Gibraltar

Kairouan

Agadir

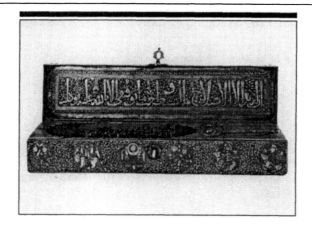

CHAPTER 11

The Islamic Book

I t is ironic that Muhammad should have called Jews and Christians "people of the book," for in the centuries that followed his prophecy and the subsequent Arab conquest of the Near East, it was the Muslims who became masters of the art of the book on a grand scale, while in Europe books and study were confined to monasteries and in Byzantium supplies of parchment limited book production. Of course, what Muhammad meant by the phrase "people of the book" were religions with written revelations; it was his admiration of this aspect of Western culture that gave the faith he founded its holy book, the Qur'ān (recitation), and eventually the impetus to bring forth its own literature and fine books.

Many aspects of production of the Islamic book and its materials were based on methods already in existence in the Near East when it was swept by Islam in the seventh and early eighth centuries, particularly in Egypt (conquered in 639–40). Arab book craftsmen learned their techniques and taste from their Coptic, Byzantine, and Jewish predecessors in Egypt, Syria, and Palestine; they also may have been influenced by Manichean books by way of Persia. Table 10 provides a chronology of the Islamic world.

MATERIALS: PAPYRUS, PARCHMENT, AND PAPER

The major surfaces on which Arabic books and documents were written were papyrus, parchment, and paper. The earliest writing, mostly short inscriptions, can be found on buildings and coins, on camels' shoulder blades and ribs, on palm bark, leather (from buffalo, sheep, and, in Persia, oxen), limestone, ostraca, linen, silk that was treated with gum and smoothed by mussel shells, and wooden boards. Script as decoration soon became a universal phenomenon in Islam—in clothing, on metal and ceramic vessels, and always as the salient architectural decoration. Because

Table 10. Chronology of the Islamic World

Dynasties and Events	Center or Capital	Date
Hijra of Muhammad from Mecca to Medina		622 C.E.
Conquest of Syria and Iraq		633–637
Conquest of Egypt		639–642
Umayyad	Damascus	661–750
Abbasid	Baghdad	750–
		to 868 in Egypt
		to 945 in Iraq
Harun al-Rashid	Baghdad	764?–809
Tulunid	Egypt	868–905
Fatimid rise in	North Africa	909
Fatimids in Egypt, establish	Cairo	969–1171
Ayyubid	Cairo	1171–1250
Founded by Saladin		1137–1193
Mamluk	Egypt/Syria	1250/60–1517
Abbasid Caliphate of Baghdad		1060–1258
Seljuk Turks move in from East, convert to Islam		956–970s
take Baghdad		1055
take Syria and Palestine		1070–1080
Crusaders	Latin Kingdom of Jerusalem	1099–1187
Mongols take Eastern territories of Caliphate (Transoxiana and Khurasan)		1219–1224
Ilkhanid (Mongols)	Baghdad	1258–1337
Timur (Tamerlane) rules (1336?–1405)	Samarqand	1369–1405
Timurid	Afghanistan, Iran	1369–1508
Safavids	Iran	1508–1534
Ottoman Turks take	Constantinople (Istanbul)	1453
Fall of Byzantine Empire		1492
Ottoman Turks conquer Syria/Palestine/Egypt		1517
take Iraq from Persia		1639

Muslim society was such a literate and highly commercial one, great quantities of writing materials always were in demand for correspondence, tax records, and other business transactions as well as for scientific, prose, poetic, religious, and legal scribal output. Although papyrus was expensive to produce and costly to buy, in the early centuries of Islam it was apparently in good supply for everyday writing until paper replaced it, although many people who used it resorted to recycled papyrus in the form of palimpsests. Papyrus codices in Arabic were rare but did exist, and there is even an extant example of a papyrus scroll from the middle of the ninth century. When papyrus was made, the factory glued to the end of the sheet the invocation of Islamic faith that also was to be found at the opening of each *sura* in the Qur'ān, the *basmalah:* "In the name of Allah, the Merciful, the Compassionate. There is no god but Allah, Muhammad is his prophet." Egypt retained her monopoly on papyrus making almost exclusively, although there were factories in Palermo and Syracuse in Sicily, and when the Abbasid caliph al-Mu'tasim established his headquarters in Samarra (836–878), he attempted to open a papyrus factory to lessen Iraq's dependence on Egypt. By that time, however, paper was already being manufactured in the eastern Islamic world and the embryonic papyrus industry on the banks of the Tigris never developed. By the middle of the tenth century, papyrus making

Spain

Dynasty, Kingdom, and Events	Center or Capital	Date
Invasions of Germanic tribes		ca. 409–
Visigothic Kingdom (Christian)	Toledo	500–711
Muslim Conquest (Umayyad Dynasty), called "al-Andalus"	Seville, Córdoba	711–717
All but northwest Spain in Muslim hands Christian population known as Mozarabs		
Independent Emirate of Córdoba		756–929
Caliphate of Córdoba		929–1031
Breakup of Umayyads		1031
"Party" Kingdoms	Badajoz, Toledo, Saragossa	1009–1091
Almoravids ("Moors") Berbers from North Africa take a smaller Andalusia	included Córdoba, Seville, Granada	1086–1145
Almohads (also Berbers from North Africa) Andalusia becomes even smaller		1150–1223
Nasrids (Arabs)	Granada	1248–1492
Reconquest		
Toledo captured by Christians		1085
Northern Spain in Christian control	Kingdoms of Portugal, León, Castile, Aragon, Catalonia	1150
Andalusia limited to southern half of Spain; Muslims in Christian kingdoms called Mudéjars ("permitted to remain" or "vassals")		
Union of Castile and León		1230
Kingdom of Aragon expands southward, also includes Catalonia		
Christians retake	Córdoba	1236
	Valencia	1238
	Seville	1248
Muslim rule limited to Granada		mid-1200s
Union of Aragon and Castile		1479
Fall of Granada		1492

waned as paper became more and more common and by the eleventh century it was a mere curiosity, at times used for decorated endsheets in books or, more practically, as lightweight pasteboard for bookbindings.

Most Arabic papyri (best preserved in Egypt, of course) come from the seventh and early eighth centuries. They are as valuable historically as Greek papyri are for an earlier age. Most of them are to be found in the National Library, Cairo; in the Archduke Rainer Collection in Vienna; and in the University of Michigan Library in Ann Arbor.

Parchment was the luxury material for Arabic books, especially for the Qur'ān, although it was not used exclusively for the holy book because the quality of paper, especially from Samarqand, Damascus, and Cairo, was exceptionally high. Because it was so expensive, parchment was used less often for nonqur'ānic manuscripts. Goats and sheep provided the hides for most parchment and vellum, although gazelle skin was also said to have been the surface for extra-fine codices. (In the Byzantine Empire of the tenth to the fourteenth centuries, parchment was made from the skin of wild asses, but it was a shortage of sheep and goats that necessitated the use of these inferior hides.) Some believe that the Arabs were the first to use lime in the processing of hides, but it is hard to imagine that this natural depilatory was unknown to earlier parchment makers. Those Islamic writers who commented on lime-curing claimed that it resulted in tough parchment and that the softness of Arab parchment was due to the use of dates in the soaking phase of its preparation. Date-cured parchment was called *Kufic,* after the same center for early bookmaking that gave its name to the script. Fine vellum, scraped very thin for writing, was called *raqq* or *riqq.* The quality of parchment certainly was as high in the Islamic Near East as it was in Europe. Sometimes parchment was dyed blue and written upon with gold ink. Parchment continued to be used longer in the western Islamic empire than in the eastern region (until the fourteenth century) because North Africa and Spain were the last Islamic lands to manufacture paper. The caliphs in Baghdad and Damascus used parchment for official documents but less frequently than they did papyrus in the early period and less frequently than paper in later times.

The making of paper in the Islamic empire will be discussed in Chapter 12. Its use was accepted fully, both for everyday writing and for luxury codices. No stigma was attached to the fine papers imported from China or made in Samarqand. One of the great advantages of paper over papyrus and parchment in the commercial and legal world of Islam was the fact that erasures could not be made without detection. As with several late medieval European and Hebrew manuscripts, the codex sometimes combined quires of paper with parchment. Papers for all kinds of manuscripts were tinted and dyed pink, purple, red, and blue from Persia to Spain. In certain countries the color of the paper had symbolic meaning: red shades expressed joy, blue, sorrow; in Syria and Egypt the death sentence was written on blue paper.

Decorated papers came into fashion first in Persia in the late fifteenth century. Either the whole piece of paper or the borders only were speckled with gold, silver, and other colors, or else marbled. These sheets were used for calligraphy only, or for pastedowns of books on the inner side of their covers, less often for the bindings themselves. Marbleized papers, along with paper itself, both of which came from China, were important contributions of the Islamic book to the Renaissance book in the West. Marbled papers, a continuous European tradition since the sixteenth century, are still popular today for endsheets, pastedowns, and bindings in the making of fine books.

TOOLS, INK, AND PAINT

The scribe's pen was a hard, closed reed, grown in the Nile or Tigris and soaked in water for strength (pl. 224). The reed could not be curved and was the length of a hand's width. The nib was cut with a sharp knife in a downward direction so that the writing edge was sloped. Various scripts were achieved by different cuts of the nib. The scribe could use the left or right side of the nib, or the upper or lower point, or the whole width of the edge, depending on his style of writing. The pen was called *qalam,* from the Hebrew *qolmos* or the Greek *calamus.* Carrying cases for the scribe's tools had an inkwell at one end (pl. 225, 226). These cases were often richly crafted, with engraved metalwork and inlays of brass, silver, and gold. Among the scribe's tools was a *liq,* a piece of wool or felt that was soaked in ink and held in the inkwell. The scribe dipped his pen into the *liq* rather than into a jar of liquid ink. The advantage of a *liq* was that it not only held the ink in suspension but it cleaned the pen as it was dipped, preventing ink from spilling. There were *liqs* for each color.

Two kinds of ink were used by Muslim scribes: soot and tannin. Soot was lampblack from animal or vegetable oils, heated sulfur, burnt papyri, or natural black earth. Glair (whipped egg white) was used instead of the usual gum arabic as an adhesive and to add lustre. For tannin ink, gallnuts of terebinth and tamarisk were employed, with vitriol (metallic sulfate) and gum or glair added, or even pomegranate rind. Metallic inks were admired but pure black ink was considered the finest. Mild solutions of yogurt or vinegar could be added to the ink to retard mold. Blue, green, and red inks were used for *sura* (divisions of the Qur'ān) headings, red

Pl. 225. Islamic writing box. Mosul, second half of the thirteenth century. Brass inlaid with gold and silver. Early Mamluk Naskhi script. "I want only to improve as much as I can, and my success depends upon Allah and on him I rely." Courtesy of the British Museum

Pl. 224. Calligrapher at his writing desk, with implements. Al-Qazwini, *Aja'ib al-Makhluqat* ("Wonders of Creation"). Turkey, sixteenth century. Naskhi script. British Library, Department of Oriental Manuscripts and Printed Books, Or. 7894, f. 18r. Courtesy of the British Library

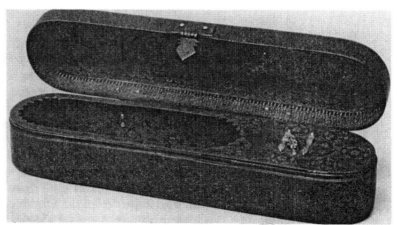

Pl. 226. Islamic writing box. Damascus, end of thirteenth or beginning of fourteenth century. Brass inlaid with gold and silver. Metropolitan Museum of Art, gift of J. Pierpont Morgan, 1917, 17.1909.822. Courtesy of the Metropolitan Museum of Art, New York

for vowels. The sources for colored inks were the same as for the basic European colors: for red there was cinnebar and red lead; for yellow, orpiment (arsenic); for green, vertigris (copper and vinegar); and for white, lead. Colored inks also were used for rubrics, flourishes, line endings, and other embellishments. Scribes could make invisible ink, too. One recipe called for milk and white water of vitriol for writing, with vitriol powder sprinkled on the script to read it. Another recipe used gall of turtle, with the letters to be read only at night. The following is a recipe for ink from an early seventeenth-century Persian treatise:

Order some soot of the best quality:
One *sir* of soot and four *sirs* of good gum.
Then, soon or late, find some vitriol and some gallnut,
Take one *sir* of the former and two *sirs* of the latter,
Pour the gum into the water, free from dust
Until it dissolves entirely, like honey water.
For a day or two whip the water and gum vigorously,

Sweeping the house from dust and rubbish,
Grind it up to one hundred hours.
Remember from me these praiseworthy words:
Rock alum is better than vitriol,
No one has understood this, besides this humble one . . .
Boil the water with the gallnuts and keep it
Until it becomes quite pure in accordance with your desire.
After this pour it in small quantities
And try it out without a fuss
Until the time when it settles
And your heart is tranquil in writing.
Do not spare labor in this.
Know that otherwise your work has been in vain.[1]

Erasing solutions were also compounded, some with vinegar and salts, some with yogurt mixed with salt in wool. But because the ink had already penetrated the parchment or paper, it was simpler to whiten or cover the error than to rub it out. One covering preparation was made of melted wax saturated with incense.

Persian painters used both gold leaf and gold paint for illumination. Leaf was made in a manner similar to that of European craftsmen. For gold paint, pieces of gold or gold-leaf filings were pounded in a mortar, then mixed with water until they settled. The water was drained off and the remaining gold sediment was mixed with saffron and dry glue or gum tragacanth. The gold surface was polished according to the effect the illuminator wished to achieve. When silver was added to gold paint, it had a greenish cast. Persian painters also used silver leaf but it has turned black due to oxidation and details painted on the silver are lost. Tin or lead was used at times as a silver substitute. It too was pulverized, with gum added. Fish and snail glue were used to fix gold and silver to paper and parchment. Honey with gum, size from scraps of hides, and glair also served as gold and silver adhesives. The brushes of miniaturists were very fine, with only a few or single hairs taken from squirrels, the throat of kittens, mongooses, or the underbelly of goats. Unlike the limited palette of Arab painters of the Levant in the thirteenth and fourteenth centuries, Persian miniaturists from the fifteenth century on took advantage of the expanded range and variety of pigments available to them. Their proximity to the source of lapis lazuli enabled them to use the real stone and not the imitation azurite that was necessary in Europe.

FORMAT

The folded sheets for the codex were gathered in quires of two, four, eight, or sixteen leaves, although at times extra leaves were added or a single sheet was inserted where the text necessitated it. Unlike parchment, one single large sheet of paper could be folded and then cut but there was no universal standard for sheet size; it varied from place to place. If the pages were very small, they could be reinforced with paper at the spine edge. To make guidelines for paper manuscripts, the scribe used a wooden frame strung with parallel wires or string to which the paper could be pressed in order to leave ruled impressions on the sheet. Such ruling frames were still in use in the Near East into this century. Because the field of Arabic codicology is not as developed as it is for Byzantine, Jewish, and European manuscripts, it is not known yet whether early Muslim scribes pricked and ruled their parchment folios in the same manner as did the scribes of Greek, Hebrew, and Latin manuscripts. They did abide by Gregory's Law for parchment, matching flesh side to flesh side and hair to hair.

One of the interesting aspects of the early Qur'ān was its horizontal format (see pl. 13, p. 11, and pl. 227). It is almost as if this book form were a deliberate continuation of the tradition of the scroll. Other reasons given by scholars for the horizontal Arabic codex are that it imitated the scroll or the monumental inscription

Pl. 227. Frontispiece of an early Qur'ān, in horizontal format. Syria or Egypt, ca. 900. Chester Beatty Library, Ms. 1406. Courtesy of the Chester Beatty Library, Dublin

panel (*tabula*), or that it could have been a reaction against the vertical format of Christian and Jewish codices. Whatever the reason, it provided a perfect background for the horizontally elongated Kufic script. This format lasted in the western Islamic empire, particularly in Tunisia, well into the eleventh century.

In early Qur'āns, the text was laid out in one-column blocks. In illustrated secular books of the thirteenth and fourteenth centuries, text is frequently inserted on angles around or even into the picture. The movement to a two-column (and even four- and six-column) layout came later and, when it is to be found in Persian books from the fourteenth century, the columns and sometimes the individual lines of writing are ruled off with frames, which became part of the decorative aspect of the page. At times, each line of text could be set against a cloud background. Later, lines of script were also written on a diagonal. Illustrations, when they did not occupy a full page, were at the top or bottom of the text or even in the center but the text was always confined to its own frames. Another feature of Persian books from the fourteenth century was that figures within the scenes at times extended outside of the frame into the margin or text (see pl. 241, p. 280). At other times, the artist shaped the frame artificially to give it an irregular aspect, or crenelated it. At still other times, there was no picture frame at all. In some manuscripts, a small space within a full-page illustration was marked off by a frame for a few lines of text or a title. All of these tricks created a vital picture space, as if the dynamism of the heroes depicted could not be contained. These shaped pictures were successful only in the hands of the best miniaturists; eventually the device became a cliché.

LITERATURE

The strength of the Arab empire until the Mongol conquests of the thirteenth century lay in the commerce of its cities. Literacy was at first a necessity but it became so much a part of the lives of this middle-class society that books for both study and pleasure on all subjects were in constant demand. The libraries built up by rulers and aristocrats were always open to those who could use them, so in this sense they were public. Scholars did much traveling from library to library, possibly seeing as many cities of their empire as academic people do today of the world. A boy started learning at the mosque school when he was seven years old. The very traditional tablet on which he practiced writing quotations from the Qur'ān resembled the *tabella ansata* of Roman times as much as it did the hornbook of colonial America (see pl. 10, p. 9).

At first, Islamic science and literature were based on the Greek tradition, which Muslims called "the ancient sciences," and, to a lesser extent, on Indian learning. Books on astronomy, chemistry, medicine, mathematics, geography, logic, metaphysics, and poetry were translated into Arabic. Works by Plato, Aristotle, Euclid, Ptolemy, Archimedes, Hippocrates, Galen, and Dioscorides thus served as a basis for Muslim science. Much of this transmission was first accomplished at the Caliph al-Ma'mun's *Bayt al-Hikma,* the House of Wisdom. Many works of Antiquity were available to late medieval and Renaissance Europe only because they had been preserved by translation into Arabic and later retranslation in Spain in the Middle Ages. To this foundation of classical learning, Muslim scholars, philosophers, and doctors added their own original thought. Arabic was the language of science in the early days of Islam, even in Persia. A number of the scientific terms we take for granted today are Arabic in origin: alcohol, alchemy, algebra, azimuth, borax, elixir, zenith, and nadir. Some Arabic scientific works were encyclopedic, among them the Persian Ibn Sina's (Avicenna) *Canon of Medicine,* which, in its Latin translation, was an essential textbook in European universities from the twelfth century on. In the Islamic empire, physicians, in addition to having the highest social status among professionals, were also scientists, lawyers, and philosophers. In the late twelfth century, men such as Ibn Rushd (Averroës) in Spain and Moses ben Maimon (Maimonides) in Egypt were responsible for introducing Aristotle to western Europe.

To the Arabs we owe our system of numerals (fig. 31). We call them Arabic but they originated in India. In Hebrew and Greek, numbers were written with letters in alphabetical order. The Romans established specific letters as numbers, which did not simplify addition and multiplication. Muslims at first followed the Hebrew and Greek systems. Although Indian numerals were introduced in Baghdad in 770, Muslim scientists did not adopt them immediately, preferring the older tradition. Mathematician and astronomer Muhammad ibn-Musa al-Khwarizmi (d. 846), who was associated with Caliph al-Ma'mun's *Bayt al-Hikma* (House of Wisdom), helped spread their use. They became popular by the tenth century. Fourteenth-century Europe adopted the so-called Arabic numerals by way of Spain. Along with numerals, the Arabs also passed along from India the decimal system and the zero, which at first was written as a small dot or a circle. In Arabic it was called *sifr,* an empty object; in Latin, *zephyrum;* in Italian, *zero;* and in English, *cipher.* Algebra, a branch of mathematics based on Greek and Indian traditions, was passed along to Europe in the twelfth century when al-Khwarizmi's textbook on the subject was translated into Latin.

SCRIPT AND SCRIBES

Calligraphy was admired above all the arts of Islam; calligraphers were accorded the same respect and honor as were artists of the Italian Renaissance in the Western setting. Calligraphy was a worthy occupation for nobility and aristocracy in all areas and periods of the Islamic empire. The professional copyist was called *warraq,* from the word for "sheet." The names of many calligraphers are known; they headed

Fig. 31. Arabic numerals. After *Encyclopaedia of Islam.* Courtesy of E. J. Brill

schools, workshops, and libraries. Sometimes they were employed by the author, at other times they were authors or scholars themselves, and they earned a decent living if their handwriting deserved it. Some were part of a large library–book production center patronized by the caliph, sultan, or shah, especially in Iraq, Egypt, and Persia and later in Turkey. Their students and later generations paid the best of them homage by copying their style and even by recording their masters' names instead of their own in their books. One of the greatest scribes was Ibn al-Bawwab (d. 1022 or 1032), who was a mural painter and illuminator before he took up calligraphy (pl. 228). A story about him reflects the scribe's multiple talents. He once found twenty-nine of a set of thirty Qur'ān volumes written by the master scribe Ibn Muqlah (d. 940) in the library in his care. This library in Shiraz belonged to a ruler of the Persian Buyid dynasty who recognized the Abbasid caliph, Baha' al-Daula. Ibn al-Bawwab bet his patron one hundred dinars and a robe of honor that he could forge the missing volume without al-Daula's detecting the fake. He set about the task by using old paper he found in the library, then copied perfectly Ibn Muqlah's handwriting in gold ink. He then took a binding off one of the twenty-nine Qur'āns for his new volume, fabricating an imitation for the original book. He won his bet, although his eventual reward was merely Chinese paper from the library. Both Ibn Muqlah's and Ibn al-Bawwab's writing techniques were used into the twelfth and thirteenth centuries; their original manuscripts brought high prices from collectors, which encouraged forgeries.

By the middle of the eighth century, several Arabic scripts, which were derived from the Aramaic branch of the Semitic alphabet and therefore composed of twenty-two letters written right to left, were in use for the Arabic and Persian tongues. The first of these scripts, written from the seventh to the thirteenth centuries, was Kufic, a square hand inspired by lapidary and numismatic inscriptions of the Nabateans (see pl. 13, p. 11). Named for Kufa in southern Iraq, the capital city

Pl. 228. Carpet page, from a Qur'ān. Baghdad, ca. 1000. Ali ibn Hilal, called Ibn al-Bawwab, scribe. Chester Beatty Library, Ms. 1431, f. 184v. Courtesy of the Chester Beatty Library, Dublin

that was a spiritual center of early Islam, the script is the one seen in early architectural inscriptions, coins, and editions of the Qur'ān. The Qur'ān often was written in multivolume sets that ranged in size from huge parchment folios read in mosques to miniature vellum books. The strokes of Kufic were black, heavy, and angular, with a strong horizontal emphasis. As time went on, the script became more ornamental, with floriated and foliated forms. The second major script was Naskhi: rounded, lighter, and more cursive in appearance, used commercially as well as for literary texts, especially on paper. By the middle of the tenth century, calligraphic rules for writing Naskhi were strict, with the height and width of each letter fixed and with ascenders and descenders having a definite relation to the body of the letter. Naskhi script began to displace Kufic in the tenth century and continued to be used for many centuries; by the twelfth century it was the most important hand, and variations on it developed. The other five major Arabic scripts were Thuluth (pl. 229), Rihan, Muhaqqaq (pl. 230), Tauqi, and Riqa'; all of them could be written simply or elaborately, knotted, and embellished with plant and even figurative forms. Calligraphers wrote treatises on their art that give us much information on the making of the Islamic book and its materials. Among these works were *Craft of the Scribes* by Abu Ja'far al-Nahhas (d. 940), *Staff of the Scribes and Implements of the Discerning* by Tamim ibn al-Mu'izz Ibn Badis (1031–1108), and

Pl. 229. Sura CXIII (right-hand page) and colophon (lower left-hand page) from a Qur'ān. Baghdad, ca. 1000. Early Thuluth script; headings in ornamental Thuluth. Ali ibn Hilal, called Ibn al-Bawwab, scribe. Chester Beatty Library, Ms. 1431, f. 283v and 284r. Courtesy of the Chester Beatty Library, Dublin

Pl. 230. Sura V, v. 5–6, fragment of a Qur'ān section, showing Muhaqqaq script. Mosul, 1306/7–1311. Chester Beatty Library, Ms. 1613. Courtesy of the Chester Beatty Library, Dublin

an anonymous treatise from about 1200 called *Writers' Aids and Intelligent People's Tools.*

A good professional scribe could turn out one hundred pages a day, which may seem superhuman compared to the efforts of the medieval European scribe. But a close look at the Arabic book reveals far fewer characters per page, and a far greater proportion of white sheet to black ink. One must also bear in mind that the Muslim scribe, working for money in addition to spiritual reward, was motivated to write faster than his monastic counterpart. In a lifetime, a Muslim scribe could write thirty-five thousand pages, filling four hundred to six hundred books. (Always allow for Near Eastern statistical exaggeration!) The average price of a book was two gold dinars but a multivolume set written by a master calligrapher could cost one hundred dinars; in rare instances single books brought that much. And the price of a book could be open to bargaining. (Two dinars paid the average monthly living expenses of a lower-middle-class family in Cairo from about the tenth to the thirteenth centuries; it could also buy the cheapest mule for transportation and a gold finger ring.) Scribes often were publishers. They operated stores or stalls in the cities of Baghdad, Damascus, and Cairo and had staffs of calligraphers and other workers, such as bookbinders and makers of ink and parchment, or paper, under their supervision. Scribes could be hired by noble, aristocratic, or wealthy middle-class patrons to enjoy home hospitality while writing a volume, although one scribe did not enjoy this arrangement, preferring to be independent and charge for his work. Calligraphers did not unite in guilds as they did in European cities.

Libraries also served as copying centers and workshops for all aspects of book production. In the early ninth century the caliph al-Ma'mun established the *Bayt al-Hikma,* or House of Wisdom, in Baghdad, also called *Dar al-'Ilm,* "House of Learning," a type of institute or academy as well as a scriptorium. Literature in foreign languages was translated, and the House of Wisdom employed collators, proofreaders, and authorizers of texts. Authors were commissioned to create their works while residing there; they were supplied with servants and scribes who took dictation. The Fatimid caliph al-Hakim (996–1021) also opened such an academy, in addition to the existing large palace library. Writing supplies were available to those who wanted to copy books in his collection, and scholars were paid while using the libraries. Similar institutes were founded in the tenth century in Basra, Mosul, and Tripoli. This caliphal patronage set a tradition for the royal book patron. Thereafter, many rulers, especially in Iraq and Persia, established library-workshops within the palace, where all aspects of book production were supervised. The librarian in charge usually was a calligrapher or illuminator. In the fifteenth century the calligrapher Ja'far al-Tabrizi served as librarian in the library founded by Timur's (Tamerlane's) grandson Baysungur Mirza, who was governor of Herat and himself a calligrapher. The artist Bihzad (1450–1525), one of the most famous Persian illuminators, was librarian at Herat for the Sultan Husayn Bayqarah around 1500, and was invited to head a new library in 1522 at Tabriz by the first Safavid shah, Isma'il (see pl. 240, 241, p. 280). In the typical Islamic library, books were shelved lying flat, one atop the other, as they were in Europe, with the title written on the fore-edge of the book. At times the shelves were divided into separate cupboards. Mosques, the *waqf* (religious foundation), and *madrassas* (colleges) all contained libraries. Palace libraries were enormous—when Saladin closed the Fatimid library after assuming rule of Egypt, it housed between 120,000 and two million books, depending on the estimates of Muslim historians. The independent Umayyad caliph of Spain, al-Hakim II (961–976), built a huge private library–production center in Córdoba, estimated as housing four hundred thousand volumes, headed by a eunuch named Bakiya. The size of libraries was sometimes measured by camel-loads of books.

Muslim scribes often left colophons with their names and the date and place of writing the manuscript. Added to this information were blessings and occasional curses, not only against those who would destroy the book but against sectarians. Students of a great master at times honored their teacher by signing his name rather than their own. Islamic manuscripts, like Muslim chronology, are dated from the *hijra,* 622, the year of the flight of Muhammad from Mecca to Medina (A.H.). There is no intercalated month every few years to bring the lunar year into harmony with the solar year as there is in the Jewish calendar, so tables are needed to calculate the equivalent Gregorian date.

The following is a colophon from a Qur'ān manuscript in the Chester Beatty Library in Dublin (Ms. K.16I):

> Has written it a sinning, self-indulging slave. He finished writing it in the district of . . . on Monday the 21st of Rajab of the year 428 [May 10, 1037]. May God have mercy on whoever invokes His pardon for the writer, for his parents and for those who use it in prayer and for the whole community of Muhammad, may God bless him and greet him.[2]

ILLUSTRATION

Because the Muslim religion is iconoclastic, there are two misconceptions concerning its art—first, that there was no religious art, and second, that figurative art did not exist at all. In fact, painting and (more rarely) sculpture were to be found in the palaces of caliphs and princes, and books were decorated with designs and miniatures. The embellishment of Qur'āns, however, like the mosque, was without human and animal figures, with ornament confined to an exuberant display of vegetal and geometric decoration, and with Arabic script as a prominent design element. So popular was one curvilinear vegetal ornament that when it spread to

Europe it became known as the arabesque: a shoot of split leaves on inorganic tendrils, rhythmically repeated or interlaced.

The earliest decorated Qur'āns from the tenth century were enhanced with frontispiece and finispiece carpet pages of abstract and geometric interlace patterns with a projecting decorative *ansa,* recalling the *tabula ansata,* the handled tablet of Roman times (see pl. 227). Thus the Islamic book also pays artistic tribute to the tradition of the schoolboy's tablet or the monumental inscription panel. Whether the carpet pages of Qur'āns preceded those of Hebrew Bibles is still a matter of conjecture, because the Hebrew Moshe Ben-Asher codex was believed by Ettinghausen to have the earlier colophon, 894–895. The fact that English and Irish Gospel books of the same or earlier age display carpet pages (the Lindisfarne Gospels even shows a rudimentary *ansa*) testifies to a possible earlier Mediterranean prototype, or an International Style of book design. Qur'āns were also ornamented with panels at the head of *suras,* at the major divisions, and at specific verses, usually the fifth and tenth, within each *sura* (see pl. 13, p. 11). Some of the early illuminators also could have been calligraphers of Qur'āns, but as artists they did not leave their names, possibly because the status of the painter was lower than that of the scribe. An early horizontally oriented frontispiece detached from its Qur'ān in the Chester Beatty Library, Dublin, shows an interlace that looks very much like the one framing the portrait of Juliana Anicia in the Vienna Dioscorides but lacking the central figures (see pl. 189, p. 236, and pl. 227). By the fifteenth century, when Persian painting was at its height under the Timurids, the typical Qur'ān opened with a *shamsa,* an ornamental medallion that contained the name and titles of the manuscript's patron and blessings for his well-being, a Near Eastern ex libris. Following that was a double page of carpet patterns, the *unwan.*

Nonreligious books, scientific and literary, were illustrated. As with their texts, the pictures in the earliest of these were derived from Byzantine Greek prototypes. Al-Sufi's *Treatise on the Fixed Stars,* based on Ptolemy's *Almagest,* was composed in 965. A copy of this treatise on paper, now in the Bodleian Library, Oxford, made by al-Sufi's son, was written and illustrated in 1009 (pl. 231). Its classical Greek-inspired drawings were varied to conform to Islamic taste; the artist transformed Virgo into a wingless Arab dancing-girl, her shoulder contorted to fit the stars in the constellation.

De Materia Medica by Dioscorides was one of several scientific manuscripts copied numerous times in the Arab world. A well-known edition in the Library of the Topkapi Sarayi in Istanbul, dated 1229, was probably made in Syria (pl. 232). Its Middle Byzantine sources are obvious when one looks at the modeling of the faces of Dioscorides and his students on the double-page frontispiece, but the garb of the students is flat and patterned and their faces are made up with beauty marks and kohl around the eyes, in the fashion of the age. The first double-page Dioscorides portrait reflects an Islamic scribal practice: students present the text they have either copied or written from dictation for their teacher's authorization. Here, however, we don't see the teacher taking his cut of the fee for this service, a known practice. The second frontispiece author portrait shows Dioscorides seated on a low stool, with his student seated cross-legged on a carpet (pl. 233). Gone is the Byzantine high-backed chair of the first frontispiece, which had resembled that of St. Mark in the Rossano Gospels (see pl. 194, p. 239). Within the manuscript's text, the depiction of plants was not always realistic; forms were simplified and stylized. This is true of other early illustrated Arabic scientific manuscripts. It is as if the model treatises were meant to serve as inspiration to the artist to create artificial patterns, and it was not the artist's task to render nature with scientific accuracy. Reminders of Byzantine manuscript painting, such as gold backgrounds, architectural frames, acanthus leaves, and single and group author portraits, can be found in this Dioscorides manuscript and other thirteenth- and fourteenth-century works made in Syria,

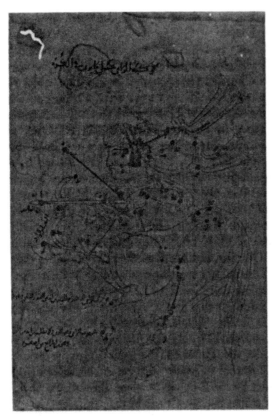

Pl. 232. Dioscorides teaching two students. Dioscorides, *De Materia Medica.* Syria or Northern Iraq, 1229. Top-kapi Sarayi, Ahmet III. 2127, f. 1v and 2r. Courtesy of the Topkapi Sarayi Museum, Istanbul

Pl. 231. Sagittarius. Al-Sufi, *Kitab Suwar al-Kawakib ath-Thabita* ("Treatise on the Fixed Stars"). Iraq(?), 1009. Naskhi script. Bodleian Library, Department of Oriental Manuscripts, Marsh 144, p. 272. Courtesy of the Bodleian Library, Oxford

Egypt, and Iraq. One can see that Ottonian and Arab illuminations were similarly based on the art of Byzantium.

One curious survival of Byzantine Christian art can be found in a popular illustrated book, *Manafi al-Hayawan,* "Book on the Usefulness of Animals," a work that can be viewed both as the fauna equivalent of the Dioscorides herbal and as the Near Eastern counterpart of the European bestiary (pl. 234, 235). Compiled in Arabic in the eleventh century by Ibn Bakhtishu, it was then translated into Persian. Folklore on real animals such as the elephant, lion, wolf, and camel is recounted, but added to it are the medicinal properties of their skin, bones, and organs as well as instructions on the preparation of prescriptions from them. Composite beasts such as the Persian *simurgh* (griffon) are also included, and humans as well, in the form of the haloed Adam and Eve in the Garden of Eden. The edition shown, now in the Pierpont Morgan Library (M.500), was written in Maragha, northwestern Persia, in 1290. In it, one can see the seeds of Far Eastern influence on Persian Islamic art not only in the Mongol facial features of Adam and Eve but in the technique of rendering trees. The flat backdrops of Arab painting were soon to give way to Chinese spatial concepts placing trees, mountains, and sky on various levels that rise upward vertically. The caliphate at Baghdad fell to the Mongols in 1258, and in the fourteenth century Mongol influence is seen in the art of the book.

Pl. 233. Dioscorides and student. Dioscorides, *De Materia Medica*. Syria or Northern Iraq, 1229. Topkapi Sarayi, Ahmet III. 2127, f. 2v. Courtesy of Topkapi Sarayi Museum, Istanbul

In addition to illustrating scientific, pseudo-scientific, and technical texts such as the *Manafi al-Hayawan, De Materia Medica, Kitab al-Diryaq* (Book of Antidotes) of Pseudo-Galen, and al-Jazari's *Kitab fi Ma'rifat al Hiyal al Handasiya* (The Book of Knowledge of Mechanical Devices), artists painted pictures for Arabic and later Persian literary works. The favorite twelfth-to-fourteenth-century work of the Arab world was the *Maqamat* al-Hariri (pl. 236). These "Assemblies" of al-Hariri (1054–1122) are collections of episodes in which a rogue-hero named Abu Zayd, disguised as someone else—a beggar, preacher, old man or woman—makes an appearance in the various cities in the caliphate, and stirs up the crowd or individuals to part with their money, either by trickery or by his clever speeches. He disappears after achieving success, only to reappear in the next *maqama*. This is a work of literary and auditory genius, one based not on plot but on verbal pyrotechnics and linguistic tricks with the Arabic tongue, such as triple and quadruple puns or sentences that can be read the same backward or forward. One would not think that this kind of literature could be illustrated. And yet it was, enough times for art historians to speak of *Maqama* iconography with prototype manuscripts. The finest version of some twelve extant illustrated copies is the Schefer Hariri in the Bibliothèque Nationale in Paris (Ms. arabe 5847), signed and dated in 1237 by the scribe and illuminator Yahya ibn Mahmud al-Wasiti (Wasit is in southern Iraq, near Basra). Many of the illustrations are assemblies of people for religious festivals, banquets, or parades, or in classrooms, libraries, shops, pharmacies, or aboard ship, in cemeteries, gardens, military camps, and caravanserais, the Near Eastern motels.

One illustration depicts a woman giving birth, a subject unseen in medieval European painting. These miniatures are drawn with a pictorial economy typical of Islamic art of the Levant of the thirteenth and fourteenth centuries. How different they are from the genre illustration of Franco-Flemish books of the late Middle Ages. They give us a sense of the middle-class Arab world, from whom the patronage for manuscripts came, in addition to the ruling class.

Another favorite illustrated book of both Arabs and Persians was *Kalila and Dimna,* or "Bidpai Fables" (pl. 237). Originally an Indian work, it is believed to have been written in the third century C.E. by the philosopher Bidpai for the moral instruction of princes. In these fables, animals endowed with human nature, such as the cowardly lion-king, the bull, birds, monkeys, and tortoises, demonstrate the consequences of their moral and immoral acts and are rewarded and punished accordingly. Each of the two jackal brothers tries to prove his point to the other—the malevolent Dimna believes that wit and cunning will win the day, while Kalila promotes honesty and harmony. Each tells a fable to elucidate his point, and other animals also tell tales within the framework tale to prove their morals. In the sixth century, *Kalila and Dimna* was translated from Sanskrit to Pahlavi, and in the eighth century it was rendered in Arabic from the middle Persian (the original Sanskrit and Pahlavi versions are lost). Later, Arabic and Persian versions were written, and ultimately the Bidpai fables were translated into Syriac, Greek, Turkish, Hebrew, Spanish, and other European languages. The work inspired many similar tales. There is a reference to an illustrated version from the ninth century but the earliest extant illustrated *Kalila and Dimna* was made in Syria in the early thirteenth century. In the fourteenth century it became a best-seller in Mamluk Egypt and Ilkhanid Persia. Timurid princes in fifteenth-century Persia continued to commission illustrated editions and it was translated anew.

The miniatures in Arabic versions of the *Kalila and Dimna* are conceived simply, like much of the illustration of Arabic scientific and literary manuscripts from the twelfth through the fourteenth centuries, with minimal landscape and architectural detail. Paper provides the backdrop, and scenes are enclosed by frames. Persian book art was far more complex and sophisticated. Patronage came from princes and governors of Mongol ancestry, who seemed to compete with each other to see whose royal library-workshop could produce the most sumptuous books. Native Persian literature was copied and illustrated on a grand scale, including historical works such as *Jami' al-Tawarikh,* the "Universal History" of Rashid al-Din; and the national epic, *Shah Nameh,* the "Book of Kings." The latter was compiled in the late tenth or early eleventh century by the poet Firdawsi, based on historical and legendary material of the pre-Islamic dynasties of Persia. One of the epic heroes is Iskander, Alexander the Great, blessed with a Persian mother. He possesses all the attributes of an Iranian hero, including the ability to slay composite beasts such as the *habash* monster, who has the fangs of a wolf, the horn of a rhinoceros, the wings of an eagle, and the paws of a lion (pl. 238). In a remarkable illustrated copy of Firdawsi's work from about 1340, known as the Demotte *Shah Nameh,* one can see how the artist absorbed Chinese style by the manner in which trees, landscape, cloud, and fire are rendered (pl. 238, 239). Yet the spatial concepts of the Demotte *Shah Nameh* are unique. Figures of men and animals are filled with dramatic energy; their bodies and actions are cut off on all sides, suggesting a great space beyond the picture frame. In a dynamic scene of the Indian army fleeing from Iskander's iron warriors, flames of gold leaf emanate from the silver-leaf horses and war chariots and riders (pl. 239). (The name "Demotte" belongs to a former owner-dealer of manuscripts, George J. Demotte, who disassembled the manuscript in the 1920s and sold each page to a different museum or library the world over.) It is interesting to

Pl. 236. The hour of birth. *Maqamat* ("Assemblies of") *al-Hariri* (Schefer Hariri). Baghdad, 1237. Standard Naskhi script. Bibliothèque Nationale, Ms. arabe 5847, f. 122v. Courtesy of the Bibliothèque Nationale, Paris

Pl. 237. The lion and the bull. Kalila and Dimna (The Bidpai Fables). Probably Syria, 1354. Bodleian Library, Department of Oriental Manuscripts, Pococke 400, f. 45r. Courtesy of the Bodleian Library, Oxford

compare this masterpiece of Ilkhanid art to the gentle little gem of European book art of the same age, the Hours of Jeanne d'Evreux (see pl. 220, p. 256).

A century later in Timurid Persia the same literary works continued to be illustrated but lyrical and decorative style replaced the dramatic, especially at Herat (now Afghanistan but then part of Persia). Figures are far smaller in the space in which they are set. Perspective is conventionalized into vertical flowered or grass-dotted landscape, with contours of mountains above and figures that cling to their edges to suggest the space beyond, topped by a solid blue or gold-leaf sky to represent the blazing sun. Trees hug the edges of the mountains and streams. In interior scenes, architecture looks like a stage set that can be folded at the will of the painter or reader. As always in Islamic art, there is sympathy and love for animals that goes beyond realism; even dragons and other mythological figures are full of life. Although landscapes are not illusionistic in the Western sense, three-dimensional effects are achieved not by light and shade but by a system of graduated colors. Iskander and other national heroes continue to appear: Isfayander, Gaymurs, Bahram Gur, and Rustam, with a specific iconography attached to each. The *Khamsa* (Five Poems) of Nizami, written in the twelfth century, was another popular illustrated work of the Timurid period, with some of the same heroes as the *Shah Nameh*. One of the greatest painters of Herat in the late Timurid period, and of all times in Persia, was the artist-librarian Bihzad. His subtle sense of color,

Pl. 238. Iskander (Alexander) slays the habash monster. Demotte *Shah Nameh*. Tabriz, 1330–1336. Naskhi script. Museum of Fine Arts, Boston, Denman W. Ross Collection, 30.105. Courtesy of the Museum of Fine Arts, Boston

Pl. 239. Iskander's iron cavalry battles the Fur of Hind (India). Demotte *Shah Nameh*. Tabriz, 1330–1336. Fogg Art Museum, gift of Edward W. Forbes, No. 1955-167. Courtesy of the Harvard University Art Museums, Cambridge

perfect composition, and elegant figure style set him above his contemporaries and later painters as well. British Library Or. 6810 and Add. 25900 are fine examples of the master's work (pl. 240, 241). The number of miniature paintings attributed to him is even greater than that from his hand.

By the Safavid Period, in the sixteenth century, book production became highly specialized. Bihzad was appointed director of the royal library in Tabriz in 1522 by the first Safavid Shah, Isma'il (1510–1524), the father of Shah Tahmasp. The library employed scribes, miniaturists, gilders, gold beaters and mixers, lapis lazuli workers, and specialists who only drew borders, which were often as decorative as the illustrations and sometimes related to them in subject.

In the Islamic world, the art of the manuscript book continued longer than it did in Europe. Double-page frontispieces that reflected the life of the royal patron had been part of the Persian book since Timurid times. A set of these painted in 1585 (now divided between the Metropolitan Museum of Art in New York and the Boston Museum of Fine Arts) depicts a hawking and drinking party in the mountains as realistically as Persian painting allowed (pl. 242). It shows us that the very rich enjoyed the same courtly pleasures as did the Duc de Berry almost two centuries earlier—the outdoor pleasure of the hunt and the indoor pleasure of collecting beautiful handmade books.

Pl. 240. Layla and Majnun at school. *Khamsa* of Nizami. Bihzad, artist. Herat, 1494. Nasta'liq script. British Library, Department of Oriental Manuscripts and Printed Books, Or. 6810, f. 106v. Courtesy of the British Library

Pl. 241. Bahram Gur slays the dragon. *Khamsa* of Nizami. Bihzad, artist. Herat, ca. 1493. Nasta'liq script. British Library, Department of Oriental Books and Manuscripts, Add. 25900, f. 161. Courtesy of the British Library

The royal Persian workshop went on producing manuscripts in the seventeenth century under the rule of the Shah Abbas I in Isfahan. Some of these were imitations of the Herat school, some were more creative. Even when handwritten and decorated books declined in quality in Persia, Persian-influenced art rose to new heights in Turkey and India. Printing did not have a great impact on Persia and the Ottoman Empire. When it finally arrived it did not inspire new and vital forms of book illustration as it did in Europe. The Golden Age of the Islamic book was the twelfth through the fourteenth centuries in the western Islamic empire and the thirteenth through the sixteenth centuries in Persia.

The Islamic book was important for its own history and for its influence on the Western book. Key elements of the modern European book of the late Middle Ages and Renaissance trace their origins to the Islamic book: its paper; its bookbinding

b. Right-hand page, Museum of Fine Arts, Boston, Francis Bartlett Donation and Picture Fund of 1912, 14.624. Courtesy of the Museum of Fine Arts, Boston

Pl. 242. A princely hawking party in the mountains. School of Qazwin, Persia, ca. 1585. *a*. Left-hand page, Metropolitan Museum of Art, Rogers Fund, 1912, 12.223.1. Courtesy of the Metropolitan Museum of Art, New York

materials, such as morocco and cordoban leather, and techniques, such as tooling in gold; its bookbinding motifs and the use of doublures and decorated pastedowns and endsheets; its marbled paper; its use of woodblocks for decoration and illustration; and its numerals, which were used eventually for pagination. Moreover, the knowledge of science and mathematics within those books educated Europe and whet its appetite to learn more. Literary forms such as the *maqama* ultimately evolved into the modern novel through *Don Quixote* in Spain. Finally, the prodigious size of Muslim libraries could only have impressed all those who saw them in Spain, especially at Córdoba, or in the Levant, where they must have amazed the Crusaders and the merchants who followed them to the Near East, and thereby inspired the European desire for acquisition that was to be satisfied only when printing was invented.

Notes

1. Vladimir Fedorovich Minorsky, trans., *Calligraphers and Painters: A Treatise by Qadi Ahmad, Son of Mir-Munshi (circa A.H. 1015/A.D. 1606)*, Freer Gallery of Art Occasional Papers, vol. 3, no. 2. (Washington, D.C., 1959), 112.

2. David Storm Rice, *The Unique Ibn al-Bawwab Manuscript in the Chester Beatty Library, Dublin* (Dublin: Emery Walker, 1955), 27.

CHAPTER 12

Papermaking

P aper links the manuscript of the Middle Ages with the book of modern times. The hand process of papermaking has been continuous since before the invention of printing and is still used today for limited and fine editions and for some private press books. It has remained essentially the same since the first mills were established in Italy. Although there were some innovations before the last century, it was only in the nineteenth century that the Industrial Revolution brought mass production to the craft. The factory where paper is made is still called a mill, whether it is a one-person operation or an enormous complex of computer-controlled machinery (pl. 243). Because papermaking, like bookbinding, is still done by hand, we will follow the story of its manufacture from the beginning to the present.

FROM THE FAR EAST TO THE NEAR EAST

Paper was invented in China. For many years Western historians accepted the following tradition recorded by a fifth-century Chinese historian. It was told that in the year 105 C.E., in the town of Leiyang in the Honan province, a court eunuch named T'sai Lun was standing by a stream and saw scraps of decomposed rags floating on the surface of the water, along with pieces of tree bark, hemp, and old fishing nets. When he saw the scum on the water caused by these disintegrated fibers, all T'sai Lun needed was some kind of screen or cloth to pick it up and allow the excess water to drain off, leaving a flat sheet of paper. The only problem with this legend, repeated in most histories of papermaking, is that T'sai Lun did not invent paper. Apparently the craft was already in existence in China for some two hundred years, since the beginning of the Western Han dynasty (221–24 B.C.E.). Archeological excavations in 1933, 1957, 1973, and 1978 have revealed examples of

283

Pl. 243. The paper mill.
Rags are sorted (*above*) and
soaked (*below*). Denis
Diderot, *Encyclopédie, ou
Dictionnaire Raisonné des
Sciences, des Arts et des
Métiers* (Paris, 1751–1780).
Courtesy of the Jewish
National and University
Library, Jerusalem

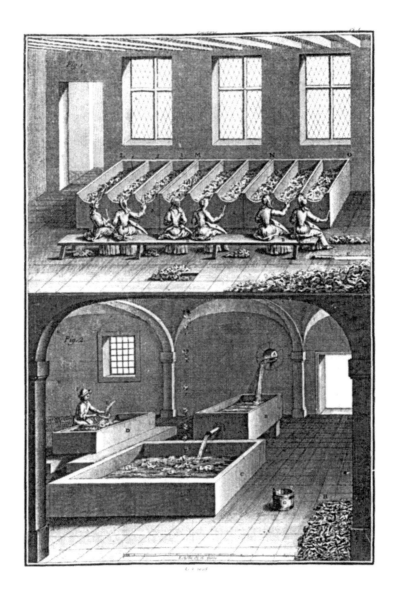

Pl. 243. The paper mill. Rags are sorted (*above*) and soaked (*below*). Denis Diderot, *Encyclopédie, ou Dictionnaire Raisonné des Sciences, des Arts et des Métiers* (Paris, 1751–1780). Courtesy of the Jewish National and University Library, Jerusalem

coarse, pale yellowish paper of vegetable fiber, all made from raw hemp. These can be seen in the Chinese Historical Museum in Beijing and in the Shaanxi Province Museum in Xian. T'sai Lun may have been responsible for transforming the industry into an official, court-sponsored enterprise, and so his name came down in history as the inventor of paper. The official Chinese version today still clings to the T'sai Lun story, in spite of research by Pan Ji-Xing on the earliest papers by means of chemical and microscopic analysis.

It is entirely logical that paper should have been invented in China, a country of many ancient technological innovations. The Chinese were literate and bureaucratic, with an urgent need for a practical and inexpensive writing surface to replace the heavy wood and bamboo-slit books used for their numerous historical and government publications. Paper was an ideal substitute for the more expensive silk, which possibly had been a writing surface since the seventh century B.C.E. The presence of the "silk" 糸 semantic indicator (radical) in the Chinese character for paper 紙 does not prove that early paper contained silk fibers. None have been found in microscopic examination of early paper. The same linguistic phenomenon occurs in our word *paper,* whose name comes from *papyrus*—although there was no papyrus content in paper, it lived on in the borrowed term.

Papermaking spread to Korea and Japan, but more relevant to the history of the Western book is its use and manufacture in the Near East and Europe. The Muslims knew about Chinese paper for some time before they started producing it themselves, and imported it even after they became experts in its production. An Arabic text, dated 1482, records that paper was first made in the Islamic Empire in the early eighth century C.E., when Muslims conquered Samarqand, a city on the trade route between Persia and China (now in Uzbekistan, U.S.S.R.). According to other Muslim historians, the impetus came in 751, when the governor of Samarqand imprisoned two Chinese papermakers after the Battle of Atlakh, near Talas. In return for their freedom, the two passed along their papermaking secrets to their captors. Before that time, papyrus had been the common writing surface in the Islamic world. Paper was a real boon to the urban centers of the Abbasid caliphate, and was of finer quality and not as easily erased as papyrus, which had been declining in quality since ancient times. As noted previously, the fact that erasures on paper could be detected easily was important to such a commercial and legalistic society, to whom law and written traditions were essential. Furthermore, paper was much cheaper to produce than the luxurious parchment, which continued to be used for Qur'āns, particularly in the western regions of the Islamic world.

After Samarqand, the next known mill was established in Baghdad in 794–795 by the Bamarkid viziers, who were soon deposed (in 803) by Harun al-Rashid, the caliph made famous in the West by the *Arabian Nights.* Harun al-Rashid was in contact with Charlemagne, who sent missionaries to try to convert him to Christianity. It is interesting to speculate on the contribution Harun would have made to the cultural life of the West had he sent Charlemagne paper instead of the white elephant that the Holy Roman Emperor requested. Charlemagne's biographer Einhard tells us his king wore linen shirts and breeches. The raw material was right there on Charlemagne's own body, but the opportunity to make paper was missed.

From the very beginning, paper was valued highly in the Caliphate. When it was well made, or imported from China or Samarqand, it assumed the prestige of parchment. Already in the ninth century there were papermaking factories in Tihama and San'a, Yemen, and in Cairo. Early Egyptian paper was made of hemp, with some linen content. Soon afterward there were mills in Tripoli, Hama, and Damascus in Syria, Tiberias in Palestine, and Tunis, Tlemcen, Ceuta, and Fez in North Africa as well as in Persia and India. Egyptian paper was famous throughout the Near East by the end of the tenth century. By the eleventh century there was a special street in Cairo where paper dealers did business. But the quality of Egyptian paper was not as high as Baghdadi paper. Damascus also became an export center in the same century, lending its name, *Damascus,* to the paper Europe and Byzantium imported. We had seen this phenomenon in earlier ages, when Pergamum gave its name to parchment and Sinope to sinopia.

The Arabs used new linen, old linen rags, hemp (ropes and cord), and raw flax for their paper, sometimes in combination. In the late-eleventh-century treatise, *Staff of the Scribes and Implements of the Discerning,* Ibn Badis described one method of manufacture. High-quality flax was separated ("purified") from the reed, moistened, and combed until it was softened. After soaking in quicklime overnight, the flax was spread in the sun to dry. The processes of soaking and rubbing with the hands and drying were repeated daily for from three to seven days, changing the limewater each time. Then it was soaked in plain water for a week, changing the water frequently so that all of the quicklime was washed out. This process served to break down and purify the fibers. Next, the damp and purified flax was pounded to a pulp by a pestle in a large mortar. Other descriptions of Arab papermaking mention that a hand-operated triphammer was used to pound hemp and rag fiber (pl. 244). A triphammer required less labor than the mortar and pestle, in the form of foot power. It consisted of a horizontal tilt-bar which, when trod by a worker on one end, caused a hammer on the other end to fall heavily upon the material to be

Pl. 244. Triphammer. From Dard Hunter, *Papermaking through Eighteen Centuries* (New York: Rudge, 1930). Courtesy of the University of Michigan Library, Department of Rare Books and Special Collections. Photo: Patrick J. Young

macerated. The triphammer still can be found in paper mills in some parts of India, Indochina and China.

Because no Arab papermaking molds have been preserved, their appearance has been hypothesized by examining the marks left on the paper itself, called laid marks, or from descriptions, such as that of Ibn Badis. One kind of mold was made of three parts: a boxlike rectangular frame, a separate screen that was set into it, and two deckle sticks that held the screen in place as the sheet was being formed. The screen was made of grass or reeds stitched together at intervals with horsehair. It was flexible enough so that after the sheet was formed the mold could be turned over onto a flat surface and the screen rolled back, leaving the sheet to dry. In another type of mold the screen was attached to the outer frame. The pulp was mixed with clean water and stirred by hand, then thrown onto the mold and dispersed to form a sheet. There may have been molds made of woven textiles as well, as there are no laid marks on much of Arab paper. It is unknown if each sheet was left to dry separately, or if they were stacked when they were still wet and pressed to squeeze out excess moisture. Finally, stacks of paper were pressed between boards.

In order for paper to accept ink without absorbing it like a blotter, sizing was necessary. The Chinese had coated their paper with gypsum, rice flour, starch, or vegetable sizes, either by rubbing or by brushing them onto the dried paper. The Arabs also used rice starch or vegetable gum sizes. The sheet was either dipped into a tub of size, or size was spread onto the sheet in powder or paste form. The sheet was then burnished on a wooden board with a pestlelike tool, with oval glass balls, with agate, or with oyster or mussel shells.

As we have seen, Islamic papermakers decorated their papers by dyeing or painting them, by speckling them with gold, silver, or colors, or by stamping designs with woodblocks. These decorated papers were used in books on the inner sides of the covers as pastedowns, and for endpapers. In Muslim Spain, pages were dyed red, vermilion, pink, and purple, and were called *Nasri* because they were first made in the Nasrid kingdom of Granada from the middle of the thirteenth to the fifteenth centuries. Marbled papers, having originated in China, were made in sixteenth-century Persia. The technique spread to Turkey. Then by the end of the century they were introduced into European books, initiating a tradition that has not ceased.

SPAIN

By the tenth century, the Muslims of Spain used paper regularly. The first Christian works on paper made in Spain are now to be found in the Monastery of Santa Domingo in Silos. They date from the last quarter of the tenth century. One is a Mozarabic breviary and missal, composed of paper as well as parchment quires (some late medieval Arabic and Hebrew manuscripts combine the two). The paper was made in the classic Arab manner, and was firm and thick, with long fibers. Size was made from rice. By 1056 there is definite evidence of a paper mill at Xàtiva, in Valencia, employing twenty workers, and one in Toledo in 1085. There had been flax plantations in the area of Xàtiva since the time of Phoenician settlement. The city was famous for its fine linen, so it is not surprising to find that its paper was admired as well by Muslim geographers and authors. With the Christian reconquest of Valencia in 1238, the craft remained in the hands of Muslim and Jewish papermakers, but their paper was taxed heavily. In the twelfth century, various towns in Catalonia took up papermaking, from Tarragona to the Pyrenees. Because the paper business was so good, wheat, corn, and rice mills and iron foundries were converted to paper mills. Catalan mills were registered in the names of their Christian landowners, but it is known that the workers were Muslims and Jews. When the owners were Jewish, they were registered as bookbinders and stationers rather than as papermakers to avoid persecution, apparently because Jews were well established in these book-related occupations in more tolerant times. They sold paper to royal and other government chanceries, monasteries, notaries, and public officers. Two families of Spanish papermakers who established their mills in the seventeenth century are still making fine paper—Romaní (1636) and Guarro (1698). Their mills were in Capellades, in Catalonia. Today there is a paper museum in this town famous for its early, excellent mills.

The mills of Valencia and Catalonia were built close to rivers so that there would be water power to activate the hammers of stampers used for breaking up rags. This eventually became the practice of all European mills (pl. 245). As one does not read of early Near Eastern mills at riverside, one assumes Valencians and Catalans were the first to use water-powered stampers. There were a few other innovations made by Muslim papermakers in Spain, who made paper from rags plus up to 25 percent hemp content. Their molds were made of hemp threads, other vegetable fibers, horsehair, or very narrow tape fixed to a wooden frame. Later, metal wires were used in Spanish molds. Early molds did not always have enough supporting ribs. This caused the wires to sag with use, leaving an uneven sheet and irregular laid marks in the middle of the paper. From the middle of the twelfth to the fourteenth centuries, Spanish and North African papermakers made identifying marks with a brush, reed, or pointed tool on the paper while it was still wet, in the form of zigzags or overlapping diagonal crosses. These "trademarks" evidently were imitations of the knife marks left by Near Eastern tanners and parchment makers. In one Arabic manuscript from 1160, now in the Bibliothèque Nationale in Paris (Ms. arabe 6499), quires were composed of very similar parchment and paper leaves with zigzag marks on both. In Spain, the proportions of the mold and the resulting sheet were first based on the size of the parchment sheet made by most Muslim parchment workers. This practice testifies to the traditionalism of the makers of book materials. The dimensions of the sheet were not standardized in Spain until the early twentieth century. In Valencia and Catalonia, size was made from wheat or rice paste. Spanish

Pl. 245. Stampers. From Diderot's *Encyclopédie.* Courtesy of the Jewish National and University Library, Jerusalem

paper was glazed with a hammer, stone, or shell, or with a roller. Frequently the sized and glazed paper was thick and shiny enough to hide the sagging laid marks and thickness in the middle of the sheet that was characteristic of early Spanish paper.

The Catalan-Aragonese empire of the thirteenth and fourteenth centuries extended to parts of Italy, Sicily, and Sardinia, and paper was exported to these locations from Barcelona and Tortosa until it was manufactured in Italy. Manuscripts in the remainder of Europe began to be written on paper in the thirteenth century. Paper in Spain was made in the classic Arab style until the middle of the fourteenth century, and it did not decline in quality until the fifteenth century. In Catalonia, paper at first was called *papel Xetavi* after the Valencian town whose white paper it imitated. Then it was called *pergamino de trapos* (rag parchment) and *pergamino de paño* (cloth parchment). A linguistic reminder of paper's Islamic origins can be found in the term still used in packaging paper. The Arabs sold five blocks of twenty-five sheets together as a *rizma* (bundle of rags). In Spain it became a *resma* or *raymarum,* in France, *reime* or *rame,* and in England, a *ream* of paper. Today's ream may consist of 472, 480 (short ream), 500 or 516 (long ream), or 526 sheets.

ITALY

The first Italian mill seems to have been established in Fabriano by the 1270s. A popular account related that one Erardo de Praga, fleeing from murder charges in Bohemia, escaped to Fabriano and erected a mill on the River Giano in 990, and his success inspired other potential papermakers. It is more likely that the first papermakers were Arabs, perhaps arriving by way of the port of Ancona. More reliable is a document on paper from 1283, which was witnessed by eight papermakers of Fabriano. There is much evidence for a thriving industry in Fabriano as well as in other Italian towns by the 1290s. Fine handmade and mold-made European paper is still produced in Fabriano, now by Cartiere (Papermill) Miliani Fabriano. (*Mold-made* is the name for paper that looks handmade, but is manufactured with care by machine.)

In the fourteenth century, papermaking spread northward. By the 1320s there were mills in Cologne, Augsburg, and Mainz, and in 1390, Italian papermakers operated the Stromer Mill just outside Nuremburg. Papermakers were active in

Strasbourg in the 1430s, and perhaps it was there that Gutenberg saw a press that inspired him to adapt it for printing. Paper mills did not operate in England until about 1495. As in Spain and Italy, other European mills always were built near an abundant supply of good, clean water. The quality of the water affected the paper; it had to be clean for washing the rags before allowing them to ferment, for mixing pulp, and for cooking size. It had to be plentiful for powering the stampers.

EUROPEAN METHODS

The technique of making paper by hand in Europe changed little from the fifteenth through the eighteenth centuries. To the classic Arab method, European papermakers introduced hydraulic stampers, metal-wire molds with a frame called a deckle, felts separating the newly formed sheets, animal sizes, and the use of watermarks. Linen rags provided the raw material. These first were sorted out and cleaned with water, bleached by boiling with lime, and left in the sun to further whiten them (see pl. 243). The cleaner and whiter the rags and the less artificial the bleaching, the better the paper. The rags were then rolled into balls and left to decompose by natural fermentation. They were then macerated in long troughs by stampers activated by a waterwheel (pl. 245). A few of these old stampers are still in use, for example, in the Richard de Bas paper mill in Ambert, France. The retted (soaked) fibers were mixed thoroughly with water to make pulp. This slurry was kept warm in a large vat as sheets were formed (pl. 246, 249B).

Pl. 246. Vatman, dipping sheets. From Jost Amman's illustrations for *Eygentliche Beschreibung aller Stände auff Erden* (Book of Trades) (Frankfurt: Feyerabend, 1568). Courtesy of University of Michigan Library, Department of Rare Books and Special Collections. Photo: Patrick J. Young

The European mold was a frame with closely strung thin metal wires, with heavier metal wire "chains" sewn at right angles. Because less fiber was deposited on these wires and chains than on the rest of the mold, faint lines appeared on the sheet. These are called *wire* or *laid lines* and *chain lines* on the paper; together they are called *laid marks* (pl. 247, 249D). To the mold the papermaker also stitched and knotted additional wires formed into various shapes: a cross, a hand, or a bull's head; armorial or kabbalistic signs or letters. These are called watermarks (pl. 247, 248). In printed books lacking colophons, watermarks are used to identify the mill and the approximate date of the paper. Works of art on paper also are dated in this manner. Watermarks were first used in Fabriano, apparently as a means of distinguishing between the paper of the many mills that were established there so quickly. In Spain, papermakers gave up their zigzag knife marks for the more aesthetically pleasing watermarks at the end of the thirteenth century, almost the same time as their appearance in Italy. The earliest Spanish watermarks are three slightly overlapping diagonal crosses, a Latin cross topped by a triangle, a rampant or passant ox, a bull, and a pear shape. (Do not forget that watermarks are logograms!) Between 1282 and 1600 there were over fifteen thousand watermarks that can be identified today. The guide for them is Charles Briquet's monumental work, *Les Filigranes* (1907), supplemented by the Paper Publications Society volumes, published in Holland.

European papermakers also introduced the deckle, a frame that fit over the mold to keep the pulp from running off the sides (pl. 249C). Arab papermakers, and the Chinese before them, at times had used two deckle-sticks to hold the screen in its separate frame during the sheet-forming stage. Spanish papermakers also used

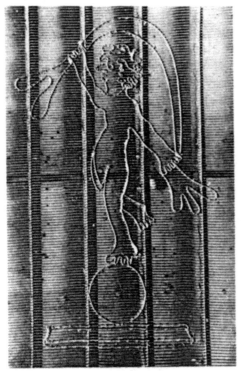

Pl. 247. Wires for watermark laced into the laid mold. Reproduced from Dard Hunter, *Papermaking: The History and Technique of an Ancient Craft* (New York: Knopf, 1967). Courtesy of Dard Hunter II

Pl. 248. Chiaroscuro (light and shade) watermark portrait of Dard Hunter. The technique is explained in his *Papermaking: The History and Technique of an Ancient Craft*. Photo from original sheet: University of Michigan Photographic Services

Pl. 249. Dipping, couching, preparing post, pressing. Joseph de Lalande, *Art de Faire le Papier* (Paris, 1761). Courtesy of Joyce Schmidt. Photo: Jewish National and University Library, Jerusalem

deckle-sticks. It is the deckle that leaves a feathery deckle-edge on paper, much admired in today's handmade paper and imitated in mold-made paper. Spanish papermakers frequently trimmed off the deckle edge.

In forming the sheet, the vatman dipped the mold and deckle vertically into the vat of pulp. He brought it up horizontally, to allow the pulp to settle on the screen, and gently rolled it from side to side in both directions, so that the fibers meshed evenly as they settled on the screen (pl. 246; pl. 249, on right). Excess water dripped down through the mold, back into the vat. The deckle was removed by the vatman to cover the next mold, as he handed the mold with its newly formed sheet to the coucher (pronounced "coocher"). In the late seventeenth century, two-sheet molds were made for smaller sizes of paper by adding a bar down the middle. The coucher turned the paper out of the mold onto a felt, a woolen blanket slightly larger than the sheet (pl. 249, center). The pile of couched papers with felts between them, called a post, was put in the press and under heavy pressure much of the water was squeezed out. The felts were removed to be used again for the next post (pl. 249, on left). The "white post," or stack of papers with no felts in between, was pressed again (pl. 249L). A pile of sheets was then hung over horsehair to dry. As mills became larger, drying was done in a loft, where it was warmer and drafts could be controlled (pl. 250). Then each sheet was sized with animal gelatin, which was known already to European papermakers from parchment manufacture. Sheets

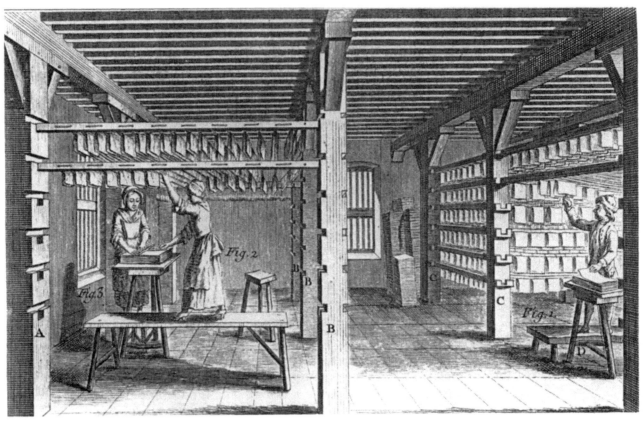

Pl. 250. The drying loft.
Diderot, *Encyclopédie*.
Courtesy of the Jewish
National and University
Library, Jerusalem

were dipped into tubs of size (pl. 251), pressed again, dried, and burnished by hand
with glass or agate as the Arabs had done, until a glazing hammer powered by water
replaced hand burnishing in some papermaking factories (pl. 252). This is illustrated
in an eighteenth-century French book on papermaking by de la Lande, *Art de faire le
papier* (1761). In the 1880s resinous sizes were introduced, not to the benefit of paper
conservation and libraries.

At least sixteen centuries passed between the time of paper's invention and its
adoption as the chief writing surface in Europe. Paper is so much cheaper and so
much faster to manufacture than parchment that it seems strange that it took so long
for Europeans to take advantage of this writing material, and to produce it once they
knew about it. There are several reasons given for the resistance of Europe to this
practical change. Some say that European Christians associated paper with the
"infidel Arabs and Jews," and did not want to have anything to do with what was
seen as their invention. Indeed, Peter the Venerable, abbot of Cluny in the twelfth
century, had great contempt for the new writing surface because of the religion of
the Jewish craftsmen who were making it. This didn't seem to bother Spanish
Christians, who were quick to compete and to break the Arab and Jewish monopoly
with the Reconquest. Others say that Europe was retarded because its inhabitants
wore woolen underwear until the fourteenth century, and it was not until they
switched to linen underwear that there eventually would be enough rags to supply
the paper mills. While this may sound ridiculous, it is a fact that linen was the fabric
for undershirts and pants of the nobility in the fourteenth century. But the truth of
the matter is that there was no great medieval demand for books or paper because
the majority of Europeans were illiterate throughout the Middle Ages. The exceptions were to be found in the monastery, or among the relatively small number
of merchants, administrators, and Jews. Parchment makers supplied enough

Pl. 251. Preparation of size, sizing sheets in the vat, pressing them afterwards. From Diderot, *Encyclopédie*. Courtesy of the Jewish National and University Library, Jerusalem

Pl. 252. *Above,* Burnishing and inspecting sheets; *below,* Glazing hammer at work. Joseph de Lalande, *Art de Faire le Papier* (Paris, 1761). Courtesy of Joyce Schmidt. Photo: Jewish National and University Library, Jerusalem

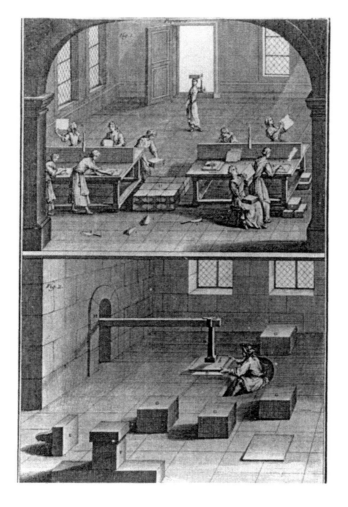

material for manuscripts until the fourteenth century. By that time, when a middle-class and university-educated readership grew, more and more ordinary books were written on paper. When printing was introduced in the middle of the fifteenth century, there simply were not enough calves, kids, or lambs to provide Europe with the material needed to feed the presses. Even if it had been in great supply, vellum was not as suitable for printing as paper although it continued to be used for a small number of deluxe printed books.

NEW RAW MATERIALS

Not that there were so many rags! The paper mills of Europe never could obtain enough flax and linen to meet the demand. Several countries prohibited the export of these raw materials because of this. In England it was a crime to bury the dead in linen shrouds. By the eighteenth century, various experiments were made to produce paper with materials other than linen, hemp, and flax. A Frenchman, René de Réaumer, made a twenty-year study, published in 1714, on how wasps build their nests, transforming wood into a paperlike structure. Few took this work and his 1742 study seriously. Shortly thereafter, an experimenting German, Dr. Jacob Christian Schäffer, published a six-volume work in 1765 showing that paper could be made from any of eighty materials: plants, moss, potatoes, leaves, stalks of plants, and even sawdust (pl. 253). Among his samples was a grapevine paper (*wyn ranken*) that he claimed contained only a small percentage of rag pulp. Analysis since

Pl. 253. Putti make paper. Engraved frontispiece. Jacob Christian Schäffer, *Versuche und Muster, ohne alle Lumpen Papier zu machen* (Regensburg, 1765– 1772). Courtesy of the Jewish National and University Library, Jerusalem

1898 has proven the opposite to be true; paper that he claimed to have "a very small" rag content really had from 15 percent to 45 percent, and paper with "no rag content" had between 10 percent and 95 percent rag. Never mind; he had the right idea—substitute what is available in nature. But Europeans still were not ready for nonrag paper. Then, in 1800, Matthias Koops took out patents in England (where so many inventions that concerned the book were patented) for paper made of straw, wood, and recycled paper. Koops invented a de-inking process as well. His book was printed on the papers of his experimental manufacture, and although he put his theory into practice, bankruptcy ended his experiments three years later. Others continued similar trials with wood-pulp paper, cooked with caustic soda (as destructive as resinous sizes), in Germany, England, and America. Finally, in the middle of the nineteenth century, wood-based paper became a commercially viable product. Between 1857 and 1860, English papermakers discovered that esparto grass from southern Spain and North Africa made a strong but thin paper that would be suitable for books—both for the printed word and eventually for half-tones and color reproductions. The best paper today is made from well-processed linen or cotton rags, or from the plants themselves—flax and cotton in the West; kozo (a mulberry), mitsumata, and gampi in Japan. The latter is not rice paper! It may be noted here that although paper has been and sometimes still is made from rice straw in China, this paper is not related to the strong but delicate-looking papers from Japan. But the name *rice paper* persists in America for Japanese kozo, mitsumata, and gampi papers.

INNOVATIONS

Even before some forward-looking paper experimenters were searching for new materials from which paper could be made, others sought ways to speed up its manufacture. In the Netherlands in the late sixteenth or early seventeenth century, papermakers thought of breaking down rags by adapting an old mill appliance that had been used for grinding tobacco and mustard seeds. This eventually was called the Hollander beater (pl. 254). It not only saved time but conserved raw materials. The older method of allowing rags to decompose by fermentation lost about a third of the fabric in the process. Not all European papermakers were quick to accept the Hollander beater because they felt a weaker sheet of paper resulted from the fibers being battered too violently and cut too short. Stampers had drawn out the fibers, enhancing fibrilation, which helped bond the sheet. But eventually the Hollander beater was adopted, and sometimes was used in conjunction with the old stampers.

In the Hollander beater, a cylinder with blades is set into one side of a long elliptical trough. The cut-up rags or other raw materials are kept circulating in water, and the fibers are broken down as they pass between the blades and the bed plate, becoming pulp. The water then can be drained to allow for storage of the pulp. The pulp is added to the vat in the desired proportion of pulp to water. It is then mixed to the proper consistency for the slurry of sheetmaking. The Hollander beater is still used today, and is considered the only machine acceptable in the hand-papermaking process. As more and more artists are turning to handmade paper itself as an art form, demand for small Hollander beaters has increased beyond the point that its originators could have imagined. Large Hollanders are part of the paper industry; smaller ones often are used in mills for experiments.

The first papermaking machine was invented by Nicolas-Louis Robert in France and patented in 1799 (pl. 255). The operating principle was that pulp was poured onto a moving mesh belt, forming a long, continuous sheet. Robert worked for the Didot printing family in their Essonnes paper mill, and the Didots financed him at first. Although Robert was awarded a cash prize by the French government, it was not enough money for him to continue improving his invention. Searching for investors, St. Léger Didot put Robert in touch with his brother-in-law in England, who showed a model of the machine to two London stationers, Henry and Sealy

Pl. 254. The Hollander beater (stampers on the left). Courtesy of the Rijksmuseum voor Volkskunde, "Het Nederlands Openlucht Museum," Arnhem, The Netherlands

Fourdrinier. They in turn hired a British engineer, Bryan Donkin, to perfect the invention, and they invested heavily in it. Donkin's machine became a success in Europe when it was marketed in 1807. A United States paper mill purchased it in 1827. Although the Fourdriniers held patents, they never profited from the machine. It was Donkin, also an innovator in other press-related materials and machinery, who continued to renew the patents as he developed practical improvements on the original patent. Robert, the inventor, died penniless. The Fourdriniers' legacy was the name of the papermaking machine, still called a *fourdrinier* in contemporary mills. Today's fourdrinier is almost a block long, with its every process controlled electronically.

The introduction of iron machinery and chemical agents into papermaking in the eighteenth and nineteenth centuries unfortunately brought to some paper a fungus, known as foxing, which appears as specks and blotches. Foxing on earlier papers had been caused by water with a high iron content. The original condition of the paper cannot be restored, but foxing can be arrested by chemical treatment, and humidity control can prevent further deterioration.

Even before mechanization, there were other changes in papermaking. One of these was a new mold introduced in the eighteenth century. A finely woven brass screen was fixed to the wooden frame. Because there were no wires and chains, no laid marks were left on the paper. Its smooth appearance gave it the name *wove*

Pl. 255. Nicholas-Louis Robert's papermaking machine. Courtesy of the Institute of Paper Science and Technology, Atlanta

paper. Long before, Chinese and Arab papermakers made wove paper, but there was no direct influence of their screens on the later European ones. Wove paper was made first by James Whatman the Elder at Turkey Mills, in Kent. But credit for its use in books is given to the English printer John Baskerville, who seems to have suggested its suitability for printing. He printed on it himself for part of his own first edition of Virgil in 1757, although he did not use wove paper in very many of his other books. English printers did not take advantage of it until the end of the century. *Papier velin,* as it was called in France, became popular with printers there, especially with the Didots. This smooth paper is still called *vellum paper,* or simply *vellum,* but it has nothing to do with the animal product (neither does baking parchment). One still may see a colophon stating that the book was printed on "vellum" or "Japanese vellum."

Another eighteenth-century innovation was the calender roll, first used in Holland, for the final smoothing of the paper (pl. 256). It not only was speedier than the hand-burnishing process but it produced a more even sheet than the mechanical glazing hammer, which vibrated as the paper was hand-held and did not apply equal pressure to each section of the sheet (see pl. 252, bottom). In early calendering, dry

Pl. 256. Wooden calender
roll. Joseph de Lalande,
Art de Faire le Papier (Paris,
1761). Courtesy of Joyce
Schmidt. Photo: Jewish
National and University
Library, Jerusalem

Pl. 256. Wooden calender roll. Joseph de Lalande, *Art de Faire le Papier* (Paris, 1761). Courtesy of Joyce Schmidt. Photo: Jewish National and University Library, Jerusalem

paper was fed through two large wooden rollers. Now calender rolls are of metal, and are fixed to the end of the fourdrinier. They can be heated, and pressure is adjustable. In the 1820s, English papermakers invented the dandy roll, a cylinder that applied an impression on wet machine-made paper to make it look as if its chain and wire lines and watermarks were an integral part of the paper. Dandy rolls, like calender rolls, are part of the modern papermaking machine.

The paper on which it is printed is one of the most important components of the book. In the contemporary printing plant, 30 percent to 60 percent of the cost of producing the book is invested in its paper. In Plantin's time (1520–1589), 60 percent to 65 percent of the book's cost was for paper, but sometimes it was as high as 75 percent. Whether it is handmade, mold-made, laid, or wove is not as important as the paper's suitability to the typography of the particular book, and its durability. Many handmade and mold-made papers that are beautiful in themselves, with obvious laid marks and watermarks, would compete with the printed text for the reader's eye. A clay-coated paper, suitable for faithful reproductions of works of art, is difficult to read when a whole page of text is printed on it. An unsized, thin

Japanese paper would allow the typography to bleed through the page in books printed in the Western manner. Because of the disintegration of highly acidic paper and resinous sizes in nineteenth-century and contemporary books, many readers and librarians now seek books printed on archival paper with a three-hundred-year life span. What will happen to those books in five hundred years? The paper on which the finest incunabula were printed will endure much longer. It would be remarkable if the readers of the future could admire our books as much as we value those of the Middle Ages and Renaissance.

CHAPTER 13

Bookbinding

TECHNIQUE:
FORWARDING

W estern European traditions of the leather-covered book, bound by hand, have remained virtually unchanged since the Middle Ages. Even the tools are similar, whether they have been fashioned anew or have been passed down by parent to child, or by master binder to favored apprentice: the sewing frame, the lying press, the bone folder, knives, and brass tools engraved in relief, mounted in handles. The difference between the handmade and the machine-made binding today is that the latter is really a case, manufactured separately from the book and glued onto the spine, which may or may not have been sewn. For the hand-bound book, the spine is sewn and the cover is applied gradually, step by step, as permanently as possible, so that the binding becomes an integral part of the book (fig. 32). The cover does not fall off the book after a number of readings, as it does in the modern case binding and paperback. There are now variations and combinations of machine and hand bindings, depending on the kind of machinery used in the bindery, on the budget, and on the aesthetics of the patron or publisher who commissions the binding.

Sewing

In binding the book by hand today, the bookbinder begins with the completed, assembled book. He or she cuts extra sheets of paper to be used as endpapers (also called endleaves or endsheets) and the boards that will eventually be attached and covered. The sewer checks or collates the signatures (or gatherings, the printed book's equivalent of the medieval quire) to make sure these sections are in the proper alphabetical order (minus *J*, *U* or *V*, and *W*), if they are so indicated by the printer. The book's spine is aligned with the sewing frame, to whose cords it will be sewn.

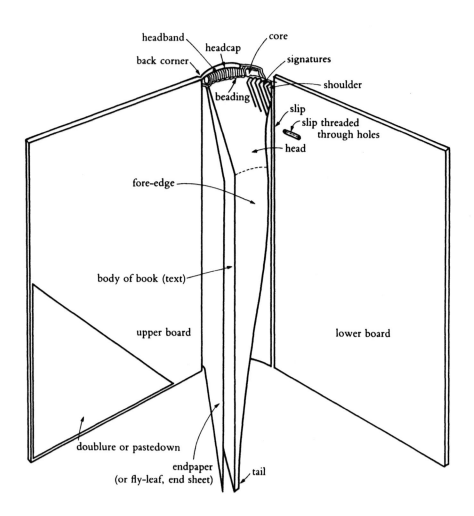

The sewing frame is strung with cords made of hemp or linen (these could have been leather thongs in the Middle Ages), tied to a crosspiece at the top and keyed-in below. The number of cords corresponds to the number of raised bands the binder has decided upon for the book, depending on its size; three to five are the average. The spine is marked in pencil to indicate where the bands will be, and the cords are adjusted to match those lines. There are no cords where the headbands and tailbands will be sewn (both headbands and tailbands are referred to as headbands). The book is set aside to await sewing, signature by signature.

The first signature is then sewn (pl. 257, center; 258). The endpapers can be the first signature, if the binder has decided to sew rather than tip them on afterwards. The first signature, set up against the cords, is held open at the centerfold with one hand. The needle and linen thread are passed through the centerfold to poke a hole at what will be the first kettle stitch. Each signature sewing begins and ends with the kettle stitch (or catch-up stitch; fig. 33). Kettle stitches connect one signature to the next near the head and tail. Later, these are connected to the headbands. The first kettle stitch is a loose end, but it is tied to the kettle stitch of the second signature when the sewer gets there. From the first kettle stitch the needle and thread proceed to the first cord. The thread is wrapped around the cord at the outside of the signature and passes back through the hole to the centerfold inside, and then goes on to the next cord to repeat the process until the kettle stitch at the other end of the spine is reached. Usually one signature at a time is sewn in this way until all are sewn.

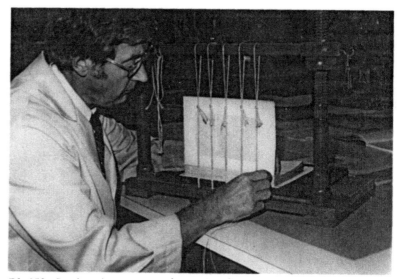

Pl. 258. Sewing signatures on the sewing frame. Courtesy of Jim Craven

Pl. 257. The bookbinder. From Jost Amman's illustrations for *Eygentliche Beschreibung aller Stände auff Erden* (Book of Trades) (Frankfurt: Feyerabend, 1568). Courtesy of University of Michigan Library, Department of Rare Books and Special Collections. Photo: Patrick J. Young

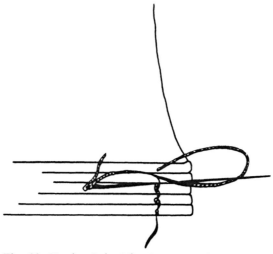

Fig. 33. Kettle stitch. After Matt T. Roberts and Don Etherington, eds., *Bookbinding and the Conservation of Books*. Drawn by Margaret R. Brown. Courtesy of Library of Congress

There are three basic sewing techniques that can best be seen by imagining one is looking down a section of the sewing frame: with single cords, as described above; with double cords, where the thread is wound around double cords in a figure 8; and with sawn-in bands, a labor-saving device that results in a weaker binding, in which grooves are made to receive the lay cords and the thread is passed in front of the cords (fig. 34). This time-saver was practiced as early as the sixteenth century. Sewing on both single and double bands was common in the Middle Ages.

The tasks of sewing the spine, gluing, rounding and backing, making the headbands, applying the boards, and covering the boards with leather are considered *forwarding,* while decoration of the cover is called *finishing.* In some binderies, particularly in France, the two aspects of binding are so distinct that the forwarder

Fig. 34. Sewing techniques. After Matt T. Roberts and Don Etherington, eds., *Bookbinding and the Conservation of Books*. Drawn by Margaret R. Brown. Courtesy of Library of Congress

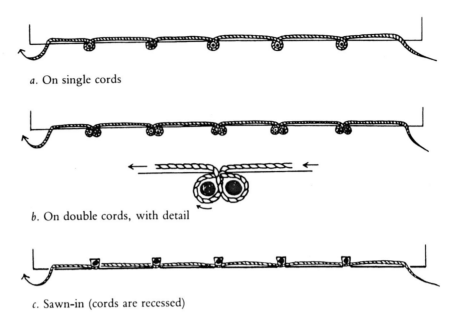

a. On single cords

b. On double cords, with detail

c. Sawn-in (cords are recessed)

never does the tooling. Most bookbinders today, when not working alone, do both forwarding and finishing with the help of apprentices who are learning the craft.

Gluing, Rounding, and Backing

After sewing of all the signatures has been completed, with endpapers sewn on in the same manner or tipped on, the cords are cut, with about two inches of cord left at the ends. These will soon be laced into the boards. Endpapers can be trimmed if they are not already the size of the book. The spine is then glued and manipulated into a slightly rounded form (rounding). The book is set into the lying press, with only a few millimeters of the spine protruding. When the glue has dried, the spine is tapped with a backing hammer (backing, pl. 259). This creates a shoulder where the boards will fit. With gluing, rounding, and backing, the spine takes on its permanent shape; ideally only the signature at the center has remained in its original place. When removed from the press, the book can be trimmed at this point if the binder has not done so before, with a plough, guillotine, knife, or chisel. Binders of the past (and sometimes today, unfortunately) in their eagerness to have smooth edges, demonstrated little sensitivity to the proportions of the manuscript or printed book by cutting off the margins. Conservators and binders today are generally more considerate, and will trim off only a minimum when it is absolutely necessary, or avoid trimming altogether.

Attaching the Boards

The plies of the leftover cords, called slips, are split with an awl and frayed with an awl or needle. Each slip is pasted and the point is twisted to thread it through the board (pl. 260). The boards have already been prepared with holes for this. Binders' board is used today, with paper pasted over the board, but originally boards were made of wood, necessary in medieval times to exert pressure on parchment to keep the pages from warping. In the Near East, Coptic and then Islamic binders favored pasteboards, made of straw and papyrus and eventually of paper. In Europe, sheets of old books were used to make pasteboard or to pad and line wooden boards. Thus, in modern times, rare manuscripts, early printers' proof sheets, or even parts of old

Pl. 259. Rounding and backing. Courtesy of Jim Craven

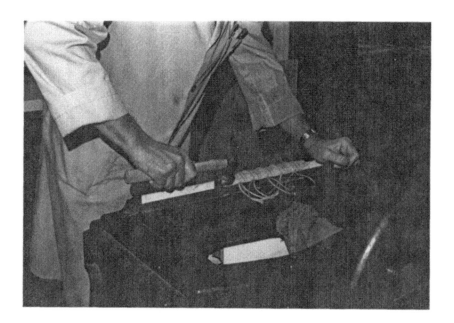

Pl. 260. Threading slips. Courtesy of Jim Craven

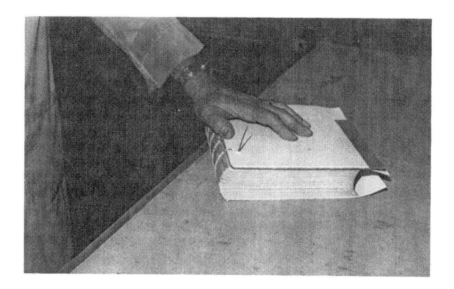

books have come to light when a book has been taken apart for conservation and rebinding. The earliest dated woodcut, the Buxheim St. Christopher of 1423, was preserved because it was binding material for a manuscript written in 1417 (see Chapter 14).

Two holes are punched in the boards next to each other for each slip to be laced in. The boards are aligned next to the spine to become the base for the upper and lower covers. The slips are laced into the boards, ending outside, with the excess slips trimmed off and hammered slightly so that they will not project.

Headbands

This is the ideal point at which headbands can be sewn (pl. 261), although some binders do so before the boards are fixed. Headbands are attached to the kettle stitches. When headbands are made by hand as an integral part of the book, two strands of different-colored thread, usually silk in the late Middle Ages, and silk or

Pl. 261. Ann Flowers
sewing headbands.

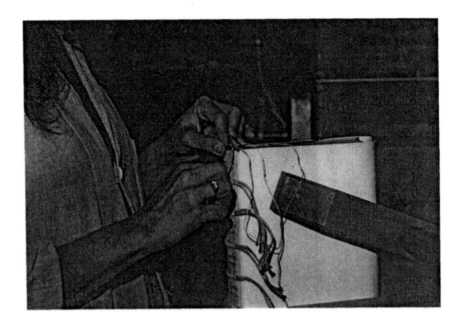

cotton or synthetics today, are twisted around each other at the head of each section, or around a core of leather, cord, or vellum, and sewn down through the fold in the section to connect with the kettle stitch. Binders do not usually fasten headbands down at each signature today, but do so at intervals of every few sections. Sometimes there is a double headband, with the second one around a thinner core, close to the first on the inside. Since the nineteenth century, many commercial binders have bought headbands manufactured on fabric tape, which can be sewn or glued to the back of the spine, to give the book a traditional look. Conservators and binders who have disbound old books report that as early as the sixteenth century there were binders who applied fake headbands. It is certainly a time-saver but does not serve the function of a real headband, which preserves the spine when the book is removed from the shelf many times with the forefinger. There were alternative materials and methods for making headbands in late medieval and Renaissance times, such as plaiting leather thongs around a vellum core that had already been sewn to the spine, but it is the silk-on-cord variety that became the norm. After the headbands are attached, the spine is lined up, that is, paper or leather is glued to it as reinforcement.

Covering

The boards are then covered with whatever material the binder has decided upon: leather, vellum, fabric, paper, or other materials. The earliest-known bound codices showed a variety of covering materials—leather or metal or ivory glued or nailed to wooden board. Leather has been considered a luxury binding material since the Renaissance, but in the Middle Ages it was the standard binding for a monastic codex. Of course there were far fewer books to bind then. Nowadays, even for fine books, leather is often combined with cloth or paper to produce a quarter- or half-leather cover. A half-leather binding will cover the spine and about one-fifth of the width of each board plus the triangular corners; a quarter-leather one will cover about one-fifth or less of the board, with no corners (see pl. 265, p. 309). Half-leather bindings became common in England in the late eighteenth century. Other materials, as varied today as they were in previous ages, can be used for covering the boards, but here we will describe the leather-bound book.

In covering the boards for a full leather binding, the single piece of leather, which has been pared down to the desired thinness and cut with enough overlap to turn in, is applied to the spine and the boards (pl. 262). While held fast but not under too much pressure, which would damage it, the leather is turned in and pasted onto the underside of the boards. Then it is turned in at the head and tail with a bone folder (pl. 263), the binder's indispensable tool. This is called a folder because its common use is for folding paper, but in the Middle Ages it could have been any flat, pointed bone tool. Sometimes there is a space between the leather cap and the colored headbands so that the latter can be seen; at other times the headcap is turned in over part of the headband, so only part of the headband shows. The bone folder is used again to smooth the leather where it has been turned in at the spine, and to shape the head and tail at the joint. Tying up the spine at the joints with string can also be done to set the headcaps. The bands may be further accentuated with a nippers (pl. 264), and rubbed and smoothed in between the bands with a rubbing stick. The raised

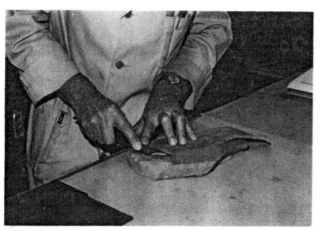

Pl. 262. Paring leather. Courtesy of Jim Craven

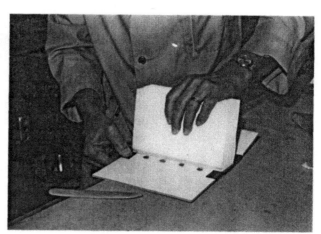

Pl. 263. Turning-in. Courtesy of Jim Craven

Pl. 264. Nipping bands. Courtesy of Jim Craven

bands may be emphasized even more by tying them up horizontally around the book; the twine will leave its pattern if this effect is desired. The binder also may tool a design in the leather over the place where slips were laced into the boards.

If the cover is of partial leather, the corners are applied first and turned in, then the cloth is cut to register and glued onto the boards. When the leather is completely dry, endpapers are trimmed further if necessary and pasted down to the inside of the cover. The book is closed and placed under weight. It is then ready for decoration, or finishing.

With each stage in the hand-bound book—sewing, gluing-up, rounding and backing, lacing-in, headbanding, and applying the cover—the book and its binding become a single integral unit.

FINISHING

Embellishment of the leather binding was and still is accomplished by cutting or tooling. Cutting is done with a knife or a pointed metal tool while the leather is damp, or with a bone folder. Lines can be made with a pallet, a tool with an elongated, straight head. Leather can be blind-stamped (impressed) with single heated tools mounted on handles with relief designs on the tip (pl. 265), or stamping can be done with fillets or rolls, tools that look like large pizza cutters. The fillet has one, two, or three raised metal bands on its wheel. When heated and rolled, the wheel leaves single, double, or triple parallel lines on the leather cover. The roll has relief designs along the wheel's edge instead of plain metal bands; it rolls out a pattern of dots, dotted lines, flowers, geometric patterns, or any small, repeated designs that could have been made one at a time with a single tool. Rolls and fillets are from 1 to 4 inches (2½ to 10 cm) in diameter and set in very long handles that can be braced on the binder's shoulder. They look the same today as they did in the sixteenth-century bookbinder's shop, as we see in Jost Ammann's woodcut *Das Ständebuch* (Book of Trades) of 1568 (compare pl. 257 and 266). Fillets may have been used as early as the twelfth century, and both fillets and rolls were in use by the latter half of the fifteenth century.

Gold tooling has been known, first in the Near East, since the eleventh century. It is done by first applying glair or size to the blind-stamped design. Then the design is covered with gold leaf, and restamped in the same place with the heated tool. More common today for gold stamping, because it is easier to manipulate, is gold on a plastic carrier that contains heat- and pressure-sensitive sizing. Gold leaf is used with rolls and fillets as well as with single tools, or with single brass letters mounted in a handle. Metal types for titles and authors can be fixed into a lettering pallet, heated, and stamped by hand if it has a handle or set in a press for stamping (pl. 267). Gold stamping must be done in a heated blocking press. Today, book manufacturers sometimes use their old letter presses, long ago phased out for text printing, for printing gold or colored titles on case bindings, which then will be glued to the products of their high-speed presses.

HISTORY

Byzantine, Coptic, and Medieval Bindings

The history of bookbinding begins at the same time as the codex itself, that is, with the Roman diptych made of wood or ivory which was fastened together with leather thongs (see pl. 17, p. 12, pl. 142, p. 166, pl. 143, p. 167). Scrolls had been encased in fabric or hide wrappers or in wooden or metal boxes or *capsae,* so the makers of luxury manuscripts in the new codex format took it for granted that their books, too, would be protected and adorned with suitable coverings. Ivory, or plates of gold or gilt silver or other metals inlaid with jewels, were fashioned separately and mounted on heavy wooden boards.

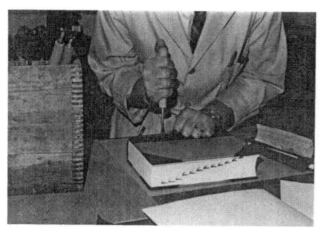

Pl. 265. Tooling a half-leather binding. Courtesy of Jim Craven

Pl. 266. Binder's tools: rolls, fillets, and pallets (*above*) in Jim Craven's bindery, the Conservation Laboratory of the Michigan Historical Collections, Bentley Historical Library, University of Michigan, Ann Arbor

Pl. 267. Name pallet. Courtesy of Jim Craven

The earliest extant leather-bound codices, from seventh- and eighth-century Egypt, first were stitched at the spine with link stitches, with their separately made leather-on-pasteboard covers glued on (pl. 268). These Coptic bindings were the ancestors of both Islamic and European leather bookbindings. A collection of fifty-two bound codices, from the Monastery of St. Michael in the Fayyum, were found in 1910 and are now preserved in the Pierpont Morgan Library in New York. Most of the bindings were impressed with metal tools. Some have cut-out leatherwork mounted on parchment that was gilded or painted red. In some, the leather was incised, blind-tooled, pierced, or dot-punched. Other leatherwork of seventh-to-ninth-century Egypt, such as saddles or pouches, shows that craftsmen also decorated leather in relief patterns and sometimes painted it red, yellow, and green. The book's leather cover was glued to pasteboards made of straw or papyrus, or a combination of the two, sometimes an inch thick. Some bindings had ivory pegs, around which leather thongs were looped, to keep the book closed. Leather thongs also were used to lift the covers, or served as bookmarks. The first *ex libris* can be found in the inside of the upper cover of one of these books: "St. Michael Archangel" is written in leather cutwork Greek letters.

Pl. 268. Coptic leather binding. On Four Gospels. Monastery of St. Michael of the Desert, Fayyum, Egypt, seventh or eighth century. Pierpont Morgan Library, M.569. Courtesy of the Pierpont Morgan Library, New York

Pl. 269. Stonyhurst Gospel (Gospel of St. Cuthbert). Dark red goatskin, Coptic-style sewing. England, seventh century. On loan to the British Library, Loan 74. Courtesy of the Trustees for Catholic Purposes Registered

Geometric and interlace patterns that characterized Coptic cover design were to continue quite naturally in Islamic leatherwork, first in Egypt and then in North Africa. It is more surprising to find a seventh-century English book cover with obvious Coptic designs. It possibly was made by an emigrating Coptic monk-binder. The book is the Northumbrian Stonyhurst Gospel of St. John, buried with St. Cuthbert (d. 687), now on display at the British Library (pl. 269). This tiny masterpiece of dark red goatskin, about 5½ inches (14 cm) high, whose relief-molded, symmetrical swirling pattern heralds the carpet-page designs of Anglo-Celtic art, has a greater affinity to North African bindings of a few centuries later than to those of the European monastery, both in its sewing technique and in its decoration (compare to pl. 276, p. 315). The oldest leather bindings from continental Europe, from the eighth century, are preserved in the Landesbibliothek at Fulda, having come from the monastery there. In their leatherwork technique, a few of these are related to the Stonyhurst Gospel binding. One, the Calmug Gospels, is also small, of the same dyed reddish leather, and sewn with the same Coptic link-stitch technique. Another, the Ragyndrudis Codex, is decorated in Coptic style but sewn on raised cords that were laced into boards in what was to become the standard European sewing method.

Leather-bound books for reading and study were kept in the monastic library, sometimes on chains to prevent their removal. The more sumptuous bindings of gold (exceptionally rare; the binding of the Lindau Gospels in the Pierpont Morgan

Library is one of the two known solid gold ones), gilt silver, or gilt copper with semiprecious stones and ivory were used in the church service or were imperial gift books. Such bindings were made for members of the Carolingian and Byzantine courts or for high churchmen. An enamel worker's technique, cloisonné, was employed for decorating fine bindings in Byzantium. The design, usually figures of Christ, the Madonna, or saints in medallions, was made with forms built up of gold threads, with enamel poured into the resulting compartments. Some Carolingian, Ottonian, and Spanish book covers are similar to these Byzantine luxury bookbindings. The wooden boards to which plaques of metal or ivory were nailed at times were so thick that they could contain relics of the saints. Gems that were set into metalwork in Byzantine fashion were not always semiprecious stones; sometimes they were made of glass, which itself was a rarity in the early Middle Ages. Pearls from European rivers, cameos, ivory carvings that were once Roman diptychs, or Byzantine plaques also were attached to wooden boards. Carved ivory or hammered gilt-silver work depicted the Crucifixion, Christ in Majesty, the evangelists with their symbols, or events from the Gospels (pl. 270). The subjects were often similar to those found within the illuminated book, as was the style. For example, one can find ivory covers with illustrations of Psalms in Reims style, resembling the Utrecht Psalter. By the thirteenth century the Limoges enamel industry supplied cover decorations for luxury bindings. In their champlevé enamel technique, the copper plaque was hollowed out, and heated colored enamel poured in and fused, with the projecting metal edges serving as outlines. Simpler covers, from Carolingian times on, were made of fabrics, such as velvet, silk, or silk brocade, or of parchment. Very few of these fabric covers have come down to us

Pl. 270. Ivory cover on the Lorsch Gospels. Virgin and Child enthroned, between Zachariah and St. John the Baptist. Angels above resemble winged Victories; New Testament scenes below. Carolingian, early ninth century. Victoria and Albert Museum, 138-1866. Courtesy of the Victoria and Albert Museum, London

because textiles deteriorated and most fabric-covered books eventually were rebound. Textiles had a better chance of surviving as doublures, on the inside of the cover.

Blind-tooled leather covers were distinctive in the twelfth and thirteenth centuries. These are called monastic bindings today even if they were made for books belonging to cathedral schools or for private patrons (pl. 271). They also can be given the name of the period—Romanesque or Gothic. Tools used for blind-stamping depicted small flowers, geometric ornaments, birds, animals and grotesques, mermaids, centaurs, and human figures. They were frequently stamped in repeat-patterns, covering the whole surface of the leather, which was calfskin or sheepskin. Spanish binders of the fourteenth and fifteenth centuries used the tiny rope tools of Islamic binders, with geometric and interlaced strapwork, in what is called Mudéjar or Hispano-Moresque style. Sometimes they combined these with Gothic-style tools. In Germany and central Europe, lines were also cut, with a sharp bone tool or with knives in a technique called *cuir ciselé* (pl. 272). Medieval leather covers frequently had heavy metal bosses driven into them to protect the leather of one book from rubbing against another as they were stacked horizontally on library shelves. Metal clasps were attached, either alone or mounted on leather straps, to keep the codex tightly closed, as much as to keep out dust as to prevent warping, a natural tendency of the parchment, especially when it was sewn tightly on the cords. Clasps and their hinges were decorative as well as functional, cut from iron, brass, silver, or gilt-silver. When books became lighter in the Renaissance, ties were used instead of clasps, although clasps remained in use. Another type of relatively lightweight book from the Middle Ages was the girdle book (pl. 273). A traveling monk could attach it to his belt and read while on horseback or donkeyback.

Islamic Bindings

To understand the history of European leather book covers since the Renaissance, it is necessary to return to the Near East, where the art of decorating leather covers was perfected. The influence of Islamic motifs, gold tooling, and inlaying of leathers came to Europe from two directions—first from North Africa, by way of Spain (Some Italian Renaissance bindings show Spanish Mudéjar influence), and then from Persia, by way of Venice. The sewing of Islamic bindings differed from the European technique (fig. 35). Quires were sewn with a link stitch, based on Coptic methods, and the separately made leather cover was pasted onto the light wooden boards or pasteboards and spine. The typical Islamic book was much thinner than its European counterpart, and did not require the secure sewing on bands of the monastic codex. It is known from a letter found in the Cairo Geniza that ready-made bindings were exported from North Africa to Egypt in the latter half of the eleventh century. The tenuous connection between the book and its cover not only encouraged the rebinding of worn-out bookcovers over the centuries, with many old ones having been stored away in mosques for posterity in geniza fashion, but it also enabled scholars and "collectors" in our own century, working in Near Eastern libraries, to remove some handsome bindings for their eventual appreciation in the West.

The typical Islamic cover had an extra protective and decorative flap that extended from the lower cover, enclosed the fore-edges, and folded over a quarter of the upper cover, in envelope fashion (pl. 274, 275). Islamic-type sewing and envelope flaps were not adopted by European binders, although in Spain, Portugal, and Yemen some Jewish binders built up the sides of the binding to form a box (pl. 276). Gold tooling was also Islamic in origin. It was mentioned in the same eleventh-century treatise that described papermaking, *The Staff of the Scribes,* by Ibn Badis (see Chapters 11 and 12). Gilt leather shoes were exported from Tunisia in the eleventh century, according to a Cairo Geniza record. The first dated gold-tooled

Pl. 271. Monastic binding (Romanesque); lower cover. On Gospel of St. John. Reddish-brown sheepskin. Paris, ca. 1150. From the Benedictine Abbey at Admont, Austria. Bodleian Library, the Broxbourne Library. Courtesy of the Bodleian Library, Oxford

Pl. 272. Cuir ciselé binding by Meir Jaffe for Hans von Thill. On Barzizius, *Epistole* (Basel, 1472). Brown hide, with blind-tooling. The binder worked in Ulm, Nuremberg, and Bamburg. Herzog August Bibliothek, 158.3 Quodl. 2°. Courtesy of the Herzog August Bibliothek, Wolfenbüttel

binding—1256—comes from Morocco (see pl. 277). By the fifteenth century, Spanish binders also tooled in gold, but infrequently, and gold tooling was known in Italy by 1480. Another Islamic binder's invention was the decoration of the insides of the covers, later called doublures when made of leather and called pastedowns when made of parchment or paper. Doublures in Persian and Turkish bindings of the fifteenth and sixteenth centuries often were as elaborate as the bindings themselves. Papers were block printed as well and, later, marbleized. The art of marbleing spread, like doublures, from Persia and Turkey to Italy, Europe, and back to the Far East, where it had originated (in China). These decorated papers are still popular today for fine books. Many binders now marble their own papers or import them from England and Italy.

The earliest group of Islamic bindings comes from the Muslim equivalent of a geniza. Fragments of worn-out covers made between the ninth and thirteenth centuries, 179 of them, were discovered in the 1940s in the Great Mosque of Kairouan, Tunisia (pl. 275). Displaying the horizontal format of early Qur'āns, they are of brown, red, or black goatskin over poplar wood boards, decorated with interlaces. One type of circular relief design was executed by setting down cords saturated with glue on the boards, then pressing the leather down and molding it to the shape of the cords, afterwards enhancing it by tooling (pl. 276). The result is similar to the central motif of the Stonyhurst Gospel (see pl. 269) and, like it, the

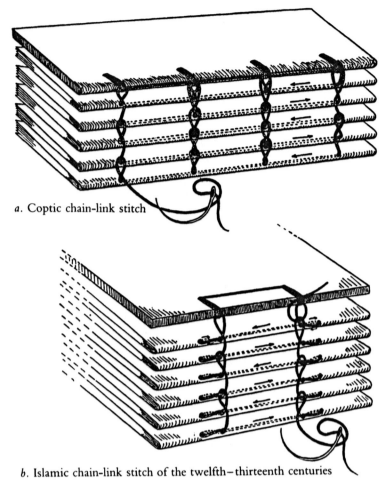

a. Coptic chain-link stitch

b. Islamic chain-link stitch of the twelfth–thirteenth centuries

Fig. 35. Coptic and Islamic sewing techniques. After Theodore C. Petersen, from *Ars Orientalis,* vol. 1. Courtesy of *Ars Orientalis*

Pl. 273. Girdle book. Breviary, written in Kastl Monastery, Germany, 1459. Doeskin, with green leather over it, brass bosses. New York Public Library, Spencer Collection, Ms. 39. Courtesy of the New York Public Library. Photo: Robert D. Rubic, New York

Pl. 274. Tunisian envelope binding, lower cover. Red leather, darkened, on poplar wood board lined with parchment. Tunisia, ninth century. The Republic of Tunisia. Reproduced from Dorothy Miner, *The History of Bookbinding, 525–1950 A.D.*

Pl. 275. Relief-tooled Tunisian envelope binding, lower cover. Black goatskin on poplar boards covered with parchment. Kairouan, eleventh century. Technique and pattern are similar to the binding of the Stonyhurst Gospel. The Republic of Tunisia. Reproduced from Dorothy Miner, *The History of Bookbinding, 525–1950 A.D.*

Pl. 276. Miniature box binding. On Hippocrates *Medical Aphorisms* and *Sefer HaPeri*. (In Hebrew; book photographed upside-down). Deep-brown morocco (goatskin), with traces of gold tooling. Lisbon, late fifteenth century. Library of the Jewish Theological Seminary of America, Micr. 8241. Courtesy of the Jewish Theological Seminary of America, New York. Photo: Jon Batista

Pl. 277. Moroccan gold-tooled binding. On a section of the Qur'ān. Red morocco (goatskin, turned brown). Marrakesh, 1256. Arab Library, Medressa Ben Yusuf, Marrakesh. Reproduced from Dorothy Miner, *History of Bookbinding, 525–1950* A.D.

Islamic design and technique are indebted to Coptic models. The favored western Islamic decoration usually was built up of small rope and dot tools or punches, which could be repeated to form an infinite variety of geometric designs, either as the central motif or as a closely impressed background for strapwork. Strapwork refers to the undecorated (reserve) geometric interlacing bands on the leather. One climax in the history of western Islamic binding came in 1256 in Morocco, where the earliest known, dated gold-tooled bindings were made (pl. 277). From there the art of gold stamping spread to Spain and southern Italy. Tanned goatskin, from that time on called morocco, became an import item sought by European binders. A variation on it took the name from the Spanish town of Córdoba. Red cordoban leather soon was as prized as morocco.

The bindings of the eastern Islamic world were more varied in their materials and often more spectacular in their designs than those of Egypt and North Africa (pl. 278). By the Timurid (fifteenth century) and Safavid (sixteenth century) periods, Persian bookbinding, which previously had been quite simple, reached its height. Covers were made of dyed leathers, some with intricate filigree patterns cut by hand, some with illustrations like the illuminations within the manuscript. Some were embossed in low relief with plaques. One favored motif that proved to be popular in Europe was a central almond-shaped medallion with four corner pieces, still considered a classic device (pl. 279). Persian binding design came directly to Venice (then to Florence, Rome, and Bologna) through trade, but also came later by way of Turkey, where binders' techniques and designs were influenced by Persian craftsmen (pl. 280). Some Turkish and later Persian binders added stones and metalwork to the leather, in Byzantine fashion. Persian lacquer-painted covers, from the second quarter of the sixteenth century, were the result of the miniaturist's art. Designs and scenes were first painted on leather. But artists soon switched to

Pl. 278. Persian lacquer-painted binding. Lower cover. Horsemen hunting deer, with falconer and attendant. Probably from a *Khamsa* of Nizami. Persia, sixteenth century. Victoria and Albert Museum, 353-1885. Courtesy of the Victoria and Albert Museum, London

Pl. 279. Filigree doublure (inside of cover). On a *Khamsa* of Nizami. Brown leather with cut medallion of the Simurgh, on a deep-blue ground. Shiraz, 1449/50. Metropolitan Museum of Art, Gift of Alexander Smith Cochran, 1913; The Cochran Collection, 13.228.3. Courtesy of the Metropolitan Museum of Art, New York

Pl. 280. Venetian binding, with a medallion of St. Mark. On a manuscript, *Del Salario del Podesta, et della sua Corte . . .* (Venice, 1574). Richly gilt red morocco. Pierpont Morgan Library, M.203. Courtesy of the Pierpont Morgan Library, New York

Pl. 281. Grolier binding. On *Augustini Steuchi . . . in Psalmos* (1550–1560). "Jo. Grolieri et Amicorum" stamped on it. Victoria and Albert Museum, L.33951938. Courtesy of the Victoria and Albert Museum, London

pasteboard that was sized with chalk, then coated with colorless lacquer, and painted with watercolors; afterwards several coats of transparent paint were applied over it.

The Renaissance in Europe, and Later

Aldus Manutius, the great humanist printer at the turn of the sixteenth century, famous for his books in small format, preferred lightweight calfskin or dyed morocco covers over thin wood or pasteboard. Thin leather straps replaced heavier metal clasps. Patterns of tiny leaves and segments of arabesques or vines were stamped in leather by the binders he patronized. These came to be known as *Aldine leaves* and eventually influenced typographic ornaments called *printers' flowers*. Their inspiration may have been in Roman monumental inscriptions. Aldus also favored either the central medallion with four-cornerpiece arrangement, or a frame along the outer edges. His prestige as a printer-publisher influenced other Venetian binders to adopt the designs of his bookbinders.

When printing began, and in the centuries that followed, few printers took upon themselves the responsibility for binding the book. It was up to the bookbuyer or the bookseller to commission the binding. Binders often worked in the same workshop as illuminators or rubricators. Gold left over from their work was removed with a gold rubber (made of rubber soaked in turpentine; now also made of synthetic crepe-rubber soaked in paraffin) and recycled. European bibliophiles had their own personal bookbinders, sometimes known by name even though they rarely left colophons. Renaissance leather covers were decorated by cuir cisé, by tooling with single tools alone or in combinations, by rolls and fillets, or by panel stamping, in which a central illustration or design was engraved on metal and stamped with a press. Panel stamping was first employed in the Netherlands in the late thirteenth century, and continued in Flemish binding. French binders adopted it in the late fifteenth century, German binders a century later. Panel stamping an entire cover was a great labor-saving device for the binder. Stamped illustrations could be bordered with tools similar to ones used since the Gothic age. Tools were reused for many bindings, and now often can identify a particular workshop. Some illustrations in cuir cisé and panel-stamped bindings have been related to specific engraving masters, who undoubtedly executed plates for stamping. The maximum tool size for effective blind stamping is about one inch (2½ cm), and for gold stamping, about ¾ inch (2 cm). A carved woodblock or a metal engraving would have to be impressed on the finished binding under the pressure of a large screw press, or the wet leather would be embossed with the metal stamp from the underside, before the leather cover was fixed to the boards. Portraits, coats of arms, imitation cameos and gems, and the lion of St. Mark, patron saint of Venice, were the favored subjects of the centerpieces of Venetian bindings, sometimes called dogale (or ducali) or medallion bindings (see pl. 280). It has not been proven whether the large binder's press preceded or followed the printing press.

Leather bindings of sixteenth-century central Europe, mounted on heavy wooden boards with pronounced bands, were sturdier and more medieval-looking than those of Italy. In addition to the handsome cuir cisé covers in black leather, pigskin continued to be a popular material in Germany since the Middle Ages, achieving the effect of delicate ivory at times. Dies with coats of arms and portraits of the patron or panel stamps of biblical subjects also appeared on the covers, sometimes painted with gold.

With the fame of Renaissance book collectors such as Jean Grolier (1479–1565), Thomas Mahieu (Maioli, d. 1572), and François I and Henri II of France, who patronized their favorite bookbinders, covers came to be classified by their owners' names as well as by the style their central motifs suggested (pl. 281, 282). But the names of their binders are well known: Etienne Roffet, royal binder for François I between 1539 and 1547; and Claude de Picques, binder for Henri II from 1548. Style

Pl. 282. Binding for Henri II. On Julius Firmicus Maternus, Jr., *Astronomicum Libri VIII* . . . (Basel, 1551). Morocco. Bibliothèque Nationale, Imp. Res. IV.186. Courtesy of the Bibliothèque Nationale, Paris

Pl. 283. Cottage binding by Samuel Mearne. On a *Book of Common Prayer* (London, 1669). Bound in 1674. Red morocco, black stain, with arms of Charles II. British Library, 7.f.13. Courtesy of the British Library

names usually were given by nineteenth-century scholars and binders. Grolier had lived in Italy, and his taste in bindings was influenced by the books he collected there. Thus, motifs of curvilinear ribbons and arabesques, rectangular concentric frames, and center-and-cornerpiece design passed into France in the 1520s and 1530s. Raised bands on Grolier's books were at times painted green, red, and white, often with the author and title stamped on the cover and spine. Some of Grolier's bindings and those in similar style were geometric, floral, or architectural, with gold tools, fillets, and rolls stamped on tan morocco and smooth calf. Design elements also were painted or dyed. Many Renaissance collectors had their names or initials stamped on their covers. Grolier liked the formula "Io. Grolier et amicorum" (as did Mahieu with his own name), gold-stamped on a painted blue panel, implying that he shared his books with friends (see pl. 281). His motto was taken from the *ex libris* of an Italian humanist who *did* share his library. It was said of Grolier that he would rather give away a book than lend it, and indeed he frequently purchased duplicate copies, making a gift of one of them. Some of his books that did not disappear altogether when his collection was scattered after his death are still in mint condition from seldom having been opened. The other motto Grolier favored was "Portio mea domine sit in terra viventium" ("My portion in the land of the living," Psalms 141:6).

By the latter half of the sixteenth century, France replaced Italy as the trendsetter of bookbinding style. Henri II sustained the collecting tradition of the French monarchy, and his initials and those of his wife Catherine de Medicis and his mistress Diane de Poitiers are repeated in compartments with crowns and fleur-de-lis on many of their books (pl. 282). Sometimes they were tooled in silver on dyed calf or morocco, citron (greenish-yellow) being a popular color. One type of compartmentalized tooling was called *fanfare* by the nineteenth-century gilder

Thouvenin, who revived the style. The name has nothing to do with the design; it comes from the title of the book on which Thouvenin found it, *Fanfares et Corvées Abbadesques* (1613). It has been associated with the French royal binders from 1578 to 1634, Nicholas and Clovis Eve, father and son, although several Parisian binders decorated covers in this style. French fanfare is characterized by compartments of strapwork filled with olive or laurel branches composed of small leaf tools (this device also appeared in French architectural decoration, seen in the Louvre). The earliest fanfare cover is on a book bound for Charles IX in 1570. The style then spread to Italy.

Red morocco was a popular covering for seventeenth-century French books; it accepted gold tooling particularly well. Morocco was at times inlaid with other multicolored leathers by cutting grooves into the cover and inserting colored pieces, creating a mosaic effect. Mosaic bindings also were to be found in later centuries in England and Spain, sometimes combined with the patron's portrait. Around 1630 another style is evident in France, called *pointillé*. Here individual tools, rolls of dots, curved lines, and leaves even tinier than those of fanfare were combined to give the cover a filigreed, jewellike sparkle. Pointillé has been associated with two names, Florimond Badier and the pseudonym Le Gascon (some believe the two to be the same person), and a profile portrait "signature."

Compared to French Renaissance books, English bindings at first seem austere. Many covers displayed the center-and-cornerpiece device. Tooling was almost exclusively in blind (impressed without gold) until the middle of the sixteenth century, with gold stamping introduced by the royal binder Thomas Berthelet about 1530. His favorite binding leather was white doeskin. The import of colored goatskin began about the time of the Restoration, 1660. Samuel Mearne (d. 1683), Charles II's binder, introduced an architectural variant known as cottage style, a triangular pediment at the top and bottom of a rectangular panel (pl. 283). It had many imitators. Other binding patterns for Charles II were derived from French fanfare or mosaic styles, with red, blue, brown, green, and white leather inlays on black morocco. All-over designs with flowers reflected the popularity of Persian carpets in Restoration England. Nonleather bindings also were valued in England. Designs, portraits, and figures embroidered on satin with gold, silver, or colored silk threads were crafted and sent to the binder for mounting on boards (pl. 284). These doll-like pictures give the cover a three-dimensional aspect. In another type of binding, transparent vellum covers were laid over paintings of mythological subjects.

Fore-edge gilding had been practiced since the Middle Ages. Gauffering, tooled decoration on gilt fore-edges, was practiced on the Iberian peninsula in the fifteenth century, and became more popular from the sixteenth century. Fore-edge painting, where the edges were painted with ornaments, coats of arms, and Christian themes such as the Madonna and Child and Baptism, had been known in Germany since the sixteenth century. It then became an English specialty (pl. 285). Charles II's portrait appeared on the edges of his books. The eighteenth-century expert in this art was William Edwards of Halifax (1723–1808), who also painted pictures on the undersurface of transparent vellum placed over white paper boards. His technique for the latter was to render the vellum transparent by soaking it in pearl ash, then pressing the part to be painted. In English fore-edge painting, landscapes, architecture, interior scenes, chess games, and other genre illustrations, which would be invisible if one looked at the fore-edge head-on, would magically appear as the fore-edge was slightly beveled. A greater feat was a double fore-edge painting; a completely different scene appeared as one splayed the fore-edge in the opposite direction.

No matter how low standards of printing were in late sixteenth- and seventeenth-century Europe, there were always some examples of magnificent bindings. By the middle of the eighteenth century, French binders returned to the

Pl. 284. Embroidered fabric binding. Abraham, Isaac, and David. On an English New Testament (London, 1625). Bodleian Library, Oxford, Douce C.110. Courtesy of the Bodleian Library, Oxford

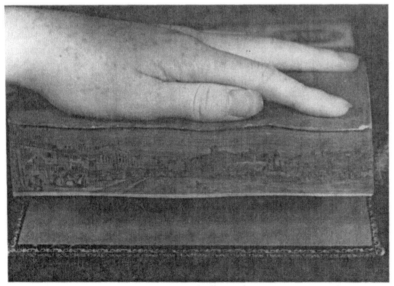

Pl. 285. Fore-edge painting, artist unknown. From *The Life and Remains of Henry Kirke White* (London: W. Raynes and Son, 1825). Courtesy of the Rare Book Collection, Library of Congress, Washington, D.C.

Pl. 286. Roger Payne binding. On *Dialogus Creaturarum* (Gouda, 1480). Binding late eighteenth century. Courtesy of the John M. Wing Foundation, Newberry Library, Chicago

sumptuousness of earlier centuries, after a brief flirtation with simplicity. Some covers exhibited ivory carvings or jewels set into precious metals. One major style in leatherwork from the eighteenth century is known as *dentelle,* a delicate imitation of lacework, accomplished by very tiny pointillé tools and fillets. Deròme le Jeune (Nicolas Denis Deròme, [1731–1788]), the third son of binder Jacques Antoine

Deròme (1696–1760) and one of a family of sixteen master binders who favored the mosaic style, was probably the best-known Parisian to bind in dentelle style. He had a distinctive little bird tool: *dentelle á l'oiseau*. The art of French binding was and still is divided into two specialties, with artisans often working in separate establishments. The *relieur* was responsible for the forwarding, and the *doreur* did the finishing, the gold tooling on the leather cover. This tradition goes back to 1581, when there were separate guilds for the two crafts.

The English expert in dentelle-like bindings was Roger Payne (1738–1797), who also favored purple endpapers and blue leather book jackets (pl. 286). The bills he presented to his patrons described his creations with little modesty. For his binding on a book now in the Walters Art Gallery, Baltimore, he wrote: "Bound in the very best Manner, & the most elegant Taste. Highly Finished with Gold Studded Borders inside magnificent. The outside Finished with two very elegant Gold Borders magnificent. The Back richly Finished with Gold Studded Work." He also wrote in a book now in the Rosenthal collection in Chicago, "Letter'd in the most correct Manner in a True Line. The Back lined with Red Morocco thin to make it open easy. Sew'd in the Best manner with Bands on the outside of the paper, Not by the usual manner of sawing into the paper at the Back the Margin is rob'd of that space." Fortunately, Payne used his tools with greater restraint than he did his pen. The greater subtlety of English bindings eventually influenced the taste of French collectors. Many sent their books to England to be bound.

Modern Times

Like much of nineteenth-century Romantic art and architecture, fine leather binding styles were eclectic. Architectural bindings either were Neo-Classical or Gothic, in cathedral style. Although craftsmanship in forwarding was still high, there were few original cover designs. Nineteenth-century innovation can be found in new binding materials, seen first in England. Mass-produced books demanded faster and cheaper binding methods. For the convenience of the retail bookseller or publisher of the late eighteenth and early nineteenth centuries, entire editions, especially of textbooks, were bound in paper boards with leather sometimes stuck over them. These came to be known as *edition bindings*. From the 1820s, cases were manufactured separately from their books, with identical covers made in quantity. Sometimes books were bound in canvas or in cheap leather, especially in roan, sheepskin that imitated morocco. The English publisher William Pickering, always conscious of book design, introduced cloth bindings on some of his books in the 1820s, although not for entire editions. By 1823, glazed calico was used, or other cloth pressed with dyed starch that was impervious to adhesive. By the 1830s cloth could be grained, and embossed or stamped with titles. These cloth bindings displayed striped, floral, and pictorial designs. Most innovations were accomplished by binder Archibald Leighton (1784–1841). Cloth casings became more popular in England and in the United States in the 1830s and 1840s for large editions, although the publisher often bound one batch at a time as the edition was sold, sometimes with different casings. Blind and gilt pictorial dies were popular for cover designs in the 1840s, with the book's endpapers painted or printed with publishers' ads until the 1890s. Many Victorian stamped bindings of cloth and leather that were charming monuments to the age are still gracing library stacks of England and America, displaying their bird, animal, vegetal, abstract, and floral motifs, with cathedrals for prayerbooks, and arabesques in all colors, including gold, silver, and black, against colored cloth (pl. 287). Even when they have darkened, they render today's cloth and imitation-cloth bindings pale by comparison. Printed paper covers were more popular than cloth in continental Europe, and this tradition has continued to the present for scholarly works.

Throughout the nineteenth century there was little change in the method of manufacturing the case binding of the cloth-covered book. Manual labor was gradually replaced by the machine, first for trimming (the guillotine) in the 1850s, then for sewing in the 1880s. By the early twentieth century, all aspects of bookbinding were mechanized: folding, gathering, cutting, rounding and backing, trimming, case making, and casing-in. Today larger printing firms take the responsibility for casing the book, providing complete book-manufacturing services to the publisher.

As twentieth-century readership made even heavier demands on publishers for more and cheaper books, paperbacks filled the need. One might say that there is nothing new in paperbacks—there were always books that the printer or bookseller never bothered to bind. Printed paper covers can be traced back to Augsburg, where a woodcut decoration appeared on the wrapper of a book printed by Erhard Ratdolt, dated 1494. Woodcuts on pasteboard covers also served as bindings of some books from Venice and Ferara in the early sixteenth century. By the mid-seventeenth century, paper covers were pasted to the spine or the endpapers, especially on pamphlets. Later in the century these often were printed. In the late eighteenth century, paperboard covers with typographic ornament and lettering became more common. Some mid-nineteenth-century novels had colored paper wrappers with pictorial designs. Popular in England were cheap works of fiction bound in glazed yellow paper boards, called yellowbacks, which disappeared by the early twentieth century. Another paperback tradition began in Germany in 1841, when Leipzig publisher Christian Bernhard Tauchnitz inaugurated a reprint series of English and American authors to be sold in Europe only. The popular Tauchnitz books are often considered the true forerunners of the modern paperback. In 1932 they inspired the Albatross library series in Hamburg (later managed by Tauchnitz), whose covers were designed by Giovanni Mardersteig, the twentieth century's finest hand-printer. In 1935 there appeared the first Penguin books, created by Allen Lane, all fiction titles. Their success begat the Pelican nonfiction series in 1937, to be followed by other flying triumphs.

American paperbacks have their own traditions, beginning in 1842, with their ups and downs until the turn of the twentieth century, when the low hardcover price of $2 drove them from the market. They were revived again in the 1920s, first with the Reynolds Publishing Company's fiction reprints at 10 cents a copy, then with the shabby squarish-format Little Blue Books at 5 cents a book. Of much higher quality were Paper Books, in the format of today's paperbacks, the creation of Charles Boni. These were distributed by the Boni brothers' Book Club beginning in 1929, with twelve books a year for $5. The best typography was sought and skilled printers were employed; Rockwell Kent was commissioned to design the covers. Ten years later, Pocket Books entered the field, with multicolored cover designs. World War II and its aftermath made paperbacks a permanent and essential part of the book market. American mass market paperback publishers have eschewed British Penguin subtlety in cover design in an attempt to catch the eye of the supermarket and drugstore shopper. (Penguin has since become more colorful.) Ten years ago a sensational, sexy illustration was the norm, even if it belied the book's content. Of late, titles in fat, metallic letters printed in relief have all but replaced pictures in an attempt to draw the reader's attention. Ironically, unsewn and pasted-on paper covers are called *perfect bindings* by their manufacturers. The books are almost guaranteed to shed their pages after a few readings. Trade paperbacks, larger and more costly, usually are bound to last longer.

Hand binding in fine leather never ceased completely during the time cloth and separately manufactured case binding became popular. The art of fine binding was revitalized in the late nineteenth century, especially by a Parisian craftsman, Henri Marius-Michel, son of a *doreur* who worked in traditional styles. Henri went on to create leather covers of Art Nouveau inspiration, with swirling floral and vegetal patterns created by onlays in brown, red, purple, gray-green, and white on citron morocco, often outlined. Marius-Michel's suggestion that a binding should reflect the contents of the book was not necessarily fulfilled in all of his own work, but it did inspire many twentieth-century binders of fine books and even ordinary paperbacks to disprove the adage, "you can't tell a book by its cover." The binders of England's Private Press Movement often preferred plain limp vellum, as they looked back to late medieval and Renaissance books for inspiration. Yet a Basilisk Press facsimile of William Morris's Kelmscott Chaucer (1975) used a Morris fabric design for its cover, manufactured by Liberty of London. Other printers of the Private Press Movement had their books leather-bound and gold-tooled in extremely fine taste. T. J. Cobden-Sanderson, who later founded the Doves Press, started his craft career as a bookbinder (pl. 288). He designed his own tools, which were relatively simple. "I charge as much for my restraint as I do for my elaboration," he once told a customer. The opposite end of the London binding spectrum at the turn of the twentieth century was represented by Sangorski and Sutcliffe's overbejeweled and gilded creations (pl. 289). This firm is still in existence, binding books with simpler covers of fine workmanship.

The twentieth century's prominent binders are persons of international reputation: Douglas Cockerell (1870–1929); his son Sydney Cockerell (1906–1987), famous for his decorated papers; Pierre Le Grain (1888–1929); Paul Bonet (1889–1971, a designer rather than a *doreur;* pl. 290); Rose Adler (1890–1959); and

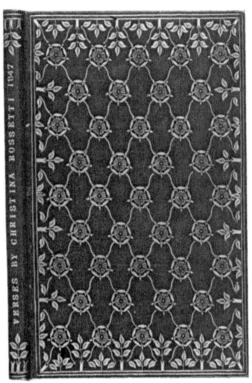

Pl. 288. Binding by T. J. Cobden-Sanderson. On Christina Rossetti, *Verses* (London: Polidori, 1847). Binding, 1885. Fitzwilliam Museum. Courtesy of the Fitzwilliam Museum, University of Cambridge

Pl. 289. Sangorski and Sutcliffe, Peacock binding. On *The Rubaiyat* of Omar Khayyam (London, 1868). Executed in 1921. Sold at Sotheby's, February 14, 1986. Courtesy of F. Sangorski and G. Sutcliffe Ltd., London and Sotheby's, London

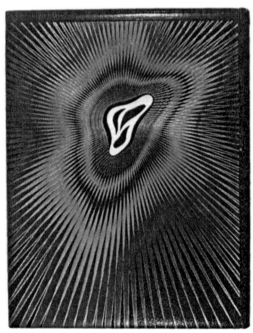

Pl. 290. Paul Bonet, designer. Binding on André Suarès, *Cirque de L'Etoile Filante* (Paris, 1933). Bound in 1939. Pierpont Morgan Library, PML 76385. Courtesy of the Pierpont Morgan Library, New York

Pl. 291. "Book Wall" by Philip Smith. Seven sets of three volumes. For J. R. R. Tolkien, *Lord of the Rings.* Oasis morocco with feathered onlays. Wiltshire, England, 1968/69. Collection of Colin and Charlotte Franklin, Oxford, England. Courtesy of Philip Smith and Colin Franklin

Michael Wilcox (b. 1939). At times their work reflects their personal interpretation of the art movements of the day. At other times they are inspired by the book's subject. From the eighteenth century, binders have more consistently stamped or printed their names onto their creations, usually on an inside cover, near the tail. At times they pasted in tickets—labels with their names.

The potential for variety in materials used for binding the book today is limited only by the imagination of the designer-binder. Just as there has been a Renaissance in hand-papermaking and calligraphy, the last few decades have seen a rise in the quality of design and workmanship in the art and craft of bookbinding. All materials are possible, from fabrics of all kinds to plastics to fur—even electronic parts and growing grass have been set into book covers. One of the most imaginative of today's designer-bookbinders working in leather is Philip Smith in England, who utilizes sophisticated colored leather inlays in a unique way. In addition to striking bindings on individual books, he has created a "book wall," a series of twenty-one covers of *The Lord of the Rings,* which, mounted together, form a picture of Tolkien's fantasy world (pl. 291).

CHAPTER 14

On the Eve of
Printing

W hen is a book handmade and when is it made by machine? Many of the mechanical devices used in making books would today be considered adjuncts to the hand process. Yet at the time they were introduced they were thought of as mechanical and technological innovations. The contemporary private-press book is almost always composed (typeset) by hand, printed by hand (often on handmade paper), and usually bound by hand, but a press and other machines are used along the way. In the Renaissance, the same book would have been considered machine-made, with its cast metal types and its printing by the platen press, duplicating the same text many times over. Metal types invented by Gutenberg about 1450 and the wooden handpress were the first steps in the process of mechanization of the book's manufacture (pl. 292, 293). Improvements on the press continued and new graphic techniques were developed in the centuries that followed. The wooden platen press was improved upon now and then, with parts added or modified. In the early nineteenth century the new cast-iron press doubled the output of printers. Soon after the iron platen press replaced the wooden one, cylinder presses were introduced. These speeded up the printing process even more, although initially few book printers made the investment in this costly equipment. The late nineteenth century saw innovations in automatic typecasting and typesetting, with Linotype and Monotype. Machine-made paper became standard, and by the early twentieth century most aspects of bookbinding could be accomplished by machine. Once the Private Press Movement was underway, its leaders, who usually had someone else doing their presswork, returned to the methods of the best incunabula printers, viewing the earlier works as well as their own books as handcrafted objects and works of art.

Today when a print is made by an artist or a print workshop by means of woodblock, copperplate engraving or etching, or another intaglio method (aquatint,

Pl. 293. Printing. Diderot's *Encyclopédie*. Courtesy of the Jewish National and University Library, Jerusalem

Pl. 292. Types, compositor's stick, galley. Diderot's, *Encyclopédie*. Courtesy of the Jewish National and University Library, Jerusalem

mezzotint, sugar lift, or stipple engraving), lithography, and silkscreen (serigraphy), it is valued by the artist, gallery, and collector as a handmade, original work of art, and not as a reproduction. But when these graphic techniques were first introduced, they too were defined as mechanical methods of printing.

Of all the graphic processes, here we will consider only the woodblock because it was used for book decorations and illustrations before books were first printed from movable type in the 1450s. Blocks had been used as a time-saver for stamping initials in late medieval manuscripts. Once they were colored in, no one paid attention to how the outlines were made. Some decorations also were accomplished by the stencil method, but use of this graphic process did not continue into the printing period, as the woodcut did. Stencil printing did not resurface until the 1930s, when serigraphy became a popular graphic medium for artists. Woodblocks also were used for a specific kind of book—the xylographic, or block, book, in which both text and illustrations were printed entirely by woodblocks.

One may say that the graphic arts (reproduction of images and texts) have been with us since the first humans of Ice Age Europe stamped or stenciled their handprints onto the walls of caves (see pl. 23, p. 19). Sumerian and Mesopotamian peoples used cylinder seals with script and pictures for printing their names (see pl. 34, p. 29, and pl. 73, p. 74). Name seals were universal in the cultures of the Fertile Crescent. Printing devices took different shapes in different areas: the scarab was popular in Egypt (see pl. 85, p. 90), the cylinder seal in Mesopotamia, and the signet ring in many areas of the Near East (see pl. 101, p. 110). The printed Phaistos Disc may have been one of a kind in Crete (pl. 294), but there were other examples of stamped vessels and bricks used in construction in the Mediterranean and Roman worlds. By the fifth and sixth centuries C.E., textiles were stamped in Coptic Egypt.

BLOCK PRINTING IN THE FAR EAST AND NEAR EAST

Block printing began in the Far East long before its sustained use in the Near East and Europe. Religious needs inspired duplication of texts in China. Over a millennium before their classical texts were block printed, Chinese craftsmen were using molds for multiplying words and designs. During the Chou Dynasty

Pl. 294. Phaistos Disc. Signs printed on clay. Text begins at top, outer rim, and reads toward the center. Crete, 1500 B.C.E. Courtesy of the Heraklion Museum, Crete. Photo: T.A.P. Service

Pl. 295. *Hyakumunto Dharani;* The Million Pagoda Charm of the Empress Shotoku, with pagoda. Woodblock printed; second earliest Far Eastern imprint. Japan, 770 C.E. British Library, Department of Oriental Manuscripts and Printed Books, Or. 60 D 1. Courtesy of the British Library

(1122–206 B.C.E.), ceremonial vessels were cast, some with inscriptions. Rubbings reproduced from cave walls and carved seals also preceded the first block printing of texts in China. Block printing must have been in existence by the eighth century. The earliest extant Far Eastern example of block printing comes from mid-eighth-century Korea, found in the Pulguk-sa monastery's Sakyamuni Pagoda in the capital of the Silla Kingdom (668–935). This Chinese *dharani* (incantations and accompanying instructions) was printed with twelve wooden blocks on paper pasted onto a 2½-inch (64-mm) wide, 20-feet (6.10-m) long scroll. It is now in the Korean National Museum. More famous (and still existing in hundreds of copies) is the *Hyakamunto Dharani,* the "million pagoda" Buddhist charms of the Empress Shotoku of Japan (764–770; pl. 295). *The Diamond Sutra,* now in the British Library, is the earliest extant printed book in Chinese (pl. 296). Its colophon states that "it was printed on May 11, 868, by Wang Chieh, for free general distribution, in order, in deep reverence, to perpetuate the memory of his parents." The book was printed with woodblocks on seven sheets of paper (9¼ inches by 17 feet; 235 mm by 5.185 m) and contains a frontispiece that is the equivalent of the Western book's author portrait. The enthroned Sakyamuni is surrounded by heavenly and earthly beings, among them the emaciated scholar Subhuti. The image obviously is reminiscent of St. Jerome and the lion. Was there a lost prototype somewhere in their mutual past, or did a scroll's author portrait pass from the Hellenistic world to the East during the Han Dynasty (206 B.C.E.–220 C.E.)? Or did the Western iconographies of Christ in Majesty and the saint with his lion come, as did halos, from the East?

Printing from movable type was invented in China long before it was discovered in Europe. "Movable types" are individually cast letters that are composed for printing and then disassembled to be reused later. Pi Sheng invented Chinese typography in the 1040s. Because of the vast number of Chinese characters,

Pl. 296. The Diamond Sutra. One of the earliest Chinese imprints. Printed by Wang Chieh, 868 C.E. British Library, Department of Oriental Manuscripts and Printed Books, Or. 8210. Courtesy of the British Library

however, it was more practical to reproduce a Chinese text with woodblocks. So the Chinese went back to block printing, which achieved its highest aesthetic standards during the Sung Dynasty (960–1279), when classic Confucian and Buddhist literature was reproduced. Chinese printing was observed by outsiders, Marco Polo among them, in 1298. No historian believes seriously that Chinese printing directly inspired the European invention. But block printing could well have had an impact on the Near East. The Persian Rashid ad-Din's *Jami' at-Tawarikh* (Universal History) of the early fourteenth century described the Chinese printing process and the nature of the government monopoly on it. Chinese paper money was in circulation all over Asia and was printed in Tabriz, the Mongol capital of Persia, in 1294. In an empire where book covers had already been stamped with tools for several centuries, it would be natural to adopt block printing. The art may have been far more common in the Islamic world than the fragmentary evidence suggests. There is a record from tenth-century Spain of the caliph sending out his proclamations to a special shop to be duplicated. More concrete testimony of block printing from the tenth to the fourteenth centuries was unearthed in Arsinoë (Crocodilopolis) in the Fayyum in the late nineteenth century. These examples of early Islamic block printing are now preserved in the Archduke Rainer Collection in the National Library, Vienna. Qur'ānic quotations and other Arabic religious texts, some of them with nonobjective decoration, are among these Near Eastern block-printed works. The Cairo Geniza also has yielded Hebrew examples of block printing on charms or amulets from the mid-fourteenth century.

Many Western scholars have assumed incorrectly that the supposed Muslim hostility to nonhandwritten Qur'āns retarded the progress of printing from movable type in the Near East after it was adopted in Europe. Some believe that earlier Muslims even prevented the spread of block printing from China to Europe. This is one of the fictions of the history of the book. It was not the Persians or Arabs who opposed printing. Rather it was the Ottoman Turkish conquerors who imposed restrictions against printing upon the Arab population. The Ottoman Turks knew full well the value of the press for disseminating ideas. It was this prohibition that squelched Arabic printing in the Near East until it was introduced by Mohammed Ali in Egypt in 1822 (Napoleon had to import presses for his own use). The Ottoman Turks had granted permission to the minorities of their domain (the Christians of Syria and the Jews of Istanbul, Salonica, and Safed) to operate presses.

If the Arab majority had been allowed to do the same, not only would the course of printing history in the Near East have been different but today's historian would be able to see a continuous development of printing from Coptic fabric stamping and leather tooling to printing on other surfaces. Metal engraving, too, another precursor of printing, was always a popular craft for decorative luxury objects in the Islamic world, and engraving existed in the Near East long before it was adopted in Europe. One of the earliest functions of block printing in Europe was the making of playing cards, the origins of which were Arab. (In the mid-thirteenth century, St. Louis complained that his Crusaders picked up the card-playing habit from the Muslims.) Although playing cards existed in manuscript form, their popular and destructible nature would have made them ideal Near Eastern consumer items to be reproduced by woodblocks and engraved plates, as they were in France and Italy (pl. 297). Unfortunately their ephemeral nature robs us of pre-fifteenth-century examples. So many inventions relating to the book came to Europe from the Near East—innovations in bookbinding, papermaking, and in literary forms such as the novel—one cannot doubt that Islamic crafts well may have been the immediate source for late medieval block printing, the forerunner of printing from movable type.

BLOCK PRINTING IN EUROPE

Fabric stamping possibly was known in early medieval Europe, but was not accomplished on a wide scale until the fourteenth century. The Italian craftsman Cennino Cennini described the technique of block printing on linen in his handbook, *Il Libro dell' Arte.* It was then employed in decorating children's clothes and for covering lecterns in churches. The earliest extant woodblock, the Protat Block, found in the Burgundy region of France and usually assigned the date of 1400 on the basis of its costumes, is part of a Crucifixion measuring 23½ by 9 inches (60 by 23 cm). It undoubtedly was used to stamp cloth, in imitation of a woven tapestry. It has already been noted that decorators of manuscripts stamped large initial letters as a time-saver. This manuscript practice continued in incunabula, where these letters were intended to be colored later by hand. In the printed book, the block could be set in the bed of the press along with the type, because both letterpress and woodblock printing are relief methods. If a woodblock initial was intended to fill the space left for it by the printer at the beginning of a book or chapter, the typesetter inserted a lowercase letter, which was printed in the large blank space, just as the scribe had done by hand in the manuscript. Many of these small printed letters are to be seen in incunabula, with or without the final block-printed capitals. The woodblock initially was a labor-saving device for the craftsman, and was not considered an artistic medium in its own right.

Materials and Techniques

Woodblocking is a relief technique. Early woodblocks were made of pear or another soft wood. The design was drawn and cut on the plank, with the grain. It could be transferred from the original on paper. The block's picture was, of course, in reverse of the resulting print. Knives, chisels, and gouges were employed to cut the wood away from the drawing, so that the thin lines to be printed stood out in relief. Ink, at first the medieval iron-gall variety, but later carbon- and oil-based, was dabbed or rolled on the block, which was set on a table. Dampened paper was placed over it, and tamped down with a frotton, a leather ball stuffed with wool or hair. The proof was then pulled to reveal the image. Printers realized early that the block could be cut to the height of the type and printed by the press along with the text. For this reason woodcuts preserve the unity of text and picture. This integrated quality of the early decorated books was lost when printers began illustrating books with copperplate engravings in the late sixteenth century and throughout the seventeenth century.

The subjects of the earliest European woodcuts were, in addition to playing cards, pictures of Christ and other New Testament figures and saints, called *heiligen*. These were printed on paper, made in monasteries or in the same workshops that made playing cards, by *kartenmacher* or *kartenmaler*. They were sold to middle-class pilgrims, especially in Germany, the Netherlands, and France, who hung them in their homes or pasted them in chests and portable dispatch boxes, or sewed them into their clothing (pl. 298). Woodcuts were colored or tinted by hand, in imitation of illuminated manuscripts, although no one would mistake one of these washed-out watercolored sheets for manuscript illuminations. In a few instances a short text accompanied the illustration, as in one of the earliest dated woodcuts, the Buxheim St. Christopher of 1423, now in the John Rylands University Library, Manchester (pl. 299). This print was preserved because it was part of the binding material of a manuscript written in 1417 in a monastery near Augsburg, a city where a *kartenmacher* was known to be active. (A print of the Madonna and four saints in the Royal Library, Brussels, is dated 1418 but may be a later copy by fifty years.) Similar woodcuts of St. Christopher in black and white and in color, and earlier and contemporaneous illuminated versions, such as one in the Hours of Catherine of Cleves in the Pierpont Morgan Library, New York (ca. 1428–1445), testify to the popularity in late medieval times of this recently decanonized patron saint of travelers. Most early woodcuts, either as single sheets or as the first printed book illustrations, show little sophistication in design and execution. Because they were intended to be colored by hand, they lacked shading. By the end of the fifteenth century, woodblock artists realized the potential of the woodcut as a black-and-white medium, not simply as a means of reproducing outlines intended to be colored and illuminated afterwards. It was then that graphic works of genius, such as Albrecht Dürer's *Apocalypse,* were created (pl. 300).

Pl. 297. Italian tarot (*tarocchi*) cards. Woodblock printed. Italy, ca. 1500. Metropolitan Museum of Art, Bequest of James C. McGuire, 1931, 31.54.159. Courtesy of the Metropolitan Museum of Art, New York

Pl. 298. The Nativity in the lid of a dispatch or alms box. Colored woodcut. France, fifteenth century. Metropolitan Museum of Art, The Harris Brisbane Dick Fund, 1928, 28.5. Courtesy of the Metropolitan Museum of Art, New York

Pl. 299. The Buxheim St. Christopher. Found in 1769 in the Carthusian Monastery of Buxheim, near Memmingen, Germany. Southern Germany, 1423. The John Rylands University Library. Courtesy of the John Rylands University Library of Manchester

Pl. 300. St. Michael fighting the dragon. Albrecht Dürer's *Apocalypse* (Nuremberg, 1498). Another woodcutter has substituted his initials, "MF," for Dürer's "AD." Courtesy of the Jewish National and University Library, Jerusalem

The artist seldom executed the print himself. After he designed it (pl. 301), the block was cut by a *formschneider* (pl. 302). It may have been the strength of the woodcutting guilds that promoted the use of *formschneider* as the executors of incunabula book illustrations. Later on it may have been lack of the technical skill of block cutting on the part of the artist who designed the illustrations. Albrecht Dürer's *formschneider* was Hieronymus Andreae, although the master cut the blocks himself at times, particularly when he was experimenting with a new technique. Hans Holbein's cutter for his *Dance of Death* series was Hans Lützelburger. Christoffel Jegher (1596–1652) was famous in his own right and as the transformer of the paintings of Peter Paul Rubens into engraved prints. Few illustrations in books from the seventeenth century on were accomplished by their designers; professional engravers did the task. The tradition of the print's execution by a special craftsperson under the direction of the artist is still with us today in print workshops the world over.

BLOCK BOOKS

For about half a century after movable types had already been used by Gutenberg, from about 1450 to 1510, there were some books printed entirely from woodblocks—both pictures and text. The text was necessarily brief. Some 317 of these xylographic books, representing thirty-one different texts, are extant. A few of them may have preceded Gutenberg's earliest printing, but most scholars now believe block books came later. They form a short-lived tradition of their own in the Netherlands, Germany, and France. At first glance, block books have an old coloring-book aspect, with their brownish oak-gall ink and their faded watercolor pictures. Usually each sheet was printed from a single block, in the same manner in which an individual woodcut was made. One block printed the double-page opening. In early block books the blank reverse sides of these printed leaves were pasted together. The now unstuck blank sides reveal that the ink and paint bled through the paper. Later, block books were printed with a press on both sides of the leaf (opisthographic printing) in black ink. Not all block books were colored.

The most popular texts saw several xylographic editions. Nearly all the books were religious, although calendars and almanacs were also printed, and one book is on the art of wrestling. The earliest block book is believed to be *Les Neuf Preux* (The Nine Gallant Knights) from France, assigned the date 1455. Other texts were the Apocalypse, in six different xylographic editions; *Decalogus* (Ten Commandments); *Cantum Cantorum* (Song of Songs); *Speculum Humanae Salvationes* (Mirror of Human Salvation); a Latin history of King David; and the *Ars Moriendi*, or the "Art of Dying" (pl. 303). Like the Dance of Death and other works of this genre, the *Ars Moriendi* had been a popular manuscript book and the subject of engravings as well, since the Black Death of 1347–48, which eventually reduced Europe's population by one-third. The text and illustrations show the reader how to prepare for death spiritually. This was accomplished by juxtaposing the Virtues and the Vices, the latter encouraging the dying man to sin, and the former, in the form of saints and angels, consoling him for renouncing temptation. One edition shows that the artist employed shading by means of hatching (parallel lines), an indication that these woodcuts were not meant to be colored. More popular than the *Ars Moriendi* was the *Biblia Pauperum,* the "Poor Man's Bible" (pl. 304). Not that poor people could afford to purchase this book; it was intended for the lesser clergy who preached to the poor. One 1465 edition from the Netherlands is dated by means of the watermarks on its paper. German and Dutch editions were programmed like the Rossano Gospels and the Bible Moralisée, with Old Testament antetypes and their New Testament heroes. Compartmentalized scenes from the Old Testament flank a central scene from the New Testament that they foreshadow, and two prophets above and below hold banderoles of explanatory prooftext. Figures with banderole texts coming forth from their lips had already been seen in late medieval

Pl. 301. The woodcut designer. Jost Amman's illustrations for *Eygentliche Beschreibung aller Stände auff Erden* (Book of Trades) (Frankfurt: Feyerabend, 1568). Courtesy of University of Michigan Library, Department of Rare Books and Special Collections. Photo: Patrick J. Young

Pl. 302. The woodblock cutter. Jost Amman's Book of Trades (Frankfurt, 1568). Courtesy of University of Michigan Library, Department of Rare Books and Special Collections. Photo: Patrick J. Young

Pl. 303. Temptation to
Impatience (*left*), and
Saints defy Impatience
(*right*). *Ars Moriendi.* Block
book. Netherlands, ca.
1450. British Library, Department of Printed
Books. Courtesy of the
British Library

Pl. 304. *Biblia Pauperum.*
On left, Isaac carries wood
for sacrifice; on right,
Elijah and widow of
Zarephath gathering wood;
prefigurations of the
Crucifixion (at center).
Block book. Netherlands,
possibly before 1450.
Esztergom Cathedral.
Courtesy of
Föszékesegyházi Könyvtár,
Esztergom, Hungary

manuscripts, such as the Rohan Book of Hours in the Bibliothèque Nationale (Ms. lat. 9471). But historians of the comic strip have considered the *Ars Moriendi* and *Biblia Pauperum* as prototypes for this modern popular art. Considering the superiority of printing with movable type over block books, it seems amazing that printers bothered with this quaint technique for so many years. Perhaps they couldn't afford, or didn't see the necessity for, the investment in typography.

In the incunabula period, most printers of luxury books attempted to make them look as much like manuscripts as possible, but by mechanical means. The Books of Hours such as those published by calligrapher-miniaturist-bookseller Antoine Vérard, or those printed by Philippe Pigouchet, could almost double for manuscripts when they were printed on vellum and colored in by hand. When printed on vellum but not colored, these books exist in a twilight world somewhere between the manuscript and the printed masterpiece (pl. 305). The manuscript aesthetic prevailed until the close of the fifteenth century, although there always were exceptions that were not inspired directly by their medieval predecessors, especially in Italy, such as the *Hypnerotomachia Poliphili* of 1499, printed by Aldus Manutius (pl. 306). In the sixteenth century, Emperor Maximilian, a great admirer of the printed book, would have his personal copy embellished by hand by one or more of the artists he patronized, including Albrecht Dürer. Calligraphers were still summoned to create typefaces. Leonhard Wagner's elegant Fraktur script, cut by Hieronymus Andreae, was printed first in 1513, but its use in the biographical-allegorical romantic poem for Maximilian, *Der Theuerdank* in 1517, was especially noteworthy because of its splendid design (pl. 307). It reaffirmed the gothic typographic tradition in Germany, which endured there well into this century. The human hand always played a major role in typographic design, as did the human mind in book design.

Pl. 305. Book of Hours. Printed on vellum by Philippe Pigouchet for Simon Vostre (Paris, 1488). Courtesy of the Jewish National and University Library, Jerusalem

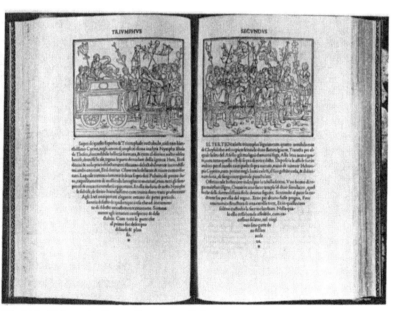

Pl. 306. Triumph. From Francesco Colonna, *Hypnerotomachia Poliphili.* (Venice: Aldus Manutius, 1499). Courtesy of the Jewish National and University Library, Jerusalem

At all times during our era of printing, between 1450 and the present day, some aspect of the machine-made book continued to be accomplished by hand. Paper was made by hand until the early nineteenth century, and it was not until the turn of the twentieth century that all aspects of bookbinding were fully mechanized. Even when new technology was introduced, not all printers or bookbinders took advantage of it, not necessarily because they were opposed to the technology, but often because it was not feasible for them to invest in complex machinery.

By the 1890s, just when all aspects of printing could be accomplished mechanically, the Private Press Movement was born. Its proponents, who considered the book a work of art, rejected mass production and returned to handmade materials and handprinting in a self-conscious way. They believed that high aesthetic standards could be achieved only through hand labor. Yet it was not the manuscript that inspired Kelmscott Press typography and illustrations (although William Morris tried his hand at calligraphy and illumination, too), but the printed book of the Renaissance. A few private-press contemporaries of Morris, such as C. H. St. John Hornby of the Ashendene Press and T. J. Cobden-Sanderson of the Doves Press, commissioned calligraphers to write and illuminate initial letters, for

Pl. 307. Melchior Pfintzing, *Der Theuerdank,* for Maximilian I. (Nuremberg: Hans Schönsperger, 1517). Courtesy of the Jewish National and University Library, Jerusalem. Photo: Albert Ben-Yaacov

at this time medieval script traditions also were experiencing a revival (see pl. 2, p. 2, and Chapter 8). Private- and fine-press printers returned to the woodcut as well, with effects different from those of the popular nineteenth-century wood engraving. The woodblock tradition continued into the twentieth century, with such masters as Eric Gill and Fritz Eichenberg illustrating books (pl. 308). And in our own time, just as the computer, camera, and laser have taken over typesetting, and offset photolithography has taken over platemaking and printing, private hand presses are flourishing and papermakers and designer bookbinders are thriving.

Although private-press books are deservedly considered handmade today by the craftspersons who create them and by the collectors who acquire them, we have defined the handmade book here as the book before printing. And so we must end here, on the eve of printing from movable type, the invention that brought so many more books into the world, and ultimately brought greater knowledge and joy to readers who love them.

Pl. 308. Daughters of Jerusalem. *Canticum Canticorum quod est Salomonis.* Illustrations by Eric Gill (Weimar: Cranach Presse, 1931). Courtesy of Abraham J. Kremer

CANTICUM CANTICORUM
Lavi pedes meos,
quomodo inquinabo illos?

DILECTUS meus misit manum suam
per foramen,
et venter meus intremuit
ad tactum ejus.
Surrexi ut aperirem dilecto meo;
manus meae stillaverunt myrrham,
et digiti mei pleni myrrha probatissima.
Pessulum ostii mei aperui dilecto meo;
at ille declinaverat, atque transierat.

Anima mea liquefacta est,
ut locutus est;
quaesivi, et non inveni illum;
vocavi, et non respondit mihi.

Invenerunt me custodes
qui circumeunt civitatem;
percusserunt me, et vulneraverunt me.
Tulerunt pallium meum mihi
custodes murorum.

ADJURO vos, filiae Jerusalem,
si inveneritis dilectum meum,
ut nuntietis ei quia amore langueo.

20

QUOD EST SALOMONIS

FILIAE JERUSALEM
QUALIS est dilectus tuus ex dilecto,
o pulcherrima mulierum?
Qualis est dilectus tuus ex dilecto,
quia sic adjurasti nos?

SPONSA
DILECTUS meus candidus
et rubicundus;
electus ex millibus.
Caput ejus aurum optimum.

21

Bibliography

The bibliography consists of books and journal articles suggested for further study as well as the secondary sources on which the individual chapters are based, or from which there have been quotations. Only exceptional non-English works have been listed. Many of the books have been reprinted, often in paperback, even where the early date alone is indicated. Names of publishers are included where the book is still in print, or where direct quotations have been made herein or figures drawn, or in the instance that the book is a Private or Fine Press publication.

REFERENCE AND GENERAL WORKS

Bibliothèque Nationale. *Le Livre.* Exhibition Catalogue. Paris, 1972.

Books about Books: An International Exhibition on the Occasion of the International Book Year 1972. Frankfurt am Main, 1972.

Glaister, Geoffrey Ashall. *Glaister's Glossary of the Book.* Berkeley: University of California Press, 1979.

Levarie, Norma. *The Art and History of Books.* New York: James H. Heineman, 1968. Reprint. New York: Da Capo, n.d.

Roberts, Matt T., and Etherington, Don. *Bookbinding and the Conservation of Books; A Dictionary of Descriptive Terminology.* Washington, D.C.: Library of Congress, 1982.

Strayer, Joseph R., ed. *Dictionary of the Middle Ages.* 13 vols. New York: Charles Scribner's Sons, 1982–1989.

Vervliet, H. D. L., ed. *The Book through Five Thousand Years.* New York and London: Phaidon, 1972.

CHAPTER 1.
WRITING

Anderson, Donald M. *The Art of Written Forms; The Theory and Practice of Calligraphy.* New York, 1969.

Ascher, Marcia and Robert. *Code of the Quipu: A Study in Media, Mathematics, and Culture.* Ann Arbor: University of Michigan Press, 1981.

Carter, Martha, ed. *Sign, Symbol, Script; An Exhibition on the Origins of Writing and the Alphabet.* Madison: University of Wisconsin, Department of Hebrew and Semitic Studies, 1983.

Chadwick, John. *The Decipherment of Linear B.* 3d ed. Cambridge: Cambridge University Press, 1970.

Diringer, David. *The Alphabet, A Key to the History of Mankind.* 2 vols. 3d ed. New York and London, 1968.

————. *Writing.* New York, 1962.

Földes-Papp, Károly. *Vom Felsbild zum Alphabet.* Stuttgart: Chr. Belser Verlag, 1966. Reprint. Bayreuth: Gondrom Verlag, 1975.

Galeries Nationales du Grande Palais. *Naissance de L'écriture; Cunéiformes et Hiéroglyphes.* Exhibition Catalogue. Paris: Editions de la Réunion des Musées Nationaux, 1982.

Gaur, Albertine. *A History of Writing.* London: The British Library, 1984.

Gelb, Ignace J. *A Study of Writing.* 2d ed. Chicago: University of Chicago Press, 1963.

Jackson, Donald. *The Story of Writing.* London: Studio Vista and New York: Taplinger, 1981.

Jensen, Hans. *Sign, Symbol and Script; An Account of Man's Efforts to Write.* New York, 1969.

Locke, Leslie Leland. *The Ancient Quipu.* New York: American Museum of Natural History, 1923.

Marshack, Alexander. *The Roots of Civilization.* New York: Macmillan, 1972.

Pope, Maurice. *The Story of Archaeological Decipherment: From Egyptian Hieroglyphics to Linear B.* New York and London, 1975.

Powell, Marvin A., ed. "Aspects of Cuneiform Writing," *Visible Language* (Special issue) 15, no. 4 (1981).

Sagan, Carl. *The Cosmic Connection: An Extraterrestrial Perspective.* Garden City, N.Y.: Doubleday, Anchor Press, 1973 and 1980.

Schmandt-Besserat, Denise. "An Archaic Recording System and the Origin of Writing," *Syro-Mesopotamian Studies* 1, no. 2 (1977): 31–70.

————. "The Earliest Precursor of Writing," *Scientific American* 238 (June 1978): 50–59.

————. "An Archaic Recording System in the Uruk-Jemdet Nasr Period," *American Journal of Archeology* 83 (1979): 19–48.

_____. "An Ancient Token System: The Precursor to Numerals and Writing," *Archaeology* 39, no. 6 (1986): 32–39.

_____. "The Origins of Writing: An Archaeologist's Perspective," *Written Communication* 3, no. 1 (1986): 31–45.

Senner, Wayne M., ed. *The Origins of Writing.* Lincoln and London: University of Nebraska Press, 1989.

Thompson, J. Eric S. *A Commentary on the Dresden Codex; A Maya Hieroglyphic Book.* Philadelphia: American Philosophical Society, 1972.

United Bible Society. *The Book of a Thousand Tongues.* Edited by E. A. Nida. London, 1971.

CHAPTER 2.
THE ALPHABET

Anderson, Donald M. *The Art of Written Forms; The Theory and Practice of Calligraphy.* New York, 1969.

Best, Jan, and Woudhuizen, Fred. *Ancient Scripts from Crete and Cyprus.* Publications of the Henri Frankfort Foundation, 9. Leiden: E. J. Brill, 1988.

Dilke, Oswald Ashton Wentworth. *Mathematics and Measurement.* London: British Museum Publications, 1987.

Diringer, David. *The Alphabet, A Key to the History of Mankind.* 2 vols. 3d ed. New York and London, 1968.

_____. *The Story of the Aleph Beth.* New York, 1960.

_____. *Writing.* New York, 1962.

_____, and Freeman, Hilda. *A History of the Alphabet.* London: Staples Press, 1953. Reprint. Headley on Thames: Gresham Books, 1977 and 1983.

Driver, Godfrey Rolles. *Semitic Writing: From Pictograph to Alphabet.* 3d ed. Edited by S. A. Hopkins. London, 1976.

Gordon, Arthur E. *The Letter Names of the Latin Alphabet.* University of California Publications: Classical Studies, vol. 9. Berkeley, 1973.

Israel Museum. *Inscriptions Reveal.* Exhibition Catalogue no. 100. Jerusalem, 1973.

Jeffery, Lilian Hamilton. *The Local Scripts of Archaic Greece: A Study of the Origin of the Greek Alphabet and Its Development from the Eighth to the Fifth Centuries B.C.* Oxford, 1961.

Logan, Robert K. *The Alphabet Effect: The Impact of the Phonetic Alphabet on the Development of Western Civilization.* New York: William Morrow, 1986. Reprint. New York: St. Martin's Press, 1987.

Mazar, Benjamin. "The Phoenician Inscriptions from Byblos and the Evolution of the Phoenician-Hebrew Alphabet," *The Early Biblical Period: Historical Studies,* 231–247. Edited by Shmuel Ahituv and Baruch A. Levine. Jerusalem: Israel Exploration Society, 1986.

Minto, Antonia. *Marsiliana d'Albegna.* Florence, 1921.

Naveh, Joseph. *Early History of the Alphabet: An Introduction to West Semitic Epigraphy and Paelaeography.* Jerusalem: Magnes Press, The Hebrew University, 1982.

_____. "The Development of the Aramaic Script," *Proceedings of the Israel Academy of Sciences and Humanities* 5, no. 1 (1970): 1–69.

Ullman, Berthold Louis. *Ancient Writing and Its Influence.* New York, 1932 and 1963. Cambridge: MIT Press, 1969. Also published as Medieval Academy Reprints for Teaching, no. 10. Toronto: University of Toronto Press, 1981.

CHAPTER 3.
THE BOOK IN THE ANCIENT WORLD: MESOPOTAMIA

Carter, Martha, ed. *Sign, Symbol, Script; An Exhibition on the Origins of Writing and the Alphabet.* Madison: University of Wisconsin, Department of Hebrew and Semitic Studies, 1983.

Chiera, Edward. *They Wrote on Clay: The Babylonian Tablets Speak Today.* Edited by George G. Cameron. Chicago, 1938, 1956. Reprint. Chicago: University of Chicago Press, 1969.

Dougherty, Raymond P. "Writing upon Parchment and Papyrus among the Babylonians and Assyrians," *Journal of the American Oriental Society* 48 (1928): 109–135.

Galeries Nationales du Grande Palais. *Naissance de L'écriture; Cunéiformes et Hiéroglyphes.* Exhibition Catalogue. Paris: Editions de la Réunion des Musées Nationaux, 1982.

Howard, Margaret. "Technical Description of the Ivory Writing-Boards from Nimrud," *Iraq* 17 (1955): 14–20.

Hunger, Hermann. *Babylonische und Assyrische Kolophone.* Alter Orient und Altes Testament, bd. 2. Neukirchen-Vluyn: Kevelaer, Butzon and Berker, 1968.

Kramer, Samuel Noah. *History Begins at Sumer: Thirty-nine Firsts in Man's Recorded History.* 3d ed. Philadelphia: University of Pennsylvania Press, 1981.

_____. *Sumerian Mythology.* Philadelphia, 1944. Reprint. Philadelphia: University of Pennsylvania Press, 1972.

_____. *The Sumerians: Their History, Culture and Character.* Chicago, 1963. Reprint. Chicago: University of Chicago Press, 1973.

Mallowan, Max Edgar Lucien. *Nimrud and Its Remains.* 2 vols. London, 1966.

Oppenheim, A. Leo. "A Note on the Scribes in Mesopotamia," *Studies in Honor of Benno Landsberger,* 253–256. Chicago, 1965.

Parrot, André. "Mesopotamian Literature," *The Arts of Assyria,* 279–294. The Arts of Mankind Series. New York: Golden Press, 1961.

Pettinato, Giovanni. *The Archives of Ebla: An Empire Inscribed in Clay.* New York: Doubleday, 1981.

Pope, Maurice. *The Story of Archaeological Decipherment: From Egyptian Hieroglyphics to Linear B.* New York and London, 1975.

Pritchard, James Bennett, ed. *The Ancient Near East; A New Anthology of Text and Pictures.* Princeton: Princeton University Press, 1976.

_____. *The Ancient Near East in Pictures Related to the Old Testament.* 2d ed. Princeton: Princeton University Press, 1969.

_____. *Ancient Near Eastern Texts Relating to the Old Testament.* 3d ed. Princeton: Princeton University Press, 1969.

Rainey, Anson F. "The Scribe at Ugarit: His Position and Influence," *Proceedings of the Israel Academy of Sciences and Humanities* 3, no. 4 (1968): 126–147.

Sachs, Abraham. "The Latest Datable Cuneiform Tablets," *Kramer Anniversary Volume, Alter Orient und Altes Testament* vol. 25 (1976): 379–398.

Wiseman, Donald John. "Assyrian Writing Boards," *Iraq* 17 (1955): 3–13.

————. "Books in the Ancient Near East and in the Old Testament," *Cambridge History of the Bible*, v. 1, 30–47. Cambridge: Cambridge University Press, 1970.

Wright, H. Curtis. *Ancient Burials of Metallic Foundation Documents in Stone Boxes*. Graduate School of Library and Information Science Occasional Papers, no. 157. Champaign-Urbana: University of Illinois, 1982.

CHAPTER 4.
THE EGYPTIAN BOOK

Baer, Klaus. *Rank and Title in the Old Kingdom; The Structure of Egyptian Administration in the Fifth and Sixth Dynasties.* Chicago: University of Chicago Press, Midway Reprint Series, 1974.

Budge, E. A. Wallis. *The Egyptian Book of the Dead: The Papyrus of Ani in the British Museum.* London, 1895. Reprint. New York: Dover Publications, 1967.

Čzerný, Jaroslav. *Paper and Books in Ancient Egypt.* London, 1947.

Edwards, Iorwerth Eiddon Stephen. *Treasures of Tutankhamun.* Exhibition Catalogue, Metropolitan Museum of Art, et al. New York: Ballantine Books, 1976.

Hayes, William C. "A Writing-Palette of the Chief Steward Amenhoteph and Some Notes on Its Owner," *Journal of Egyptian Archaeology* 24, no. 1 (1938): 9–24.

Hendriks, Ignace H. M. "Pliny, Historia Naturalis XIII, 74–82, and the Manufacture of Papyrus," *Zeitschrift für Papyrology und Epigraphik* 37 (1980): 121–136. Commented upon by Eric G. Turner, "An open letter to Dr. I. Hendriks," *Zeitschrift für Papyrology und Epigraphik* 39 (1980): 113–114.

Hussein, Mohammad A. *Origins of the Book: Egypt's Contribution to the Development of the Book from Papyrus to Codex.* Leipzig, 1970. (*Origins of the Book: From Papyrus to Codex.* New York, 1972.)

Johnson, Malcolm. *The Nature and Making of Papyrus.* Barkston Ash, Yorkshire: Elmete Press, 1973.

Lewis, Naphtali. *Papyrus in Classical Antiquity.* Oxford, 1974.

Lichtheim, Miriam, ed. *Ancient Egyptian Literature; A Book of Readings.* 3 vols. Berkeley: University of California Press, 1973–1980.

Ragab, Hassan. *Le Papyrus.* Cairo: Dr. Ragab Papyrus Institute, 1980.

CHAPTER 5.
THE HEBREW BOOK

Avigad, Nahman. *Hebrew Bullae from the Time of Jeremiah: Remnants of a Burnt Archive.* Jerusalem: Israel Exploration Society, 1986.

Avrin, Leila R. *The Illuminations of the Moshe Ben-Asher Codex of 895 C.E.* Ph.D. diss., University of Michigan, 1974.

————. *Micrography as Art.* Jerusalem: Israel Museum and Paris: Centre National de la Recherche Scientifique, 1981.

Barkay, Gabriel. *Ketef Hinnom: A Treasure Facing Jerusalem's Walls.* Israel Museum Exhibition Catalogue no. 274. Jerusalem, 1986.

————. "The Divine Name Found in Jerusalem," *Biblical Archaeology Review* 9, no. 2 (1983): 14–19.

Beit-Arié, Malachi. *Hebrew Codicology.* 2d ed. Jerusalem: Israel Academy of Sciences and Humanities and Paris: Centre National de la Recherche Scientifique, 1981.

————. "Palaeographical Identification of Hebrew Manuscripts: Methodology and Practice," *Jewish Art* (formerly *Journal of Jewish Art*) 12–13 (1986–87): 15–44.

Blondheim, David Simon. "An Old Portuguese Work on Manuscript Illumination," *Jewish Quarterly Review* 19 (1928): 97–135 and 20 (1929): 283–284.

Comité de Paléographie Hébraïque. *Manuscrits Médiévaux en Caractères Hébraïques Portant des Indications de Date jusqu'à 1540.* Edited by Colette Sirat and Malachi Beit-Arié. Paris: Centre National de la Recherche Scientifique and Jerusalem: Israel Academy of Sciences and Humanities. 4 vols. to date, 1972– .

Driver, Godfrey Rolles. *Aramaic Documents of the Fifth Century B.C.* Oxford, 1954.

————. *Semitic Writing: From Pictograph to Alphabet.* 3d ed. Edited by S. A. Hopkins. London, 1976.

Gutmann, Joseph. *Hebrew Manuscript Painting.* New York: Braziller, 1978.

Haran, Menahem. "Bible Scrolls in Eastern and Western Jewish Communities from Qumran to the High Middle Ages," *Hebrew Union College Annual* 55 (1985): 21–42.

————. "Scribal Workmanship in Biblical Times, the Scrolls and the Writing Implements," *Tarbiz* 50 (1980–81): 65–67. (In Hebrew)

Herzog, Isaac. *The Royal Purple and the Biblical Blue.* Edited by Ehud Spanier. Jerusalem: Keter, 1987.

Israel Museum. *Inscriptions Reveal.* Exhibition Catalogue no. 100. Jerusalem, 1973.

Mazar, Benjamin. "King David's Scribe and the High Officialdom of the United Monarchy of Israel," *The Early Biblical Period: Historical Studies*, 126–138. Edited by Shmuel Ahituv and Baruch A. Levine. Jerusalem: Israel Exploration Society, 1986.

Narkiss, Bezalel. *Hebrew Illuminated Manuscripts.* New York, 1969.

Porten, Bezalel. *Archives from Elephantine: The Life of an Ancient Jewish Military Colony.* Berkeley, 1968.

————, and Yardeni, Ada. *Textbook of Aramaic Documents from Ancient Egypt. 1. Letters.* Jerusalem: The Hebrew University Department of History of the Jewish People; Texts and Studies for Students, 1986. Distributed by Eisenbrauns, Winona Lake, Indiana.

Posner, Raphael, and Ta-Shema, Israel. *The Hebrew Book: An Historical Survey.* New York: Amiel, 1975.

Sabar, Shalom. "The Beginnings of Ketûbbah Decoration in Italy: Venice in the Late Sixteenth to the Early Seventeenth Centuries," *Jewish Art* (formerly *Journal of Jewish Art*) 12–13 (1986–87): 96–110.

Sirat, Colette. *Les Papyrus en Caractères Hébraïques Trouvés en Egypt*. Paris: Centre National de la Recherche Scientifique, 1985.

Vermes, Geza. *The Dead Sea Scrolls in English*. 2d ed. Harmondsworth: Penguin, 1979.

_____. *The Dead Sea Scrolls; Qumran in Perspective*. London, 1977 and Cleveland, 1978. Reprint. Philadelphia: Fortress, 1981.

Vorst, Benjamin. "Parchment Making—Ancient and Modern," *Fine Print* 12, no. 1 (1986): 209–211, 220–221.

Welles, Charles Bradford. *The Excavations at Dura Europos. Final Report V, Part 1. The Parchment and Papyri*. New Haven, 1959.

Wiseman, Donald John. "Assyrian Writing Boards," *Iraq* 17 (1955): 3–13.

Yadin, Yigael. *The Temple Scroll: The Hidden Law of the Dead Sea Sect*. New York: Random House, 1985.

_____. "Tefillin (Phylacteries) from Qumran (XQ Phyl 1–4)," *Eretz Israel* 9 (1969): 60–85. (In Hebrew)

Schubart, Wilhelm. *Das Buch bei den Griechen und Römern*. 2d ed. Berlin, 1921. 3d ed., with additions by E. Paul. Heidelberg, 1961.

Skeat, Theodore Cressy. "The Use of Dictation in Ancient Book Production," *Proceedings of the British Academy* 42 (1956): 179–208.

_____. "Early Christian Book-Production: Papyri and Manuscripts," *Cambridge History of the Bible*, vol. 2, 54–79. Cambridge, 1969.

Thompson, Edward Maunde. *Handbook of Greek and Latin Palaeography*. 3d ed. London, 1906.

_____. *An Introduction to Greek and Latin Palaeography*. Oxford, 1912. Reprint. New York, 1966.

Turner, Eric G. *Athenian Books in the Fifth and Fourth Centuries B.C.* London, 1952.

_____. *Greek Manuscripts of the Ancient World*. Princeton, 1971.

_____. *Greek Papyri; An Introduction*. Oxford and Princeton, 1968.

_____. *The Typology of the Early Codex*. Philadelphia: University of Pennsylvania Press, 1977.

CHAPTER 6.
THE GREEK AND
HELLENISTIC BOOK

Avi-Yonah, Michael. *Ancient Scrolls*. Cassell's Introducing Archaeology Series, 4. London, 1973.

Bickerman, Elias J. "The Colophon of the Greek Book of Esther," *Journal of Biblical Literature* 63 (1944): 339–361.

Chadwick, John. *The Mycenaean World*. Cambridge, 1976.

Diringer, David. *The Hand-Produced Book*. London, 1953. Reprinted as *The Book before Printing; Ancient, Medieval and Oriental*. New York: Dover Publications, 1982.

Grant, Michael, ed. *Greece and Rome: The Birth of Western Civilization*. London: Thames and Hudson, 1964. American edition: *The Birth of Western Civilization: Greece and Rome*. New York: McGraw Hill, 1964.

Hadas, Moses. *Ancilla to Classical Reading*. New York: Columbia University Press, 1954.

Harvey, F. D. "Literacy in the Athenian Democracy," *Revue des Etudes Grecques* 79 (1966): 585–635.

Knox, Bernard MacGregor Walker. "Books and Readers in the Greek World," *The Cambridge History of Classical Literature*, vol. 1, *Greek Literature*, 1–41. Edited by P. E. Easterling and B. M. W. Knox. Cambridge: Cambridge University Press, 1985.

Lewis, Naphtali. "Papyrus and Ancient Writing: The First Hundred Years of Papyrology," *Archaeology* (July-August 1983): 31–37.

Metzger, Bruce M. "The Making of Ancient Books," in his *The Text of the New Testament*, 3–31. Oxford, 1968.

_____. *Manuscripts of the Greek Bible: An Introduction to Palaeography*. New York and Oxford, 1981.

Pinner, H. L. *The World of Books in Classical Antiquity*. Leiden, 1948.

Roberts, Colin Henderson. "Books in the Graeco-Roman World and in the New Testament," *Cambridge History of the Bible*, vol. 1, 48–66. Cambridge, 1970.

_____, and Skeat, Theodore Cressy. *The Birth of the Codex*. London: Oxford University Press for the British Academy, 1983.

CHAPTER 7.
THE ROMAN BOOK

Avi-Yonah, Michael. *Ancient Scrolls*. Cassell's Introducing Archaeology Series, 4. London, 1973.

Bowman, Alan K. *The Roman Writing Tablets from Vindolanda*. London: The British Museum, 1983.

Dilke, Oswald Ashton Wentworth. *Roman Books and Their Impact*. Leeds: Elmete Press, 1977.

Diringer, David. *The Hand-Produced Book*. London, 1953. Reprinted as *The Book before Printing; Ancient, Medieval and Oriental*. New York: Dover Publications, 1982.

Grant, Michael, ed. *Greece and Rome: The Birth of Western Civilization*. London: Thames and Hudson, 1964. American edition: *The Birth of Western Civilization: Greece and Rome*. New York: McGraw Hill, 1964.

Hadas, Moses. *Ancilla to Classical Reading*. New York, 1954.

Kenney, E. J. "Books and Readers in the Roman World," *The Cambridge History of Classical Literature*, vol. 2, *Latin Literature*, 3–32. Edited by E. J. Kenney. Cambridge: Cambridge University Press, 1982.

Lewis, Naphtali. "Papyrus and Ancient Writing: The First Hundred Years of Papyrology," *Archaeology* (July–August 1983): 31–37.

Metzger, Bruce M. "The Making of Ancient Books," in his *The Text of the New Testament*, 3–31. Oxford, 1968.

Pinner, H. L. *The World of Books in Classical Antiquity*. Leiden, 1948.

Pliny the Elder (Gaius Plinius Secundus). *Natural History*. Translated by H. Rackham. 10 vols. Loeb Classical Library. London: William Heinemann and Cambridge: Harvard University Press, 1948. Reprinted 1968.

Reichmann, Felix, "The Book Trade at the Time of the Roman Empire," *Library Quarterly* 8 (1938): 40–76.

Roberts, Colin Henderson, and Skeat, Theodore Cressy. *The Birth of the Codex*. London: Oxford University Press for the British Academy, 1983.

————. "Books in the Graeco-Roman World and in the New Testament," *Cambridge History of the Bible,* vol. 1, 48–66. Cambridge, 1970.

Schubart, Wilhelm. *Das Buch bei den Griechen und Römern.* 2d ed. Berlin, 1921. 3d ed., with additions by E. Paul. Heidelberg, 1961.

Skeat, Theodore Cressy. "Early Christian Book-Production: Papyri and Manuscripts," *Cambridge History of the Bible,* vol. 2, 54–79. Cambridge, 1969.

————. "The Use of Dictation in Ancient Book Production," *Proceedings of the British Academy* 42 (1956): 179–208.

Thompson, Edward Maunde. *Handbook of Greek and Latin Palaeography.* 3d ed. London, 1906.

————. *An Introduction to Greek and Latin Palaeography.* Oxford, 1912. Reprint. New York, 1966.

Turner, Eric G. *The Typology of the Early Codex.* Philadelphia: University of Pennsylvania Press, 1977.

Welles, Charles Bradford. *The Excavations at Dura Europos. Final Report V, Part 1. The Parchment and Papyri.* New Haven, 1959.

CHAPTER 8.
LATIN SCRIPT

Alexander, Jonathan James Graham. *The Decorated Letter.* New York: Braziller, 1978.

Anderson, Donald M. *The Art of Written Forms; The Theory and Practice of Calligraphy.* New York, 1969.

Baltimore Museum of Art. *Two Thousand Years of Calligraphy. A Three-part Exhibition Organized by the Baltimore Museum of Art, Peabody Institute Library and Walters Art Gallery.* Baltimore, 1965.

Bischoff, Bernhard; Lieftinck, G. I.; and Battelli, G. *Nomenclature des Ecritures Livreques du IXe au XVIe Siècle.* Colloques Internationaux du C.N.R.S.; Sciences Humaines IV. Paris: Centre National de la Recherche Scientifique, 1954.

Boyle, Leonard E. *Medieval Latin Palaeography, a Bibliographical Introduction.* Toronto: University of Toronto Press, 1984.

Brown, Michelle P. *A Guide to Western Historical Scripts from Antiquity to 1660.* Toronto: University of Toronto Press and London: The British Library, 1990.

Calligraphy Review. (Journal; before Fall 1987, *Calligraphy Idea Exchange*) Edited by Karyn L. Gilman. Norman, Oklahoma, 1983– .

Drogin, Marc. *Medieval Calligraphy: Its History and Technique.* Montclair, N.J.: Allanheld and Schram, 1980.

Fairbank, Alfred. *A Book of Scripts.* Harmondsworth: Penguin, 1949.

————. *Calligraphy and Paleography: Essays Presented to Alfred Fairbank on His 70th Birthday.* Edited by Arthur Sidney Osley. New York, 1966.

Gordon, Arthur E., and Gordon, Joyce S. *Album of Dated Latin Inscriptions.* 4 vols. Berkeley, 1958–1965.

————. *Contributions to the Palaeography of Latin Inscriptions.* University of California Publications in Classical Archaeology, no. 3, 65–241. Berkeley, 1957. Reprint. Milan, 1977.

Goudy, Frederic W. *The Alphabet and Elements of Lettering.* 1918. Reprint. Berkeley and Los Angeles: University of

California Press and London: Cambridge University Press, 1952. Reprint. New York: Dover Publications, 1963.

Grey, Nicolete. *A History of Lettering; Creative Experiment and Letter Identity.* Oxford: Phaidon, 1986.

Hatch, W. H. P. "The Origin and Meaning of the Term 'Uncial,'" *Classical Philology* 30 (1935): 247–254.

Hayes, James. *The Roman Letter; A Study of Notable Graven and Written Forms from Twenty Centuries.* Chicago: Lakeside Press, R. R. Donnelley & Sons, 1951.

Ireland, Robert. "Epigraphy," *A Handbook of Roman Art,* 220–233. Edited by Martin Henig. Oxford: Phaidon, 1983.

Johnston, Edward. *Writing & Illuminating, & Lettering.* London: Pitman, 1906. Reprint. New York: Taplinger (Pentalic), 1977.

Johnston, Priscilla. *Edward Johnston.* London, 1959. 2d ed. New York: Pentalic Corporation, 1976.

Kirchner, Joachim. *Scriptura Latina Libraria.* Munich: R. Oldenbourg Verlag, 1970.

Lowe, Elias Avery. *Handwriting: Our Medieval Legacy.* Rome: Edizioni di Storia e Letteratura, 1969.

————, ed. *Codices Latini Antiquiores: A Palaeographic Guide to Latin Manuscripts prior to the Ninth Century.* 11 vols. Oxford, 1934–1966. Supplement. Oxford: Oxford University Press, 1971.

Morison, Stanley. *Italian Writing-Books of the Sixteenth Century.* Edited by Nicolas Barker. London: The British Library, 1990.

————. *Politics and Script: Aspects of Authority and Freedom in the Development of Graeco-Latin Script from the Sixth Century B.C. to the Twentieth Century A.D.* Edited by and completed by Nicolas Barker. Oxford, 1972.

Ogg, Oscar (intro). *Three Classics of Italian Calligraphy; An Unabridged Reissue of the Writing Books of Arrighi, Tagliente, Palatino.* New York: Dover Publications, 1953.

Osley, Arthur Sidney. *Scribes and Sources: Handbooks of the Chancery Hand in the Sixteenth Century.* Boston: Godine, 1980.

Parkes, M. B., and Watson, Andrew G. *Medieval Scribes, Manuscripts and Libraries; Essays Presented to N. R. Ker.* London: Scolar Press, 1978.

Payne, Ann. *Medieval Beasts.* New York: New Amsterdam Books and London: The British Library, 1990.

Peabody Institute Library, Baltimore. *Calligraphy and Handwriting in America, 1710–1962.* Exhibition Catalogue. Caledonia, N.Y., 1963.

Standard, Paul. *Arrighi's Running Hand; A Study of Chancery Cursive.* New York: Taplinger, 1979.

Steinberg, Sigfrid Heinrich. "Medieval Writing Masters," *The Library,* 4th ser., 22 (1942): 1–42.

Stiennon, Jacques, and Hasenohr, Geneviève. *Paléographie du Moyen Age.* Paris: Armand Colin, 1973.

Thompson, Samuel Harrison. *Latin Bookhands of the Later Middle Ages, 1100–1500.* Cambridge: Cambridge University Press, 1969.

Tschichold, Jan. *An Illustrated History of Writing and Lettering.* London and Basel, 1946.

Ullman, Berthold Louis. *Ancient Writing and Its Influence.* New York, 1932 and 1963. Cambridge: MIT Press, 1969. Also published as Medieval Academy Reprints for

Teaching, no. 10. Toronto: University of Toronto Press, 1981.

_____. *The Origin and Development of Humanistic Script.* Rome, 1960.

Victoria and Albert Museum. *The Universal Penman: A Survey of Western Calligraphy from the Roman Period to 1980.* Exhibition Catalogue. London: Her Majesty's Stationery Office, 1980.

Wardrop, James. *The Script of Humanism.* Oxford, 1963.

CHAPTER 9.
CODICES MANU SCRIPTI:
BOOKS WRITTEN BY HAND

Bibliologia; Elementa ad Librorum Studia Pertinentia (series). Brepols, 1983– .

Bibliotheca Palatina. *Scriptorium: Book Production in the Middle Ages,* by Vera Trost. Exhibition Manual (University of Heidelberg). Heidelberg: Distributed by Kurt Ziehank, 1986.

Blondheim, David Simon. "An Old Portuguese Work on Manuscript Illumination," *Jewish Quarterly Review* 19 (1928): 97–135 and 20 (1929): 283–284.

Borradaile, Viola, and Borradaile, Rosamund. *The Strasbourg Manuscript: A Medieval Painter's Handbook.* Hollywood-by-the-Sea, Florida, 1966.

Le Bouveret, Suiss, Saint Benoît de Port Valais (Bénédictins du Bouveret). *Colophons des Manuscrits Occidentaux de Origins au XVIe Siècle.* 6 vols. Fribourg, Switzerland: Editions Universitaires, 1965–1982.

Codicologica; Towards a Science of Handwritten Books (periodical). Leiden: Brill, 1975– .

Cohen-Mushlin, Aliza. *A Medieval Scriptorium; Sancta Maria Magdalena de Frankendal.* Wiesbaden: Otto Harrassowitz, 1990.

Delaissé, L. M. J. "Towards a History of the Medieval Book," *Miscellanea André Combes.* vol. 2. Cathedra Sancti Thomae Pontificiae Universitatis Lateranensis, no. 4. Rome, 1967.

Drogin, Marc. *Anathema! Medieval Scribes and the History of Book Curses.* Totowa and Montclair, N.J.: Alanheld and Schram, 1983.

Eco, Umberto. *The Name of the Rose.* New York: Harcourt Brace Jovanovich, 1983.

Egbert, Virginia Wylie. *The Medieval Artist at Work.* Princeton, 1967.

Gilissen, Léon. *Prolégomènes à la Codicologie: Recherches sur la Construction des Cahiers et la Mise en Page des Manuscrits Médiévaux.* Ghent: Editions Scientifiques Story-Scientia, 1977.

Gumbert, J. P. *The Dutch and Their Books in the Manuscript Age.* London: The British Library, 1990.

Harmon, James A. *Codicology of the Court School of Charlemagne: Gospel Book Production, Illumination, and Emphasized Script.* European University Studies Series 28/History of Art, vol. 21. Berlin/Frankfurt am Main: Peter Lang, 1982.

Herzog, Isaac. *The Royal Purple and the Biblical Blue.* Edited by Ehud Spanier. Jerusalem: Keter, 1987.

Humphreys, K. W. *The Book Provisions of the Medieval Friars, 1215–1400.* Safaho Foundation for Promotion of Bibliographic Research, Safaho Monographs, vol. 2; Studies in the History of Libraries and Librarianship, vol. 1. Amsterdam: Erasmus Booksellers, 1964.

_____. "The Provisions of Students' Text-Books in the Later Middle Ages," *Das Buch und Sein Haus,* vol. 1 (*Erlesenes aus der Welt des Buches*), 61–76. Edited by Rolf Fuhlrott and Bertram Haller. Wiesbaden: Dr. Ludwig Reichert Verlag, 1979.

Jones, Leslie Webber. "Where Are the Prickings?" *Transactions and Proceedings of the American Philological Association* 75 (1944): 71–86.

_____. "Pricking Manuscripts: The Instruments and Their Significance," *Speculum* 21 (1946): 389–403.

_____. "Ancient Prickings in Eighth-Century Manuscripts," *Scriptorium* 15 (1961): 14–22.

_____. "Prickings as Clue to Date and Origin: The Eighth Century," *Medievala et Humanistica* 14 (1962): 15–22.

Leclerq, Jean. *The Love of Learning and the Desire for God: A Study of Monastic Culture.* 3d ed. New York: Fordham University Press, 1985.

Lehmann-Haupt, Hellmut, ed. *The Göttingen Model Book: A Facsimile Edition and Translations of a Fifteenth-Century Illuminators' Manual.* Columbia, Mo.: University of Missouri Press, 1972.

McKitterick, Rosamond. *The Carolingians and the Written Word.* Cambridge: Cambridge University Press, 1989.

Madan, Falconer. *Books in Manuscript: A Short Introduction to Their Study and Use.* London, 1893. Rev. ed. London: K. Paul, Trench, Trubner & Co., 1920.

Manuscripta: A Journal Devoted to Manuscript Studies. St. Louis: St. Louis University Pius XII Memorial Library, 1957– .

Martin, Henri-Jean; Chartier, Roger; and Vivet, Jean-Pierre. *Histoire de l'Edition Française.* Vol. 1, *Le Livre Conquérant du Moyen Age au Milieu du XVIIe Siècle.* Paris, 1982.

Merrifield, Mary P. *Original Treatises on the Arts of Painting.* Vol. 1. London, 1849. Reprint. New York: Dover Publications, 1967.

Metzger, Bruce M. *The Text of the New Testament.* 2d ed. Oxford, 1968.

_____. "When Did Scribes Begin to Use Writing Desks?" *Proceedings of the XIth Congress of Byzantine Studies, 1958,* 355–362. Munich, 1961.

Parkes, M. B., and Watson, Andrew G. *Medieval Scribes, Manuscripts and Libraries: Essays Presented to N. R. Ker.* London: Scolar Press, 1978.

La Production du Livre Universitaire au Moyen Age; Exemplar et Pecia. Edited by Louis J. Bataillon, Bertrand G. Guyot and Richard H. Rouse. Paris: Centre National de la Recherche Scientifique, 1988.

Rand, E. K. "How Many Leaves at a Time?" *Palaeographica Latina* 5 (1927): 52–78.

Reed, Ronald. *Ancient Skins, Parchments and Leathers.* London, 1972.

_____. *The Nature and Making of Parchment.* Leeds, 1975.

Reynolds, Leighton Durham, and Wilson, N. G. *Scribes and Scholars: A Guide to the Transmission of Greek and Latin Literature.* 2d ed. Oxford, 1974.

Rouse, Richard H. and Rouse, Mary A. "The Verbal Concordance to the Scriptures," *Archivum Fratrum Praedicatorum* 44 (1974): 5–30.

————. "*Statim Invenire*: Schools, Preachers, and New Attitudes to the Page," *Renaissance and Renewal in the Twelfth Century*, 201–225. Edited by Robert L. Benson and Giles Constable. Cambridge: Cambridge University Press, 1982.

————. "Alphabetization" and "Codicology" in *Dictionary of the Middle Ages*. Edited by Joseph R. Strayer. New York: Charles Scribner's Sons, 1982–1989.

Saenger, Paul. "Silent Reading: Its Impact on Late Medieval Script and Society," *Viator* 13 (1982): 367–414.

Scheller, Robert Walter. *A Survey of Medieval Model Books*. Haarlem, 1963.

Scriptorium: International Review of Manuscript Studies. Brussels, 1946/47– .

Skeat, Theodore Cressy. "Early Christian Book-Production: Papyri and Manuscripts," *The Cambridge History of the Bible*, vol. 2, 54–79. Cambridge, 1969.

Steele, Robert. "The Pecia," *The Library*, 4th ser., 11 (1930–31): 230–234.

Theophilus. *On Divers Arts*. Translated by J. G. Hawthorne and C. S. Smith. Chicago, 1963.

Thompson, Daniel V. *The Materials and Techniques of Medieval Painting*. New York, 1956.

————, and Hamilton, George Heard, trans. *De Arte Illuminandi: The Technique of Manuscript Illumination; Translated from the Latin of Naples MS. XII E. 27*. New Haven, 1933.

Vezin, J. "Observation sur l'Emploi des Réclames dans les Manuscrits Latins," *Bibliothèque de l'Ecole des Chartres* 125 (1967): 5–33.

Wolfenbütteler Abhandlungen zur Renaissance Forschung. *Buch und Text im 15 Jahrhundert – Book and Text in the Fifteenth Century*. Wolfenbüttel: August Herzog Bibliothek, 1981.

Zerdoun Bat-Yehouda, Monique. *Les Encres Noires au Moyen Age (jusqu'a à 1600)*. Paris: Centre National de la Recherche Scientifique, 1983.

CHAPTER 10.
MANUSCRIPT ILLUMINATION

Alexander, Jonathan James Graham. *The Decorated Letter*. New York: Braziller, 1978.

Avril, François. *Manuscript Painting in the Court of France: The Fourteenth Century (1310–1380)*. New York: Braziller, 1978.

Bologna, Giulia. *Illuminated Manuscripts: The Book before Gutenberg*. New York: Weidenfeld and Nicholson, 1988.

Calkins, Robert G. *Illuminated Books of the Middle Ages*. Ithaca: Cornell, 1983.

Cockerell, Sydney C. *Old Testament Miniatures: A Medieval Picture Book with 283 Paintings from the Creation to the Story of David*. New York: Braziller, 1969.

D'Ancona, P., and Aeschlimann, E. *The Art of Illumination*. London, 1969.

De Hamel, Christopher. *History of Illuminated Manuscripts*. Oxford: Phaidon Press, 1986.

Delaissé, L. M. J. *A Century of Dutch Manuscript Illumination*. Berkeley, 1968.

Diringer, David. *The Illuminated Book: Its History and Production*. London, 1967.

Dominguez Bordona, Jésus. *Spanish Illumination*. Florence, 1929. Reprint. New York, 1969.

Dupont, Jacques, and Gnudi, Cesare. *Gothic Painting*. Cleveland: Skira, 1962.

Engelbregt, J. H. A. *The Utrecht Psalter: A Century of Critical Investigation, 1860–1960*. Utrecht, 1965.

Goldschmidt, Adolph. *German Illumination*. 2 vols. Florence, 1928. Reprint. New York, 1969.

Grabar, André. *Byzantine Painting*. Geneva: Skira, 1953.

————. *Early Medieval Painting*. New York: Skira, 1957.

————. *Golden Age of Justinian*. The Arts of Mankind Series. New York: Odyssey Press, 1967.

Harthan, John. *The Book of Hours: With a Historical Survey and Commentary*. New York: Park Lane, 1977. (*Books of Hours and Their Owners*. London: Thames and Hudson, 1977.)

————. *The History of the Illustrated Book: The Western Tradition*. London: Thames and Hudson, 1981.

Hubert, Jean; Porcher, Jean; and Volbach, W. F. *The Carolingian Renaissance*. The Arts of Mankind Series. New York: Braziller, 1970.

James, Montague Rhodes. *The Apocalypse in Art*. London, 1931.

Kren, Thomas. *Renaissance Painting in Manuscripts: Treasures of the British Library*. New York: Hudson Hills, 1983.

Meiss, Millard. *French Painting in the Time of Jean de Berry: The Late Fourteenth Century*. 2 vols. London, 1967.

————. *The Limbourgs and Their Contemporaries*. 2 vols. New York, 1974.

Melot, Michel. *The Art of Illustration*. Geneva: Skira and New York: Rizzoli, 1984.

Metropolitan Museum of Art Bulletin, "Jean Pucelle." (Special issue) vol. 29 (Feb. 1971), 253–284.

Miner, Dorothy E. *The Development of Medieval Illumination as Related to the Evolution of Book Design*. Catholic Life Annual 1 (1958). Reprint. Baltimore: Walters Art Gallery, 1958.

Mütherich, Florentine, and Gaehde, Joachim E. *Carolingian Painting*. New York: Braziller, 1976.

Nordenfalk, Carl. *Celtic and Anglo-Saxon Painting: Book Illumination in the British Isles 600–800*. New York: Braziller, 1977.

Oakeshott, Walter. *The Two Winchester Bibles*. Oxford, 1981.

Pächt, Otto. *Book Illumination of the Middle Ages: An Introduction*. New York: Oxford University Press, 1986.

Randall, Lilian M. C. *Images in the Margins of Gothic Manuscripts*. Berkeley and Los Angeles, 1966.

Robb, David M. *The Art of the Illuminated Manuscript*. South Brunswick and New York: A. S. Barnes and Company, 1973.

Salmi, Mario. *Italian Miniatures*. New York, 1954.

Thomas, Marcel. *The Golden Age: Manuscript Painting at the Time of Jean, Duke of Berry*. New York: Braziller, 1979.

Valentine, Lucia N. *Ornament in Medieval Manuscripts: A Glossary.* London, 1965.

Van Moé, Emile A. *The Decorated Letter: From the VIII to the XII Century.* Paris, 1950.

Weitzmann, Kurt. *Ancient Book Illumination.* Cambridge, 1959.

————. *Illustration in Roll and Codex.* Princeton, 1947.

————. *Late Antique and Early Christian Book Illumination.* New York: Braziller, 1977.

————. *Studies in Classical and Byzantine Manuscript Illumination.* Chicago, 1976.

White, Terence Hanbury. *The Bestiary: A Book of Beasts: Being a Translation from a Latin Bestiary of the Twelfth Century.* New York, 1954. Reprint. New York: Capricorn Books, 1960.

See also facsimiles of individual manuscripts (e.g., Josua-Rolle; the Book of Kells; Utrecht Psalter; Le Psautier de Saint Louis; the *Très Riches Heures* of Jean, Duke of Berry) and the Braziller series, "Eastern and Western Manuscript Illumination" (Avril, Alexander, Nordenfalk, Mütherich, Thomas, Weitzmann, etc.) NOTE: Skira books here and in Chapter 11 have been reprinted by Skira-Rizzoli, New York. Arts of Mankind series are published in England by Thames and Hudson.

CHAPTER 11.
THE ISLAMIC BOOK

Arnold, Thomas Walker, and Grohmann, Adolf. *The Islamic Book: A Contribution to Its Art and History from the VII–XVIII Century.* London and Florence, 1929.

Atil, Esin. *Kalila wa Dimna: Fables from a Fourteenth-Century Arabic Manuscript.* Washington, D.C.: Smithsonian Institution Press, 1981.

Behzad, H. Taherzade. "The Preparation of the Miniaturist's Materials," *Survey of Persian Art,* vol. 3, 1921–1927. Edited by Arthur Upham Pope. (Part of "Painting and the Art of the Book," 1809–1944). New York and London, 1939. Reprint. Tokyo, 1964.

Bosch, Gulnar K. "The Staff of the Scribes and Implements of the Discerning: An Excerpt," *Ars Orientalis* 4 (1961): 1–13.

————; Carswell, John; and Petherbridge, Guy. *Islamic Bindings and Bookmaking.* Exhibition Catalogue. Chicago: The Oriental Institute Museum, University of Chicago, 1981.

Brian, Doris. "A Reconstruction of the Miniature Cycle in the Demotte Shah Nameh," *Ars Islamica* 6 (1939): 96–112.

Ettinghausen, Richard. *Arab Painting.* Cleveland: Skira, 1962.

————. "Manuscript Illumination," *Survey of Persian Art,* vol. 3, 1937–1974. Edited by Arthur Upham Pope. New York and London, 1939. Reprint. Tokyo, 1964.

Grabar, Oleg. *The Illustrations of the Maqamat.* Chicago Visual Library, Studies in Manuscript Illumination; Text-Fiche Series no. 45. Chicago: University of Chicago Press, 1984.

————, and Blair, Sheila. *Epic Images and Contemporary History: The Illustrations of the Great Mongol Shahnama.* Chicago: University of Chicago Press, 1980.

Gray, Basil. *Persian Painting.* Cleveland: Skira, 1961.

————, ed. *The Arts of the Book in Central Asia.* London, 1979.

Grohmann, Adolf. *From the World of Arabic Papyri.* Cairo, 1952.

Herzfeld, Ernst. "Die Tabula Ansata in der Islamischen Epigraphik und Ornamentik," *Der Islam* 6 (1916): 189–199.

James, David. *Islamic Masterpieces of the Chester Beatty Library.* Exhibition at Leighton House Gallery, London. London: Art and Archaeology Research Papers for the World of Islam Festival Trust, 1981.

Minorsky, Vladimir Fedorovich, trans. *Calligraphers and Painters: A Treatise by Qadi Ahmad, Son of Mir-Munshi (circa A.H. 1015/A.D. 1606).* Freer Gallery of Art Occasional Papers, vol. 3, no. 2. Washington, D.C., 1959.

Pedersen, Johannes. *The Arabic Book.* Translated by Geoffrey French, and edited by Robert Hillenbrand. Princeton: Princeton University Press, 1984.

Rice, David Storm. *The Unique Ibn al-Bawwab Manuscript in the Chester Beatty Library, Dublin.* Dublin: Emery Walker, 1955.

Safadi, Yasin Hamid. *Islamic Calligraphy.* London: Thames and Hudson, 1978.

Schimmel, Annemarie. *Islamic Calligraphy.* Institute of Religious Iconography, State University Groningen, Iconography of Religions, Section 22, 1. Leiden: E. J. Brill, 1970.

Weitzmann, Kurt. "The Greek Sources of Islamic Scientific Illustrations," *Archaeologica Orientalia in Memorium Ernst Herzfeld,* 244–266. (Princeton Institute for Advanced Study). Edited by George C. Miles. Locust Valley, N.Y., 1952.

CHAPTER 12.
PAPERMAKING

Amman, Jost, illus. *Eygentliche Beschreibung aller Stände auff Erden.* Text by Hans Sachs. Frankfurt: Sigmund Feyerabend, 1568.

————. *A True Description of All Trades, Published in Frankfurt in the Year 1568.* (Facsimile of book-related woodcuts) Brooklyn: Merganthaler Linotype Co., 1930.

Barrett, Timothy. *Japanese Papermaking: Traditions, Tools, and Techniques.* Appendix by Winifred Lutz. New York: Weatherhill, 1983.

Bosch, Gulnar K.; Carswell, John; and Petherbridge, Guy. *Islamic Bindings and Bookmaking.* Exhibition Catalogue. Chicago: The Oriental Institute Museum, University of Chicago, 1981.

Briquet, Charles Moïse. *Les Filigranes; Dictionnaire Historique des Marques du Papier dès leur Apparition vers 1282 jusq'en 1600.* 4 vols. Paris, 1907. Reprint. Amsterdam: The Paper Publications Society, University Library Amsterdam, 1968. [For supplements to Briquet see the Paper Publications Society, *Monumenta Chartae Papyraceae Historiam Illustrantia: Or Collection of Works and Documents Illustrating the History of Paper.* 14 vols. to date. Amsterdam, 1950– .]

Ch'ien, Ts'un-hsün. "Papermaking," *Science and Civilisation in China,* vol. 5, part 1. Edited by Joseph Needham. Cambridge: Cambridge University Press, 1985.

Diderot, Denis. *Encyclopédie, ou Dictionnaire Raisonné des Sciences, des Arts et des Métiers, par une Société de gens de lettres.* Paris, 1751–1780. Partially reprinted as *A Diderot Pictorial Encyclopedia of Trades and Industry.* 2 vols. New York: Dover Publications, 1959.

Grohmann, Adolf. *From the World of Arabic Papyri.* Cairo, 1952.

Haemmerle, Albert. *Buntpapier.* 2d ed. Munich: Callwey, 1977.

Hunter, Dard. *Hand Made Paper and Its Water Marks: A Bibliography.* New York, 1917. Reprint. New York: Burt Franklin, 1968.

————. *Literature of Papermaking: 1390–1800.* Chillicothe, Ohio, 1925. Reprint. New York: Burt Franklin, 1971.

————. *My Life with Paper.* New York, 1958.

————. *Papermaking in Pioneer America.* Philadelphia, 1952. Reprint. New York: Garland, 1980.

————. *Papermaking: The History and Technique of an Ancient Craft.* New York, 1943. Reprint. New York: Gannon, 1978.

————. *Papermaking through Eighteen Centuries.* New York, 1930. 2d ed. New York, 1947.

"Kaghad." *Encyclopedia of Islam.* Vol. 4, 419–420. Leiden: Brill, 1974.

Lalande, Joseph Jérôme de. *The Art of Papermaking.* (*Art de Faire le Papier.*) Paris, 1761. Translated by MacIntyre Atkinson. Facsimile ed. Kilmurray, Ireland: Ashling Press, 1976.

Library of Congress. *Papermaking Art and Craft.* Washington, D.C., 1968.

Loeber, E. G. *Paper Mould and Mouldmaker.* Amsterdam: The Paper Publications Society, 1982.

Mason, John. *Papermaking as an Artistic Craft.* Leicester, 1963.

Morris, Henry. "Jacob Christian Schaeffer," in his *Pepper Pot,* 53–86. North Hills, Pa.: Bird and Bull Press, 1977.

New York Public Library. *On Paper: The History of an Art.* New York, 1990.

Pan, Ji-Xing. *History of Papermaking Techniques in China.* Beijing: Cultural Relics Press, 1979. (In Chinese)

————. "On the Origin of Papermaking in the Light of Newest Archeological Discoveries," *IPH Information* (Bulletin of the International Paper Historians) 15, no. 2 (1981): 38–48.

The Paper Maker. (Journal) 1932–1940. Kalamazoo, Mich.: Paper Makers Chemical Corporation (1932–1936); Wilmington, Del.: Hercules Powder Company (1936–1940). Frequency varied.

Schmoller, Hans. "Panoply of Paper: On Collecting Decorated Papers," *Matrix* 3 (1983): 5–20.

Turner, Sylvie, and Skiold, Birgit. *Handmade Paper Today.* London: Lund Humphries, 1983.

Valls i Subirà, Oriol. *Paper and Watermarks in Catalonia. Monumenta Chartae Papyraceae Historiam Illustrantia,* no. 12. 2 vols. Hilversum, Holland: The Paper Publications Society, 1970.

(See also various works on the history of paper printed by Henry Morris at his Bird and Bull Press, formerly in North Hills, now Newtown, Pennsylvania.)

CHAPTER 13.
BOOKBINDING

Amman, Jost, illus. *Eygentliche Beschreibung aller Stände auff Erden.* Text by Hans Sachs. Frankfurt: Sigmund Feyerabend, 1568.

————. *A True Description of All Trades, Published in Frankfurt in the Year 1568.* (Facsimile of book-related woodcuts) Brooklyn: Merganthaler Linotype Co., 1930.

Avrin, Leila. "The Sephardi Box Binding," *Scripta Hierosolymitana* 29 (1989): 27–43.

Bonn, Thomas L. *Under Cover: An Illustrated History of American Mass-Market Paperbacks.* Harmondsworth and New York: Penguin, 1982.

Bosch, Gulnar K.; Carswell, John; and Petherbridge, Guy. *Islamic Bindings and Bookmaking.* Exhibition Catalogue. Chicago: The Oriental Institute Museum, University of Chicago, 1981.

Cockerell, Douglas. *Bookbinding, and The Care of Books: A Textbook for Bookbinders and Librarians.* London, 1901. Reprint of 5th edition (1953). London, 1971.

Diderot, Denis. *Encyclopédie, ou Dictionnaire Raisonné des Sciences, des Arts et des Métiers, par une Société de gens de lettres.* Paris, 1751–1780. Partially reprinted. *A Diderot Pictorial Encyclopedia of Trades and Industry.* 2 vols. New York: Dover Publications, 1959.

Diehl, Edith. *Bookbinding: Its Background and Technique.* New York, 1946.

Donnelley (R. R.) and Sons Company. *A Rod for the Back of the Binder.* Chicago, 1928.

Duncan, Alastair, and de Bartha, Georges. *Art Nouveau and Art Deco Bookbinding: French Masterpieces 1880–1940.* New York: Abrams, 1989.

Ettinghausen, Richard. "Near Eastern Book Covers and Their Influence on European Bindings," *Ars Orientalis* 3 (1959): 115–131.

Foot, Mirjam. *Pictorial Bookbindings.* London: The British Library, 1986.

Goldschmidt, Ernst Philip. *Gothic and Renaissance Bookbindings.* London, 1928.

Harthan, John P. *Bookbindings.* 2d ed. London, 1961.

Hobson, Anthony. *Humanists and Bookbinders; The Origins and Diffusion of the Humanistic Bookbinding 1459–1559.* Cambridge: Cambridge University Press, 1989.

Horton, Carolyn. *Cleaning and Preserving Bindings and Related Materials.* Chicago, 1969.

Jackson, William A. "Printed Wrappers of the Fifteenth to the Eighteenth Centuries," *Harvard Library Bulletin* 6 (1952): 313–321.

Johnson, Pauline. *Creative Bookbinding.* Seattle, 1964.

Lehmann-Haupt, Hellmut. *Bookbinding in America.* Portland, Maine, 1941.

McLean, Ruari. *Victorian Publishers' Book-bindings in Cloth and Leather.* London, 1974.

Middleton, Bernard C. *A History of English Craft Bookbinding Technique.* New York, 1963.

————. *The Restoration of Leather Bindings.* Rev. ed. Chicago: American Library Association, 1984.

Miner, Dorothy. *The History of Bookbinding, 525–1950 A.D. An Exhibition Held at the Baltimore Museum of Art.* Baltimore, 1957.

Needham, Paul. *Twelve Centuries of Bookbinding, 400–1600.* Exhibition at the Pierpont Morgan Library. New York, 1979.

The New Bookbinder (Journal). London: Designer Bookbinders, 1981– .

Nixon, Howard M. *Bookbindings from the Library of Jean Grolier: A Loan Exhibition (British Museum).* London, 1965.

_____. *Five Centuries of English Bookbinding.* London, 1978.

Petersen, Theodore C. "Early Islamic Bookbindings and Their Coptic Relations," *Ars Orientalis* 1 (1956): 41–64.

Roberts, Matt T., and Etherington, Don. *Bookbinding and the Conservation of Books, A Dictionary of Descriptive Terminology.* Washington, D.C.: Library of Congress, 1982.

Sarre, Friedrich Paul Theodore. *Islamic Bookbinding.* London and Berlin, 1923.

Smith, Philip. *New Directions in Bookbinding.* New York: Van Nostrand Reinhold, 1974.

Thomas, Henry. *Early Spanish Bookbindings, XI–XV Centuries.* Illustrated Monographs 23. London: Printed for the Bibliographical Society at the Oxford University Press, 1939 (for 1936).

Tidcombe, Marianne. *The Doves Bindery.* London: The British Library, 1991.

CHAPTER 14.
ON THE EVE OF PRINTING

Amman, Jost, illus. *Eygentliche Beschreibung aller Stände auff Erden.* Text by Hans Sachs. Frankfurt: Sigmund Feyerabend, 1568.

_____. *A True Description of All Trades, Published in Frankfurt in the Year 1568.* (Facsimile of book-related woodcuts) Brooklyn: Merganthaler Linotype Co., 1930.

Biblia Pauperum. Facsimile Edition of the Forty-Leaf Blockbook in the Library of the Esztergom Cathedral. Introduction, notes, and subtitles, Elizabeth Soltész. Budapest: Corvina Press, 1967.

Blumenthal, Joseph. *Art of the Printed Book, 1455–1955: Masterpieces of Typography through Five Centuries from the Collection of the Pierpont Morgan Library.* New York, 1973.

Brunner, Felix. *A Handbook of Graphic Reproduction Processes.* 2d ed. Teufen, Switzerland, 1964.

Bühler, Curt F. *The Fifteenth-Century Book: The Scribes, The Printers, The Decorators.* Philadelphia, 1960.

Carter, John, and Muir, Percy. *Printing and the Mind of Man; A Descriptive Catalogue Illustrating the Impact of Printing on the Evolution of Western Civilization during Five Centuries.* London, 1967.

Carter, Thomas Francis. *The Invention of Printing in China and Its Spread Westward.* New York, 1935. 2d ed. rev. by Carrington Goodrich. New York, 1955.

Cave, Roderick. *The Private Press.* 2d ed. New York: R. R. Bowker, 1983.

Cennino d'Andrea Cennini. *The Craftsman's Handbook. The Italian "Il Libro dell'Arte."* Translated by Daniel V.

Thompson, Jr. New Haven, 1933. Reprint. New York: Dover Publications, 1954.

Ch'ien, Ts'un-hsün. *Written on Bamboo and Silk.* Chicago, 1961.

Diderot, Denis. *Encyclopédie, ou Dictionnaire Raisonné des Sciences, des Arts et des Métiers, par une Société de gens de lettres.* Paris, 1751–1780. Partially reprinted as *A Diderot Pictorial Encyclopedia of Trades and Industry.* 2 vols. New York: Dover Publications, 1959.

Eichenberg, Fritz. *The Art of the Print: Masterpieces, History, Techniques.* New York: Harry N. Abrams, 1976.

Eisenstein, Elizabeth L. *The Printing Press as an Agent of Change.* 2 vols. Cambridge: Cambridge University Press, 1979.

_____. *The Printing Revolution in Early Modern Europe.* Cambridge: Cambridge University Press, 1983.

_____. "From Scriptoria to Printing Shops: Evolution and Revolution in the Early Printed Book Trade," *Books and Society in History,* 29–42. Papers of the Association of College and Research Libraries Rare Books and Manuscripts Preconference, 24–28 June 1980, Boston. Edited by Kenneth E. Carpenter. New York: R. R. Bowker, 1983.

Febvre, Lucien, and Martin, Henri-Jean. *The Coming of the Book.* London, 1976. (*l'Apparition du Livre.* Paris, 1958)

Fine Print (Journal). Edited by Sandra Kirshenbaum. San Francisco, 1970– .

Gaskell, Philip. *A New Introduction to Bibliography.* New York and Oxford: Oxford University Press, 1972.

Goldschmidt, Ernst Philip. *Medieval Texts and Their First Appearance in Print.* Oxford, 1943. Reprint. London, 1965.

Haebler, Konrad. *The Study of Incunabula.* New York, 1933.

Hind, Arthur M. *A History of Engraving and Etching from the Fifteenth Century to the Year 1924.* Boston and New York, 1924. Reprint of 3d ed. New York: Dover Publications, 1963.

_____. *An Introduction to a History of Woodcut.* 2 vols. London, 1935. Reprint. New York: Dover Publications, 1963.

Hirsch, Rudolf. *Printing, Selling, Reading, 1450–1550.* Wiesbaden, 1967.

Holman, Louis A. *The Graphic Processes: Intaglio, Relief, Planographic: A Series of Actual Prints.* Boston: Charles E. Goodspeed Company, 1926.

Lehmann-Haupt, Hellmut. *Gutenberg and the Master of the Playing Cards.* New Haven, 1966.

McMurtrie, Douglas. *The Book: The Story of Printing and Bookmaking.* New York: Oxford University Press, 1948.

Mardersteig, Giovanni. *The Officina Bodoni: An Account of the Work of a Hand Press.* Edited and translated by Hans Schmoller. Verona: Edizioni Valdonega, 1980.

Matrix (Journal). Andoversford, Gloucestershire: The Whittington Press, 1981– .

Thompson, Susan Otis. *American Book Design and William Morris.* New York: R. R. Bowker, 1977.

Wolfenbütteler Abhandlungen zur Renaissance Forschung. Buch und Text im 15 Jahrhundert – Book and Text in the Fifteenth Century. Wolfenbüttel: Herzog August Bibliothek, 1981.

Index

Prepared by Pamela Hori

Leila Avrin is a faculty member at the School of Library and Archive Studies at the Hebrew University of Jerusalem. In the fall of 1991, she will be the Louis and Helen Padnos Visiting Associate Professor of Judaic Studies at the University of Michigan. The author of *Micrography as Art* (CNRS/Jerusalem, 1981), Avrin has published numerous articles on the book arts. She holds a doctorate in art history and an M.L.S. from the University of Michigan and has chaired the Israel Bibliophile Society since 1980.

The text is composed in the typeface Bembo, originally designed and cut in 1495 by Francesco Griffo of Bologna for the Venetian Renaissance printer Aldus Manutius. Three years later, Griffo perfected it by thinning the letters and modeling the capitals after Roman inscriptions. Bembo can be seen in the Aldine masterpiece *Hypneroto-machia Poliphili* (1495). The face served as a typographic inspiration for centuries; in 1929 it was revised by the Monotype Corporation as Bembo, Series 270.

CPSIA information can be obtained at www.ICGtesting.com
Printed in the USA
LVOW090054040113

314325LV00003B/30/P